CW01500063

Sacred Intent

Genesis Breyer P-Orridge

*Conversations and Travels
with Carl Abrahamsson*

1986-2019

With 50 photographic portraits

TRAPARTbooks

ISBN 978-91-984512-6-9

Trapart Books
PO Box 8105
SE-104 20 Stockholm
Sweden

info@trapart.net
www.trapart.net
www.genesisporridge.com

Table of Contents

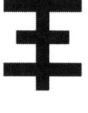

Introduction to Sacred Intent

In 1984, I started subscribing to information stemming from the "occultural network" Thee Temple Ov Psychick Youth (TOPY) in London. This odd constellation was rumoured to be a mix between a magical order, a philosophical think tank, and an archive for truly occult information – in the sense of it being hidden or ostracised by those who maintain power through a status quo, because of too much potential transgression capacity.

This network was also connected to a band called Psychic TV. Or vice versa. Moving through different styles – from ethnic, tribal, Western experimental to fairly traditional rock music at the time – "PTV" toured and generated interest not only through their avant garde music and videos, but through hundreds of eloquent interviews about magic, politics, art, cultural engineering, and many other things.

I found it all extremely exciting, and was already a fan of the main spokesperson: British artist Genesis P-Orridge. His previous projects C.O.U.M. Transmissions and Throbbing Gristle ("TG") provoked the hell out of performance art and the music industry, respectively. Whatever P-Orridge conceived of, or touched and developed, became food for thought not only for me as a young Swedish intellectual but also for the world. He not only knew how to elegantly reformulate obscure theories; he also knew how to get them into the limelight of public attention.

Being a young fanzine editor at the time, I used my interest in Psychic TV as a door-opener into the TOPY Headquarters at 50 Beck Road in Hackney, London. On a cold November day in 1986, I visited the P-Orridgean household for the first time to talk about music and magic. When I left, nothing was quite the same. I not only respected P-Orridge as an artist and "conversationalist" even more, but had also come to the insight that what TOPY was doing was simply so unheard of and "new" that I definitely wanted to be a part of it.

The glamour of magic also appealed. Master magician Aleister Crowley and fellow Brit sorcerer Austin Osman Spare were integrated in the TOPY "corpus," but that museum of arcane magics was not enough. The ideas of William S. Burroughs and Brion Gysin about how to apply artistic methods (perhaps most specifically the "cut-up" method) to magical creation (and vice versa) were also integrated and championed, and opened up a whole and brave new world of synergies and connected dots for me. Magic should not be a secluded phenomenon allowed only within a designated time and space, but rather an all-immersive lifestyle that challenges all one's inhibitions, and allows for a development towards, and an eventual merger with, whatever existential ideals one may have. It may sound simple but it certainly isn't! But here at least was a group of contemporary and very creative individuals who were joyously experimenting with the very building blocks of existence. Guerrilla magicians creating art to change the future!

No sooner than I was back in Stockholm, I set up "TOPYSCAN" – Thee Temple Ov Psychick Youth Scandinavia. I spoke with P-Orridge (now being Genesis or just "Gen") often, and wrote letters to London and other "Access Points" of the network. I was suddenly part of a miasmic vortex of philosophy, art, occultism, and the free exchange of information as a way of life.

In 1988, I revisited London to interview Gen again about TOPY and current affairs. This interview ended up in my new publication: *The Fenris Wolf*. This was just one example of the multi-creative expressions that many people in the TOPY environment produced: books, records, cassettes, videos, magazines, events and many other things. This power of manic manifestation became a glue that held the network together, while also inspiring others to create in a similar spirit.

After some five years of being the administrator of TOPYSCAN and later also TOPYEUROPE, I felt a need to focus on other things. Strangely enough, Gen felt the same thing at the same time; as did Tom Banger, the administrator of T.O.P.Y.N.A (the North-American branch). It was some kind of inexplicably synchronised farewell to this first phase of TOPY, and we lovingly accepted it as such.

During these years, a real friendship had developed between Gen and myself. In 1989, I followed him and then wife Paula P-Orridge on their spoken word tour of Scandinavia. Upon the return to Stockholm, we recorded an album called "At Stockholm" (by Psychic TV & White Stains, which was my band together with audio wizard Thomas Tibert at this time). Gen had also written diligently for the following issues of *The Fenris Wolf*. Even if the TOPY structure had dwindled, our creativity was still very active.

Making that first album, and watching (and listening to) Gen perform his unique spoken word-magic made me realise not only the potency of words but also the actual power of delivery. This is equally evident in all the thousands of interviews that have taken place over the decades. Gen's ability to be eloquent, combined with a seductive voice, combined with the extended seduction of integration of the interviewer ("it is not only a talk but a real conversation") all merge into one of the most efficient tools in the P-Orridgean artistic box. In a way, the initial flamboyance means attraction, and then the words seep out and draws you closer. Persuasion as an artform.

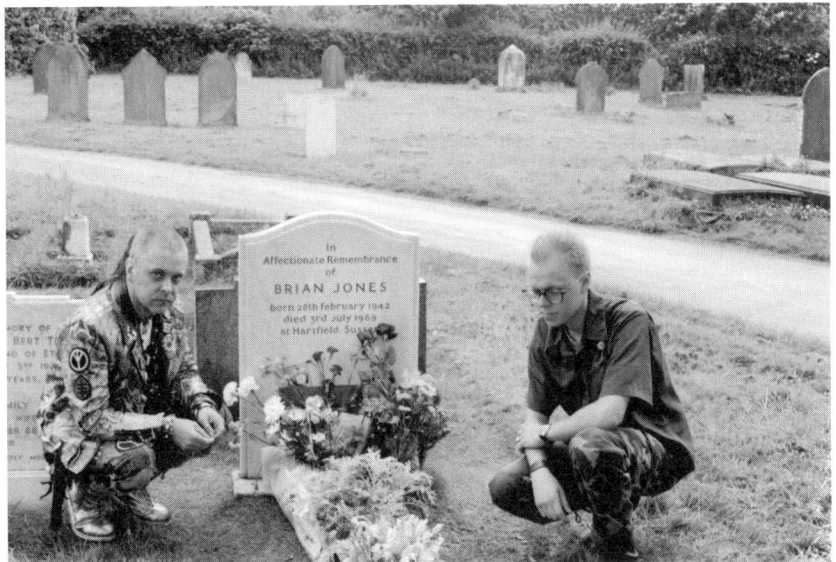

Genesis P-Orridge and Carl Abrahamsson, Cheltenham, 1988

This meta-level of integrating content and signal into a poetic form made me want to collaborate on something substantial and "long term." What better phenomenon than that of the interview in itself?

Next we met was in California in 1993. I was on a magical mystery tour of sorts, while Gen was now living in exile. Warned not to return to the UK by Scotland Yard and his civil liberty lawyers, he was also going through a depressing divorce and trying to find new bearings in life. Not a good time to talk about lofty ideals and optimism.

Considerably better was the meeting in Stockholm in 1998. Not only did that trip bring the debut performance of his new musical/spoken word project Thee Majesty. It was also the first time I met Gen's new partner, American performance artist, legendary New York dominatrix and nurse Jackie "Lady Jaye" Breyer. Being solidly situated in New York, a re-emergence into an art world left behind in the mid-1970s seemed considerably easier than from rural Northern California. And I could tell: Gen's inspiration was flying high.

We had a great time, but the pace of touring and socialising in general didn't allow for a proper interview this time either. Although there was at this point e-mail as well as cell phones, that still didn't equal a face to face meeting and conversation. On this we both agreed, and decided to start meeting up at different places in the world, with the expressed purpose of one day making a unique form of travel book out of it all.

Sacred Intent

In 2000, we began in Kathmandu, Nepal. And now it was a different story altogether. When you have a current affairs kind of talk, it usually gets locked in time. But when you know you want to move both backwards and forwards in time, it's invaluable to have something as timeless as a book in mind.

Then we just rolled with it. Talking about Gen's past, present, future, projects, ideas, the origins of ideas, methods, meetings, influences and many other things. This process has continued up until the very end of 2019; integrating key moments and developments; good as well as bad, happy as well as sad. Interviews one-on-one, as well as some open lectures and talks. Optimistic and altruistic as well as, occasionally, dystopic and puzzled.

There have also been related spin-off projects throughout the decades. In 2004, the follow-up to "At Stockholm" happened: the album "Wordship" by Thee Majesty & Cotton Ferox (my musical project at the time, again with Thomas Tibert). In 2016, I made a documentary film about Gen and his work, called "Change Itself." In 2018 I published Genesis's interviews with and texts about British-Canadian "Beat" painter-author Brion Gysin in a book called *His Name Was Master*. In 2019, the third spoken word album happened: "Loyalty Does Not End with Death" (this time simply as/by Genesis Breyer P-Orridge & Carl Abrahamsson).

On February 22nd, 2020, Genesis Breyer P-Orridge turns 70. This book is meant to be a gift of sorts for that special occasion. A gift to fans and partakers of the ever inspiring creations stemming from the P-Orridgean mind, and also to that mind itself – and the body and soul that tag along for the ride.

For me, it's been a joy, pleasure and honour to have worked so closely with an artist so unique in so many ways: in approach, in form, and in content. The overall creative umbrella here is always one of "sacred intent." Art is made to make magic happen. Magic is made to make art happen. Seldom, if ever, in the history of art and culture has this proto-creative equation been expressed clearer than in the life and work of Genesis Breyer P-Orridge.

Finally, on a personal, formal, editorial note: at the height of the Breyer P-Orridge "pandrogeny" project, Genesis preferred to use a feminine perspective/denomination. Hence "she" and "her" became predominant in conversations and writings. Although I fully respect this, I always had a hard time changing it around in my mind – very likely because Gen had been imprinted on me as a male. I have therefore consistently stuck to my own perspective when referring to Gen in the third person in this book.

In a life-long attempt not only at mutating culture and language but also the very view of "self" and its fluidity, Genesis often refers to himself in the plural. Hence "I said" more often than not becomes "We said."

In accordance with the "timeline of life," I have changed the short versions of the name at the beginning of each answer from "GPO" to "GBPO," from 2000

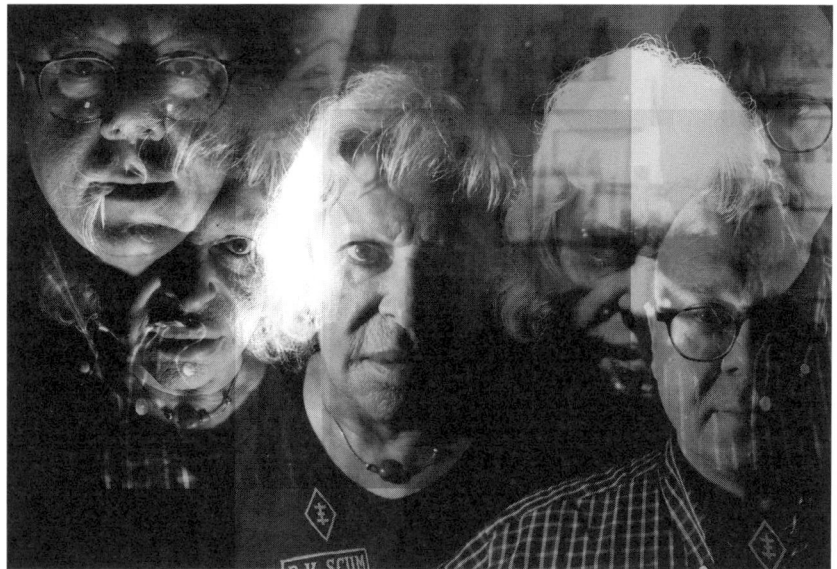

Genesis Breyer P-Orridge and Carl Abrahamsson, New York, 2018

and onwards. In regard to the concept of Pandrogeny, this is how it's spelled: Pandrogeny. When referring to one individual, couple, or entity "immersed" in Pandrogeny, it's one "Pandrogyne."

I would like to convey my thanks and praise to the following people who have been of invaluable assistance in the development and manifestation of this book: Vanessa Sinclair, Margareta Abrahamsson, Sofia Lindström-Abrahamsson, Mikael Prey, Henrik Møll, Ryan Martin, Edley O'Dowd, Lady Jaye Breyer P-Orridge, Trilochan, Benedikte Lindström, Vera Nikolic, Andrew M McKenzie, and Christian Kount. And, of course, to Gen.

Carl Abrahamsson, Stockholm, January 2020

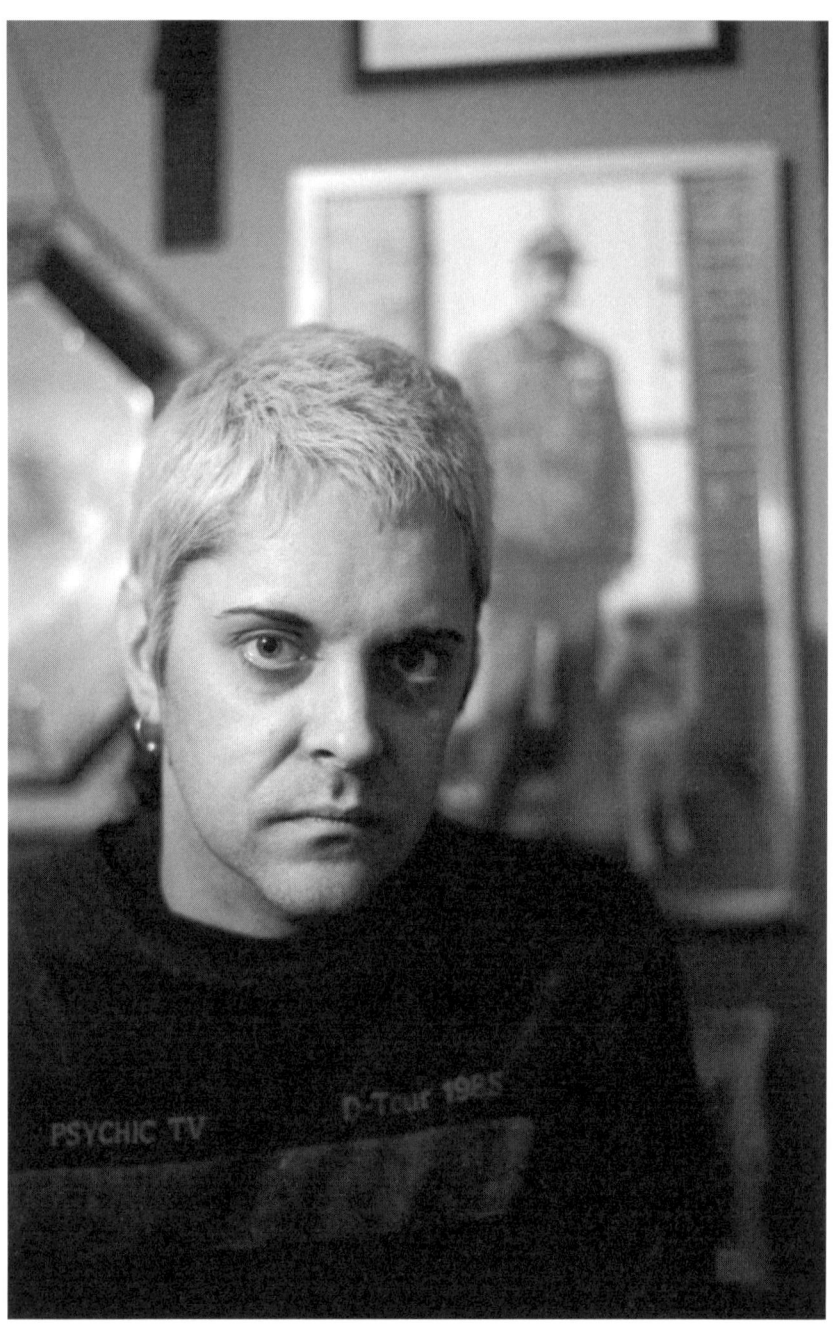

50 Beck Road, London 1988

London, November 9th, 1986

After having been a Temple Ov Psychick Youth "subscriber" for some years, I decided I wanted to interview Genesis P-Orridge for my fanzine Lollipop. *I was very curious about TOPY and what Psychic TV were up to, but I couldn't help bringing up Genesis's previous and highly influential project: Throbbing Gristle, or "TG."*

GPO: It was me who actually said it was time to end TG.

CA: Were there any hard feelings?

GPO: Oh yeah. I don't think it really reads very well though. My main concern with people is their attitude. While things can at any given moment be fun and entertaining or absurd or strange, the reason people do anything should be very honest. Their motivations should be to grow and wake up as much as they possibly can, and share that attempt to wake up with everyone else and communicate that.

CA: They didn't?

GPO: Not in my opinion, they didn't. It wasn't sudden though. It went on a long time. I had this house back then, and I used to be down here copying all the cassette tapes and doing a lot of mail. They all had jobs and were out earning a lot of money, which they kept for themselves. Chris and Cosey[1] helped a bit with copying tapes and day to day running, but they always made sure that the money that they were earning went to them. I was still on the dole and working here; just growing away from people.

CA: So it was more like you drifted apart than a split-up?

GPO: I suppose so, in retrospect. We started to drift apart and then I realised that

---

1 Chris Carter (b 1953) and Christine "Cosey Fanni Tutti" Newby (b 1951): members of Throbbing Gristle.

Sacred Intent

I was the only one honest enough to say that it was finished. Also, TG seemed to have become irrelevant; it had made its point. To keep going would have been like becoming an institution.

CA: Except for the fact that you started making videos with Sleazy,[2] did you at this time have a concept for what was to become Psychic TV?

GPO: I always do. It was already scripted. Before that, when we had C.O.U.M. Transmissions, I already had Throbbing Gristle worked out. The group after Psychic TV has a name as well.

CA: What will that be?

GPO: I'm not going to tell you that (laughs). You'll have to wait and see. But next year, instead of being Psychic TV, it's going to be Psychic Television, the full word.

CA: To show what?

GPO: That we're expanding both as a record label and book publisher. Also, the films and videos will become more clearly important. The nice thing with this project is that there's room to change it within the original idea, whereas with TG it was a very particular thing. It could only be TG but nothing else. It was either that or nothing. That's why it had to split up, whereas with Psychic Television, it can change and develop into all directions. That's why I prefer it as a project.

CA: What do you think of the TG days now, in retrospect?

GPO: Emotionally painful and creatively quite good. It's become a legend. It's historical. I'm pleased that people find it relevant. I think it's a shame that there are so many other groups that try to be a pretend version of TG. They haven't understood the basic idea of TG, which was to grow and change and develop and evolve, for better or worse. It's better to change than stay the same. Never to accept anyone else's opinion and never to accept anyone else's answer or anyone else's morality. To always ask first. If you agree with them on the evidence and experiences you've had, then fine. But never to go "Yes" for the sake of it.

---

2 Peter "Sleazy" Christopherson (1955-2010): member of C.O.U.M., Throbbing Gristle and early Psychic TV before he went on to form the project Coil together with Geoff "Jhon Balance" Rushton (1962-2004), also an early member of Psychic TV.

CA: So you had Psychic Television already worked out. Did it crystallise itself as a group immediately after TG?

GPO: It was always meant to be an idea that different people worked on. That's why it says on the record, "For the realisation of this project, Psychic Television were..." I'd lost interest in the idea of a fixed line-up because it does end a group, like with TG. No one else could have joined TG. We couldn't have had one person left and carry on. When any individual in it was dissatisfied, that was the end of the group. Whereas with Psychic TV, in theory, it could carry on even if I were dead. It's a concept that belongs to all the people who decide to use it. That's why the styles change and the particular emphasis of any given year changes, depending on who's involved and working with it. I'm the director, if you like, a creative or artistic director, and I can veto someone's continuing involvement in the project. Beyond that, anyone who's in it at any given time can and does affect the sound and the things that get done. Since August, we've reverted totally back to the beginning. We're working on the project as it was first stated, which will be to start releasing videos regularly, to start releasing more books regularly, to communicate more with other organisations, both magical and rebellious, wherever they may be, and to communicate more with people generally. Whether it's magazines, TV, radio or at parties or wherever it may be.

CA: The reasons why you haven't done this is because you've been touring and recording too much?

GPO: Not too much. We deliberately decided to spend 1986 changing the outside world's perception of us. The people interested in PTV most of the time had a good faith in our ability to make decisions even though it might appear that we were doing something very strange or contradictory.

CA: Was that one of the reasons why you decided to create something musically more light-hearted?

GPO: Oh yeah. We decided to be a rock'n'roll group for a year. It worked, because instead of the music press permanently just slagging us off and saying we were horrible, evil people, they turned around and said, "Hey! These are good records, I like them. Therefore they must be alright..." Which is equally ridiculous. Because you make a good single doesn't mean that you're a good person anymore than if you make a weird noisy record you're a bad person. Having been aware of their basic simplistic attitude, we decided to play a game with their way of looking at things.

Sacred Intent

CA: It seems that when you were in TG, you as a person got a lot of attention. It seems that this is coming back now. You're in the gossip columns of the music press almost every week now, with stories about how your snake ran away, the big boat party, etc. Are you pleased with that?

GPO: Not really. That's why we've retired for four months. It was getting stupid. That's the bad side effect of deliberately wanting to appear to be a rock'n'roll band. They start to write about you like they do about all the other rock'n'roll bands. "Seen at such and such a place, having a cup of tea in a café..." Anything you do, they put in a gossip column. That drives people mad. It drives me mad. You get bored with it. We're hiding away for a few months until people forget. Then it'll be interesting when we re-appear. They'll probably go, just as we will, "It would be nice to have a PTV event again..." We want it to feel fresh for us because then we'd assume that it'd be fresh for people in London or everywhere else too.

One key strategy that we have embraced and used from C.O.U.M. onwards is this: If it seems people have become familiar with one of our strategies, then our next move must be the diametric opposite whenever possible. Always contradict your previous statement or action. Avoid the expected. You can have too much of a good thing. You've got to have the self-discipline to know when to stop and disappear and work on something else. Now, we're half way through a new, proper LP. "Thee Starlit Mire" is about half done. We're trying to raise money to finish it.[3]

CA: What will it be like, musically?

GPO: It will be more like "Force the Hand of Chance,"[4] in that it will be actual tracks. It's only the third actual official Psychic TV album. Not many, when you think about it. Although there are a lot of PTV records, this is only the third album. It will be part of the set dealing with magic, or a magical perception of life. The proper albums are like textbook records. It was mainly written during the last two years, so it will be using songs and more musical structures for that particular purpose. It'll be a fusion of the first two. I know the title of the fourth LP, which is called "Thee Big House." They're always metaphors. The big house is where you get to. Each LP is almost like a chapter of a book. The book is a theoretical book.

CA: Are you pleased with the two first chapters?

GPO: Yes, I think they are good records. I think "Force the Hand of Chance"

---

3 This album was eventually released in 1988 as "Allegory And Self (Illustration In Sound)."
4 The first album by Psychic TV, released in 1982.

sounds more relevant and more interesting now than a lot of people thought when it was released. I listen to it more now than I did then. I've started playing it again, as if it's by someone else. I just like it as a record.

CA: "Message From Thee Temple" certainly got me interested.[5]

GPO: That was a very influential track, yet totally different in style to what anyone would expect. It proved that people do want to think and do want to listen and do want to be given more ideas than just rock'n'roll.

CA: Are you going to use binaural (holophonic) recording again?

GPO: We didn't think we could because the guy disappeared.[6] But we met him on tour in August in California. He gave us his card and said he'd still like to work with us. I would imagine that would be for the "Big House"-LP. The new one is already half done without "Ringo."[7] There will be one or two holophonic effects on it though, because we have some on tape already. But "Thee Big House" should be holophonic. That's the ultimate place that you should try and get to.

CA: What's the main advantage of holophonic recording?

GPO: It's more emotional. You can actually transmit feelings and sensations quite literally as opposed to trying to describe them with music. It's a big advantage if you're trying to talk about how people feel and exist and what it's like to be alive. We want to make the records accessible. People should be able to put it on and listen to the whole LP and enjoy listening to it. Later on, they can realise that these words aren't quite the normal words they'd expect. What are they actually about? Why is the cover like that? What are these extra bits of paper that are in it?

CA: That must be a more effective means of "propaganda" than with TG?

GPO: Oh yeah. TG was a sketch in a way of its own time. Psychic Television to me is the most appropriate name for this era anyway. It's the perfect name for a group now. It includes technology and the most powerful medium of television, with the idea of the unconscious or the instinctive mind, the not-controlled person.

---

5 A text/statement about the philosophy of TOPY included on the first Psychic TV album.
6 Hugo Zuccarelli, developer of the holophonic recording method.
7 "Ringo" is a three-dimensional model of a human head used for recording "holophonically."

CA: Is that also where the term "hyperdelic" comes in?

GPO: Hyperdelic is not going back to "psychedelic." The idea of psychedelia was to expand consciousness and expand one's idea of what was going on in the world and what was possible. Hyperdelic is a way of saying, "Let's go even further and even more totally out there and let's use every bit of technology, video tape, Polaroid camera and computer we can find to do it." So that we just get lost in this technological dream explosion.

CA: Do you use a lot of technology in your music-making?

GPO: We have an "Emulator 2" on stage and we use Fairlights in the studio, and some computers. Anything. We all have small cassette recorders. I've got several of them, in fact. When Genesse, the second baby, was being born, we videotaped the whole birth. Six hours of video. We tape-recorded it as well. We have the actual groan of the baby coming out, the actual moment of a birth. That's the beginning of "Thee Starlit Mire." "Force the Hand of Chance" is saying these are the different ways of looking at the world, this is how we feel. "Dreams Less Sweet"[8] is the battle between the world as you've been told it is by society, education, parents and the world you feel inside: your world. Side one of "Dreams Less Sweet" is the supposed real world and side two is our world. "Thee Starlit Mire" is the decision to live in your own world. If you like, you are reborn into the starlit dimension, where anything is possible. Where you can face all of the different aspects of your character. Having done that, you apply all those things to creating a world quite different and which makes more sense and is more real. That's "Thee Big House."

CA: You even had a deal with Warner Brothers?

GPO: We had a deal with Warner Brothers for "Force the Hand of Chance," with CBS for "Dreams Less Sweet," RCA for "Good Vibrations."[9] Maybe someone else for "Thee Starlit Mire". We're becoming like The Sex Pistols (laughs). We only do one-record deals with them. I think they've caught on to the idea (laughs). We'll have to wait and see. Parallel to that, we're working on the idea of the film "Godstar."[10] For that, we're trying to raise a quarter of a million pounds, believe it or not.

8 The second Psychic TV album, released in 1983.
9 A cover of the Beach Boys song, released as an EP in 1986.
10 "Godstar" was a single released in 1984, but also the name of a bigger project celebrating Rolling Stones guitarist Brian Jones.

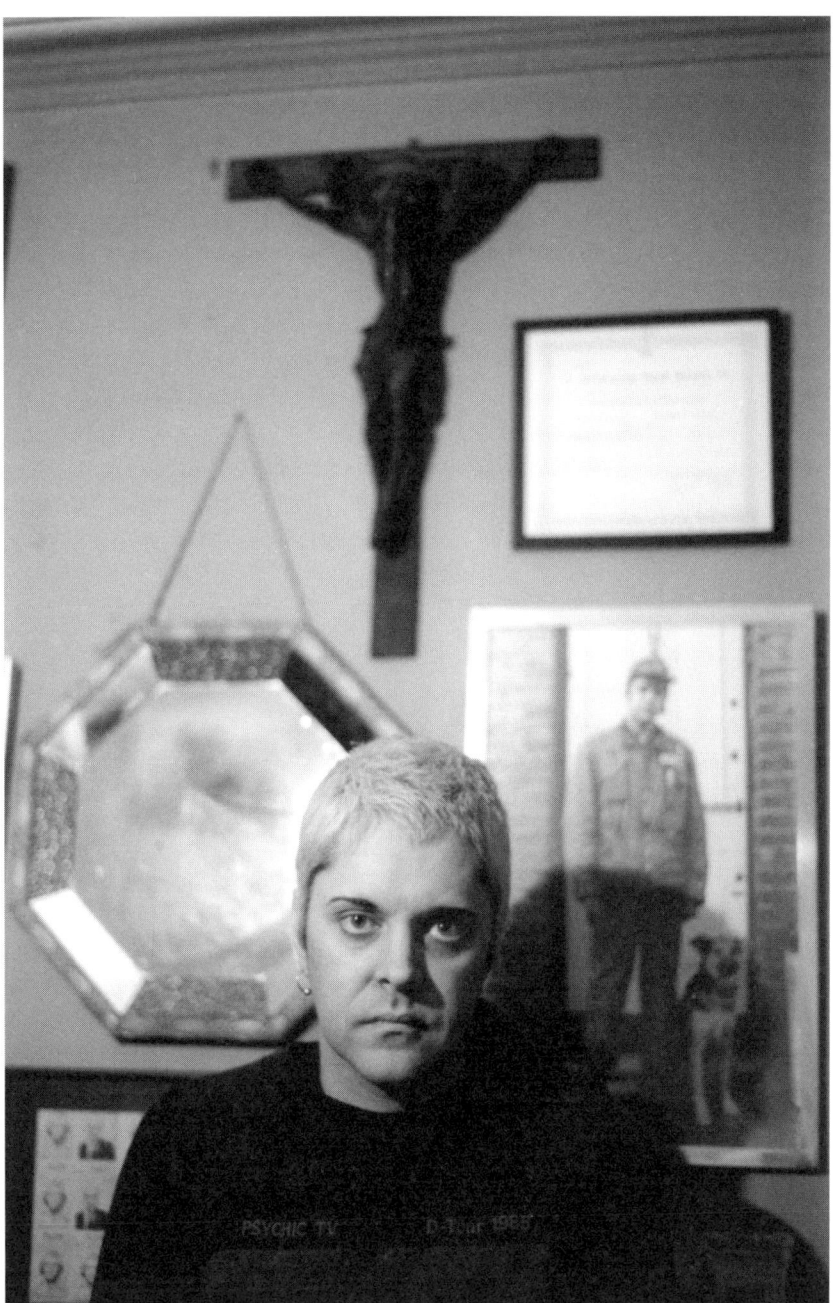

London, 1986

CA: You haven't started shooting yet?

GPO: We've done bits, but we have to get on more properly with it now. We need at least lumps of money. There's somebody we've met who raises money for films and who likes the idea. They're trying to raise money from investors to make it properly.

CA: Will it be like a regular feature film?

GPO: It'll be like "Eraserhead" or something like that; an underground but feature film.

CA: Who'll play Brian Jones?

GPO: Possibly his son Julian. We're in contact with him. But more likely is that it will be someone who doesn't look like him whatsoever. That'll probably be better. It's about him as a scapegoat or a victim or as a symbol of all of us, fighting. In his case, he was destroyed. We will at least try and make people realise that it's a parable, a story, and that now, twenty years later, we'll try not to get destroyed.

CA: Have you heard any reactions from the Stones' side?

GPO: Mick Jagger hates it. He's still trying to suppress it. Radio One was playing "Godstar" and it was going up in the real charts, which was an amazing feat for Psychic TV and my own indie label Temple Records. Then Mick Jagger got his office to contact Radio One and said quite categorically, "If you continue playing this record, you will never ever receive any Rolling Stones press releases, copies of any records, white labels or interviews ever again." If they'd said that to me, I would have said, "Great! Fantastic! What a relief..." But unfortunately the people at Radio One actually think The Rolling Stones are still important. So they said they wouldn't play it anymore. They stopped playing it. We found out that Jagger is actually bald on top, like Eno. He was spotted at a hair salon with a hair piece discussing how he was having a hair transplant. We found out the name of his hairdresser. We sold the story to one of the daily newspapers. "Baldy Jagger needs a cure!" So that was one piece of revenge we've already had. We were so pleased when we found out that he was bald. "Thee Psychick Youth Nett Work" will always win! Bill Wyman we've met, and he seems to just be neutral. A bit embarrassed but not "anti." I think he remembers Brian Jones.

CA: I really can't understand why they should react so negatively. It's a tribute.

GPO: Mick Jagger was always a rival of Brian Jones. Whether Brian Jones committed suicide, just died, was murdered, whatever it was... Mick Jagger was certainly better off with Brian Jones not being around. He got Brian Jones out of the group. Even on just that level, he's embarrassed to be reminded that he'd been so careless and ruthless. He carried on a sadistic emotional campaign against Brian Jones.

CA: The fact that you're so fascinated with Brian Jones, does it have to do with things like the fact that he also knew Brion Gysin,[11] or that he was interested in many of same things as you are, or...?

GPO: It's everything. He's the perfect vehicle. He's the point where all the different threads and ideas meet. He's a great symbol for us to start talking about lots of things that we believe in. Yet he's a real person who's remained interesting and mysterious. The whole story has not been told. It does draw a parallel to what we think are the best bits of the 60s, which are the looking and the experimenting and the not accepting of what even a pop song should be. It can be absolutely anything. Some pop songs of the 60s were appalling but some of them were absolutely radical. The radical ones would still be radical today.

CA: "Satisfaction" is still a great song about existential frustration.

GPO: It was banned in a lot of places. "Let's Spend the Night Together" was banned too. "Sympathy for the Devil" is another one. For a little while they hung out with Kenneth Anger as well.[12] So, it's just a useful story. Some write stories or songs for the sake of it. But for us, every song, event or story is chosen because we can then talk about ways that people behave and see the world. And ways to look out from inside yourself and understand better that the things that are done to you are used to control you. It makes sure that you can try and keep some kind of self-respect and ability to develop as an individual.

CA: When you're making films, what inspires you? Particular filmmakers or dreams, or...?

GPO: Mainly it's subconscious images, dreams and cut-ups. When in doubt, chop things up. Things you find interesting, things that appeal. If you don't have a storyline but lots of interesting images on videotape, all of which for no reason

---

11 Brion Gysin (1916-1986), British-Canadian painter and author, and one of P-Orridge's main sources of inspiration and mentors.
12 Kenneth Anger (b 1927), American filmmaker and occultist.

appear to have some power even if you can't analyse it, then you jump them all together and you start to see a story, even if there was none originally. It gives the idea of a story. When you play live, the music is changing so you don't want it to be a particular story, you want it to have open ends and holes in it so the audience can fill those gaps in themselves, and associate them.

CA: When you set up a show, is it very important that sound and images are somewhat synched?

GPO: We've tried it both ways, and it tends to work better when it's not synchronised. What we want to do is continue researching and try a combination of both. If there's a certain piece of music that we think that we'll play all the way through a tour, even if it's an improvised instrumental, then it might be worthwhile having two or three prepared mixes of video for that one section. That way, the audience is never sure when it's synchronised and when it's not. At one moment it can be totally synchronised and maybe even triggered by the Emulator or something, so that it pulses to the beat. Then it can go random again. I think it's just more stimulating for the audience that they're never sure. And for us too. It's much more interesting for us never to know when it's synched.

CA: How would you characterise a perfect gig?

GPO: It's just the way you feel. It's got nothing to do with whether the music was good or the films were good. I would like the audience to feel like as if they'd taken a very exciting, totally optimistic drug and had the best sex they'd ever had in their life. That's how I'd like them to feel (laughs).

CA: Do a lot of people come backstage afterwards and let you know how they feel?

GPO: In Britain and in most places there's a very family-like atmosphere between the people on stage and the people in the audience. The front rows are usually the most enthusiastic. Some of the people are part of what we call "Thee Sex Tribe." They follow us around and tend to do what they call "sexual terrorism." They strip off and dance and do all kinds of things. The sexual tribe is growing considerably. What's interesting is that the girls don't act as heterosexual girls or lesbian girls. They just act in a sexual way. Boys who otherwise would never kiss a boy might kiss a boy and not feel embarrassed or inhibited at that moment. That's the healthiest part of all. They feel free from any inhibitions at that period of time. There is a temporary, yet very strong, suspension of any Either/Or, male/female definitions. It's a zone of *new sexuality*.

CA: Do you encourage that from stage?

GPO: Oh yeah (laughs)! I started to behave like that more on stage, and that seemed to trigger other people to behave like that off stage, in the audience. We noticed that and then encouraged it. We want to carry on having a "voodoo," tribal section at the end of the gigs. Maybe even have the gig and then stop and say, "We're going off for ten minutes and then we're coming back and anyone who wants to stay for a pagan ritual can stay..." Maybe even get people to start bringing drums along so that everyone could just drum until they're exhausted and see what kind of mental states and sexual states they can get into. You can never tell which places get that way. In Detroit, we were really exhausted and we didn't think that we wanted to play the club because it didn't look very interesting. Yet that was the most sexual night of the whole US tour.

CA: Were they people who knew about Psychic TV?

GPO: Not really, most of them. That was what was so strange. It was basically a black club. There were white teenagers there too and some knew about us, but not many. We all felt really horny afterwards and so did the audience. There were all of these people trying to get off with each other and fuck straight away. They couldn't help themselves. That was great. There's no way you can predict which one will be that way.

CA: Do you know of any other bands who get that effect?

GPO: When we played the Town & Country Club, most of the stage managing was done by people who'd worked with Killing Joke. One would expect that they could generate something along those lines, according to their theories and whatever. But the stage people said they'd never seen anything like our concert. "I wish Killing Joke gigs were like this!" (laughs) I think Killing Joke are one of the more exciting live bands from Britain still. But I think they're a bit too macho. Maybe that's why, because it's so male dominated? They do talk about women being subservient. They're very sexist. That's probably why they don't get that response. With Psychic TV, there have been, and still are, girls involved in the group on stage. There's no sort of role playing going on. I don't try to act out anything that's macho. I'm just as happy to touch a boy at the front as a girl. Nobody feels excluded. Nobody feels they're being stereotyped or projected at. Most people are aware that we are quite openly interested in sexuality and in the power of that: its ability to break down conditioning.

CA: What do you enjoy the most? Playing live or dealing with things here?

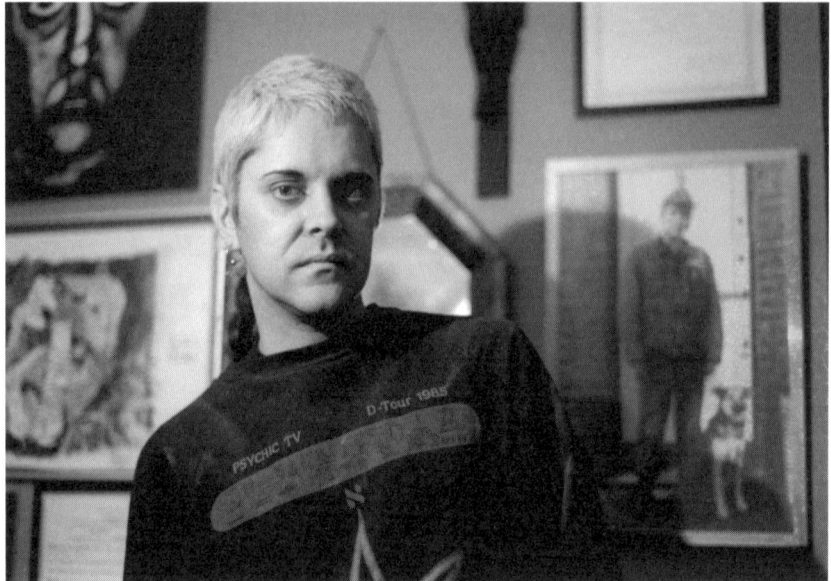

London, 1986

GPO: I like it all. I wish there were three of me, so I could do them all of the time. When it's like that in Detroit and it goes really voodoo and when nobody's in control and yet it's not anarchic... When it's got its own life and it's spiralling in this sexual and mental energy, then it's incredible. Then it's *Kundalini* energy to a power of ten!

CA: Even good rock'n'roll shows can do that.

GPO: That's one reason why we started experimenting with the rock'n'roll techniques. One thing that is worth noting is that, when we started, we tried working with ritual music, ethnic music, different types of music from different countries. We thought that if we could integrate that with our music, we would probably get the effect of tribal music. But we didn't really. It was much more intellectual. When Sleazy and Geoff left I decided to try another technique, which was rock'n'roll with Alex Fergusson.[13] Here we are with a really good guitarist, so let's try that. That's when it started to get very tribal and very sexual. I mean, rock'n'roll means fuck. That's when I got thinking about things like the early Rolling Stones. They were the first rock'n'roll band that I got interested in. It's like the

---

13 Alex Fergusson (b 1952) was a member of Psychic TV between 1981 and 1987.

22

first time you have sex or the first time you have an orgasm. The excitement of a real rock'n'roll gig is sexual excitement. That was what we realised and that's when the revelation came. We'd been trying intellectually but it was actually all about instinct and gut feeling. If there's a good riff... I know, it sounds really corny... But if there's a really good riff and a good mix and if the people on stage are putting every single ounce of energy into it, and projecting that at the audience and basically saying, "I want to fuck you all! If I could, I'd fuck each and every one of you..." Then, it works. That was why Jim Morrison was that kind of person. That was what he projected at his audience.

CA: Do you have any other favourite rock'n'roll bands?

GPO: Some of the early Stones stuff. "Satisfaction," "Jumping Jack Flash" and that era before Brian Jones died. That was very sexual. Because of Brian Jones' way of dressing, also quite androgynous. It wasn't just male. Afterwards Mick Jagger turned it around to the male thing again. "Mick Jagger, I am a man, I am a cock..." That's boring. I used to like The Velvet Underground and I still like them as a group and I think they were very influential in terms of breaking down styles. But they weren't very sexual as a group. I find them less satisfying now, creatively, than I used to. Because of this change in the way I look at music now.

CA: They must have influenced your show though?

GPO: Oh yeah. I also think early Soft Cell were quite interesting. I've never had any Led Zeppelin records but I'm beginning to rate Led Zeppelin, certainly conceptually, as a very, very good band, although I used to hate them when they were going on. Mainly without listening though. When I saw it in the media at the time, it was just naff. Heavy Metal posing around. But having seen some early clips of them... They were totally over the top. I saw an old clip on some program recently and it was just like noise, crazy. They were also a group who tried to put ideas and philosophies into their music.

CA: Except for people making music, are there any others that have inspired you?

GPO: Brion Gysin mainly, I'd say. And Austin Osman Spare,[14] who was a minor English occult figure and painter. He influenced Aleister Crowley[15] a lot but worked on his own. He was never a member of any group. I like his paintings and

---

14 Austin Osman Spare (1888-1956), British artist and occultist.
15 Aleister Crowley (1875-1947), British author and occultist.

I like his writings. He died in the late 1950s. But, in popular culture, everything that comes through. Even "Eastenders" and what you're watching on TV, what you read in different newspapers; just about everything influences us. We're like a sponge. We're not snobs about it. We're always greedy for more information and more images and more ideas and more ways of looking at things. Even if we don't like them, it's good. We just keep on absorbing things.

CA: You mentioned that you get ideas for the films subconsciously. But are there any directors that have inspired you?

GPO: I like Visconti but I only really like one film: "The Damned." That film works; it's really claustrophobic and decadent. I like odd films really, more than filmmakers. I like bits of Kenneth Anger but not all of it. I like bits of Warhol but not all of it. And I like things like "Aliens" too, and "The Texas Chainsaw Massacre." I like trash more than I like intellectual stuff. I like things that hit me straight away and I feel something. I'm not out to prove my own mental prowess to myself or anyone else.

CA: Have you worked with any professional filmmakers?

GPO: We've worked with Derek Jarman, John Maybury, Akiko Hada, and Ceryth Wyn Evans. They all make promo videos and films for the British Film Institute and Channel Four. They all supply images and films for us and work with us. I met Derek Jarman in 1969, and everyone influences each other. It cross-fertilises. I've always used superimpositions. Even in TG we did that. Even before I saw any of Derek's films. It's a mix of all of us wanting to express images that are very rich. The only way to make them that rich is to have more than one layer. That's primarily why that happens. We all influence each other and no one's bothered about ownership. We work and donate soundtracks to them and they give us images to cut up, for the same purpose. Sometimes they watch films that we've done all on our own and are influenced by them. It doesn't worry any of us. We see ourselves as a collective, really. Psychic Television is the collective expression of various underground film- and video-makers in Britain. It's not just us as a rock band. All of them in their own right make their own films too, which are finished works by them. But sometimes they give bits of those back to be re-used through Psychic Television.

CA: Do you have your own editing equipment?

GPO: We don't own anything. We'd like to, but we rent it when we need to do something.

CA: Do you like to research what kinds of effects things like superimpositions can have?

GPO: It was through researching the dreamachine[16] that made us interested in that. We would like to find ways of making television have the same effect. We want to have people watch television with their eyes closed but still see pictures. That's what we're aiming for. But to see different pictures at different times. Which is what happens with the dreamachine.

CA: One could use drugs...

GPO: Yes, but then you become illegal and the authorities can close you down. But if you could find a trick where people can use some commonplace thing like a light-bulb or a television set to have the same psychedelic experience, how do they ban that? Then they've got a real problem. Are they going to ban television? A dreamachine just uses a light-bulb.

CA: How does it work?

GPO: It's a column that has holes at mathematical intervals. It spins and the light-bulb is inside the column. You have your eyes at a certain distance and look at the bulb through your eyelids. It's not like a strobe that just flashes. The light is coming out in a curve. It gets more intense as it goes past. It triggers off the alpha waves of the brain, and the dream cycle is activated while you're awake. When you open your eyes, you can stop it. It has the same effect as LSD. Not as frightening because you never lose control, but visually the same. Not necessarily mentally the same, but visually the same. We're building them very robust so that we can have them at the front of the stage. People who don't want to watch the films can just close their eyes and trip out on the dreamachine while we play. We're also going to have a hypnodisk at the front of the bass drum. If you stare at it, you hypnotise yourself. Then you dream again very vividly, while you're still awake. It's going to be more intense both visually and physically. There will actually be parapsychological experiments going on during the concerts.

CA: If you can manage to put people in a trance, what would you do with them?

GPO: Well, it's not a passive trance. It's an active trance. They're still awake and

---

16 The Dreamachine was invented by Brion Gysin, and is basically a light-source contained within a spinning cylinder with holes in its sides. The pulses of the light stemming from the revolutions of the cylinder affect the human brain in a hallucinogenic way.

aware. The least they will do is have very interesting visions. One would hope that it would sink in with the sexual side. It would make them feel less inhibited about what they were feeling physically, and start to actually do things to themselves or to each other. It's research.

CA: How are you looked upon among more traditional magicians?

GPO: We always thought they'd assume we were really silly and feel angry and threatened by us. In fact, what's happened this year is that they've started to get in contact with us to say they want to work with us and become our allies. They respect the way we're doing things. While they're not necessarily working in the same way, they feel we are sincere and quite skilled in what we do. We are just a modern expression of the same tradition. That's good. We've been having meetings with several of them. Just several people involved in traditional magic, that's about as much as I'll say. So that's interesting. Even Francis King[17] has recommended us to organisations in America. When we were on tour all over America, various magical organisations came to the gigs and made contact. We're still in contact with them. One organisation in particular, based in New York, that has a mailing list of 22,000 people, are now sending out catalogues of all of our material to all their people. It's all beginning to happen exactly as we hoped it would. Of course, they should wait and see what we're like. One LP and a few interviews is not enough to make any sense. It's ironic that it's five years since we started, which is two plus three.[18] It has a life of its own and it seems to be keeping its own schedule. We're sceptical of some of their techniques and their belief in gods and demons and all that. But a lot of it is just language. What we call "Thee Museum Ov Magick."

One thing that we have already agreed on is to try and fight against the Parliament and against the Church here for the right to have a pagan temple in London, where we can have non-Christian burials. At the moment we can't. At the moment, you can't have the burial or the ceremony that you want. If we can get a building and have it recognised by the government, then different organisations could use it. When I die, I want to able to say to people around me, "Let's work out a Temple Ov Psychick Youth Death Ceremony..." That's what I want. I want the right to that. Why not? Muslims can, Jewish people can, but not pagans. That's wrong. The pagans were the original inhabitants of Britain anyway, just like the American Indians in America. The Christian church seems more interested in politics and money rather than belief. That's why the born-again Christians are so conservative. They're not interested in religion, they're interested in

---

17 Francis King (1934-1994), British author.
18 A reference to William S. Burroughs's and Brion Gysin's fetishising of the number "23."

power, money and morals, which is just big business protecting itself. Because it's scared really. It's the last ditch protection of big business.

CA: How powerful do you think TOPY could become?

GPO: Well, we're not looking for power. We're looking for freedom of choice. There are about 4,000 TOPY subscribers in the whole world, but it's going to increase through these mailing lists and through the fact that we now have a headquarters in Holland and one in Denver, Colorado. When I say headquarters, I don't mean that it's all grand yet. However, there are three permanent bases of activity that are all interconnected. By the new year, we'll all be linked by computer. Then there are other organisations that we work closely with, some in London, some elsewhere in the world, who already have quite strong organisations. We're trying to act as a catalyst, to get rid of people's differences of detail, about what they believe and what they want to achieve as individuals. That's fine, but I say that we should go for the things that we definitely agree on, which is to be recognised as having the right to be a pagan, and the right to a way of death. And also to challenge the Christian church and repressive governments everywhere. To fight for some social values too... just very basic ones. That seems to be beginning to make sense to a lot of people. It's not because it's our idea. These things happen only when they are inevitable; when everyone feels the same way.

CA: Are there a lot of people who aren't interested in the music who get in touch?

GPO: Oh yeah, definitely. There hasn't been an attempt really by people involved in magic or the occult to really communicate with young people when they're teenagers. There's never been that kind of "crusade" before. That's something quite new for groups to decide to do that. Magical groups usually consist of twenty people who are all very academic, almost like university professors who live very normal straight lives the rest of the time. I think it's time to go out on the street and show young people that it's relevant. It may be the best technique to use for them to fight what they've been trying to get away from. It's a way out from all the shit we've had since the 50s that young people have tried to fight with rock'n'roll and fashion.

CA: Do people react differently in different countries?

GPO: No, they don't, really. Amazingly, you can get Japanese people jumping around and be sexy as well as Americans and Canadians... Everywhere. It's a very primal urge and response. That's why it works and that's why it's such a good vehicle for ideas too.

CA: How come you chose to re-record "Roman P"?[19]

GPO: We tried to play it live the way it was on the original record but we couldn't do it that way. It didn't work. Alex Fergusson did a different arrangement of it live. After about a year of playing it faster live, we realised that people jumped around and had a good time to it. So we thought we'd record it. It seemed amusing to do a cover version of your own song. You asked how big TOPY can get – it tends to spiral quicker as it moves on. Once more people put in things like projects, that attracts other people who put in more. It's an accelerating increase.

CA: Can you manage that then?

GPO: One of the reasons we're rebuilding now is to expand our efficiency, to be able to use the next three-four months learning how to make the fewest possible mistakes in the office. All the information should be written down as clearly as possible. We'll have a computer with all the addresses in. If we want to send a letter just to people in Scandinavia, we can hit a button and it'll print the addresses. We're trying to think of every possible way to cope as far as we can. If it gets too big for this headquarters, we have to have another. If we get a bigger building, which is one of our plans, we can centralise all the activities.

CA: How many Psychick Youth are there in London?

GPO: Very hard to say because there are people who think they are and dress as if they are, and they're complete idiots. They probably go around boasting that they are. Then there are people who appear completely ordinary and who'd never say they were psychick youth, but to us they are. It's what you do and it's your attitude and the energy you put into trying to grow and express things. That's what makes you a psychick youth, not how you look or whether or not you do a ritual on the 23rd of every month.[20] That's interesting but that doesn't prove anything either. Nothing means anything if the person's an idiot. The value is that they're actually trying to be awake and trying to learn and trying to expand themselves and through that project it out into the real world. There's no point in doing it just for yourself. Obviously you're trying to improve and develop yourself and remove as many neuroses as you can, so you become more effective and more balanced and more able to do things. When you do that, it's no good doing it for

19 A Psychic TV single originally released by Sordide Sentimentale in 1984, and then re-recorded and re-released in 1986.
20 Reference to one of the central TOPY rituals: performing a sexual "sigilising" at 23.00 hrs on the 23rd of every month. For more information about these aspects of TOPY, please read Genesis P-Orridge et al, *Thee Psychick Bible*, Feral House, Port Townsend, 2009.

yourself. What's the point? You have to take that big gamble of projecting it into the real world. Then you get criticism. People say, "I don't like it... That's stupid..." Then you have to learn to have so much courage and faith in yourself and what you believe. Even if criticism can disappoint and disillusion you, at the end of the day you still know that the way you're trying to work and live is the right way to work and live. Even if everyone says you're stupid. That's what we're doing. It does involve caring for people too. Selfishness has no place in Thee Temple Ov Psychick Youth. The people who tend to be told to go away, either from Psychic TV or from TOPY, are the people who use it just for themselves and don't want to share and don't want to grow and don't want to do boring work as well as exciting work. I don't mind knocking down walls. I don't think that just because I'm Genesis P-Orridge I have to do all the exciting work. I'm happy to sweep the floor and knock down a wall and make a cup of tea as well. Everyone should feel like that. There is no more important or less important job. There's just, "What has to get done? Who can do it? Let's get it done as quickly as we can and let's do more and more and more..."

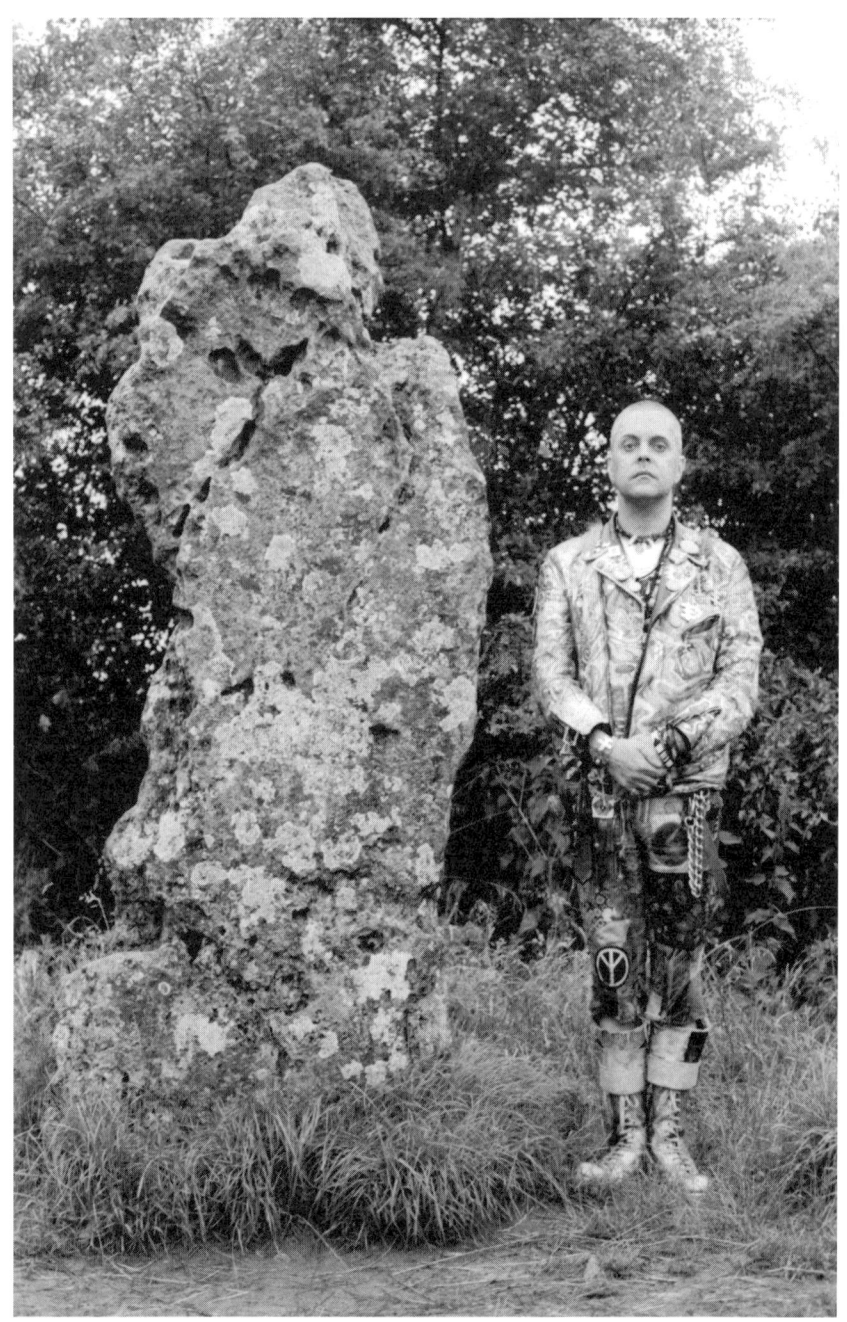

The Rollright Stones, 1988

London, July 6th, 1988

After an outing to the pagan site the Rollright Stones, and a visit to Rolling Stones founder Brian Jones's grave in Cheltenham, we had the following talk during a break at "Times Square Studios" in London, where Gen was recording new acid house tracks together with Dave Ball (of Soft Cell fame).

CA: Why is it, do you think, that people can't or won't understand what Thee Temple Ov Psychick Youth is doing?

GPO: Why would so-called professional journalists get themselves into the position of deciding in advance what they're going to like? Which is what they actually do. They've made up the story. Why would someone who would probably, in other circumstances, say that they're an intelligent person? Who are they serving by focussing on people who do not have any power to speak in response and then these writers deliberately distort, hurt or even knowingly destroy the lives of those people who they have probably never met? The psychology of that behaviour on a mass level is very disturbing. It's far more disturbing than what we may or may not be doing in private for our own philosophical reasons. That's the bit that's scary. Not what we're doing or not doing. How do they justify it to themselves when they go home? What do they do when they're lying in bed or watching TV or having a coffee? How can they just sit there, knowing that they do not care about the truth? Or are they so utterly perverted and morally corrupt that they actually believe there is a justification for that behaviour? Do they actually feel so totally right that they're the equivalent of a fundamentalist terrorist? Or the equivalent of the person who assassinated John Lennon? Because that's the level they're at in terms of behaviour. They're no different than "The Son of Sam," who'll invent a glossary of terms, a pseudo-raison d'être in order to justify random violence. It's just random media violence. It's terrorism basically. Blackmail and terrorism. And if one actually took one of these people to a rational court of law and prosecuted them, those would have to be the charges. Intimidation, protection racket, blackmail, violence and abuse, child abuse. When they attack families they're also threatening the children as well. I'm sure, if you went up to them and said, "Do you enjoy being a child abuser?" they'd say, "What are you talking about? You're mad..." That's what they're doing. Caresse[1] has to go to school. She may well get intimidated by other people at school. She goes to a normal primary school. That's the bit that's really disturbing. Why do they decide to pick on us? Because we choose not to be secretive. That's the irony. I'm sure they'll try and imply that we're all very secretive. But, as you know yourself, anyone who wants to send in five pounds can get the same information from us as anyone else. And has been able to for seven years. So we've not exactly been secretive. Far from it. What we try to do is make available more information of an esoteric or behavioural kind to give people more options as to what they can choose to be like. They may choose to be totally normal. There's nothing wrong with that. But they may also choose to be less normal, given that they find out what else is possible. I think that they are scared, presumably of our power, that it may be growing.

It's one of the great ironies of Western civilisation that honesty is one of the things feared most. All the churches and religions in the West fear honesty, because they're based on intimidation and the threat of infinite violence when you die, which is a very bizarre thing to base a religion on. Eternal violence to your spirit and soul. I think we're very honest people. And I think that terrifies a country that is conditioned into dishonesty. People at the very top of the pyramid are totally dishonest and corrupt. And also privileged enough to do whatever they want in private and cover it up afterwards, whether it be Watergate or visiting prostitutes or whatever. Occasionally they hand over a scapegoat to the media, in order to cover up a much larger amount of corruption and cesspool behaviour. But primarily the privileged ruling classes of all types are allowed one morality and the rest of us, who are not true human beings – according to them, we're a lower breed – are not allowed to do what they tell us not to. So if they say, "You're not allowed to have gay sex," 99.9% of the population are legally not allowed to, by that 0.1%. And if we don't like that decision, we're physically intimidated by armies, police, courts, the press, mass media and economic threats as well. So if you really look at the whole process, it's political. It's about political control. And obviously, we have for 20 odd years spoken out very clearly against control: political, behavioural, social and economic. It's not very surprising that one or two puppets of the powers that be have been trained and placed in those positions because they're so stupid. They can be convinced that they are a part of a moral crusade.

CA: Would TOPY ever take sides in a party-political stance?

---

1 Caresse P-Orridge (b 1982), Genesis P-Orridge's first child with Paula P-Orridge (b Paula Brooking, 1963). Their second daughter is Genesse P-Orridge, born 1985.

GPO: We would never support one or another party, because we go on a pragmatic level from the cause itself, whether it be animal rights or children's rights or whatever. This week it could be rhinos and the next it could be a community nursery. One of the things that always surprises me is how few people have bothered to note how much overtly political action we take, both in our relationship with the media and in our day to day life. We still tend to believe in that old 1960s saying: "No matter who you vote for, a government gets in."

CA: Psychic TV get quite a lot of good reviews and a lot of attention. Isn't there ever anything positive on TOPY?

GPO: In Britain? No, not really. In the world, yes. We've had good positive response in America and Japan and Germany, all over. But at the same time there's also usually an anti-response, because what we're doing is deliberately challenging the status quo. And we're challenging inherited moral values, saying, "I refuse to accept that you, the authorities, the educational system, my so called elders, my social parents, know implicitly what is or is not right and wrong."

We tend to follow the American Indian philosophy that women and children are sacred and should never be abused and attacked. And that everybody – male, female, child, animal and the ground that we walk on – are a part of a food chain and a survival chain. You can't separate any of those elements at all. As soon as you attempt to separate them, there is somewhere a form of death. If you build a concrete city over the land, you have separated the people in the city from the earth and in some way a part of their spirit and the earth's spirit on that spot will die from that separation. And thereby you can start to see why people in the cities are so neurotic. They're not in contact with the vast part of their environment anymore. They cannot physically or psychically touch it a lot of the time. That must be very damaging.

People say, "Why rhinos?" Well, the child of a rhino that's killed this week is the child of the woman next door in ten years' time. Because I honestly believe that the authorities in Britain and all the countries in the world are now terrified of the onrush of an ecological, economic and medical explosion of disasters. The scale is so immense that their old techniques of lying and intimidating will be irrelevant very soon. It will be down to the people on the street to invent new ways to survive, if possible. And it won't even be a rebellion against authority. It'll just be, "How do we stay alive?" And at that point Thee Temple is trying to set up a structure, a philosophy, which re-teaches the concept of a contemporary tribal appreciation of life, so that you do realise that when we talk about caring it's not enough anymore to care for your nearest and dearest. You have to care for anyone who gives you respect. That tribe is not in the old sense of all living in one small tented village. That tribe is spread, scattered across the globe, and

Sacred Intent

it's a tribe of those who attempt to perceive what's happening. And, in their own mind, not contribute to the damage anymore where possible. It's not the normal old-fashioned tribe, because the world has changed. If we were all in the Amazon basin and they weren't knocking it down, we could probably build a village and live in it as a tribe. But it's not like that. We live all over the world at the moment, but there are, and have to be, methods of regaining the best aspects of tribal living, which is pooling resources. Those with the rights skills do that job, because it saves time and effort. If somebody knows how to do computers, they do the computer for everyone. And somebody else who can cook, cooks for everyone. They have equal value. There is no hierarchy anymore. There's just, "Who gets things done and who doesn't?" If someone can write, then they write the story and history of the tribe. And in return they get fed. It's very simple, basic re-learning of how life actually is. Because that process is going on all the time, but it's being clouded and disguised and camouflaged so much by the way the authority-side and conditioning-side of society has gone, that it's very hard for anyone to grasp it or see it anymore.

CA: Do you feel optimistic about it?

GPO: I think that Thee Temple can at the very least leave behind various useful starting points, working models and information. That's why the book publishing is going to be important, and that's why things like records and tapes and so on are important. Interviews are less and less important. We're at the level now where we just do it. Talking about it is usually a waste of time and energy. You sit down and think, "Should I talk to a music journalist who's ill-informed and prejudiced for three hours or should I go out and help a child to the hospital?" I would go and help the child because it's more important. And soon that's going to be what we're all thinking about. It's odd, because whilst it can appear to be very unselfish, in actual fact it's not. It's also totally selfish, because we're trying to learn as fast as possible how to all survive and get the most to survive for all of us and the people we can get in contact with. It's one of those interesting philosophical contradictions, that in order to be self-preserving one has to be totally selfless wherever possible. And that is something that works on the American Indian level. We learned so much from just being with that American Indian shaman Nomad for just two-three days, about how to look at things in circles. You have your own individual person circle and then other people have theirs, and no one really has the right to invade anyone else's circle. Then you have a larger circle of a family, and then the tribal circle, and then the natural circle, which is the entire planet.

The other thing we learned was something that confirmed what we've always felt and dealt with, which is that dreams are an equal reality to so called waking reality. And they're part of more circles. The concept of invasion into anyone else's circle has become clearer. Exactly what is happening to us now with *The Sunday People* is a kind of rape basically.[2] I see people who perpetrate that, day in, day out, week in, week out, year in, year out, as the most despicable examples of modern capitalist society. Because they should know better, and they do the most vile hurt in the least possibility of anyone calling them to task. They go and do an article on an old man who likes "Alice in Wonderland." That was in last week. And they say he's a paedophile because he likes "Alice in Wonderland." Yet you can go to all these bookshops in Britain and buy books with pictures of Lewis Carroll and of girls. Who decides when it's OK to like them purely as aesthetics and it's OK to like them slightly more?

CA: You had the same problem with the artwork of the TG album "D.o.A."[3]

GPO: Yes. It's never gone away. We always said Throbbing Gristle was dealing with the concept of reporting – journalism in a way – and in the representation of information, so that people are prejudiced one way or another, by what you tell them about the information. That information war is still going on. In a way far more violently, because there are more desperate people around.

CA: So the ideal might be to have a "Psychick Colony" somewhere?

GPO: The ideal is to have psychick colonies. If you have one colony, only one bomb is needed to destroy it. You have Psychick Youth colonies for those who want to make the gesture of devoting 24 hours a day of their life forever to standing up and saying, "I believe that this is one of the solutions to the problems that are coming and already have arrived." It's also a way of re-learning humanity, because this is psychotherapy, psychodrama, behavioural therapy, stress therapy... all those things. A family unit is a hell of a stress; learning to deal with four or five people. To learn to deal with twenty people is unheard of in our society, and it's pathetic really that it's so hard for people. But at the same time people can be a part of Thee Temple and totally integrated on the surface with the way things go on day to day; working in television, working anywhere. But aware in their own minds that when they make decisions that in any way involve morality, that they can choose that which gives rather than excludes.

Our society seems to be involved in a perpetual attempt to exclude minorities, or exclusion of different ways of thinking. And yet all the great leaps for-

---

2 *The Sunday People*: a British tabloid.
3 Included artwork for Throbbing Gristle's "D.o.A. – The Third And Final Report" album (1978) showed a young girl with her panties visible.

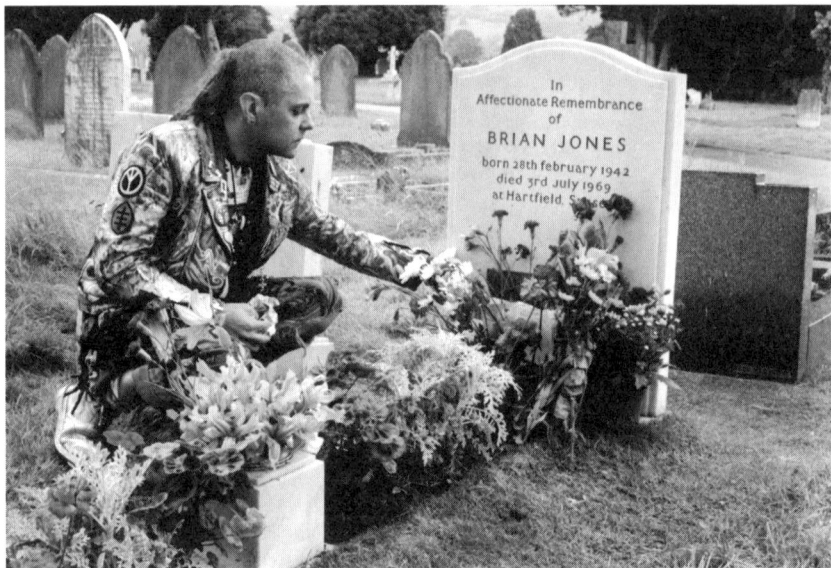

Cheltenham, 1988

ward philosophically, scientifically, politically are made by those who come up with the non-status quo ideas. The radical, renegade idea is the idea that always, so far, has saved the human race, quite literally. The thing that has never saved any civilisation is violently shoring up the old order. There is no evidence ever throughout human history of that working. And yet these morons at the top of the pyramid continue endlessly to repeat this loop of more violence, more authority, more repression, over and over.

Take the fundamentalist Christians, who come around crucifying non-Christians. The evidence was that Jesus, who was one of a small number of radicals, if you accept the story at all for the argument's sake, was crucified and destroyed with his band of people. But did it stop the idea? Of course it didn't. They can't read their own evidence, these people. They just turn their back and run away. You have to go a long way back in history, or you have to go across the globe and you have to look at the examples of what we're always told are primitive cultures, to discover where there is a healthy integration of all the aspects of life. From giving birth to dying to illness to madness to menstruation to puberty to celebration, all of these things; dreaming, being awake, making music, making food, all those things are integrated in such a way that there is a permanent sense of balance and harmony. We call that a "primitive" culture! And then we look at our culture, where we have germ warfare, permanently institutionalised violence by the police and the army and the psychiatrists and the politicians.

And we have people put in concrete blocks and we have the persecution of any minority that says, "I don't agree." We call that civilised. It may sound like a very simplistic thing to say, but sadly that simple observation is still considered to be anarchic, dangerous, subversive, destructive, Satanic. If that's Satanic, then yes, I'm a Satanist. But what does that mean? I don't believe in any gods. I believe that gods are early attempts at psychology; trying to understand the light and dark side of human nature where you go right inside yourself, beyond dreams and into those recesses which we should look into. But we're out of practice in our culture. And you give it names. That helps when you're telling stories, because they come from a time when there was primarily no written history. You can tell people something much clearer with a parable than with the very abstract theory of mathematical formulas. You tell a story about a squirrel and a rabbit to a child and they remember it. If you say "x-3y-v," they'll go, "What?" That's where that comes from. I've got nothing against using that terminology to explain how human beings are, and how they can relate, and how they can support and expand each others' consciousness.

CA: Most of the pagan gods are just aspects of human nature.

GPO: Of course. Why do you think that dogmatic Christianity's basic ethic is so terrified by pagans? Because it works as examples of behaviour. Christianity's basic tenet is "Be good now, or else we'll punish you forever and ever when you're dead. And we may punish you while you're alive too!" That's an incredibly sick, social pseudo-religion. It certainly has nothing to do with the ecstatic mysticism of the original Christianity, the Gnostic Christianity, which of course was destroyed by the Romans and Saint Paul. Paul was the equivalent of a CIA agent, who literally killed off the rival disciples and then mutated and totally altered the philosophy for his own ends, and for the ends of Rome. What happened then with the Christian church? It became the Roman church. Romans basically sent in their own agents and subverted the idea. From then on it was a Roman bastardisation for political and social ends.

We're scapegoats. It's odd that I keep being picked on in Britain. I don't think I'm very important. I don't even really flirt with or contact the media anymore. I just get on with trying to honestly develop a way of life that can be applied in different territories. Like with you, you're going to go to Scandinavia and you're in Scandinavia. I'm not Scandinavian, so I'm not trying to impose my vision.

Here's what I've discovered. I'm 38 years old and for all of my faults I have spent most of those 38 years searching determinedly and genuinely for ideas that work and ideas that help. Not everyone maybe, but some people. If they work and if they make any kind of sense, the only way to check is to give them to other people and see if it works. If it helps one or two or ten or fifteen, that's a massive improvement of what most people do in their life to help anyone. If it helps a few hundred or a few thousand, that's incredible. But it doesn't prove anything about me, except that some of my observations of the way life goes on were correct enough to relate to other people, who then, hopefully, expand upon it in their own way and in their own experience and develop it further.

I think your idea of mixing in the Scandinavian gods and myths is brilliant. Just as in America it should bring in the American Indians. And if it was Japan, they should try and look into Japanese cultural history; Shinto or some obscure little group of mystics that someone has remembered but who were also trying to have an integrated constructive and functional way of life that included the concept of total mental and psychic evolution. I'm interested in human beings evolving beyond this primitive state of violence, into a state where if somebody stood up and said, "I'm a politician" or "I'm a priest" or "I'm a colonel," everybody would just burst out laughing and walk off. And that one individual would be able to do nothing about it, because nobody would understand what they were talking about anymore. It'd be irrelevant. "What does that mean? Religion? Never heard of that. Armies? Fighting? For the sake of it? Why?" It should be irrelevant by now, because it's stupid, it's uneconomic, it serves no purpose except destruction. If everyone were trained, taught, given the example of pooling all their skills, ideas, resources and knowledge in order to get the best for everybody, they would get the best too. Not being selfless, but being totally and utterly selfish in a way. Then there'd be no problem at all, anywhere. It wouldn't become viable as a thing that could happen. It would be beyond the vocabulary of anyone's experience. Somebody said, "Look, we can't chop down the Amazon basin, because it's just bad news for everyone." Then everybody should go, "Yeah! I don't want to bloody die! Don't do it!" The biggest answers are so simple. If we live in a world where people are being trained to be selfish, let's tell them that this is the ultimate selfish idea. It's called "Getting the most out of your life, for the least cost, and staying alive. And no one hurts you!" It's so obvious, if you just go back and check anybody's history anywhere. When do the problems come? When they refuse to share a bit of food, a bit of information, a bit of skill. That is why my new t-shirt design has a smiley skull surrounded by the words "SAVE WILD LIFE – SAVE YOUR LIFE!"

CA: In Western societies today, you vote for a party every third, fourth, fifth year or so. But when you've voted for "your" party, you can't really control what happens.

GPO: Of course not. Also, in Britain there hasn't been a government with an actual majority of vote since the Second World War. There are three or more parties. It's the number of seats they get, not the number of votes. The Tory party usually gets about 30% of the votes, but they get the most seats because a lot of the people don't bother to vote, and a lot of people vote for the other two parties. So you have a situation where 70% of the people who live here have a government they voted against. That's a really odd situation. The 30% who voted for the minority government, as you say, half of those at least, once they've made that gesture of voting, can do nothing about what actually happens. They could suddenly be disenfranchised and told, "You're never going to vote again!" Which I suspect will happen in the next ten or fifteen years. I really suspect that it's certainly more than an equal chance that, in Britain, voting will become no more than a cosmetic charade, as it is in Russia and everywhere else. It's even possible that the Tory party might declare the equivalent of a one party system. The way they're going on, they're doing that without bothering to declare it anyway. Same in the U.S.A.

CA: Do you see Acid House as a good vehicle to affect people on the dance-floor?[4]

GPO: Oh yes, that, but actually it's the first time in years that I've heard a style of music that I've actually enjoyed. We've been saying since the first hyperdelic things that we wanted to find a fusion between psychedelic attitudes and technology, to take *hyperdelic* one step further than *psychedelic*. We spent most of last year experimenting with different ways of achieving that. With "Godstar" and the other things we got the "hyperdelic rock" effect, but not a true dance-floor effect that was contemporary and worked regardless of itself. It was last September-October that we recorded the "Superman"-record.[5] A long time ago. At which point there had been no articles at all in Britain about Acid House, or even House, bar the Soul-type of House music. The words hadn't even been coined by the press yet in the U.K. – only in Detroit and Chicago clubs. We always said that the best ideas are those which are inevitable. Like TG and Industrial music were inevitable. That's why it took off and that's why it made sense to so many people. The same thing with House. The faster speed works on the body in a much more overt way. TG and Psychic TV and many other people have learned, a long time ago, that spinning in tapes on a very constant rhythm is interesting. So, in a way, it's just what we've always done. It's ironic that the solution we were looking for was what we did anyway. Just honing in on one aspect of it, which was the repeated rhythm. More extreme use of effects, with found information laid on

---

4 At this time, Genesis P-Orridge, various members of Psychic TV, and their own label Temple Records were involved in the dance music/culture "Acid House" that was instrumental in/as a re-booted and extended "summer of love," ca 1987-1989.
5 One of the 12" records that made an impact on the Acid House/club scene in the UK.

top. That's what "Jack the Tab"[6] is and that's what the "Superman" record is, with Timothy Leary talking all the way through.

CA: Where does the term "Jack the Tab" originate from?

GPO: A guy called Richard Norris, who started Bam Caruso, the psychedelic re-release label, and he also started the magazine *Strange Things*, came up with that. He came to interview us for *Strange Things* and I was telling him how we were working on these ideas for Acid dance and so on. He really got into the idea of it and said, "Let's do something together. Let's really push this together and join forces, Bam Caruso, Temple Records and you and me." Castalia is the name I suggested for the label. The Castalia Foundation was where Timothy Leary and everyone used to do their experiments. Whenever we're together we just come up with these phrases. He came up with "Jack the Tab." We thought that was a really good one. Then he rang me up one night and said, "Somebody asked me what Tab means." And I said "Techno Acid Beat," which came straight out of the top my head without a thought. And now they're calling it the Detroit Acid House "Techno". And yet this was in February or so.

I would argue that the reason that that's happening for me is a result of the way Thee Temple works, in analysis and ability to have a cumulative increase in intuitive abilities, which is what is the best side effect. It's just amazing how much is happening to you everyday, even though I always knew it was possible. The day that you and I went to see Brian Jones' grave, I was sitting in the car and I almost said something to Paula, but something interrupted my thought. I was going to say, "Remind me next week to buy 'After The Goldrush' by Neil Young," because I used to have that record and I really liked it and I wanted to listen to it again. On Monday I went into the office and there's a fax from New York saying, "Would you like to contribute a track for a compilation album for charity which will all be covers of Neil Young songs?" I hadn't thought about Neil Young since who knows when. I just faxed straight back and said, "I'm already working on it!" It's getting more and more constant, that kind of thing. It gets more and more. All I can say is, persevere, because I've been doing this for twenty years and it's getting to be constant now.[7]

CA: It's a wonderful feeling.

---

6 The name of another of the Psychic TV-related Acid House release, which also became a term or "meme" in itself.
7 In 1997 Lady Jaye Breyer P-Orridge named this synchronistic phenomenon the "Ov Course Factor" or the "Of Course Factor."

GPO: It's great, because you realise that you are actually beginning to control events, or at least to be so linked with them that you have fastest response. Often the people who survive in survival situations are the ones with the fastest response: finding the food, turning round in time not to get hit by a lion, whatever it may be. Knowing to move just before someone's going to attack you. That's the sort of faculty that we all once had. If you go back to the American Indians, they'll wonder why you bother to talk about it, because to them that's a day to day way of life as it's always been. It's rather sad that in Western society we have to remember how to be that way. But it's still useful. Even in this technological society it's very useful. And when I get that review of "Jack the Tab," it just confirms what I felt, because that LP is exactly the product of trusting that intuition.

CA: I spoke to someone at Temple Records and they said that the original "Thee Starlit Mire" album is going to come out soon.

GPO: That one is coming out as a limited edition picture disc called "Allegory And Self," which is an Austin Spare title. It'll come out as a normal album here and in America as well. A lot of the material on it is still very interesting, and it really needs a commentary, because every track on it was built in order for it to appear to be accessible musically, and lyrically quite simple, bar two tracks, but actually every single track is very specifically about a certain element of magic. It really is allegories and parables about magic. So it's the third album basically. The third proper album.

CA: How come it took so long for it to come out?

GPO: I felt subconsciously that it needed to wait, in order for us to be more clear about what it was and whether it worked. When we listened to it again after not listening to it for a year, it still sounded really good. It's good. We're activists, as you know. That's why I coined the phrase "Occulture", which I think is a very good word. It's a combination of the "Occult," in its widest sense, and "Culture." I've been involved in a total war with culture since the day I started. And that's not changed. I am at war with the status quo of society and I am at war with those in control and power. I'm at war with hypocrisy and lies. I'm at war with the mass media. I'm at war with every bastard who tries to hurt someone else for its own sake. And I'm at war with privilege and I'm at war with all things that one should be at war with basically. And I'm at war with every kind of Either/Or. And parallel to that I believe in genuine loyalty, genuine caring, genuine love and genuine creativity. And genuine integration of one's life and all those constructive things which also ought to be obvious. I've always said, "I do the obvious." It's just that most people don't have the courage. That's it in a nutshell. That's what

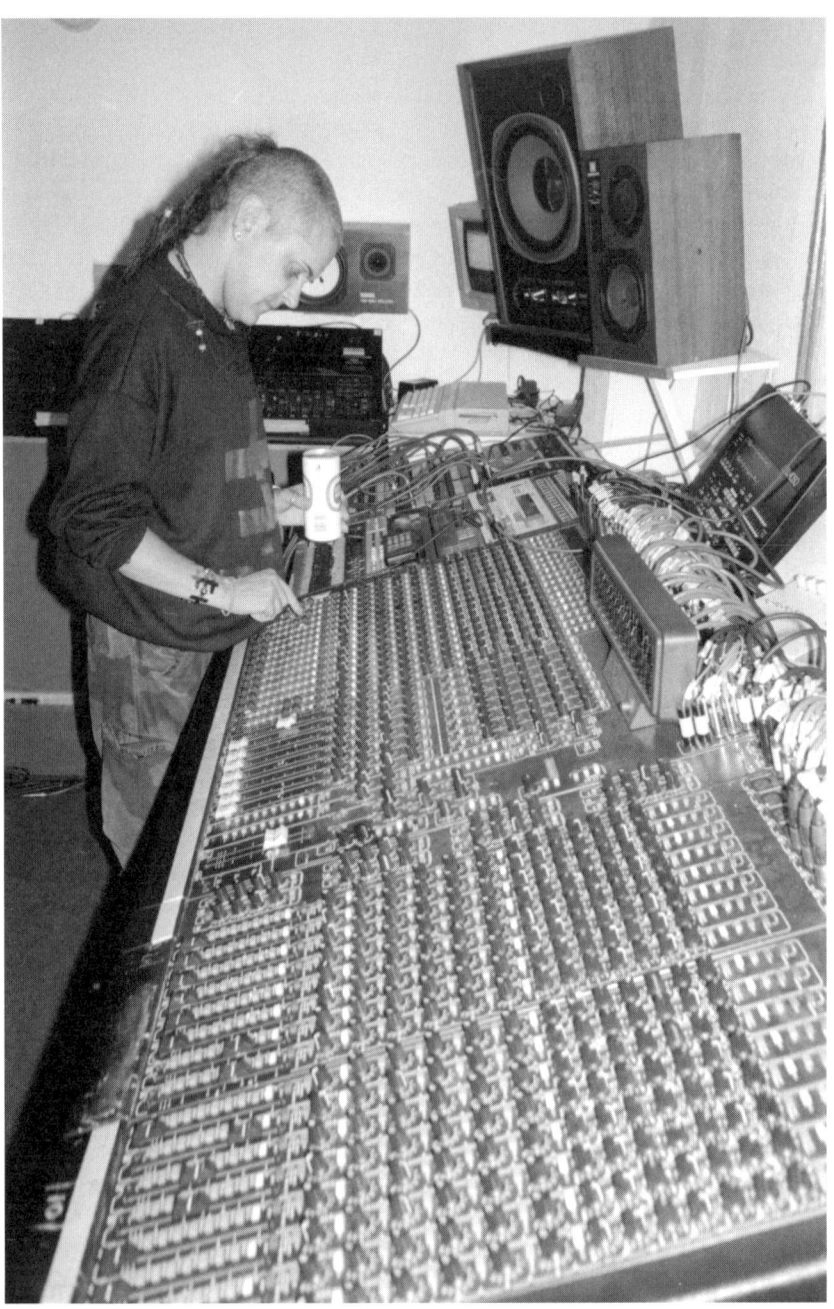

Times Square Studios, London, 1988

terrifies people, because one day they'll be aware, not because it's coming from me or because I'm more or less clever than anyone else, but just that message that we've talked about is very powerful like all radical messages. They're incredibly simple and massively powerful once a lot of people have listened. It's not that hard to turn somebody's ear. That's why they try to stop people from coming to concerts, and that's why they try to stop them from buying records; that's why they tell them not to read what we write. Because every time someone comes to a concert and listens to the records, then the odds increase that everyone's going to start going, "That makes sense!" And once that spiral starts, there is actually the possibility of infinite expansion. And as we're not the owners of it... Even if they get rid of us, the message can carry on living, like all messages. We're merely the transmitters of that message. It came to us via a lot of people: Brion Gysin, William S. Burroughs, Austin Osman Spare, Grandmother, every American Indian, every Aboriginal; everyone who's honest with themselves passed on that message. What we're trying to say is to the whole of society, "For your own survival and for your own increase of happiness, be honest! Before it's too late..." Because the other way won't and does not work. It's a choice. It's that simple.

CA: I suppose a lot of people will always associate Psychic TV with the more cryptic sounds, like on the first two LPs. What do you have to say to those people?

GPO: The same message. Everything we do is allegory. Everything that I construct.

CA: Reflections of what's happening?

GPO: Exactly. Also, they are more complicated and sophisticated than we give them credit for. That's the nature of art. Sometimes the best way to tell somebody something is not verbal; it's symbolic. And the way you build something like the "Dreams Less Sweet" album, the actual structure of it, is the message. The way it's made and the contradictions and the surprises. That's the message and it's not something you can speak, as with a lot of art and a lot of creative expressions. If it was just as simple as speaking, no one would write any more books or paint any more paintings or make any more music, except as celebration. But human beings are complex, and in our society the unconscious mind has been deliberately separated from the conscious mind. We're trying to bring them back together, to make them healthy. Sometimes the only way is through hieroglyphs. People should stop trying to understand or make sense of a lot of those messages in the superficial way, and just accept that they are statements and messages from intelligent people. There therefore has to be intelligence in the way they're made.

Therefore... don't worry about it! Just let it happen, listen to it, and it will tell you its own story. It's basically a description of how life is.

CA: What do you hope that people will think when they listen to Psychic TV and read TOPY material in 50 years from now?

GPO: I hope they'll think we were intelligent (laughs). And that it'll be useful to them. We try to be functional. I think that so far, without blowing my own trumpet, that the work I've done up to date is still considered to be viable and influential. I see no reason why that should alter.

CA: A lot of the TG material is still ahead of most bands.

GPO: Even now. If you listen to "20 Jazz Funk Greats," there are even a couple of tracks that are like Acid House. It's interesting. And "Heathen Earth," the long one with the violin, is like Acid House too. And "Distant dreams" and "Adrenalin." "Adrenalin" is really close to Acid House. I like "Distant Dreams." The spoken parts are like pure, genuine existentialism, which is really hard to get. It's really deadpan and I like how it works. "These times, they are just passing..." Those sorts of lyrics sound really easy and use really normal words, which is one of my favourite hobbies. To make things sound really ordinary and yet be one of the most precise, accurate and, sort of, hard-edged descriptions of some element of reality.

CA: When you're writing your lyrics, or poetry, do you work very hard and scribble over and over, or is it more like a flow of words coming out that you won't change?

GPO: That was written straight down.

CA: Is that the most common way for you to work?

GPO: Most common. Occasionally, I go back and change it, but not usually adding any extra information. Like with mixing, it's the same. That's just a skill that I've developed over twenty odd years of working. It's like Burroughs once said, "People think that all they have to do to write a good novel is to do a cut-up. But the skill is knowing what to cut up and how much to cut up and where to put each section." That's something that involves the aesthetics of the mind that's doing it. That can't be taught and it can't be learned and it can't be copied.

CA: What you are doing with sampling is basically cut-ups. It's interesting.

GPO: It all keeps coming back. The reason I think ritual is so useful in our society is that it's a behavioural cut-up. We have normal patterns of behaviour. When you do a ritual you cut up the way you would normally respond. You reach thresholds of behaviour you would normally avoid. You're in a situation you're not used to. You're actually doing to your responses, your behaviour, your perceptions and your emotions and your psychic abilities the same thing that a cut-up does to words, or sampling does to music. That's why it's so important. That's why Brion Gysin's message about cut-ups is one of the most important statements and discoveries made this century, because you can apply it to video and television and anything else. You can see what controls and what de-controls. And where you are and how big you are and how you exist, your shape, your depth and everything else. You can actually build a holophonic, holographic image of yourself and your place in the world via cut-ups. That ability is the most radical, magical, artistic, physiological statement there has ever been for a long time.

CA: And the sampling unit is the technological device for it.

GPO: And the Dreamachine. Brion Gysin was an alchemist; there's no question. He was the equivalent of the figures in Gothic novels; the roving *Zanoni* alchemist who just had immense knowledge and passed it on verbally to the next generation of people. That's actually what he said to me in Paris. In most of the secret initiations it's always called "touching hands." What you do is take their hand and say, if it's someone who has knowledge of what they're saying, "I pass to you all my knowledge freely for you to make use of and develop." That's what he said to me in Paris, because he trusted us. Even William S. Burroughs wrote in a letter that we were people dealing with the most important aspects of communication that he'd met.

CA: It's well organised and not just an interest.

GPO: It's genuine. It's the real thing. They can't bribe us. They can't give us money. They can't scare us off. What can they do? Their tricks don't work. They can kill me, but it's too late. They can hurt me, but it's too late. I don't own the idea; it's not living in me. I'm just a little bit of the process that keeps alive and moving. That has happened all through human history.

CA: "Thee Psychick Youth Nett Work..."

GPO: Exactly! It's not the Genesis P-Orridge network. Although sometimes people try and do that, it's just another attempt to discredit it and make people scared of it. That's a pity, but at the end of the day there are enough people who are intelligent enough to see around all those games and think, "I've met Gen. That's not his trip. He's trying to give..." And that's what I do. I try to give.

CA: A lot of young people today seem very frustrated. They don't know what to do. All they do is walk around and criticise.

GPO: I think Thee Temple can become the best vehicle in post-industrial society to find a new form of belief structure and behaviour structure. That's the difference. You can have both, without being forced to sign manifestos, like "the ten rules." There are some basic tenets. We are overtly, and we accept and admit it, anti-Christian. With good reason, we believe. And we are anti-control. And we are pro-the development of some kind of new sexuality, where people absorb and develop their female and male aspects. *Pandrogeny*, as we call it. Both in the way they behave with each other, their ability to allow their feelings to come through if they're male, or develop their strength if they're female. And so on. Evolution. Sexuality is not the same as sex, which is another thing our society throws all the time. I'm sure that *The Sunday People* will say it. This is one of their favourite word games. "So, you're into the power of sex?" and you say, "No, sexuality!" Which is quite different from the sex act. Sexuality need never involve an orgasm or the sex act. We're interested in the evolution of the shamanic vision of the world as a whole. Ecology, behaviour, the tribal idea. Those platforms and all the obvious spin-off concerns you would get if you use the word "control," then you're talking about all forms of media and language. If you imagine all the lines going off from each of those words – sexuality, control, shamanism, anti-Christianity – they also all just join up in the big web again. It's all the same thing. How to have dignity as a human being and how to be positive and useful as a human being and how to avoid being degraded and abused as a human being.

CA: You're also going to start publishing books now.[8]

GPO: It's just a very useful way of preserving information and ideas, and spreading it around the planet so it's harder to get rid of it. If you print 1000 copies and they destroy 900, hopefully there's 100 around somewhere that may eventually become useful. Just like in Crowley's case. Most of his books were in small numbers, but now they're in tens and tens of thousand copies, for better or worse. It doesn't matter. The fact is it survived. The thoughts survived, primarily because he printed books. The same with Austin Spare. He's just coming into his own now. He's become more influential. I have to say partly because TOPY has gone

8 A reference to the TOPY-related publishing company Temple Press.

on about him so much. He's become hip. That's fine. There are times when we quite deliberately make use of and manipulate the concept of fashion and hipness, like with Brion Gysin. Basically, it's an invocation.

CA: And Burroughs as well.

GPO: Burroughs as well. You invoke and say the name enough times and eventually people go, "Burroughs? Who is this Burroughs I keep hearing about?" They keep hearing about it, because you keep saying it. That's a magical technique that goes back to the beginning of time, but used in a new way, via mass media and fashion. But it's still invocation, it's still a mantra. It's a mantra to get a specific result, which is interest in that person's knowledge. We do that all the time and we do it quite well.

CA: What are your upcoming projects?

GPO: The "Godstar"-book on Brian Jones. A book on Brion Gysin, based on my interviews and archive.[9] And a book called *Sex, Power and Magick*, which is the history of C.O.U.M. Transmissions and the origins. We want to do three books. One is *Sex, Power and Magick*, which is about C.O.U.M. Transmissions. One is *Power, Sex and Magick*, which is about Throbbing Gristle. And the last one is *Magick, Sex and Power*, which is about Psychic TV and Thee Temple Ov Psychick Youth. It'll be a three volume series. The first one is finished. There's also another book we want to do with Zev,[10] which is linguistic, searching for the Mother tongue and translating various so called holy texts back to their original meanings. What you discover is that they're all, even the "Song of Songs" in the Bible, about Tantric sex and sexual magic. We also want to do a really quick scrapbook called *The Unwholesome Earth Catalogue*. It'll be press cuttings, photos, clips, bits by anyone. It'll be a big scrapbook. And then, once a year, a journal. A serious literary, journalistic compilation book on anything that seems to be useful that should be published, whether it's an article by a journalist that couldn't be printed by Fleet Street, or an esoteric essay on Thee Temple, or a review of a painter who should be remembered. An occultural magazine.

CA: *The Equinox* for the 1980s?[11]

---

9 Eventually published in 2018 as *Brion Gysin: His Name Was Master*, by Trapart Books, Stockholm.
10 Zev (born Stefan Weisser, 1951-2017) was a percussionist and occultist, and part of the TOPY network. The project mentioned here manifested as the book *Rhythmajik*, published by Temple Press, Brighton, in 1992.
11 A reference to Aleister Crowley's series of esoteric and philosophical publications, published between 1909-1913.

Sacred Intent

GPO: Like a mix between *RE/Search*[12] and *The Equinox*, I suppose, but hopefully a bit more radical and provocative, about the state of the entire world. So those are a few projects. Enough to get on with. We also want to print *Thee Grey Book*[13] in different languages. Once we do that, then every TOPY "Access Point" can sell the same book and raise money for themselves that way. That should be quite useful, just like a bible. It'll also be an interesting statement about the idea of the global network. And it's of interest to everyone.

CA: What are the Psychic TV shows like nowadays?

GPO: In London, they're a bit more "extravaganza," because we have more resources here. On a good day there's anything up to 20 video monitors, two or three 16 mm projectors, lighting effects... Basically as many visual, retinal stimulations as possible. The films and the videos are primarily what we make ourselves rather than just found stuff. If it's found stuff, it has to be very interesting or specific. Paula has a flight-case with six cassette decks as well as percussions. We've been using sampling keyboards, but now we want to wire up the drum-kit too to the computer, so when Matthew[14] is playing the drums we can have any sounds we want for rhythm. What we're aiming towards is to become a very contemporary form of tribal celebration music. Ritual music, to have the same effect as "voodoo" trance. And the possibility of it becoming endless, when people involved want to keep on going. There are unfortunately a lot of limitations in terms of the rock venue and promoter at this stage. But we think it's better to make a so-called rock concert of an hour and a half, as an example of what could be possible, than not do it at all. And then occasionally, as things improve, find locations where we can promote and control it all so we can have the option of going on all night.

---

12 A San Francisco-based publication that presents thematic issues on underground culture. Of interest here, mainly issues no. 4/5 (on William S Burroughs, Brion Gysin, and Throbbing Gristle etc, 1982) and no. 6/7 (*The Industrial Culture Handbook,* 1984).
13 *Thee Grey Book* was the main book/pamphlet expressing the ideals and methods of TOPY. Re-published later in Genesis P-Orridge et al, *Thee Psychick Bible*, Feral House, Port Townsend 2009.
14 Matthew Best, drummer of Psychic TV between 1985 and 1999.

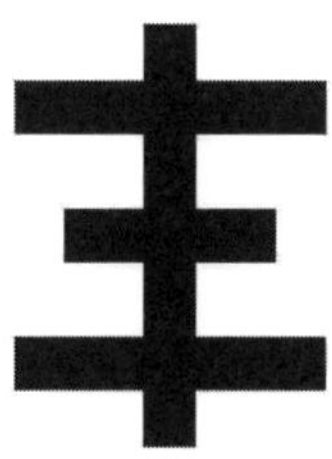

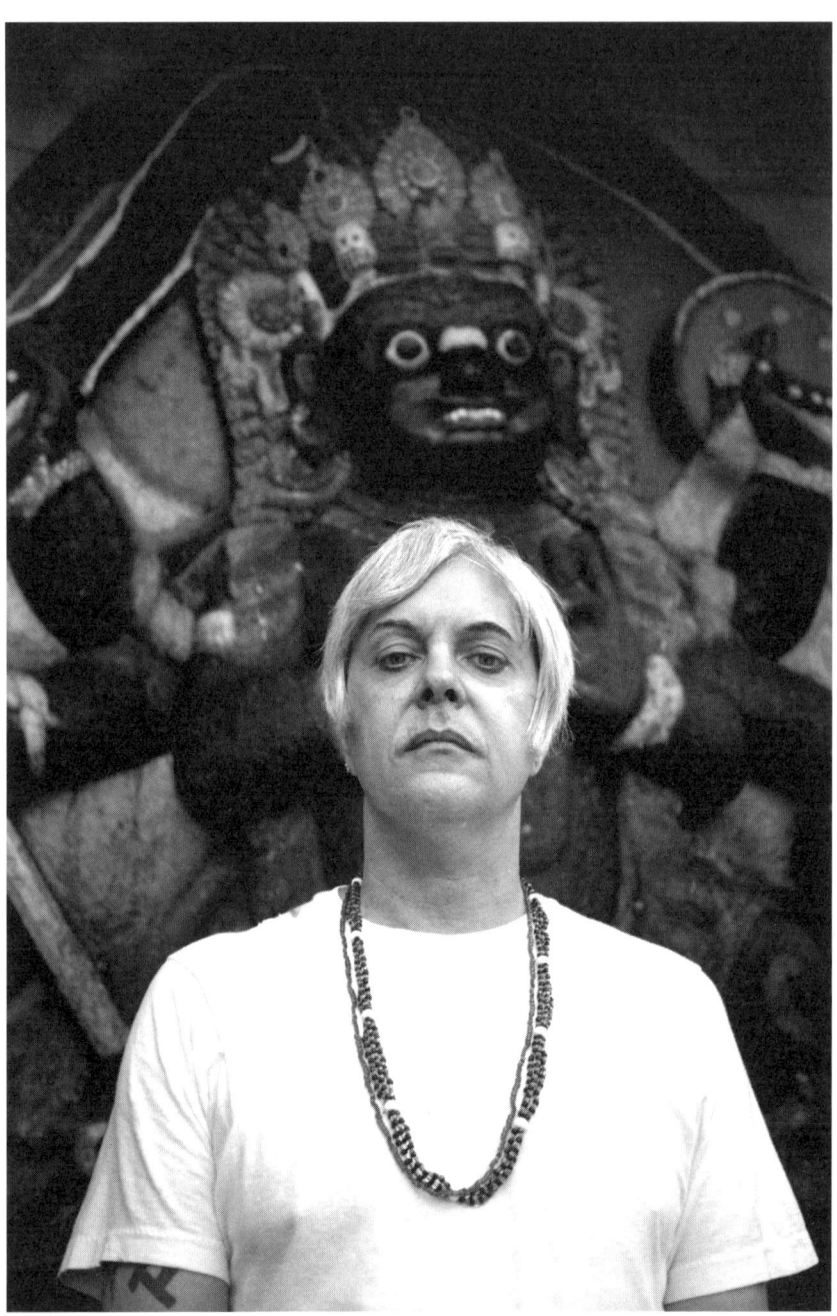

Kathmandu, 2000

Kathmandu, September 23rd, 2000

After having tried to do more structured interviews during American and Swedish meetings in the interim years between 1988 and 2000, we decided to actually make a series of interviews in different locations of the world, and eventually make a book out of it. The first sessions were recorded in Kathmandu, Nepal.

CA: Now we're in Nepal, in Kathmandu, and this is the beginning of, I hope, many sessions leading on to something really good. It might be logical and also interesting to hear about the first time you were here. What were the reasons for your coming here?

GBPO: I came here towards the end of 1991 so it's been three times three: nine years. Gosh, why I came here... When I was probably around nine years old my father gave me a copy of *Seven Years in Tibet* by Heinrich Harrer. I was always getting sick and running out of books to read. So he gave me that book to read and said, "You might like this." I was absolutely fascinated. Even at that age I couldn't put it down. It was like watching this incredible movie. I just entered the book. The whole story and the descriptions of the mountains and the culture made a permanent impression, quite definitely. From that moment on I know I was looking for more information about Tibet. Not as a focussed search but it was always there, present in the shadows of my consciousness. That's never gone away, that fascination with whatever that represented to me. I think one thing it represented was that some of the stories, legends, ideas, the music, the discipline as I understood them at that age, was that they all resonated quite deeply with me. It had nothing to do with anything I'd been presented with before that. There was no reason why I should feel like that. There was nothing on the television at that time, there were almost no books on the subject. Harrer's book was the only one that was easily accessible at the time that dealt with Tibet. There were no recordings, nothing. From eleven or twelve onwards I started to seek out alternative information in the forms of novels, books, pictures. I'm not sure exactly when it was but it was sometime during the mid-60s that I came across a recording of Tibetan music. Again, it was like an explosion inside my head. To me, it seemed completely logical. Far more logical than Western music and far more logical than jazz or rock'n'roll. It seemed to be a very pure description of what sounds and music are supposed to be doing. I had no way to articulate that; I had no real language at the time. Again, it was very visceral and my nervous system was quite literally receiving the information. I think that was exactly what was happening.

To sidetrack for a minute... A guy in America called Mario Pazzaglini was probably the expert on alien writing and alien texts in the world. Including Crowley's *The Book of the Law*, but also the *Urantia* book, channelled letters from housewives in Nevada, bits of apparent UFOs with inscriptions in the metal. He said that one of the grave mistakes of earthly culture as we know it, and particularly in the West, is that we expect alien, extraterrestrial texts and messages, inter-dimensional messages, to make sense in our language, to be translatable into English. Which, of course, is farcical. He said that after all his research, including meetings with His Holiness the Dalai Lama and many, many people, he understood it's because they're not written languages in the same way that we consider language. They quite literally reprogram the nervous system. That same effect I believe is what the Tibetan culture had on me.

In the very early 1970s, I suppose, I'd got hold of one or two albums of Tibetan music. It was still very hard to find. I came across a University bookshop somewhere that had one, maybe two albums of Tibetan music. I used to play them as often as the Velvet Underground, for the same kinds of reasons. Then somebody told me that there was going to be a concert by Dr. Alain Presencer at Ronnie Scott's club in Soho. It seemed like an unlikely place. He'd be playing singing bowls and Tibetan instruments. That came afterwards actually. Before that, I was going down Portobello Road. In my mind, I was visualising a Tibetan thigh-bone trumpet. Somehow I'd gradually stripped away all the different sensations and fascinations and reduced down my immediate obsession to the thigh-bone trumpet. I was walking down Portobello Road, daydreaming about a thigh-bone trumpet. All of a sudden I stopped dead in my tracks, as one does, and turned to the left. I saw this little arcade with small stores that I'd never ever been in before. I just had to go inside. I walked right to the end of the arcade. There was a tiny stall there. I looked at the floor, still being in a semi-trance. I looked up and there was this trendy looking man, with slightly long, black curly hair, a little moustache. Just below his hands were some singing bowls. I said, "Wow, I didn't know anyone had any singing bowls..." I started to talk to him about it and how much I loved Tibetan music and how I couldn't find anyone who knew anything about it. He introduced himself as Dr. Alain Presencer. Then I remembered that I'd heard an album of the singing bowls of Tibet, which was basically him showing how they all sounded. It was more like a library record. I jumped up and down and told him I had a cassette of his recordings. It was so fantastic to finally hear what all the instruments sound like. I got all enthusiastic and said that I was looking for a really beautiful singing bowl and, even more importantly, a thigh-bone trumpet. He looked at me and said, "Well, this bowl..." He took one from underneath and said it was a much more special one than the ones I'd heard before. I've still not really seen one like it since. It's really thick. It's made out of five metals, including gold. Really heavy. He played it for me and I'd never really seen one played before. People have to remember that when this sort of thing happened in 1970-71, it was very unusual to be this interested. There were very few Tibetans coming over to the West at that time. There wasn't that much information. As the old saying goes, it just blew my mind. I could not believe I'd finally found someone who knew what they were, and who had some and could play them! Three things at once. To cut a long story short, he seemed to decide that I was truly interested, beyond just curiosity. I asked how much the bowl was and he said, "Normally, it would be very expensive, several hundred pounds, but you can have it for whatever you have in your purse." That was about thirty pounds. He said it was meant to be with me. Then he pulled out a thigh-bone trumpet out from underneath and he played that for me as well and showed me how to play that. I played it straight away, not very well but I managed to play it enough for it to make some real notes. I still haven't seen one quite the same. It's so minimal. It's just bone, incredibly polished from being held. There's no metal mouthpiece, just a bit of wax. It still, to this day, smells of where it was burned. It smells fresh. He said it was well over 300 years old and that it was incredibly special and that it was a real one. That it was either a holy man or a murderer or a virgin. One of the three things. There's a bit of skin around the bell, which he said was yak skin, and a little band of brass. I got that basically as a gift, more or less. It was one of those blurred, unreal moments. It was after that that I read in the paper that he was also doing a performance, which I still have the tape of somewhere. I saw him again and said, "Thank you so much!" I haven't seen him since. I think he was Canadian. He was a fortuitous being that intervened. Am I meandering too much?

CA: Not at all. It's highly interesting.

GBPO: I used to play it for myself when I did rituals. I always used to think about it as being incredibly powerful and talismanic for me. No matter what else happened to me, those two items, to this day... If there were a fire in the house or an earthquake, those would be two of the things I'd grab. They're that important to me. The bowl itself, according to him, was for smashing the heads of demons. A banishing note. Also, I've come to realise that it's for breaking people's neuro-linguistic loops, migraines, headaches, shattering complexes and traumas, emotional and physical. The more I thought about it and looked at it and listened to it and worked with it, the more I came to the conclusion, again without any real literature to go by, that it must be, on a more mundane, functional level, releasing endorphins. Very specific ones. That very pure note had a very specific metabolic effect. One of the reasons I'd been so affected by the music itself was that that's one of the ways it works. It really does go into the body and dance with the cells. Depending on the thickness of the skin and the flesh, the muscles and all the other elements that make up a human body, it penetrates different levels and generates subtle and less subtle releases of chemicals and synaptic firing at different rates. It can actually palpitate. If you've got one frequency of the body, at say seven cycles per second, and it's at nine, it will start to beat with the body. The body will start to come to its frequency. Which is incredibly powerful stuff. This is marvellous and very radical neurological engineering. My respect and fascination just grew. These people have figured out how to engineer the internal workings of the body long before we even knew that it had those workings. They can make, without real forges, without proper kilns, these perfectly formed tools. Sonic, psychic hygiene... mundane, medical tools, basically just in hard earth, that are absolutely precise, razor sharp and miraculous. They can say that, "This one will do this and that one will do that..."

He also had one at Ronnie Scott's that had been given to him by His Holiness the Dalai Lama. He used to go into Tibet before anyone was allowed to go in there. He used to go with the rebels who were still fighting, and brought some things out that way. He would even be asked to go to a particular monastery and rescue something, a specific bowl or whatever it might be. This one he played and it made a very high note with some other thing beating. Beating in a particular way. It was called the Sirius bowl, the star. That was the frequency of that star, they say. He went to one of the big radio telescopes where they were just starting to pick out frequencies and start to analyse everything. They recorded his Sirius-singing bowl and looked at the print-out. Then they recorded the frequency of Sirius. It was exactly the same. How the hell did these "primitive" people from this medieval culture or anyone know a) what the frequency was, because it's inaudible, and b) then create it audibly and still keep it precise? I feel really honoured that the singing bowl I have is from the same source and is one of those special ones. It's not just the average, common singing bowl, it's a precise one. Built with precise work.

The thigh-bone trumpet eventually surfaced into our popular culture with "Force the Hand of Chance" by Psychic TV. Purely as experiment. What would happen if we did 23 layers of this Tibetan thigh-bone? The thing that got really exciting was that I was doing some very intense, very focussed ritual work with Miss Jackie and Baba Raul Canizares.[1] It was very specific work for healing

---

1 Baba Raul Canizares (1955-2002), author and leading practitioner of Santeria in New York. Founder of the Orisha Consciousness Movement, and friend of the Breyer P-Orridges'.

someone who was incredibly sick. I suddenly felt this compulsion to take out the thigh-bone trumpet, which I only play in ritual situations now, and to start playing it again. I became possessed by a Tibetan spirit and played it like I've never played it before or since. I played it like a master. While it's terribly tragic that it didn't get recorded, because I've never heard anything quite like it, I guess it wasn't meant to get recorded. We live with it. Then something I'd never done before happened. I started to do something that certainly sounded like Tibetan chanting and talking and praying, through the thigh-bone trumpet. Again, it was so fluent and there was no hesitation. Suddenly out came this deep, deep language with strange notes during the whole ritual. Baba Raul was absolutely stunned because he'd never heard anything like this. He had never seen me do this before. He knew it wasn't me. Later, he went and spoke with the spirits and they said it was Drukpa Kunley, and that this bone had belonged to him. It was ambiguous the way he said it was his bone. We don't know if it was one he played or if it's his thigh-bone. There's no way for us to really be sure. It seems sensible because the spirits assume you know what they mean. I'd never even heard Drukpa Kunley. I'd tried to find different ways to spell it. It's happened three times so far. He came through a Misa[2] saying that whenever it was necessary for him to come through for healing he would be available. It was his thigh-bone and I was supposed to have it. It was time for me to start to work with it in a much more focussed and considered way.

CA: Do you ever see yourself as a vehicle? All through your adult, creative life, you have gone through different kinds of arts but with the same kind of attitude. Do you give that perspective any kind of viability – that the actual trumpet could actually have helped change things and your own directions without you consciously knowing it?

GBPO: Absolutely. I hadn't thought of it before. But it makes sense. If it's affecting the nervous system and imprinting it without one's knowledge – like looking at a text without knowing what it means, like hieroglyphs – it must absolutely have done that. Then you start, "Why did I get the trumpet?" How come it was so easy and out of the blue? It was the right person who taught me. Why would that one person pick this little skinny, apparently hippie, guy? The things were worth a lot of money. He basically gave them away.

CA: I've come to the conclusion that one of the most essential magical qualities is to be at the right place at the right time. Would you agree?

---

2 A spiritism session where a medium is possessed by Santeria spirits with messages for those present. Started by Alan Kardec, a 19th Century mystic.

GPO: Yes, I would agree. The symmetry of the universe and all the other universes that intersect in this particular place we're in, is so beautifully structured, so perfect in both the mathematical and emotional way that yes, the greatest of anything that one might call a magician or a baba or a saddhu or a holy person... Whatever the word we want to use... The really impressive quality seems to be the utter simplicity of the key events. The more that one makes friends with all that's symbolised by "23" and supposed random chance... All the lessons I got from Brion Gysin, which is that there is no random chance and yet, "How random is random?" That very puzzling contradictory spiritual bumper sticker becomes almost ludicrous in a place like Nepal. When people say, "I know this guru who a hundred years ago could manifest things...," you think that it sounds a bit far-fetched. But, again, it's that whole thing of language. Sometimes you don't have to pull it out of thin air. Sometimes you manifest it merely by sitting in a coffee bar and being open enough to see in the body movement of a passer-by that they're different. And then to be open enough to say, "Hi! You look interesting..." That might be exactly the person who has the next piece of your jigsaw puzzle. That openness to instant and very subtle shifts in one's immediately surrounding consensus reality, that's when it gets really exciting. It's one of the hardest things for people to do. They want one plus one – I do this and get that. That turns out not to be how it happens, really. That's how you train yourself sometimes to become open but at some point something else happens. Something much more difficult a) to pass on, and b) to articulate. Those who understand the classic thing, they've also found the same thing happening. It's recognition rather than teaching. One of the first things William S. Burroughs said to me was, "Write every day..." In a way, ritual is like that. The reason you write every day or do ritual is for health – magical, physical, emotional health. One can gradually crawl forward in terms of learning in an evolution, a growing... One can crawl but one can also be so prepared and so completely open to any adventure and possibility that when little flashes of illumination, that are so vital, happen, or when certain things pass in front of you, you recognise the ones that are significant and you embrace them. That is something that you can only be prepared for by the way that you build yourself.

I have now come to the conclusion that, as beings, we really are here to build our souls in a very particular way. That's a word we'll have to perhaps look up later. We are here to build our SELF, in big letters. All the choices we make have consequences and all the ways we choose to look, the things we allow ourselves to hear, increase or decrease our abilities to unfold beyond certain points. When you really start to look more and more into all the different rigorous spiritual disciplines, most of them will at some point get to the wordless place, where it's a dance. There's a dance with more than appears within the body. It's a dance outside the body. It's bigger than the body. We are projecting and extending beyond the physical body. For some people it could be knowing when someone's watching you in a room. A simple example of that sensation. Being on the street and feeling someone has bumped in to you although they weren't near enough. All those sensations are more precisely how we describe them than we realise. I somehow knew they were in the room watching. Yet that is "parapsychology." Everyone's felt that some time. "I knew they were going to phone before the phone rang." Everyone says they've had that experience. "I was thinking of you and you just rang me." Any scepticism about the extension beyond the body and consciousness leaking way out beyond what we think it's contained by... I think every human being has experienced some version of that.

CA: To what extent do you think the soul or the self needs the body to train?

GBPO: Well, it apparently does. It sometimes mystifies me. But I have to accept that it does. I think we should come back to that, because you were asking me about Nepal. It's a big question and we should come back to it. All these different things had happened, step by step, touch by touch, to the point where I've included in my ritual work, in my metaphysical thinking, in my talismanic relationship with the universe... Particularly these two sacrosanct items. When we were doing TOPY, people who were sigilising[3] and got to three sent in sigils, we sent them Tibetan buttons as a gift with no explanation. The theme was always coming in. I was always re-introducing and assimilating and having it be part of the bigger picture. Then Malik from TOPYSTEEL[4] started telling me about Samye Ling, the Tibetan Buddhist monastery in Scotland. He said that he'd gone there and it had been really helpful for him when he was having a difficult time. He said I really should go there. I thought it sounded a bit new agey; my sceptical self. It might be hard for people, the notion that despite the fact that I have this romantic relationship with existence, I also have a very sceptical side. Sometimes I'm almost over-sceptical, just because something seems too easy. I used to worry, from a Western, Protestant ethic, about when something came on a plate. Did it have the same value as when it was hard to get? Now I don't worry about that anymore, as you know. Lady Jaye has since taught me to always accept all gifts. But for a while I used to actually think that, "That wasn't hard enough! What's wrong here? Why isn't it difficult?"

I knew of Samye Ling but didn't know exactly where it was. Somewhere between Edinburgh and Glasgow, and this was 1989 I think. I decided to do a camping trip. We used to always take Caresse and Genesse on camping trips and

---

3 A method of integrating, for instance, a graphic or other symbol into one's subconscious during an ecstatic (quite often sexual) magical ritual.
4 One of the many TOPY Access Points.

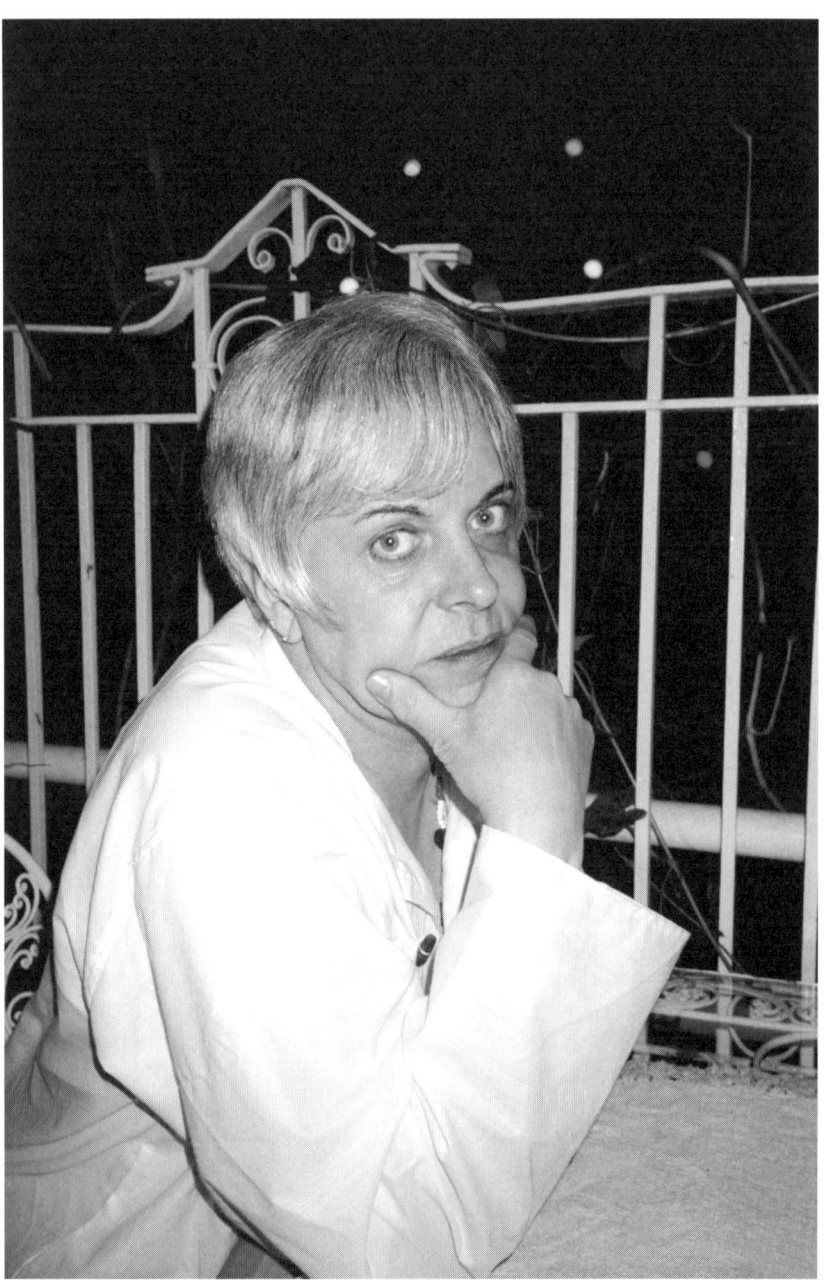

Kathmandu, 2000

go to stone circles and stone sites. We'd get survey maps and find even the small ones... all these amazing places. In 1989, we decided to take the children up to Scotland. Looking for fabulous places. We rented a little mini-van so we could just camp anywhere we felt like. One particular evening we got lost. I was driving, it was night time, and I think I was trying to get to Edinburgh. I don't recall where I was trying to get to. Just driving and it was very much like a Zen trip, in the sense that wherever we ended up, we slept. This is where it gets very odd and fascinating. I'm driving and driving and it gets darker and darker. There are no houses anymore, just forests. I have to drive slowly because of animals, deer and rabbits in front of the headlights. I wasn't concerned because I knew that in the end I could just pull over and wait for daylight. I was feeling awake and rather enjoying seeing the animals.

Some time late evening I see a figure dressed in grey robes at the side of the road, hitchiking. What on earth is anyone doing out here at this time of night? I slowed down, a little suspicious, thinking this could be some crazy person. A man, no easily specific age, in grey. He wanted a lift and I said, "Sure. Where are you going?" and he just said that he lived "up there," pointing forward. I thought it was very odd. No village, just "up there." He sat next to me but I couldn't focus on him. No matter how hard I tried, I couldn't really see what he looked like. He talked to me but I couldn't recall what he had just said. I was somewhat mystified and a little suspicious. I can't place who or what this man is. There was something very mysterious, something that troubled me. But not in a frightening way. I just couldn't make sense of why I was concerned about this experience.

All of a sudden he said, "That's where I live!" and I just saw trees. He said that his house was there. As he was getting out, he asked if we were looking for Samye Ling. I said that not really, no, but said I might go there one day. He said it was just up the road. I looked and indeed there was a house among the trees. He got out and walked away. I thought that I'd better ask him exactly where the monastery is, so I jumped out of the van. He'd disappeared. I thought it was getting weird. I turned to Paula, and she said that she thought he was dead, that he was a ghost, but she was too scared to say anything. I thought he was a ghost too. But we guessed it must mean we should go to Samye Ling!

This is the whole thing that we were talking about. Being ready to go, "OK, no matter how irrational this experience is right now, that's not important. The important thing is that somehow I've been directed..." I drove along the road and as we passed a church I saw a sign saying "Lockerbie," which is the little village where that passenger jet crashed after a Libyan operative had smuggled on a bomb killing everyone on the plane and a lot of people sleeping in their beds. Then I saw some Tibetan prayer flags and some lights and somehow we had found Samye Ling. We drove inside, pulled up the van, and this really jolly nun came up and said "Hi! I'm Annie Wong Mo." I said that we'd come to visit and asked if it was OK if we stayed a while. No problem. We could have dinner very soon, she told us. That would be great to have dinner with Tibetan monks, and the European ones too of course. We walked in with her and felt really welcomed and had a really friendly, happy time. Suddenly the nun stopped and looked at me and at the table, rather curiously, and said, "That's odd... They've laid a plate for Lama Yeshe. He's the retreat master, but he never comes out for dinner. Very rarely." It transpired that Lama Yeshe had instructed the monks and nuns preparing dinner, before we even knew we would be ending up there, to lay a plate for him and four people who would be his guests. I've never found out whether it was him on that road or one of his familiars or projections. But I have to, at least, put that into the realm of possibilities. If it wasn't one of his thought forms, then how else could he have led us there? It's this fantastic good fortune. Suddenly, from thinking I might go and check it out, to sitting with the guy.

He was brilliant. He put all my suspicions at rest and just completely seduced me in the best possible way. I've likened him since then to being a dolphin. Being with him was very similar to being with the dolphins. The sensation of him looking in your eyes, inside you... It was like he was going through the index file cards. Every memory, where you were before, where you come from, the future, the past and who knows how many dimensions. And always with a giggle! Giggling and laughing is always a good sign to me. In my experience, some of the wisest people have laughed a lot and made fun of everything. Quite the opposite of pompous.

CA: The Dalai Lama is a very fine example of that.

GBPO: Yes. And also very humble in the best possible way. The laughing, wise person. I stayed there with the children quite a long time; a few days. We even considered buying a house near Samye Ling because I enjoyed it so much. We did some rituals, some prostrations, some praying and got to know all of the people. At some point before I left he said to me in a private audience that I had to go to Nepal. He told me that they had a monastery in Kathmandu and that they had soup kitchens for all the refugees.

CA: Which Tibetan school or tradition was that?

GBPO: You know, I can't remember. I'd have to check my notebooks. It's been so long since I looked. First I thought it was a bit presumptuous... "You should go to Kathmandu..." But it was one of those classic NLP, mystical, hypnotic... Whatever you want to call it... He programmed me. The idea didn't leave me. From then on it became the next pilgrimage, the next spiritual, magical pilgrimage. It didn't take that much persuasion! OK, now I've got somewhere to go with a reason to go. I rarely travel without a specific reason. I think that travel broadens the mind because one goes with the intention of broadening it. One can also go and come back with no new information. Going to a place like Ibiza and seeing it doesn't always broaden the mind.

So that's how I got to Nepal. The sequence of events, more or less, that got me on a plane to Nepal, bringing great big bundles of clothes that we collected through TOPY. We got fantastically high quality clothing through TOPY and carried it all the way there. They had a small area in the monastery to warehouse it. They made sure it went to the most useful places. If you just gave them away to the kids, they would sell them.

When we first arrived we inevitably took pity on these filthy starving kids aged around six to eight, begging barefoot near the start of winter. Paula bought new, cheap but strong sneakers for two or three of them on behalf of TOPY. Much to our surprise the same kids appeared a couple of days later back in bare feet. The Nepali monks explained to us that they had sold them, or had them stolen by bigger kids. Our Western thoughts and pity processes were useless there. Of course!

CA: What are your impressions on returning to Nepal?

GBPO: The first thing I've noticed is that there seems to be a lot less beggars, surprisingly. I expected more because I thought that the more tourists, the more beggars. But it seems the beggars have gone elsewhere. There used to be dozens of Indian beggars that came up from Northern India specifically to Kathmandu for the easy pickings. They seem to have more or less disappeared. Or on the road from the visa place to the Royal Palace, there used to be a lot of Indian beggars there too, and around the corner in Thamel[5] too. I don't see those people anymore. There were also a great many newly-arrived Tibetan refugees, many wearing traditional costumes and traditional jewellery. They would tend to congregate at Boudenath Stupa because it was one of the places that everyone knew of. That would be both colourful and sad because the quickest way to get any money at all would be to sell what they'd carried over. Which would tend to be their most prized personal possessions. There was this very affecting and melancholy mix combined with the joy of being free and having arrived at the destination. People would be parting with talismans for some rupees. Hairpins, locks, daggers. They would go inside their clothes and drag out something. There were a lot of beggar children around Boudenath who really did live in the streets. They kept warm by sleeping with dogs. I don't know where those people are. I don't know if it's a sign of success and social progress or whether they've been moved

---

5 A part of Kathmandu popular with tourists.

to less visible sights. It certainly appears as if things are policed more. Just having to pay to go into Boudenath is a big change, even if that's only for tourists. There was a lot more dirt and a lot more activity actually on the street, going from Chhetrapati towards the river where the Vajra Hotel is. There was much more of people living in makeshift huts, washing in the street, cleaning in the street, cooking in the street, using the street as a toilet. That seems to have disappeared to a great extent. The garbage tends to be piled on the corner of a street instead of all around. There's an attempt to clean up and be more hygienic and aware of some of the causes of illness. Whether that's just in Kathmandu, I don't know. There seems to be a lot more organisation and things seem more consciously commercialised. There are more renovated buildings. There's a higher level of European and foreign people.

In a way, all the things that might have tended to discourage someone else from coming here were all the things that excited me. I was very excited to see all the levels of life being active and lived out on the street, in through the doors and into the buildings. It was very much as if the spirit of life itself was just leaking through everything; from the very smallest creatures living in the street to the incredibly baroque, psychedelic paintings of the temples. You could literally glance from a golden Buddha to a blood-soaked Kali, then to a child crawling in garbage and then look up and see someone drive past in a diplomatic car. I fell in love with the way Nepalis and Tibetans live a total integration of spiritual devotion and mundane daily life. For me, that kaleidoscope of extreme differences becoming one unity is just a beautiful metaphor of how my experience of life is. In a very real sense, every action, every still moment, every loud barter and every quiet prayer is an entirety; a completeness like the period during an eclipse when it is total. All these contradictions are an energised chaos, yet also an organic, molecular lack of motion. Nirvana perhaps?

That is, in different forms, and perhaps less extreme, the trip here. The turn-on, so to speak. Devotion flows within everything. You may see a goat being beheaded in a ritual performed by a priest for a woman dressed for her day job at the office. Old ladies shopping see nothing out of the ordinary. A porter carries a refridgerator on his back wearing plastic flip flops and rests by a statue of Ganesh in a shrine between the doors of two homes. There is no separation. Life is art/spirit and art/spirit is life. Which is why I was so fascinated with the idea of the Aghori.[6] Trilochan[7] told me about it. The path of no distinction, where everything is the same. No matter how different it might appear, it's all ultimately

---

6 The Aghori Baba is a group of ascetic practitioners associated with magic, necromancy etc. Although looked down upon by orthodox Hindus, local people revere them for their magical and healing abilities.
7 Trilochan is a revered baba and cultural celebrity in Kathmandu, associated with the "Hippie Trail" of the 1970s, and a friend of Breyer P-Orridge's. Trilochan is also revered Sun Yogi.

just molecules and atoms dancing together, held by unseen forces. Kathmandu and Nepal are, in a sense, exactly that. They're not distinct from the greatest things in the universe. And they're made up of the simplest in terms of behaviour and belief, and the needs of life. Nepal really is the gateway to all other worlds, I think. Both literally and figuratively, symbolically. It's unique in that there are 36 tribes, four castes... It's the only country in the world where Hinduism is the official religion. But Hinduism here happily incorporates Buddhism and vice versa. You can go to Swayambhu and there's a temple with the sacrifices, and you have Buddhist iconography as well on that same temple, and prayer wheels spinning around the edges.

There are many parallels between Trilochan and me. We just kept coming up with them, with different names between the Yoruba and the Orisha and the ones here. I'm not academic enough but the parallels and the similarities are striking. Even one of the babas gave me a card saying he was from "Orisa," and the original word is *Orisa*. So there's a place here where the holy people and the babas go to perform rituals, and there's the beads and the different colours and meditations and the fact that there's blood sacrifice in both. There's a very clear connection. It's well known that the culture from the North of India worked its way all around and through Africa and then through Spain. Nigeria has the Dogon, who are an ancient culture. These two paths are probably the oldest surviving paths, the Nepalese and the Yoruba. I'm including Tibetan Buddhism in that as well. I think that Tibet and Nepal are one in a sense now with the refugees and the migration.

CA: So you're suggesting more of an Asian genesis rather than an African one? In terms of this specific kind of religion?

GBPO: I don't think anybody knows. My feeling is that everything could have begun in one place. Certainly, biologically they've traced DNA back to just two people in Africa, one male and one female. I don't think that's necessarily the interesting conjecture. I think the real conjecture is to learn to believe that all sincere religions – and to be sincere they have to believe in generosity, kindness and love rather than violence and imposition – are the same. The myths and the stories they tell have originated for the same reasons. That's really what I get from the connections between the Orisha consciousness and Hinduism and Buddhism and animism. They're the oldest ones; they're pre-Egyptian. Neither of these two paths really get the attention that one would expect based just upon how old they are – the lineage. I really think that it's because Europeans for centuries have believed that it could not be possible that there was knowledge in Africa, because these people appear "primitive." It could not be possible that there's wisdom and knowledge in Nepal or Tibet because these people appear to be savages and medieval. Most of the lack of understanding and appreciation has been pure post-Christian racial and intellectual prejudice.

CA: Could it be that the strength of Hinduism and the strength of Buddhism and the resurgence in the West of African religions has to do with the fact that they're essentially non-missionary? They attract people who specifically want to find things out themselves?

GBPO: I think it's significant that they are non-missionary. I don't think that's the only reason for the resurgence though. I think part of the resurgence has literally to do with the migration of populations. In the United States, the way things are going, soon half the population will be speaking Spanish. The semi-official religion of many of these peoples has always been versions of Santeria. The same in Cuba and in all those places where slaves were brought from Nigeria and other places in Africa. With Buddhism one could argue that the reason the universe created a situation where His Holiness the Dalai Lama had to choose to leave Tibet was precisely because the West needed the psychic healing and hygiene of Tibetan Buddhism. Luckily for us all, because it's been such a tragedy in so many ways, there is at least one silver lining to the Chinese version of the holocaust. People run around chasing some cocaine dealer from Nicaragua, spending billions of dollars on the drug war and turn a blind eye to their favourite trading partner China. They have very methodically committed genocide. Somehow they think that sterilising people doesn't necessarily mean killing them. They're just making it impossible for the people, their language and their unique culture to survive and grow. That's a crime against humanity. The rituals at Swayambhu, with the flowers, the chanting, the beads and the liquids, the candles and the fires, the stones and so on are integral to representing the forces of the gods and goddesses. All that is very familiar if you've started to work with Orisha consciousness in any way. In the same way, all the colours seem to be parallel too. I think the other thing that makes them similar is the idea of practising every day, and that the gods and goddesses, the divine beings, are in no way offended or belittled by the idea of your involving them in everyday life. Even mundane activities like cooking and making decisions. All those things are completely reasonable and necessary to the practice.

I can't stress enough how incredibly important it is that people try to live every minute of every day of their lives with the sense of something divine. And that it's surprisingly more liberating than people might imagine. You might imagine that once you spend your whole life, every day, aware of all these other forces that are in balance, and that you also have to be in balance, that that might seem restrictive and difficult. But in fact it's quite the opposite. It's the classic truism of many religions, which is that once you let go of trying to be in control,

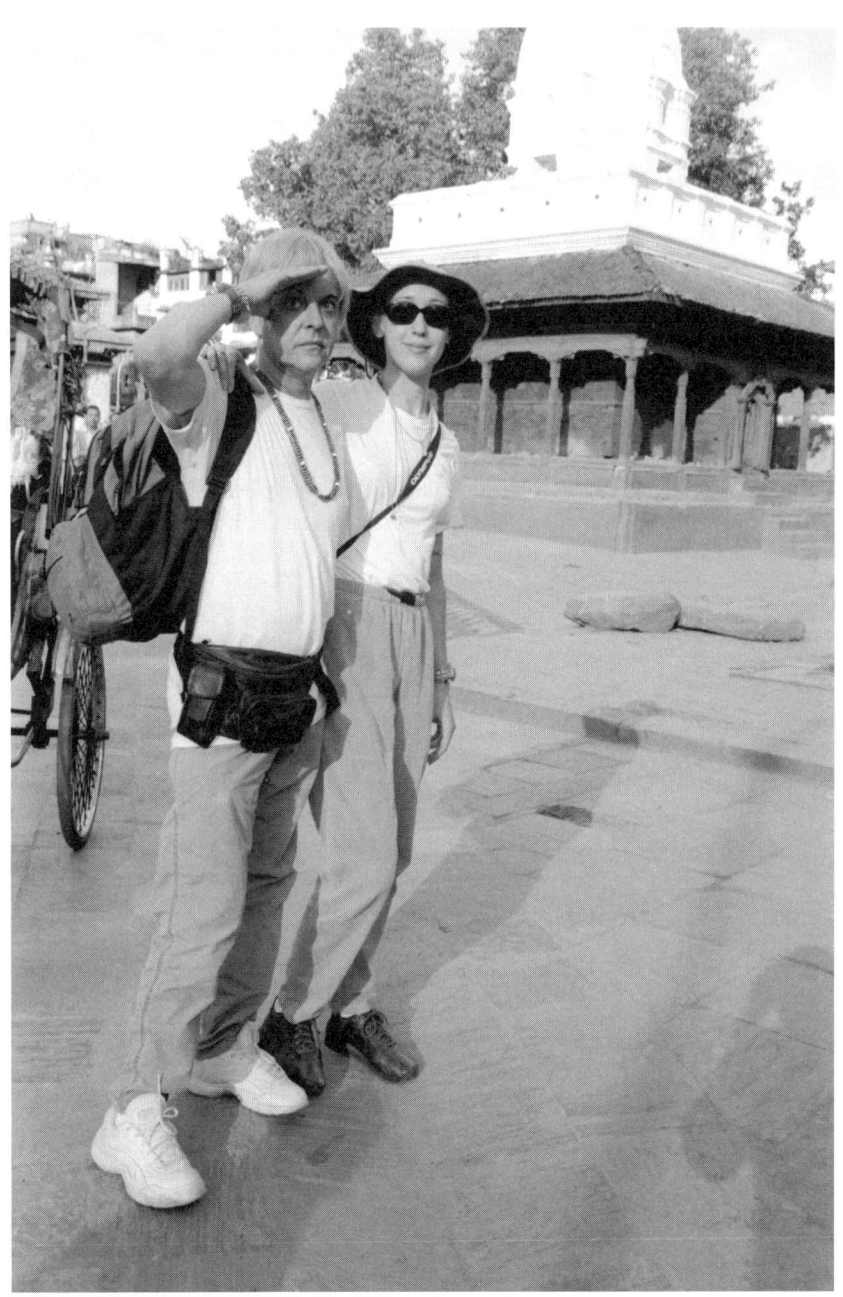

Genesis P-Orridge & Jackie "Lady Jaye" Breyer, Kathmandu, 2000

you have as much control as you want. You have it because you're in partnership with the unimagined, as yet, forces, whether they be mathematical, literal, metaphysical, biological... There is no doubt in my mind that this universe, in which this particular planet is a section, is the most impossible-to-conceive kaleidoscope of geometry and colour and consciousness and being and life force – the living spirit. It actually all exists outside, except on this planet. This planet is most remarkable for having linear time. Grant Morrison, who wrote "The Invisibles," had a very good explanation of how to think of the human body. The body is a time suit. Our spirits reincarnate on this planet in bodies, in time suits. Time itself, linear time, is such a brutal environment that even with time suits we are broken down as it ages and destroys us. A time suit lasts usually under 80 years. Once you imagine that your human body is like a deep diving module, you know that once you go outside you get crushed by the pressures. It's a little bit like that being here. When we're in the womb we remember being part of God and still in bliss. We have certain connections with parents and friends through the skin and through the blood and the thoughts of the people close. Then we forget that because we're inside linear time. The less the children sleep all day and the more they try and communicate with words, the more they become aware of their time suit bodies. And the less they remember the divine. That separation has been used for centuries by those who would control everybody. One of the classic tragedies of the last 2000 years is that those who possess power and exercise that power have conspired to gradually convince more and more human beings that the material is the only form that there is. There's only the material world and therefore you have to look after your body because it's real. You should try and get money because it's real. What they've done is ultimately now becoming a global plague. Everywhere you go on this planet, every culture is being invaded by this idea, which is that things that appear solid and appear to be here now, in measured time, are more valuable than anything else because there is nothing else. The underlying theme of the global expansion is completely atheist and completely materialist in a way that we have never seen before.

CA: There's a lot of awakening going on at the same time, and there are a lot of avenues for spreading inspiration for illumination, etc. Do you see any of these as being an action and any other as being a reaction? For instance, is the new age movement a reaction stemming from the control aspect, or vice versa? Is the control aspect tightening the screws now that it's easy to see that something is going on that could potentially be threatening?

GBPO: I hate to sound trite, but all of the above. I think the people in control have, since the 60s, which we can refer to as a phenomenon I think... Well it was the 50s too and the Beatniks... Basically, it was post-war, post-atomic bomb.

That's my real feeling. What gets labelled as the 60s was just the very visible outpouring of something that began with Hiroshima and Nagasaki. People in control were taken by surprise, I think, by the speed with which the alternative culture spread. One reason it did spread so quickly was the advent of offset litho printing, which is not often given the credit it deserves. Suddenly, Gestetner sten-cil and offset litho became cheaper, which meant that people could save up their small amounts of money and print at least one issue of a magazine. Traveling was also getting easier so people could carry the magazines with them and give or sell them to other people. The whole backbone of the alternative movement at that time was the underground magazines, and people travelling with them. And the improvement in the postal service, to a lesser degree. But mainly people traveling and getting cheap printing. The reaction of the people in control was to prosecute the magazines all over America and Europe for obscenity and includ-ing sexual material and try and jail the writers. This is also forgotten by a lot of young people. The authorities wanted to suppress everything and everyone that seemed to be an enemy. That's how they operated with culture then. To see an enemy and attack it and try and destroy it. What's happened since then though is that they've changed the tactic in a very disturbing way. It's disturbing because it's effective and people don't seem to have woken up to it yet. They now realise that they have no enemies. There is no need to target one group as the enemy. It can still be used as a more primitive tactic, a bit like using a shotgun when you've got smart bombs. One keeps one's arsenal of weapons. But the real strategy now is to coerce, to assimilate, to mimic, and especially to bribe instantly anything that appears to be successful and popular with rebellious youth, and a potential enemy. If somebody is doing punk rock, you sign them to a major label. You don't say, "Oh dear! Let's stop them..." If somebody is making a radically fresh political statement, you ask them to join your parliamentary committee to give you advice, and give them a salary and publish their papers and say how won-derful it is that people are thinking of these things. You put them on talk shows on television and you make them friendly and familiar like Santa Claus. They are seduced or reduced. Either way, it doesn't really matter. That combined with the new mass media; with TV that they never lost control over, like they did with the printed press. They made laws in advance against pirate radio stations once they saw that might happen. Pirate television never took off. They closed down the new mass media. The first thing they didn't seem to have control over was "The Well."[8] It operated just like the underground press. When I first had my e-mail account, it was at The Well. It was just basically people writing to each other. It was a free zone. It was an ad hoc free zone and the telephone wires worked like people traveling. Packets of information were passed around. And people were

---

8 The Well was one of the first substantial internet communities.

of course travelling too. As Timothy Leary said, "One of the great things about the web was that you could move your brain around the world without leaving your house." That's still true. Still one of his very astute statements. You didn't have to get on a plane with a big bag of underground newspapers. You could send them instantly for ten cents or less. And no one could censor it. It was back to the underground press idea.

But it was also Timothy Leary's house that I was invited to, in the strategy of the new world order. I was invited to speak to several people who were investigating the nature of the world wide web for Bill Gates. They said that he had told them that they could have a budget of whatever his shares made in one day. It turned out to be ten million dollars that day. They got that budget to travel around America physically and interview the leading lights of the newly appearing Internet community, which was John Perry Barlow and the people at *Mondo 2000*, like RU Sirius, and Timothy Leary. He told them about me and invited me over. It turned out, once they, who shall remain nameless, started talking to me, that they'd been given the task to privatise and police the internet and make it into a commercial venture, where people could protect their investments. Their smaller project, and I use the name as a joke, was the questions, "What would be the next gadgets that the hip people would want? How would they like the technology to go? What kind of hardware?" That was when I realised that it was on its way to be over. When people are spending ten million dollars to figure out how to control that new medium, and this is just one person, you realise that again, they see early on what could be an enemy. Then they co-opt it, and some of the leading experts and originators. They get semi-free information and then they close it down. That's much more insidious and much more dangerous... That's actually what's going on with this global economy: globalism.

Globalism used to be the word that struck fear into every free nation. I seem to remember that the First and Second World Wars were supposedly fought against globalism. Good cooperative behaviour between different tribes. We're already part of the Third World War. It's going on right now. It's going on in an invisible way. It may well be, and I would subscribe to it, that we are in the process of a chemical reaction: a fusion. The way I describe it is that whilst in one way it seems arbitrary that we just hit 2000-2001... As we live in a measured time environment, no date is insignificant. As the universe ultimately is describable as mathematics, then numbers and dates are significant in some way. I would argue that they're alive. With the advent of the splitting of the atom and the advent of computers and all that those imply, and also with the mapping of the human genome... Those three things are both the ultimate evidence and achievement of the old way and also inherently have the potential of triggering a new way. That's the point where we're at right now. Quite literally. Not because of different stories in different mythological books, and not because of fear and loathing or blind enthusiasm. I just think that one's logic and one's deduction takes you to this point. If we assume that all holy people and all the babas live outside of time as well as in their human time suits, then of course they can access the oracle and they can access the entire timeless form and shape of some part of this universe that they're connected with. It's quite reasonable that they would predict certain crisis points; certain significant moments where change is possible, where really important millennial shifts can happen in terms of the unfolding of human history. Most of them have picked somewhere around now.

If we use as an example the information that's doubling faster and faster, and the population too... And that's another story too. Are we just pods of information? At some point in the next ten years information will double instantly. And after that, before itself. It sounds awfully like a piece of metaphysical, Tibetan-Buddhist literature of ideas. That's the other thing that's happening. People are being forced by their own powers of deduction and by the evidence that they experience in their mind and body to try and describe their world. And as they do, they become mystics by default. Whatever lack of discipline or discipline one may actually exercise when one begins to deduce and reduce the possibilities of what's happening whilst here in life, one becomes a mystic. And one becomes aware of the mysticism of life. Because one has to say things that only make sense based on one's actual inter-dimensional perceptions. And the attempt to put them together like two slides and see the beautiful symmetry when they slip together. What one expects of one's life from the universe and what one tries to do with it. If the two fit perfectly, that's equal to a mandala. If they don't fit perfectly, you still see little bits in a jigsaw puzzle that could become the mandala. That's when people get excited and that's when they start coming to places like Nepal and not being disappointed. Because all of that goes on here as a matter of course. It's not even really worth mentioning. The villagers we went to today, they would just say, "Of course! Of course it's nothing less than timelessness and of course there are things we don't understand and that intervene on our behalf when we ask them nicely, just like good parents."

The other war that I think is going on is the war of those ultimately kind beings, no matter how bizarre they may seem to us, and whatever the other powers are that are the bad trip of this flattening out into global control and mediocrity. Ultimately, that's where you lose yourself. If anyone's Faust, it's the old way. The absolutely materialist, globalist old way that still believes that money is power, and that if you don't agree, it's absolutely reasonable to hurt, kill or in other ways destroy someone else who does not agree. That's the old way. That way, on the surface, is spreading like a virus, in terms of other governments and other control systems adopting it. They're adopting an infected method. There is no philosophy. We're in the age of the godless in terms of those who supposedly take care of society. One of the most abhorrent phrases I have ever heard is right-wing republicans who're saying they are "compassionate republicans." The two just don't go together. There's no room for a compassionate politician. Gandhi would not be able to do that work now because they got wise. There is a war. The war that used to take place in the heavens is coming to the earth but in an unusual way. I think that a lot of the old gods and goddesses have reincarnated and they are here right now in human bodies. Maybe not even aware that they are who they are but they're here. It's such an important crossroads. Because they're here, people can feel their warmth, like a fire, even though they don't have a name or a sign. I believe people feel that spiritual warmth, that sense in certain people that they truly want to make something sacred and holy happen with their lives; no matter how difficult it is, no matter how many mistakes they make. Within them, ultimately, is that intention. Those people warm the souls of the people around them, even the angry souls, even the sceptical souls, even the greedy souls are warmed by them. I've seen it over and over. It's never wasted. Some of those who are warmed share that with others. That's where the other medium is. It's become another invisible medium. I don't think they're all reincarnated necessarily in the obvious places and in their own previous religions. They're reincarnated where they're needed, and then they meet. That's the new way.

The new way is that all the gods and goddesses are here together to destroy evil and greed and stupidity because there's no need for it anymore. No one needs to believe in it anymore. All of us can see through the mass media the evidence and what's wrong and what's stupid and what is glorifying the mundane and cosmetic. Each human being can fight a huge part of the war by believing that the universe is kind, by believing that it is not stupid or weak to give love beyond just one's own immediate family. You can love unconditionally and not get hurt. The final part of the new way is knowing that one is richer by sharing that which one has with others who have other things than if one is just a millionaire on one's own. For example, Trilochan will have his holy area here in his holy land. Through Trilochan, holy land has been acquired, through his warmth and fire. People have been drawn to his fire and made it possible for his dream which is a dream of many people manifesting that in holy land. In the same way, we can have a place in America. We can have a farm and you can have a place wherever you are. Each of us has a house and we all have a house. In Morocco we have a house. If someone asks me how many houses I have, I'd probably answer that I have about eight houses. One in Nepal, one in Morocco, one in Sweden, one in New York, one in upstate New York, one in San Francisco. We all have those places. Maybe eight, nine focussed people, with their fire that is such a strong compulsion that they cannot stop themselves despite all those around them who claim to know better and telling them it's the wrong path. Those people suddenly have a global network, and all of them know, of course. We all know that it's the same story. I stick to the original statement from years ago: "Everyone is telling the truth all the time."

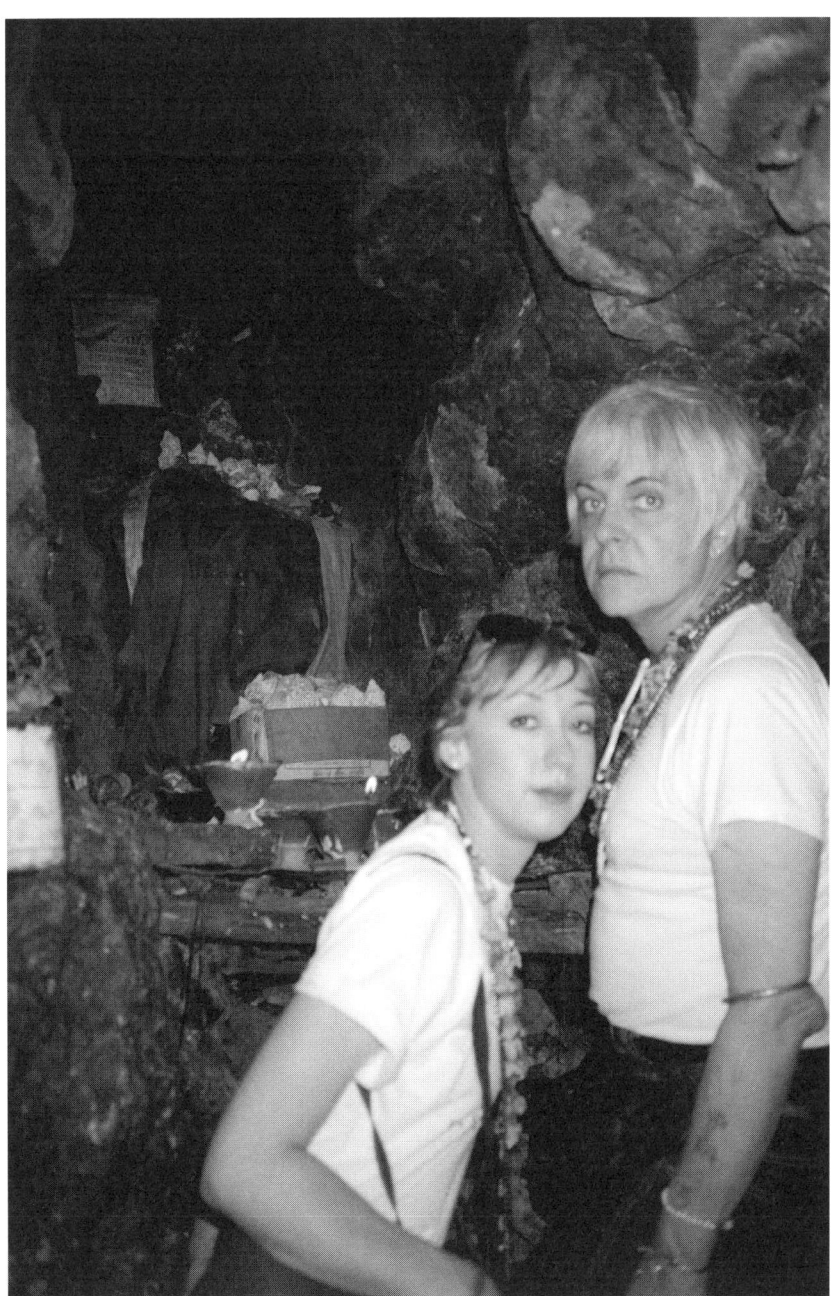

Kathmandu, 2000

All that matters in the end is that it's fire and that it's elemental energy; a transforming energy. That's all we need to know. The next new way on is to accept all the truths and not worry about the names. To love all the names. They're all the names of us and they're all the names of God and all the names of the universe. All the names of whatever they may or may not be. When you surrender to that, where it doesn't matter, and where even matter doesn't matter, then you suddenly see this pattern. It becomes simpler and simpler. Power comes to you. Things you need come to you exactly when they're needed. Not before. You can't get greedy this way, because it won't come before the right time. This is the *Of Course Factor*. It's like, "How come I get it when I don't want it?" The real trick of the truth is teaching yourself to say what you need. That's really hard. I still make this terrible mistake, where I'll say something which is only half of what I was thinking. It doesn't communicate. If I stop myself and if I'm humble enough to admit that I couldn't communicate properly, trying to say what I was actually feeling in my heart when I said that... "I wish you wouldn't do that because..." Instead I'd say, "Could you turn off the television?" What I really mean is that, "I'd really appreciate if you'd notice that I'm trying to do something and you turned the television on." What you really want to communicate is being noticed and respected. That's where it's harder to find the path. In the West maybe it's different. I know a lot of confusion happens because people try to say short bits; short versions of what they mean.

There's an invisible help here because that's how the universe works. In the West everything is built solid and big and impressive There's a whole attempt to convince people that that's what's real. If you have these fabulous big strong structures then it must be OK. "It's alright because we're in control, because we can still build big houses..." This is the time of the gods; this is the classic time of the gods and they are walking here yet again.

One of the puzzles of being on this planet in human bodies is that you forget who you were before. That's one of the agreements you make when you're reincarnated. Some very few holy people remember.

CA: The main thing that made the Second World War different from the previous ones was the atomic bomb. The reaction to that started a new era in which this philanthropic, magical resurgence is taking place. Do you think that all of these positive things could in any way have been inspired or affected by forces outside our planetary sphere?

GBPO: Absolutely. That's it. There's no question in my mind that the gods and the goddesses and the spirits and all kinds of beings, they all exist here too. They're all connected here too. Ultimately, everything we touch and feel and think is made of God, in the truest sense. From nothing, which was God unawakened, came something, which was God becoming aware of itself. From then on, everything that's unfolded since then has to be, by logic, made of God. The universe is God experiencing itself. It's a joy for God to experience this universe. It's a joy for all the gods and goddesses and human beings to enjoy being. We are part of that being. They are concerned for their own beings, as they feel everything. We can feel everything if we become awakened enough too. Some people go mad because they feel everything and they're not trained. They end up in mental hospitals because they experience everything. No one knows what to do or how to stop it. Even by their thoughts they can be involved in what's happening, just as by our thoughts we can make things happen. Even in mundane ways. We've seen it on this trip. We think of something and suddenly someone walks up to us with that thing. It's to the point where it's laughable. One of the reasons why it happens more frequently or more visibly in Nepal is because of the unorganised chaos. It's an embracing of a system of the universe, which says "it shall come to you." You're actually just navigating infinite pathways simultaneously. You can't see what your largest spirit, your potential being, is already experiencing. If we keep reincarnating through infinity we have all evolved too. This bit is just the exact moment that is a part of what it's experiencing. From my personal experience I also see other parts of my evolution. Looking back now, I know there are other parts of me that are already in this person's way future and also way past. But they're happening now too. Therefore it's all happening at once. I've been in those other-dimensional states and I've seen one unfolding into my possible future. And I've seen another one and been able to adjust a change in the future because of the learning I'm having now; the compassion I'm beginning to feel now. I can see the other me before I learned a little compassion. If I know that that much can happen now, then if I can find a place of true, simple compassion and truth and kindness, I can resolve all my futures and pasts and be at one with the beatific. In that way I can share the fire with others. That's what happens when we get babas, gurus, saints and holy people. They are in all of us but they're still here too.

CA: We talked about the "soul" the other night. Does this reincarnated energy have an integrated identity according to you?

GBPO: I believe so. I believe that we are already like angels or greater beings. Those greater beings are both what we were before time began to be measured here, and they're also what we can become after time is measured here. For reasons that I haven't fully resolved in my own mind, those beings chose to build or create this particular dimension that we think of as earth, because they still wanted to learn and grow. There is no end to what is possible. For some reason it seems there was some form of agreement that this would be what would happen next. It's difficult for those beings, because that's what they want. If you zoom back far enough and if you imagine this universe and this planet and even a war going on while you do that, and you go far enough back and just look at the whole universe, it's always beautiful. It's always perfect. It's always immaculately balanced. That's why you sometimes hear certain scriptures and holy writings say, "In the end suffering is nothing." Because in the end the universe is innately fabulous and perfect and balanced. Our ego tells us that what happens here is more important than anything else. Just as when people say "the end of the world," they really mean "the end of human beings." Yet they have the audacity to say "the end of the world."

CA: I agree. I believe in an identity moving along. However, one thing I haven't really figured out is the exponential increase in population. Where do the new ones come from?

GBPO: Remember Tom? Tom from T.O.P.Y.N.A.?[9] He had a very funny explanation: "They just throw in cheap souls from elsewhere..." It could be cats and dogs from other dimensions... The flotsam and jetsam from other universes get thrown in. I've heard other people suggest that there are literally soulless beings on the planet as well. My personal theory so far is that greater beings can incarnate in more than one body at the same time. There could be a million souls reincarnated at once, all over the world. As it happens, that's what the Orisha consciousness suggests as well. Which is why different people have the same head. The Tibetans are coming to a similar conclusion with their theories on rinpoches coming back. Sometimes someone becomes a rinpoche simply by being a son or daughter of already incarnated beings. Somebody like Howard Bloom, who's an atheist, would say it's because we are just literally clever ants, and all creatures are simply organisms that replicate in order to take up the maximum territory, at all cost.

CA: When we were in India in 1996, we asked many Tibetans-in-exile a set of standard questions, hoping to get some kind of insight.[10] In some specific questions, they all answered the same thing so that could very well just be dogmatic training.

GBPO: Here's an answer that just came to me. Given that I believe that I.T.,[11] which is a supreme creator, that from which we all came, and also that through

---

9 Tom Banger was the main coordinator of TOPY North America.
10 Reference to the work of first expedition of the Institute for Comparative Magico-anthropology in India in 1996, researching the view on ritual and magic within the Tibetan religious communities in Himachal Pradesh.
11 I.T. = "Imaginary Time. Where TIME is that which EMITS," a P-Orridgean formulation of "God."

infinity facets of all possible concepts of the future, and many times of incredible beings... "Supreme Creator" is not a literal being to me. Probably not an entity. The first book of the *Bible* is the book of "creation," which is a proces; an energy or alchemy beyong our comprehension. Perhaps I.T. is better described as "a supreme creation"? It's the perfect playground for learning, and that the only form of truth, wisdom and evolution even for an awakened being to become more awakened is through experience and suffering and being on the material plane, then there's no shortage of new soul material. Just make some more. We don't know how many other universes and dimensions there are praying to have the experience of being in a body in order to learn, in order to learn knowledge and humility, whatever it may be. We would again be arrogant to assume that reincarnation is only by human for humans.

CA: Then we're in the Buddhist world again, with the concept of "sentient" beings of many different kinds.

GBPO: Absolutely. That would be my intuitive guess right now. There's no shortage of beings in infinity that might wish to experience malleable materialised human form. The Aghori "path of no distinction" has had a big influence on me. It helped me a lot in working my way through my own dead ends. Until I came to Nepal I was more of an existentialist. I didn't really believe in God. I believed things worked and I did believe in magic. But I believed it was only in the human brain and its own potential. We have no idea how things work. I never doubted that magic works, and I always had visions with information, but the only model I was given when I was young was the Church of England – and that felt wrong. People say they felt uncomfortable as a man so they became a woman or the other way around. I used to say that I felt uncomfortable in a body. From early on I remember thinking, "What is this place? What is this flesh?" I had this feeling that I didn't want to come because I'm really too confused in a body. Somebody told me I had to go. Like a messenger. The maps don't work until you understand them. It's one thing to have a map of the underground of London but quite another thing to get on for the first time and find your way. And in Paris, and in New York. When I had my maps I started truly looking, trying to get to a new place. Once I'm on that train, it's fine. The map is a little bit of help but it doesn't get me there. That's a metaphor.

CA: And you can meet a lot of other travellers.

GBPO: Absolutely. Sometimes they're trying to get off at the same station, which is very nice. That's where we all are right now. I used to put it like this to make it easy for people... If we stick with the subway, there's all these different stations

Sacred Intent

and all these different lines. There's even the "circle line" in London. You can go to sleep on it and years later you'll still be going round. I used to say that it's like a big fun fair with lots of different rides. You could see each other and wave at each other or shout, "I see you over there!" And one can be on the same ride at the same time too. That has to do with this particular intersection between infinite time and measured time. For reasons best known to the universe a lot of people are on the same ride at the same time. More than usual. They see each other, even though they're all from different cultures and look different, we see each other straight away. And feel the warmth. Feel your own kind. And some of us are alone. That's why I do what I do. That's why I do music and books and per-form and travel. It's to send messages out like a beacon or a torch, a lighthouse. Saying, "There's one over here! Come over here and I can probably help set you up with someone over there..." We're doing that function at the very least, I hope. I've always felt since I was a child that there had to be special holy places where people could go to so that they could feel less alone and feel that, "It's OK, you're not crazy..." Without sounding like science fiction, I've always felt like politicians and people who like power for its own sake, or money for its own sake, are part of a different species. Maybe their particular species also has to reincarnate, and they're assholes. Absurdly amoral.

CA: How did you first come into contact with the Orisha consciousness? What was it that attracted you to it or vice versa?

GBPO: Through Miss Jackie. She'd already been involved to a degree. At some point she went for a reading in the East Village, and she met Baba Raul Caniza-res. But I had already become very curious about it. Now, it seems like it was inevitable. At one point she went to see Baba in his shop, and I went with her. That was the first time that I met him. Sometimes I'd just drop in and chat be-cause I was always wandering by anyway. We'd have discussions. I thought it was interesting that he had a wide diversity of books. Madame Blavatsky, Crowley, and very academic books on Hinduism and Buddhism. Lots of scribbled notes in there. They were books he'd actually read many, many times. He had a very good knowledge of Judaism and the Christian Bible. A wide-ranging knowledge of all things metaphysical and spiritual. I got more and more curious and felt more and more magnetically drawn to the system in a way that I hadn't been in any other system. It was a different kind of magnetism. In all the others it was about information but this was more visceral. There was a resonance that had nothing to do with charismatic personalities. It was like an awakened memory, a sense of remembering who I used to be. This was something that I used to be. This was something that I used to be involved in. It was connected to me in a deep, beyond-human way. That was one of the first times that I started to feel that my

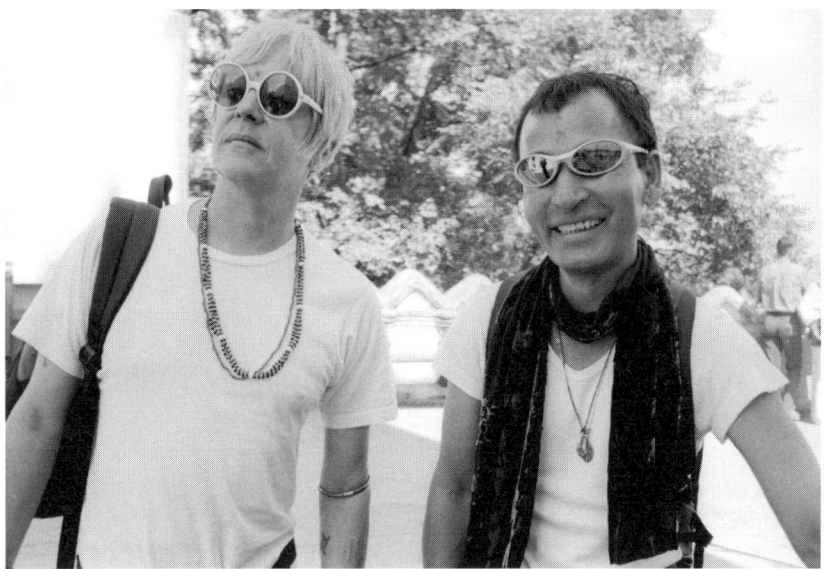

Genesis P-Orridge & Trilochan, Kathmandu, 2000

mind and body were actually connected. As opposed to the body being something that moved around and needed minimal attention in order for the brain to continue its thinking. I was very fortunate to have a partner and a spouse who was so clear-headed whenever I asked questions. There was no mystification. No one was asking for a declaration, or that I should do certain things or that I'd have to convert someone else. There was nothing I had to sign or any kind of fundamentalism. It's just a very practical view of life. You have a relationship with God, a supreme creator and you have relationships with the gods and the goddesses and spirits. You learn that there are spirits that want to be incarnated but who can't. An example of Orisha consciousness and Hindu beliefs connecting.

There are a lot of small things that we have noticed, just by talking these past few days. Down to calling holy people "Baba", the necklaces, daily practices. There are many connectors that make it clear that it's part of a picture that gets closer to an original picture. One day I decided, just out of intellectual curiosity, to ask Baba to do a reading about who my primary Orisha was. In all of my life, as you know, number three has been my number and I used to write things with a big E, and my altar was always red and black, and the ritual room was always red and black. There were so many things. There's no way you can fake a reading like that, the odds are just billions to one. It came out as Eshu, which is red and black and the number three. It was a classic case of "Of course!" There was also the sense of getting one piece or a vision beyond my human life. You know, "That's

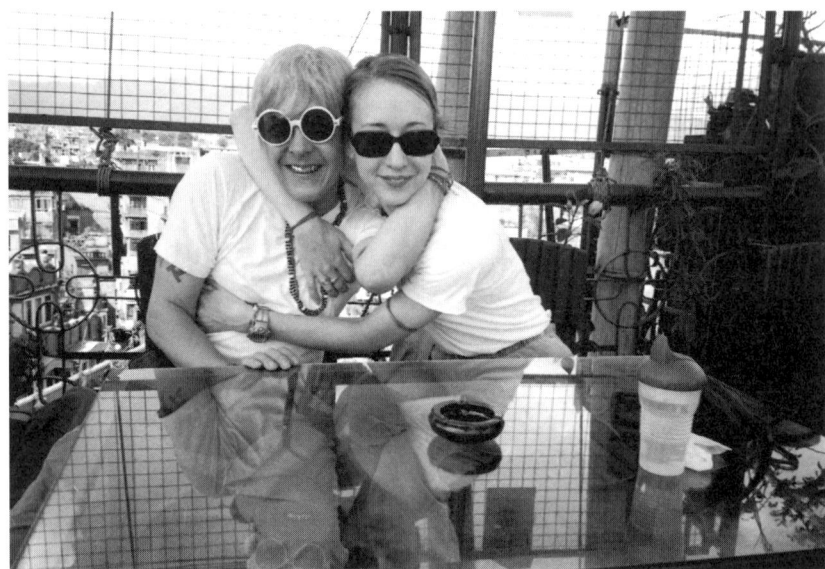

Kathmandu, 2000

why, all my life, I've put stones in these circles and that's why I've always done things like that and why I've been allergic to coconut..." The coconut is Eshu, the symbol of Eshu, so I'd be eating myself. Everything was absurdly appropriate. It seemed almost too ridiculous that all my life I'd been trying to understand the universe when in fact it already understood me. I just hadn't got the information. To the credit of this way of life, and to my faith that there was a structure and that there was something more than I'd been told, in every sense of the word, it led me to travel and seek out the unusual. I would recommend that to everyone, to always seek out the irrational and the unlikely and the unusual. Quite often, very clear examples of universal truth are right there. I was very blessed. I finally met people who could make sense of the insanity I'd been experiencing.

CA: Now that you've had this insight and you know so well that it's Eshu, can you see any specific Eshu-traits in any of the main projects you've been involved in?

GBPO: Oh yes. The crossroads represents the communication and the creativity. Eshu is a trickster. He's the only person who knows the location of God, the location of the Supreme Being. All the other orishas and gods and goddesses have to go through Eshu because he's the one that goes back and forth with messages. It's very much about communicating with all religions and all beings, in order for them to better communicate with the divine. It may sound strange to some people, but that is what I always thought art was about. I always thought you became a monk or an artist; that those were the two best choices in life: to be overtly holy or to be creative. That to me is a holy act. The raw material of the creativity had been life. I wanted to squeeze divinity out of every aspect of life and equalise the dark and light and just see what was really there. Which is why the Aghori path is so interesting. It suggests the same thing. You equalise everything in order to make true judgement. Which, to be fair, is a little bit like Scientology and the E-meter. You equalise all the emotional reactions in order to better judge and make choices. It also seems I was blessed to be born in this body in 1950. I saw television appear, I saw cars become common and telephones really become common. I saw 78 rpm records become vinyl, and vinyl become CDs, and CDs become mp3s. The hardware of society from the pre-war to the postwar. I've watched all the postwar with an awareness that it happened. I was old enough to actually see it and remember it happening. A fantastic position, in terms of perspective to be in when observing culture. Culture and its reaction to spirituality. I remember things like the Cuba crisis and being told I might be blown up by an atom bomb on the way to school and leaning on the glass of the school bus, wondering what it would feel like if it melted when the bomb went off. People really believed that day that they were going to be annihilated. I lived through that experience; an entire culture believing it was going to be annihilated within that day. When I speak of that concept of the atomic bomb changing everything I speak from personal experience, not just from speculation.

Eshu is also most close to Shiva in this Hindu culture. I was always drawn to Shiva things. I always went to Shiva things, tridents and lingams. That's Eshu too. Between all of the different things I was drawn to and the way I made my life up until then, it was very much a classic Eshuesque scenario. That's why I'm so hopeful now between the old way on and the new way on. The great side-effect of globalising mass media is that there is this fantastic spontaneous network between all the isolated kind and positive, creative beings. There's one more chance for them to team up and make a web themselves. A web of their own. I think the fact that it's called the "web" is really on our side. The naming of it is really positive for the forces of creativity. Everyone is going to see which their archetype is and which true tribe they belong to. I even sometimes wonder if a certain number of greater beings weren't, either as an experiment, or marooned for a particular need or experience, the original beings on this planet. As they experienced and as they thought and as they articulated and made language amongst themselves and went through the process of unravelling whatever it was that they were here to puzzle out, that they created what is sometimes known as the "twelve tribes". The various peoples of the earth came from various beings that would not come from the same origin. That's something else that's being played out here too. The resolution of those different initial source beings. The resolution of it can be changed by it taking place here in measured time. That's very important. There's a point where it goes beyond logic and becomes irrational. A lot of people retreat and hide in themselves and inside the status quo. But eventually, at some point, you have to just follow your obsessions and follow the things that draw you and trust the feelings you have.

I always knew there was a reason why I had to be involved with something that has to do with Tibet. I just knew that Tibet was part of my jigsaw. The same with Nepal. I knew I had to come to Nepal. I always felt there was a piece of my mandala missing, which explained my own position in the metaphysical disciplines. That there was a general day-to-day belief system and communication with the divine system that would work very comfortably for me. I tried lots of different ways of thinking. I looked at them and read about them and made contact with them and I even invented one of my own. You get a great sense of relief when you come across your home system. That's really what they are: home systems. The ones that work for your nervous system, the ones that resonate with the same frequency. That's an example of when time gets saved; measured time. When you can actually lock into a system that consciously takes care of the day-to-day stuff and maintain the constant awareness of the other. Then you can really get down to some creative work. It's a bit like meeting your soul mate in a relationship. You don't have to worry about that game again. You have to always work at it and be aware of it and regenerate it every single day. But the searching is necessarily finished. A completed search and a relief of having found an emotional relationship home and a spiritual system home. Each time this happens you have more of the mundane time freed up.

CA: It's interesting that when these kinds of meetings happen, one usually refers to that experience by saying that "no words were needed." The resonance is so strong and the communication is already there...

GBPO: A lot of people talk about life as if it's happening to them; as if things are being done to them. They don't have any control, everything is happening. "This happened to me today and it made me miserable. They sent me these bills..." It's as if life is something that's done to you. As soon as you really grasp the idea of it unfolding as a beautiful thread or a carpet unrolling... Once you experience that as a sensation and as a vision you know that nothing is being done to you. Even events that seem unpleasant as they happen when you look at them from the huge picture, the flowing, the unfolding, they're just one part of this incredible, beautiful process. It's such a great big step to move away from being a victim of life happening to you, to being the soul watching its own beautiful growth and unfolding. One of the biggest things you can do in your life is just to make that move away from life merely happening to you. Better to be a witness to your own unfolding. You're not in control but you're witnessing it. In the best sense, on a really good day you witness it outside of yourself. It's a big beautiful box of senses and ideas and memories and all of the genetic history down to the first people... Everything is contained in the nervous system. You can love and have orgasms that no one knows what they are. You can read books about people you want to meet, and you can travel, and then it's all a joy when you realise that that's one of the big and simple realisations... What you really are is a sensory experience machine for all these other beings. Through you, each of us experience this moment too. What a fantastic machine this is, in terms of being able to travel through the senses...

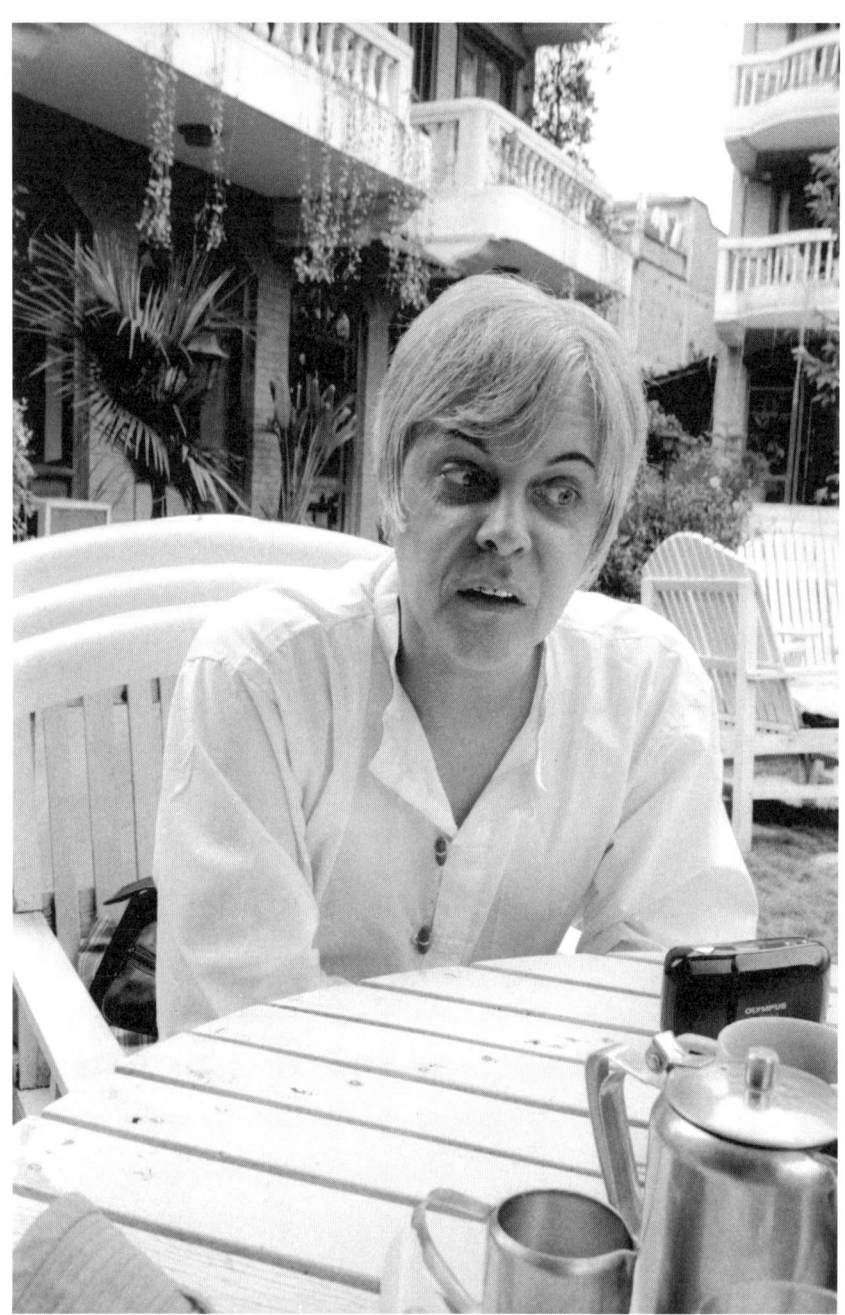

Kathmandu, 2000

Kathmandu, October 3rd, 2000

CA: Since you at an early age defined a will, a desire, a motivation to become an artist, I'm curious to know, now that you've been active as one for such a long time, where you would place yourself in art history?

GBPO: For many years, one word I wouldn't use was "art." I thought of artists from an early age as saddhus or holy persons. It seemed to me that it was a divine gift from the universe. It was sacred in a very real sense. What had once been religious art was less obviously so. I would argue that Jackson Pollock and some of the other abstract expressionists in New York were equally as spiritual. That thread does run through a lot of the more interesting art that lasts longer. Even Warhol remained in a very real sense Catholic, and Dali as well. In the case of someone like Picasso it was more sheer passion and fervour for the art itself; the act of creation. That's one of the greatest gifts: the gift of being blessed with the potential to do creative things. It's a very high calling. Everything I've done was done with that in mind. It was always about creating a new universe. Not just making things. At the moment, in terms of an art-historical context or cultural historical context... As the waters settle I think that for at least a minority there is a consensus that some of the things I've been involved in have been significant and influential in a very real sense. I would suggest my conception of Industrial Music, my triggering, with you and others of a contemporary occult revival with TOPY, and of course pandrogeny with Lady Jaye are all examples of this. What I dubbed "Cultural Engineering." All those ideas have gone global and lasted ever since.

I feel mainly that I'm in the tradition of the beatniks. The beatnik writers, and even more particularly like Brion Gysin, who was perhaps more successful in getting attention. It's the renaissance-man-idea, which in the 60s we called "transmedia." The idea of being able to apply oneself to any material and do something that is, in a sense, a poem. Whether we move chairs around in a room or pick up grass and put it down in a different place but with great consideration, or to actually take two or three pieces of imagery and join them together in a way that never existed before. All those kinds of things are essential parts of living. They're the equivalent of breathing and eating; in my life anyway. I think that the original form of living was the same. What we think of as primitive or outmoded cultures and people... It's not even worthy of a conversation that one includes one's sense of the universe, one's belief systems in spirits, divine beings and gods, animisms, stones, whatever it may be... All those different things are absolutely and certainly included from the moment of waking and going to sleep and even considering what one might dream whilst asleep. To me, a healthy life is a creative life. In the West, the artist represents the closest thing we have to the wandering holy man. I think that Allen Ginsberg, despite many of his over-indulgent weaknesses, really was the first to spot that change in our appreciation of popular culture and its link with serious literature and art. Something had happened in society; the moving and traveling and all those things we discussed before about the inter-communication. There was also a breakthrough in the early 50s. He spotted the holy madman and the holy poet, and saw them as schematic figures. I don't think that influenced me as much as it confirmed my beliefs. When I came across the beatniks I was reading actual lives, actual experiences, still living, which was a nice change. Theoretically, they could be just down the road. And that's what they turned out to be. That just absolutely confirmed what I thought in my heart; what I'd always been seeing in my mind and my imagination. There was a viable way. There was still room for the bohemian, wandering, creative and spiritually seeking person.

CA: I think in many cases the lifestyles and the attitudes have been more interesting than the actual work created.

GBPO: I think in most cases that's true. Although Jack Kerouac originally was one of my introductions to all of that, I now find him intensely boring and unreadable. I cannot read it, not even for nostalgia's sake. But at age 15, it's perfect science fiction or social fiction.

CA: It's like Salinger's *The Catcher in the Rye* in a way. It's so great when you're a teenager but now it feels rather trite. Kerouac was quite revered from the beginning and was integrated in an American literary mind. He's affected current writers and some of them have certainly taken it on, further. But he does feel a bit caught in his time.

GBPO: What's nice about that is that he dreamed of being a famous and influential writer. He achieved that, mainly posthumously, but enough in his lifetime to realise that he'd succeeded. He worked incredibly hard at it. That's something people forget. You can have that mimicry where people think, "Oh, if I travel and if I take drugs and if I get strung out and go to Morocco, I will be just like William S. Burroughs and immediately, by default, write a masterpiece. Or I will go to jail for something stupid and become Jean Genet." The great mistake so many people seem to make is that if they mimic something, the work involved is not necessary.

The uniqueness of the lives that they revere is that it's usually based upon a reckless abandon to creativity. Where one's own mortality is literally at stake sometimes. That's when a lot of people make decisions to back off. Or when suffering is involved and poverty is involved. Even then, that's not enough, just because you become poor or suffer. That doesn't mean that you're going to have a revelation. It requires discipline and constant work; constant searching and a refusal to become habitual about almost anything. Or to at least question one's habits constantly. To try and always refine one's actions, so that the maximum happens with the minimum interference and disruption from the status quo. It's like a martial art in the end. One has to balance and duck and dive and think, improvise, really look. And ultimately look at oneself more than anything else in terms of criticism and listen like crazy. Look and listen all the time. And love listening and looking. One has to truly adore looking at anything and everything that's going on. Listening to everything and imagining it as raw material. That's actually what it all is. The five senses are supplying us very beautifully with endless disassembled and assembled information. The senses are actually cutting up all the time, as Burroughs and Gysin so rightly said. We spend a lot of our mental energy trying to assemble linear information from that cut-up. One of the great jumps that's been made in the last 15 years is the complete embracing of cut-up and sampling concepts and techniques via mass culture. Brion Gysin would probably be joyful and rather amazed to see how far those ideas have spread into every aspect of culture and advertising, film-making, and general media. A lot of the reasons why it's done that is because a lot of the people at the core of changing those media are aficionados of Burroughs and Gysin.

CA: Exactly. It's really stunning to see the work of those two guys and your work, I think. It's been thematically concerned with showing people how it's done. Not just using it but also showing how it's done. The impact that has had is utterly fascinating.

GBPO: Huge. Huge impact. It still amazes me. Looking at television almost anywhere, I can see those techniques so brightly within the way people sample things. The speed that television's increased to makes many children's programs and even adult programs so incredibly fast in the editing that it becomes a sensory cut-up. One assembles fragments of a half-hour program rather than watching it in linear time.

CA: I don't know to what extent Gysin sensed that these things were happening towards the end of his life. Somewhat through your work, I assume. Burroughs, I don't know if he really cared. He seemed quite neutral.

GBPO: Well, William didn't seem to be particularly concerned with legacy or effect. He was more into giving clear and well considered, precisely written analyses of how different media operate and how they're applied by politicians and mass media. All the ideas of control. Those were some of the key concerns he had, but he was very self-contained. But I think he was pleased with himself, in regard to what he managed to achieve.

Brion expressed great relief when we began to proselytise some of his work. I used to go and see him. He was pleased because I actually got things done. I'd go and see him and say that we'd organised for *Here To Go*[1] to be published. We did manage to get it published. I also predicted to him at the time that if it got published somewhere, someone would pick it up and republish it. Which is what happened too. He had no real interest in actually bothering to get recognition and working the media to his advantage. In the end, although he, as most of us at times do, felt a little hurt or a little bit frustrated by the lack of recognition or credit, or that the ideas aren't expanded upon as much as would seem possible, he really didn't care. Not enough to make the effort. He was ultimately an artist's artist who compulsively created and thought and wrote to the very end. I saw him in the last week of his life. I was sitting and talking to him and drinking tea. He was showing me new notebooks and things he was writing and playing me tapes with ideas for songs. Then he looked at his watch and said, "You have to go out and have some coffee or something for an hour. The undertaker is coming to measure me for my coffin." That was what was happening then. That was a very odd feeling! I was aware that he was dying but to be suddenly confronted with it that literally with someone who still appeared bright... I went out and then came back. The undertaker had left. That's when he said that he was just tired of being here. He was tired of the pain. Emphysema is terrible. Just like a lot of the babas and the gurus are able to do, he decided exactly when he was going to leave his body. And he did, within a few days. He had a very magical relationship with how he worked with creative acts, and how he envisioned himself. With the patience of the wise, I think he was confident enough in the deep content of what he was trying to express, that he knew that it would have its time in some form or another. He was very pleased to have a whole new generation, with all of us, coming up and taking those ideas exactly as he wanted it. Not just mimicking but expanding upon them and experimenting with them and applying them in less likely forms than he'd imagined, through video and rock music.

So I guess I would like to feel that I'm in that particular lineage, but there are

---

1 *Here To Go – Planet R:101: Brion Gysin interviewed by Terry Wilson,* Quartet Books, London, 1982.

other bits of me. There's a bit of a surrealist in me. There's some of the 60s and the Warhol era, in a very numb way. It's something I always include in many aspects. I always thought of Throbbing Gristle as a completely Andy Warhol-based media experiment. It worked again. I took his blueprint and assembled it, edited it, adjusted it to my own particular needs of the moment. It was very effective. He's a bit like John Cage. I prefer to read John Cage's books than listen to his music. A lot of the time with Warhol, I prefer to look at his strategies than stare at his pictures.

CA: It's also amazing to see what a neutral façade can achieve.

GBPO: There are so many ongoing lessons coming from Warhol, as well as the beatniks. Those are, to me, the most important 20th century artistic movements. I think of Warhol as a movement because he collected a lot of people around him. Warhol was a movement rather than a person. Which is why the neutral façade works so well.

CA: People projected on to him what they perceived him to be. He would just go, "Mmm, that's great."

GBPO: That's right. He was almost the Nike-logo for the Factory. He was such a caricature in such a witty and dry way that he could also represent the corporate logo of the Factory for all the other people there; the ones that were working there or hanging out there. They could utilise that logo to their own ends with his consent. That was something I worked with on each project, a logo, for very much those kinds of reasons. Ultimately, all work should be capable of being non-verbal as well. One has just a symbol in the end. That can, as you said, represent anything that someone else wants it to be. They can enter completely from their own self-perceived universe. That gives people a sense of a certain protection in the unknown. What you really do is build an unknown universe and then get a somewhat familiar doorway in so that they can, at least in the beginning, feel familiar enough to appreciate and absorb some of the new experience. Then you can retreat and use that as a key to re-enter, both in their own mind and their own conscious, literal events.

CA: Did you ever meet Warhol?

GBPO: No, I never met Warhol, surprisingly. I expected to, because I usually end up meeting people somehow. The only one I met was Billy Apple when he was going through his crazy period. He left the Factory in a bout of speed paranoia. I think I bumped into him some time in the very early 70s in London, when I

Sacred Intent

was visiting Nicholas Bramble[2] in the Gay Lib Street Theatre. A lot of interesting people went through Nicholas's flat in Colville Terrace, near Portobello Road. I also met Bishop Ondine via Jerry Dreva, and corresponded a few times before he died back at his parents' place, I believe.

CA: Did you see that recent book of Billy Name's colour photos from the Factory? The power of freeze-framing time. I think one of the reasons for Warhol's fame, and the Factory's too, was that it was all so well documented.

GBPO: Yes, and shamelessly.

CA: That's one way of doing it. The diametrical opposite is of course to not be available at all.

GBPO: The Duchamp version. That's also someone one would have to consider. With Throbbing Gristle we went for the document-everything-approach. With C.O.U.M. Transmissions it was somewhere in the middle. Most of the documentation of C.O.U.M. was random chance. Other people would be taking photographs and we'd ask if they'd send us copies. The documentation was primarily whatever anyone sent. It was very much a smashed mirror in terms of what C.O.U.M. was really like. It was arbitrary. Who could be bothered and who would be kind enough? Once in a while we'd have an automatic camera going off, so there was no photographer at all, just photographs. All those approaches work. One of the tricks is to know when to become withdrawn and inaccessible whilst considering if there's something else one wants to say. That's one of the big differences between my approach and that of most people in modern art. In modern art, for a long, long time, since the late 60s I think, the basic strategy for most people seem to be to find one thing that everyone says is good and then just keep doing it. And they try and do it as long as they can so that they can make as much money as possible. A lot of young artists see Warhol as an example of celebrity and riches. They're not really interested in much else. There's no depth to their perception of what he achieved at all; of his commentary on American life.

CA: Would you consider anyone else in that sense? Damien Hirst comes to my mind, Jeff Koons perhaps... People who seem to be very conscious of the business aspect at all times.

GBPO: And Gilbert & George. Even though I love them, I think they're very shallow. They have become very rich. They applied it in a very effective way.

---

2 Nicholas Bramble, British artist, sculptor and activist.

I like them because they have a great sense of humour and self-parody. They added a new element, so that's why they're original. I can't even be bothered thinking of names and I don't think it really matters either. Everyone can tell, going into a gallery, who's doing that trick. As Brion Gysin said, "Do not speak ill of the dead!" Sometimes people's imaginations die long before their bodies. It's definitely a disadvantage to change, in terms of appreciation and effectiveness in the art world or the music business or whichever side that money comes from for creativity. It's rather ironic and to me puzzling that so many people discuss the idea of change and growth and development of their ideas, and yet so few would dare to actually attempt to keep changing. Many people have said to me, "Why did you stop just when it was becoming a success? Why didn't you just keep going for two more years, so you'd get money?" That's the only reason, to be more famous. That's the big, big downside of contemporary culture. It has been polluted to an immense degree by a facile interpretation of Warhol that serves the purposes of those, again, who would prefer to have us not thinking. Now, there's a big, big carrot... If you make music, your only conscious desire is to be on the television as much as whoever is popular at the moment. Britney Spears, Backstreet Boys or Abba. The only purpose of creativity is to emulate the success financially, and the media coverage. Madonna is a good example. People want to be Madonna. Britney Spears actually said that that was what she wanted to become: a second generation Madonna. That's it. That's all she wanted to be. To dress up and jump around on television. The effect of that in the way that the culture feeds society is damaging.

I really believe that the integration of the divine, the spiritual and the metaphysical in whatever form or discipline, combined with free-flowing intuitive creativity, are the life's blood of culture. And that culture is the skeleton, the solid structure of society and life. Those two things have to be really, really powerful and well-nourished or the body becomes an ugly distortion and weak and crippled and sick. That's what we're seeing in terms of the disgracefully greedy culture we're living in. I'm appalled at the shallow amorality of Western culture. No matter what the superficial disruption of the harmony of Nepal might be, it's an oasis of common sense in the most valuable sense of the expression.

CA: Was there a specific time or occurrence when the spiritual and art got linked in your life? I think you mentioned a car ride in *Wreckers of Civilisation*[3] that became an important experience?

GBPO: Yes, but that was actually after I'd already had the intersection of the

---

3 Simon Ford, *Wreckers of Civilisation – The Story of C.O.U.M. Transmissions & Throbbing Gristle*, Black Dog Publishing, London, 1999.

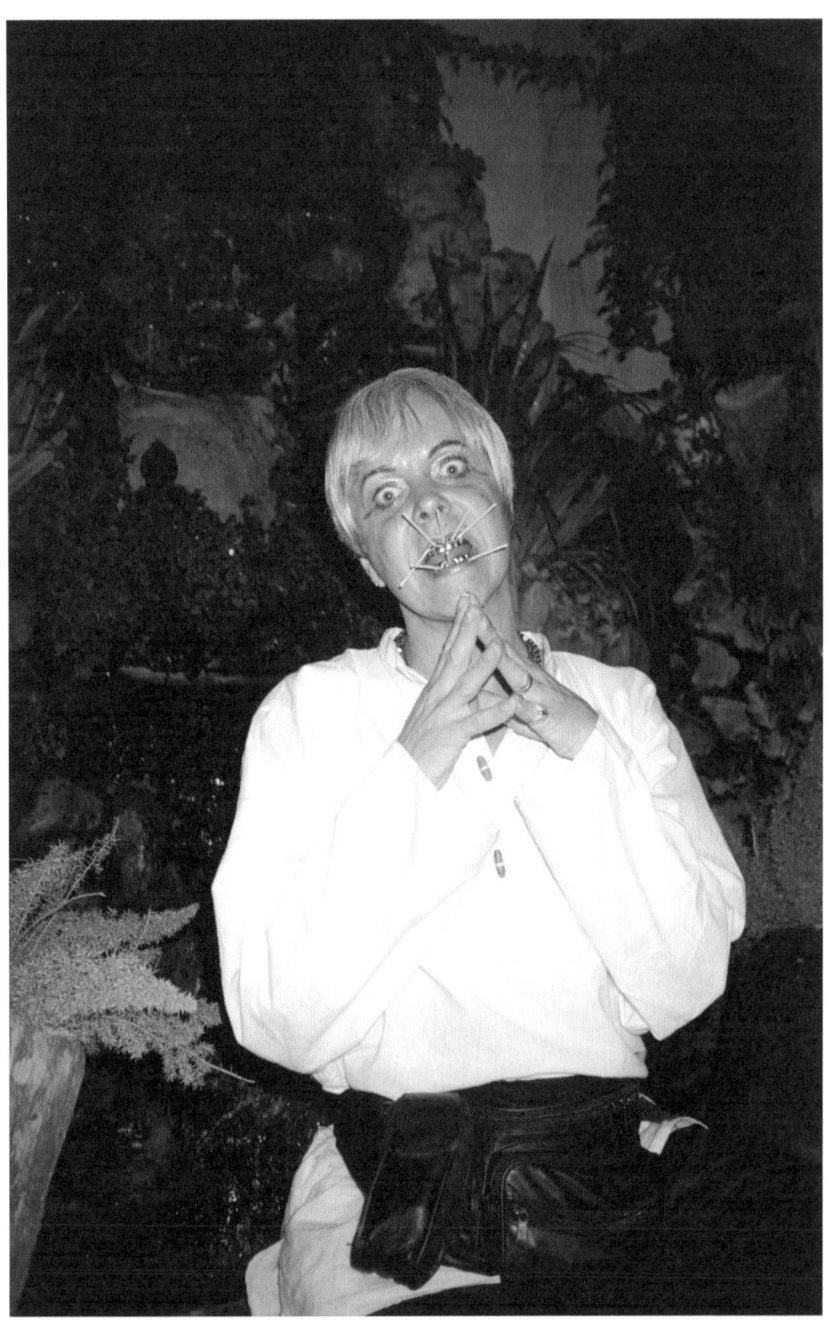

Kathmandu, 2000

divine and creativity. There was never a question of a choice between the two. Before that moment I knew that creativity in some form was possible: painting, writing, drawing, thinking... From a very early stage, when going to the countryside for example, I'd move rocks around and make patterns for hours in a very ritualistic manner in a complete trance with nothing else in my mind. I would get more pleasure and satisfaction in the sense of being alive from those kinds of activities than the usual ones I was expected to be excited by. I was perhaps seven or eight years old. I already felt that a lot of what was around me was very mundane. That was never ever a question. It became stronger because I got confirmation in reading Buddhist texts and they seemed to me to be fantastic poems. Poems talking about the weirdest speculations about what the universe and the consciousness and thinking could be. Then there was a general increase in ideas of consciousness and expansion that was part of the culture through the drug explosion of the 60s, around which there was obviously a lot of propaganda when I was in my early teens. That was also a very strong current of thought.

I think that the experience you refer to was the first true and very clear out-of-body, inter-dimensional experience. It was very, very separate from what we would think of as normal life. A truly consciousness-changing experience. I just realised recently that it was basically a flicker experience. I don't remember any flicker but I do remember that I was in the back seat of the car with my eyes closed, leaning on the window. All of a sudden, I wasn't in the car; I was flying along next to the car, through the hedge that I'd been staring at. Interpenetration. I realised that it was quite feasible for the body and its molecules to pass through other molecules. There was no reason why that shouldn't be possible, because I was doing it at that moment. Then I started to see pictures and images. It was as if I was downloading an incredible amount of information to my brain, really fast, and hearing certain voices saying certain key words. Reinforcing some of the ideas as it went in. It lasted a long time, half an hour or more. I got back into my own body and just sat in the car speechless. My parents thought I was in a bad mood so they didn't bother me. When I got back to the house I just started writing down everything I could remember. That was the basis for C.O.U.M. Transmissions.

C.O.U.M. Transmissions, to me, was always about that relationship between the universe, the divine, the unexpected possibilities of the mind and the human body and the realisation that there were no boundaries of the human body. There were no fixed modes of behaviour or perception at all. It was a complete sham. What I was looking at every day was so arbitrary it was absurd. That was when it really struck home. It's never left me. Every time I wake up I am somewhat disappointed that the room looks pretty much the same. "Damn, I'm still trapped in what I believe it looks like but I know it doesn't look like that. There can be many other ways." Ultimately it's transparent and has no solidity whatsoever.

That's something else I think we really experience here in Nepal. That most people walking around, from the beggars to the intellectuals, from the high to the low castes, have no problem switching from ideas in conversation of Maya, the illusion, and Nirvana, and the fact that all of this is temporary and a way to learn and build a life. It is absolutely universal and unquestionable that this is an absurd and strange construct in which we appear to move and exist. I felt at home because I didn't feel a need to explain myself to anyone, because they already knew. I didn't have to discuss conceptual, existential matters because it was obvious to everyone that that was how it was. When things were discussed they were discussed with enthusiasm, joy, humour and reverence and with a real sense of tolerance. What better place to be than somewhere where those are the main qualities of everyday life? Whether you are dying of leprosy or you are the king? Is that not a fabulous map of how to live life? And where to navigate with one's consciousness? I just breathed this huge sigh of relief. I immediately thought, "I could stay here for years and never be bored." Because every day someone somewhere is doing something fantastic or thinking something fantastic or creating a craft piece through some fantastic skill. Again, skill is considered as a norm. Almost everybody here can create something beautiful with their hands. Cooking, carving, sewing, colouring, embroidering, building... I just find that so thrilling and energising. I even walk through Thamel and see all the shops with the eye-candy. That's fabulous and really nourishing. Then I see the people who are making those items and they are, if there is such a thing, really ordinary everyday people who don't think anything of the fact that they can make perfect replicas of antiques or that they can sew really fast and do abstract screen prints on backs of T-shirts and not even know what they are. I really appreciate that. I find that very nourishing for my soul to be in a place where excelling is considered unquestionably what you're supposed to do. Even if you're a beggar, you excel at it. If you're a hustler, you excel at it. If you're a waiter, you excel. The concept of reaching for that level of excellence in all actions is dramatically different to the West, where it seems people try and get away with the least to receive the most.

CA: We have become used to the term "information society." For you, does that basically just mean information being shuffled back and forth, and used as leverage for power?

GBPO: Yes, it's just a pipeline. There's a misconception that if you have every piece of information ever recorded in one spot simultaneously, one will somehow become superior. It is, of course, bullshit. It's the old story of the cut-up again. Anyone can do a cut-up but the quality of the raw material and bits that one chooses in sequence is the real skill. Uniqueness comes from taking the unlikely path rather than the simple path or the easier, less demanding path. That's what I find really unpleasant and rather tasteless in the world wide web is that it's used so very much as a convenience. A way to do even less to get some kind of gratuitous reward. It's addictive, just like all the great products; like cigarettes and drinks. You are never satisfied, you can never get enough. It never really gives you what you want and it's never as good the second time.

CA: Is there anything on your long artistic path – a method, process or a project – that you feel disappointed with? Something that didn't work out as planned?

GBPO: Yes. What springs to mind, in all honesty, was the "Godstar" project; the hyperdelic part of Psychic TV. I would really like to know what would have happened if the Rolling Stones office and BBC radio had not colluded in preventing the "Godstar" single having national airplay, as it was supposed to. I also regret having the money from that project ripped off by our ex-manager. We never got any of the money back in order to finance the "Godstar" movie. That record generated about 150,000 pounds in profit, on our own label. Now, that would be half a million pounds; more than enough to make a really good test segment of the movie. Jon Savage was going to co-write the script with me. We got one of Brian Jones's sons to at least consider being a look-alike. We also found someone in a small underground band in London who looked like him. We'd done all the homework. That I would have liked to have happen. It was a project ahead of its time. It would have been influential in an underground way. There are people in South Africa now, working on an independent surreal documentary, a factional, fictional documentary inspired by the metaphor of Brian Jones's life. That sounds like a very good way to deal with it. The South Africans have already said that they wanted "Godstar" to be the theme song for their film. They want me to be involved because they said they were inspired by the fact that there were other people out there feeling the same way. Perhaps it's the classic thing where the universe picks its own time? It will all happen as I hoped it would through people I didn't know I would meet, some 20 years later. At the moment, that project would be the one that springs to mind most obviously. We got very close!

CA: So someone else can then manifest an idea that you've had, which is better than it not manifesting at all. Talking about Jones makes us go back in time, both to 1985 and to the 1960s. Do you think science can make us go beyond the strictly personal perception of time?

GBPO: Well, they've slowed down time. They've literally managed to slow down time. They pushed some subatomic particle through some lead and it came out on the other side before it went in or as it went in. It's bizarre. Technically speaking, time went backwards. There's a Japanese scientist who has slowed down the speed of light, upon which all physics is based, in a lab. A repeatable experiment. Again, no one really knows what that means, if anything. But I'm sure that if you went out on the streets of Nepal and asked someone if they knew that time isn't constant and that there is no fixed speed of light, they would go, "Yes... Of course I know that... We've known that for 10,000 years... What's the big deal?"

CA: Scientists use empirical methods; they measure and repeat experiments. In our current mythology there is really no such thing as "random." If you apply this methodology to cut-ups and see what leaks through, and if one studied deeper and further, what do you think one would find? Scientists have even started to use concepts such as "God" and "Creation". Do you think there's a parallel line between science and art, to be able to actually get to the core?

GBPO: In terms of creativity within the culture, and what we think of as all the versions of the arts, and alchemical science, which is theoretical science... They are both mystical, hermetic traditions.

CA: That's something apparent among early Gnostics too; trying to find out where ideas actually come from.

GBPO: The Gnostics are very close to the depth psychologists too, the post-Jungian people. There was a guy who wrote *A Blue Fire*, that new hip psychologist.[4] He's fantastic. They're theoretically about psychology but he himself says very clearly that he's discussing the concept of the soul and layers of consciousness. That psychology is basically a camouflage for mysticism. And it's great that finally the camouflage is being discarded, and that they're looking at people in a totally different and metaphysical way, and at the relationship that each person has with the soul. I think again that we live in a fascinating intersection, both with the information doubling, and with science confirming that nothing is real and that all is speculation and even using language that is culled from Buddhist texts and Eastern texts. And then you have the artists who are, on good days, trying to conceive of and package the unspeakable. I don't mean that in terms of horror but rather literally that which can not be said.

We're at this wonderful moment where everything is being opened up in a Pandora's box of possibilities. As we've been saying for ten to fifteen years, if the universe becomes infinitely quaquaversal and life becomes more and more holographic and quaquaversal, then the best skills to have are those which are unspecific; where you are not taken by too much surprise when the apparent

---

4 James Hillman, *A Blue Fire*, Harper Perennial, New York, 1997.

veil of your reality opens and something strange comes through. In a sense, I really think that those of us who are trying to be awake are in preparation for the unexpected and the unknowable so that we can, to some degree, cope with another step up in the realms of existence. This particular phase, this larval phase of being trapped in corporeal bodies and believing in solidity is coming to an end. That's probably what all the prophecies really mean. They don't mean an end of the world or the end of the species but an end of this phase of being. It's probably a release from ignorance as much as a reunion with that which we call "God." If we're honest with ourselves, to a great degree we are now mimicking all the qualities that we've described as "God." We can be infinitely present all over the world through various media.

CA: Science has caught up with that, in terms of genetic engineering... It's become malleable.

GBPO: That's what I was going to say. You have the genome aspect. They say literally that they have "the book of life," with God's mathematical and logical equations and that it's now written down. We can be omni-present and omni-powerful and we can design life and we can bring life from nothing. We can look beyond matter and into the infinite. For all we know, we are the god engine finding itself and being self-aware.

CA: A very Luciferian principle.

GBPO: Probably. But I suspect that being the experience of divine instigation, the eye-blink as I think of it, of what we think of as "God." The flash of the moment of nothingness becoming potential matter and life. The thing that was really for the first time a visceral, literal, muscular and quite an experiential way, completely immersive. When this happened to me I actually felt the sensations of the divine and being almost surprised by this moment of self-awareness.[5] The consciousness had been there before but it hadn't really known it was there. Whatever happened at that very first flash I think was equally of value as to what it is and everything that has come since. The entire unfolding is equally that of God, as of all other possible materials and beings that exist in this and many other universes. That it is an experiential gain for all, including God and all gods. That's part of what is hidden in all the myths. It's part of a secret code underneath the ideas of rebellion and knowledge. That's where that almost Haiku-element in that poem I wrote comes in:

---

5 This experience had been documented in *Gnosis* no 32, San Francisco, 1994, pp 48-54.

First I.T. was
Then I.T. knew it was
And that was I.T.

That is, to me, the inner code of the story of creation. That is also the inner code of the artist. First it is, like another cluster in an apparent existence. Then it knows it was and it changes to the past tense, where one has the sense of past, present and future of being and being self-aware. And that really is it, in terms of the process. From then on, the being aware of existence and the insatiable pleasure of experiencing it all is the core of existence; the core of the reason to exist, for me. Art and all the other things are tenuous, temporary skins around that; they just fix it in some way. As much for my benefit of remembering that the present is a flowing thing. They're just all snapshots, ultimately. They just anchor us to that little bit we might need right now because we're not evolved enough. It gives me just enough anchors not to disappear completely in speculation. I also feel that one of the duties of anyone who wants to understand anything, is to share what they feel they've learned, no matter how banal or incomprehensible it might seem. We all know and feel in science that we don't often know why equations work for a long time. I work with that principle. If it seems to have an effect or if it seems to be useful as a tool or a functional way of navigating life, then I am honour-bound to offer it out to my fellow human beings.

CA: That's also another equation: The more you do of that, the more you'll get.

GBPO: Yes, it seems to be that way. I think also that one is illuminated by that fire; the one that makes one a little bit more visible and a little bit more attractive to other people in the sense of a flame and moth, but not for destructive reasons.

CA: You are almost incredibly productive. Every manifestation, all the products, the projects, everything that you've been involved in, surely stem from ideas. Where do ideas come from in your case?

GBPO: A lot of it is deduction. I spend a massive amount of time running ideas between two or three different voices in my mind, like tapes. Like a rather dull TV-debate. I can set up these three experts: the idea, the Devil's advocate and the random person. I run the idea and listen to them discussing it and taking it deeper and deeper. Every so often, all of a sudden there's like a clang where all three are in agreement, that it's somehow effective or somehow relevant enough to merit further investigation. Then it goes up one level in the consciousness.

CA: But still... What the panel is debating is an idea.

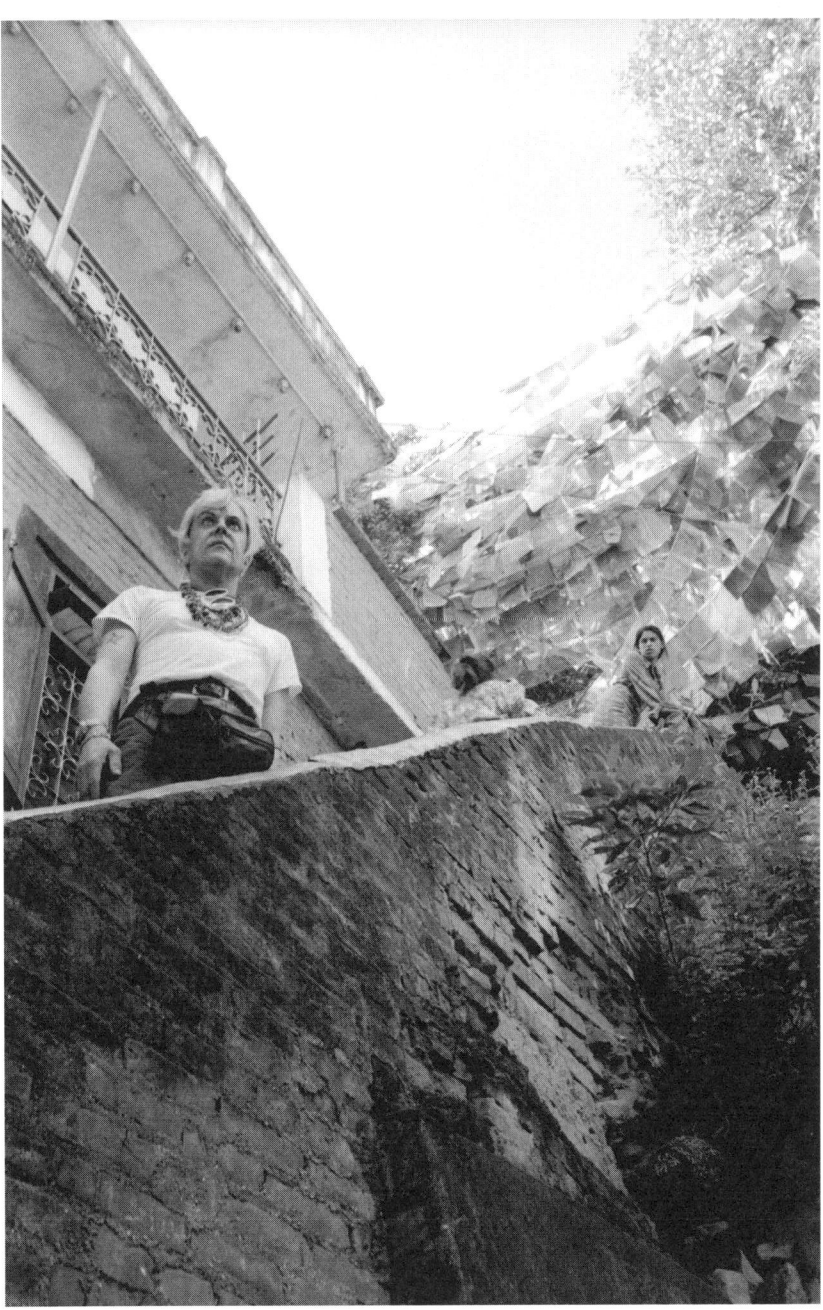

Kathmandu, 2000

GBPO: Which comes from questions, basically, more often than not.

CA: So there are no meditational flashes or "possessions" or...?

GBPO: Yes, but those are primarily decorative. There are random intersections because I do collages and cut-ups. I take for granted that my mind is assembling and cutting up everything that's going on. That's feeding it too. It ends up in a reservoir. That reservoir of all these impressions and combinations, none of which I take as fixed... I don't assume that people will always look the same or that things will happen in the same way or there's any reason why a chair can't float on water... Everything is possible and everything is true. That's the basic first level for letting input into the reservoir. I then tap it by asking questions. Those are triggered by boredom or by humour or by a phrase. Writing in the diary, perhaps some word may stumble out in a line in a way that I didn't expect. That will set up the first set of questions. Which is why I think that writing and collaging and taping and listening are very, very, very important. A first step to be always really fluent in manipulating material, sculpting material. Something triggers the questions, and the questions start to build the formulation of potential ideas. Then I start to deduce both why I'm curious about the idea and extrapolate what would happen in terms of forecasting if I decide to put that idea into some form of action and make it concrete. Sometimes, just the mental exercise of forecasting to the end is satisfying enough and I discard it completely as a project, even though I know it would have worked. Or I'll put it to the side in a notebook, in case one day I'm stuck on a rainy day. That's it really. The idea of the divine inspiration I would think of more as being a divine channel and that there are agendas outside of my own conscious and unconscious processes that are being fed in. They are in the invisible and the act of faith that one makes is also an element of creativity.

CA: Do you look at the input that you get as thematically changing, depending on what kind of pantheon, magical system or spiritual way of thinking you're working with? You have passed through different phases of experimentation where a certain language has been applied, a certain pantheon has been applied...

GBPO: Not really. I think that ultimately that's why this new project, "Thee Majesty," makes sense. The majesty of art, the majesty of being alive or the majesty of the universe and of what is divine and of ordinariness and of this fabulous little planet – the strange intersection of what appears to be a planet – was always what first launched me into trying to communicate with people and trying to communicate with whatever else is here. And with myself. What's more likely to have happened was that I was a little bit embarrassed early on. I was embarrassed about the idea of saying that C.O.U.M. was based on a spiritual idea. It wasn't very hip. Also, I was so disappointed in the art world and the general cultural world when I finally accessed it in my late teens. I was so utterly appalled at the lack of integrity and the lack of spirituality that I reacted against it. I felt, at the beginning, a certain anger and frustration into my approaches with art. That's really what has gradually ebbed away more and more. I hope that I now actually openly and publicly integrate how I really feel about trying to do music and art.

All the different pantheons, systems and concepts that I've utilised as meta-phors or as practical systems, are all still enclosed and contained in everything I've done so far. I think of them all as amicable with each other. I think there's a game of the gods but I don't see that as a war of the gods. If there is a war it's almost a conceptual rebellion about ideas. A healthy dialogue rather than a win-all or a lose-all, binary heaven-and-hell idea or thought fabric. I would be at that point. I feel far more directly assisted by the Orishas than I've ever felt in any other system. I feel they're very alive and very responsive and very active and colourful and robust and funny. There are a lot of fabulously hilarious trickster stories. Whether it's an incredibly complex and sophisticated neurological level or just the infinite memory of every part of life since DNA began recording, it doesn't really matter much. I tend to believe that beings can be creative by belief and repetition. That's part of how faith and magic, sorcery and divinity work. And Sainthood. All those things come from clarity of intent, repetition and un-swerving kindness and belief. Those fuel the divine. Those are all qualities we know we should aspire to in ourselves and in others.

As you get closer to actually seeing something in your own mirror, you start to let go of a lot of the safety nets and the secret compromises and realise that you have nothing to lose by actually saying what you really think. As you say what you really think, you discover that people are attentive, and at the very least usually respectful, even if they think you're a wild guru or a crazy child or they simply don't agree. Often when you try to adjust or dilute, something that might seem brutal in terms of how you feel about life, you're far more likely to get to be attacked, aggression and even violence. That's where what becomes sophisticated becomes simplicity again. Hesitation dis-integrates.

CA: Honesty protects?

GBPO: Honesty protects. It's how we used to say, "Magick defends itself." I think it's true. In the end, you ultimately just spend your life waking up and hopefully asking yourself who you are. Even more importantly, asking "What do I want from this? What do I really want? And when I have had everything I tried to do, how will I view this the day I die?" If I was given that moment to review everything I've done, how will I feel about my life? Will I feel embarrassed and guilty and afraid of things that were not resolved? Will I regret the consequences of ill-considered actions? We all do stupid things and it takes us forever to begin to wake up. If we move forward slowly, letting go of some of those things, and we see that there's a progression towards less and less sense of consequence and less and less sense of ill-considered actions, then we can probably relax and surrender to what happens next. You have to judge your life every day as if you're just about to die. A Sufi saying. I try to look at it at the end of each day. Something exists that was done with a creative intent that was not there when I woke up. A line or a drawing or just a photograph that I cut out of a magazine or a meal or a kiss and a hug from someone you didn't expect. It can be very simple but it is always powerful.

CA: We passed by a blood sacrifice in the street today. The word sacrifice means to "make holy." That element is present in the Orisha consciousness too. Don't you find it strange how people react when they actually see life and death? How both life and death have become almost taboo? Where people go to hospitals to give birth, as if it's some kind of sickness? Tourists being appalled at this serene moment where a simple goat is made holy?

GBPO: And its spirit is given the freedom to incarnate in a higher being. I was initially curious to see how I would react to a sacrifice done with sacred intent. It was a new thing, although I'd seen it here in Nepal before. One of the memories I always used to mention to people was, when they asked me what it's like here, that it's very psychedelic and the underlying theme of everything is devotion. What was fabulous even on the first day was that I was walking down the road along what I nick-named the dead-dog river. I looked across the river and there would be cremations taking place, with some children being cremated and eventually swept into the river. Dogs and pigs would wait to be able to eat bits and pieces that floated ashore. Further down the river would be women doing laundry and someone else cleaning their kitchen pans, ready to make breakfast. You'd walk past all of that, and the next thing you'd see would be a little restaurant with some workers having chai tea and smoking cigarettes and gossiping before they started their long day. There would be sewage along the road, with another huge pig eating the sewage and a leper with no finger asking for money and the a shop with beautiful, beautiful bead-work and embroidered T-shirt shop with Grateful Dead T-shirts and then someone wandering along with a goat, and then sacrificing it and spreading the blood and then carrying on to work. That, to me, was, in a nutshell, the joy of Nepal. Something that was so primal and made so much reasonable sense to me and my nervous system. All my reasoning capacities were just frozen. Not in a numb way but they were just suspended.

I accepted this information, one piece after another and realised the whole idea of the Aghori Baba. The path of no distinction. It was all one. It was all the same. That was a very spiritual moment, where I felt the texture of the flesh of God almost. It's all spinning in cycles and circles and it's all the same. Ultimately, we all get born and we all die. That was my first experience of sacrifice, seeing the goat dragged along the street. No one else was even turning. A very precious moment. The second time was with the Orisha. I had no problem having an open mind but I was surprised at the beauty and the potency and the deep reverence for life that was involved. None of the discussions, and none of the prayers, and none of the perceptions were about death. It was all about giving life, saving life, healing life, sharing life and being appreciative for having life. Blessing all that is sacrificed by all beings for our chance to experience life. That's what goes on. It's important to note that it tends to be mainly the Buddhists who sometimes criticize the taking of life. If they're really sincere Buddhists, they live by that principle, and I can understand that point of view. I admit to being puzzled by the concept of taking a life when I'm back in my Western mode and Western reality imprint, which is so deep. Christians are the most vocal opponents.

CA: Which is strange, because their entire religion is based on blood sacrifice.

GBPO: And human sacrifice even. The lamb of God. Not only is their religion based upon blood sacrifice, it also celebrates blood sacrifice every Sunday, with communion. As I like to point out to Christians, what do they think happens on Christmas Day? In Britain and America and elsewhere? They sacrifice hundreds of millions of turkeys and chickens and pigs simultaneously to remember the birth of the blood sacrifice. Is it OK just because they don't soil their hands? Is it OK just because they don't watch? Because they don't pray about it? Because they don't revere the soul of the being that's dying for them? They can never answer. They just go, "It's not the same…" The answer is, "Of course not, because you're afraid to be part of that which is sacrificed." So until they end their own sacrifices, and we're not even talking about the sacrifice of millions of human beings who dared to disagree with a word or two in a particular edition of the Bible, I fail to see that the human species anywhere is really beyond sacrifice. Perhaps the whole power of sacrifice is to not forget the process that gives us life. Through all times, so far, we have lived through the sacrifice of animals and this is what reminds us of that they give themselves to us so that we may live. Doesn't that sound rather like the Bible? Isn't that what they say about Jesus? The ultimate sacrifice, real or metaphorical, of a being… Blood sacrifice somehow consecrates change, and also reinforces one's realisation and affirms one's needs to live life in a metaphysical, magical and spiritual way. That must include creativity.

CA: What would you say, just from your own personal experience, constitutes the state of mind that the ritual brings, or the actual physical change happening?

Is it the state of mind induced that's the creative principle or the physical substance?

GBPO: I think the state of mind is the principal result. But in a sacrifice there's a bridge between the material world and the inter-dimensional world. The sacrifice represents oneself too; that you also will die, you also will sacrifice your body ultimately, in order to return to that which is other. Which is why there's so much power in it. And, of course, even in the Tibetan religion, in the more hidden sorcerer-aspects and in the Bon and some of the animist traditions, they still carry on. They basically have "cakes of light"[6] and they include blood. Sacrifices do occur even in the Buddhist traditions. So at certain times both the oracle and the sacrifice are integral to the oldest religions. The only real argument against any of these ways of focusing and serving the universe is that they are literally old. Perhaps we don't need to do things the same way anymore? One of the things I find so healthy about the Orisha consciousness is that it's dedicated to looking into and seeking a way to maintain the relationship with the Orishas and actual sacrifice because there's so much sense of change. It is a new way on. I am very hopeful that a new treaty with the Orishas is feasible. That of course would be blasphemy in the major Church of Santeria, but all things must pass. Even in long-held traditions.

CA: Especially in them!

GBPO: I tend to assume that what's really going on is that we have another thousand years to deal with. These thousand years are about ways that consciousness will change, that are absolutely outside the realm of our imagination, and that the human body itself will be seen and used as entirely malleable and adjustable. And something of an obsolete organ, a little bit like the appendix or men's nipples. We will reach a level of some of the more visionary science fiction, where we can knowingly do what some of the highest lamas and rinpoches can do, which is leave our physical bodies and travel and explore and learn whilst maintaining some sense of identity and the possibility of return. Retrieval of information outside the body. That will become commonplace, just as it already is here.

CA: We have talked about needing the body to be able to work. What we can see, mainly in the Western culture, I guess, is a degeneration of the body with cancer and other diseases, and obesity. Do you think a higher state of mind could help control the body more and possibly even mutate it?

---

6 Reference to Aleister Crowley's "Gnostic Mass" and his Thelemic religion, in which the communion contains ingredients of life rather than those of a symbolic death.

GBPO: That may well be part of the equation. A tremendous culling of the species will reactivate the metaphysical view, and that there will be new dark ages, followed by new middle ages, followed by a renaissance. That renaissance will be unrecognisable from what we might expect it to be right now. A lot of the developments in cosmetic surgery and genetics and other forms of body alteration and cloning are going to play a very important part in the evolution of this species. Most people, I think, are afraid to really consider what's going to happen. I actually find it very exciting and enervating to imagine having infinite options in terms of shape, form and ability on a physical plane. And at the same time having infinite options as to how to apply the neurology of the brain and consciousness; having far, far more choices and doorways. We'll probably have a whole new species: those who leave bodies frozen or leave them completely and decide to just travel to other universes; those who allow other people from other universes into their body, knowingly and consciously to confer with us. A lot might happen.

I hope that there will also be an end to the binary gender as well. That's one of my pet topics. That split, that separation, is becoming anachronistic and psychologically unhealthy in the species. It's one of the main contributors to conflict and friction on a very deep level. Ecstasy too, but ecstasy can be enjoyed by two hermaphrodites just as much as by two people of apparently different gender. I would vote for an entirely hermaphroditic species. The choice to be whatever version of gender one wants. It would not exclude ecstasy or union in any form. I think it would be a big up-stepping of magical intent and activity. It seems it's prophesied in the hermetic traditions everywhere and in the alchemical traditions. Even the Pope last year declared that God was male and female. Again, by deduction. It must be. I honestly believe that one of the programs in our structures on the deepest level is to become one again, to become the image of God. If learning is the process, then the end result is again to become the image of God, with the qualities of God and to share them with God knowingly instead of by accident. To choose to make union with the divine as opposed to accidentally existing. How's that so far?

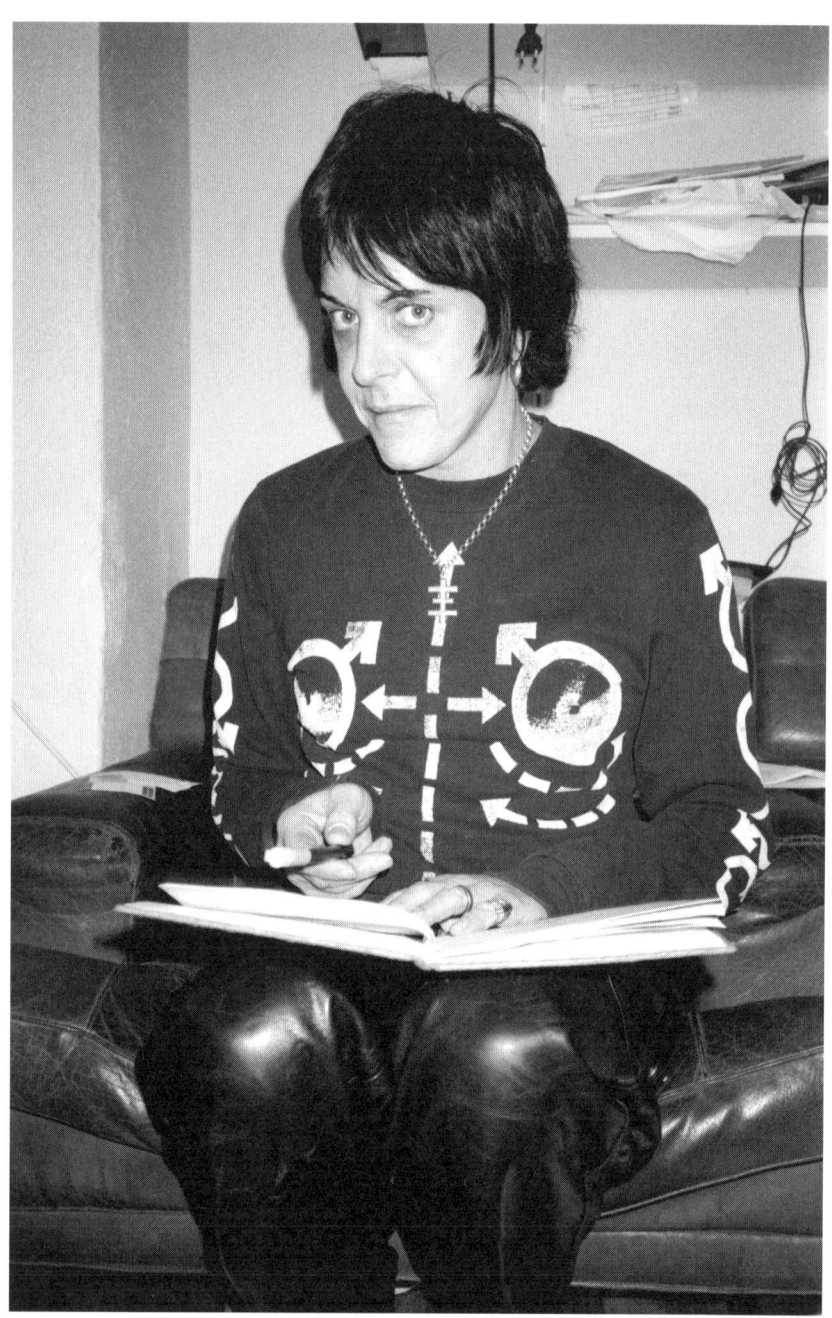

Stockholm, 2002

Stockholm, February 3rd, 2002

While I had brought Genesis over to Stockholm to record a new album together with my musical project Cotton Ferox, we also arranged a lecture evening at Fylkingen, a classic venue for experimental art in Sweden. This was a sold out evening that also featured an exhibition of records covers and other related art. During the evening, Genesis showed slides and videos from C.O.U.M. and onwards, and talked about central concepts.

GBPO: Okay, well I decided to do something I've never done before, just for the hell of it, which is to show the secret art that I've been making for the last 30 years. You probably, if you do know anything about me, imagine that I'm a musician or I pretend to be a musician if I'm correct, and so I've decided to not mention music at all. So, be prepared for that. I have something here, and it's not actually one line or one story but merely a series of strange collisions that one can either surrender to, and exploit the pleasure, or try and impose form and shape on something and end up frustrated, angry and even bitter. I can tell you right now, I am not frustrated, I am not angry, and I am not bitter. I've had so much pleasure that this is the story of my pleasure. And if it's in any way appealing, I would suggest that you look for your own pleasure, build it carefully and then present it to someone else. And that might well make life more fun.

In the end, there's only one thing that really takes place while we're alive and that is the act of making something that was not there before; whether it's a relationship or a piece of music or a room that you live in... Looking at things differently and trying and trying to see something as if it was never there a minute ago – it might not be there in another minute's time.

So I wanted to tell you something, which is that I actually murdered Neil Megson a few years ago, and I've been intrigued by this ever since. I wrote something, a few weeks ago which perhaps will explain my dilemma. I've been thinking more and more lately, "where is Neil?" Neil Megson was the person that I was born and named as by my parents, and in 1965 Neil Megson invented a game. He invented a character, Genesis P-Orridge, and he let him loose into the world. In the beginning Neil was being Genesis, and Genesis was responsible for what the Art was and for the creativity, but Neil was the puppet-master of this alter ego and he was in control. But then, as Genesis took himself more and more seriously, or as Neil did, he changed his name. People would meet him and it was only Genesis they were speaking to. And there was no Neil any more. There was a point then when Neil was actually forgotten by Genesis.

It's a strange question that puzzles me now: does Neil still exist? Why was he erased and murdered by Genesis? Almost like one of those monsters in a movie, a parasite that takes over and completely absorbs, like "The Blob." Perhaps the Creation does take over the Creator, and I'm not really sure if Neil exists anymore, and I wonder what he thinks about Genesis, if he could... I'm Genesis; I killed Neil. I wonder if I went back to ask him to look at what he became as Genesis, would he still make the same decision? Or would he not want to be erased by Art? Or was it the determination, the dedication to living Art and Life as one that made Genesis exist? I don't know where Neil is, and I wonder if Neil created Genesis and Genesis has now completely absorbed everything that was Neil and perhaps the only way to solve this question is not to be Genesis any more. But I'm stuck here now.

One of my first inspirations would be Andy Warhol and the idea that celebrity and personality can become art. That is why I invented a character like Genesis P-Orridge – to see what would happen if you actually lived the piece of Art instead of making it. So I spent quite a lot of time in the early 60s in London in a commune that was basically a psychotherapy commune. The rigours of that particular place are significant, I think, in that you were not allowed to sleep in the same place two nights in a row; there were no beds; the toilet and the bath were one big room so that you were always visible when you were doing anything intimate; the clothes that everybody had were in one large box, and each morning the first person to get out of their sleeping bag or off the floor would put on the clothes that they liked and become a character suggested by this chosen outfit, and the last person to wake up got what was left. At any moment during the day you could say to another person, "Stop! Why are you eating food with a knife and fork; have you no imagination? Is there no other way to eat food? Why did you eat bread today? You've eaten bread before. Have you no imagination? Why is your hair the same today? Why is your name the same today?" I learned later that this "stop game" was an idea coming from Gurdjieff. And I actually observed people having nervous breakdowns and become catatonic. I found it very exciting and enjoyed it a great deal, and in fact took it to my own extremes and lived on the roof and leaped on scaffolding and hanging on strings and chains.

What I realized was that nothing was really fixed; nothing was permanent and, most importantly, the personality and the ways in which we behave are just as flexible and easy to manipulate as paint or photography or collaging or sculpture, or sand. What we think we are is completely arbitrary and is mainly inherited from what everybody tells us that we are and that's another reason that

I decided to destroy myself. I wanted to find out what would happen if I began with a name that implied something and allowed it to lead me into new situations where I would guess and improvise and rebuild moment to moment what might happen next for that character, and that's the character that presumably to some degree has appealed to or created curiosity in you.

The thing that's important to remember is that there is nothing unusual about this process. You're all actually building yourselves right now. When I was at that youth place today,[1] it struck me very clearly there that the younger people are trying to build a life for themselves, but they were building themselves from the outside in; they were building themselves with things that they thought represented ideas – instead of letting the ideas build them in ways they haven't seen before. It was like a parade of moments from television. It was a beautifully naïve event, and yet I wondered if anyone has said to them at school or at home, "you don't have to be that way; you can be any way that you want."

And really, that's the only message that I can have for any of you here: look at everything that happens to you, look at any moment in which you've inhibited yourself, and ask "why am I inhibited? Why do I stop at this point? Am I embarrassed to be naked? Is that because I don't like my body? Or is that because I think I should look like somebody else's body? Is there a reason that I don't have sex in public? Is there a reason that I don't sleep in the street?" If we think about behaviour it's no different to writing down a nursery rhyme. We simply take what we expect and then we live the expected.

So I would like to just try tonight to help you see evidence of breaking all those usual habits and looking at the world with a fresh eye... The first video... This is the first time it's been seen in 25 years. It's from 1974 C.O.U.M. Transmissions, and it's the beginning of the process of me coming to terms with being in a body and refusing to accept any of the boundaries that I had inherited from the adult world.

[Video screening]

The first thing that happened was that I realized that reality is truly just a series of choices, and each of us as a being is just a continuing series of choices that we make. And each one of you here tonight is actually a completely separate universe. All our universes are intersecting and meeting, and you're aware that I'm here and I'm aware that there are people here and we're having a vaguely similar experience. But as soon as you leave the room there is no proof that either of us exist and the common experience is over, and that's when you're with someone

---

1 Lava, Kulturhuset, Stockholm, where P-Orridge talked and played records for an interested crowd of young people.

else and their universe continues with you.

This is very important, I think, in your life: in the end, you are born alone and you live in one universe that is yours alone; and you will pass on from that apparent universe alone. And what you build during the time you appear to be here is absolutely your responsibility. And no one but you should choose what that is – because only you are there all the time. No one else. The rest are just visitors who never see the world; the universe that you are. It's yours, and if you don't choose to build it the way you really want, you're wasting the time you have. That's something I think is very important to bear in mind, because you can take that idea, and if you truly live it, you can start to feel awake and alive and in contact with things that otherwise you just miss. And that's what Art is. Art is built in your universe; temporarily you're having control of it. No-one else, no-one, has the right to build your universe! And don't let them ever, ever teach you otherwise.

Now the next thing that became incredibly important for me was to understand something that I could only call magic. I've tried to find better words or less fashionable, more fashionable words, but in the end it's "magic." It's a process… And I was introduced to the idea of magic, in terms of finding a process to make choices and build my universe and have control over it, from William S. Burroughs and Brion Gysin. In my personal opinion they are probably master magicians of their particular age. And the reason is that they were doing something that is happening in most of the work that I will show you today, and they came up between them with an idea that some of you may have heard of called the "cut-up" – that basically nothing is linear, nothing goes from A to B, nothing is as it seems. We try and impose shape, and we try and impose order, but in fact we live in a completely chaotic state. And to get a clearer, more accurate picture of what's happening, the more we smash and fragment what appears to be solid or logical, the closer we get to what might really be going on. The original ways that the beatniks, with Brion Gysin, applied the cut-up was very literally cutting pieces of paper, reassembling them and then re-reading what they said, and one of the classic moments on tape of William S. Burroughs is when he gets a letter from his lawyer in London and it's a letter all about book deals and money and bills and percentages, and you hear him slicing up the paper and he says "Let's see what they really say…" and as he starts to read it he basically goes something like "Money money my money not your money my money…" They all start laughing… Basically they see the message which is they are getting nothing.

[Video Screening]

The Dreamachine is a very simple device, you'll see it, and you'll get the idea really quickly… As Brion Gysin said, it's the only artwork you look at with your eyes closed. That's a radical thought, and it's a radical piece of equipment because

108

it just uses a light bulb, and the light comes from a sequence of holes in a cardboard tube and they strobe on the eyes in a certain rhythm and frequency and with your eyes closed you hallucinate. If you use it long enough and if you relax enough you will travel to other dimensions and begin to see landscapes, archetypal figures, creatures from fiction and myth that you might have thought not possibly be real. And of course, they cannot possibly be real but that's what they think about you. And who is watching who, and who's at which side… I don't know. I have no way of being sure that when I'm apparently awake it's any more real than when I'm asleep. And I don't think you do really. If you think you do, maybe you're limiting what happens.

[Video screening]

What was happening at the very beginning of being Genesis, was cutting up behaviour, cutting up personality, cutting up every aspect of inherited ideas of reality, and the strength to do that came very much from the process that the beatniks gave to the world, and the cut-up in particular as a magical process. You cannot remember often enough that you are a series of choices, and that in an ideal situation you should erase everything that you imagined you were and start to build your own world.

The process of doing this is strange, in that the art and the artist in this day and age have become one thing. The human body and the artist are actually falling out of what was once a canvas and into the world itself. And so, the life that one lives is the Art in a very real sense. And the life that one lives therefore should be joyous, and it should reveal mystery and change every aspect of how we deal with being alive.

I don't know how it is for everybody else, and maybe I'm just fucked up, but I am still absolutely shocked that I'm in a human body. It blows my mind to wake up and see edges to me, because I don't have edges in my head. One of the reasons I've worked on my own skin and worked on this strange canvas is to try and understand where I begin and where I end. It seems that this is something like a mobile cluster of biological systems that move something else around, and the something else is the consciousness; the sense we have of existing and being a person, of having an identity. If that's the case, then the body is, to some degree, holding us back from what might happen. I think for a long, long time I was angry at the restrictions of having a human body, and sometimes I think I probably still am. Even more so, I'm angry at the idea that there are genders and that there are certain expectations of how this cluster works and how it's supposed to behave in relation to other clusters. And once I have resolved the idea that there is some solidity to the thing that I live inside, and that is temporary, and this being an incredibly brutal environment in linear time and gravity and space – it's so brutal that it is almost like wearing a diving suit – in order to experience we come in bodies and the experience we have is a blessing that we might never have again. And once more I'll just urge you: don't waste that time.

I don't have many things to tell you. I don't know that much. But I can share my questions with you and I can share some of the things that seem to help make sense of this. You don't know how long you've got. You don't know if you're going to come back. You might believe you will; I think what you believe tends to make things happen. But given that there tends to be a pattern to this physical stuff, work with it, find out how to control it, take power over it for yourself, build the world yourself, take identity and choose what it is for you.

[Slideshow]

As we experiment with this strange thing we call life, what we tend to find happens is that there are ways to communicate in non-verbal ways and to bypass the usual expectations and controls the society tries to use to define and maintain its power, with reference for what it wants us to behave like.

This is a very important man: an Aghori Baba. This Aghori Baba lives in a cave by Pashupatinath in Kathmandu and he tends a fire. It's a fire dedicated to the Hindu deity Shiva, and the fire has been burning for more than 1000 years without ever going out. And each Aghori Baba takes on the honour of maintaining the fire. The path of the Aghori is in a very real way linked to the process of magic and art in the way that I'm trying to completely and generally explain. The path of the Aghori is a path of no distinction, and the simple way of explaining that is that everything is exactly the same or completely different. And so, for example, an Aghori Baba would eat human shit and eat a beautiful meal of chicken and vegetables and actually taste the same thing, because taste and value are absolutely imposed by us. Nothing is innately different from anything else. He might drink petrol and then drink water and it would be the same experience. It's a very rigorous, difficult path but the idea behind that is that we absolutely choose what we want to have happen. There are no real lines. No good and no bad, and no black and no white, and no female and no male, and no dead and no alive; there are no edges. It's a very, very liberating thing and it's like coming home to a new house and suddenly it all makes sense.

I was really very lucky when I spent some time with the Aghori Baba. He gave me some of the ash from the fire and asked me to take it back to America, which I have. And sometimes I take the powder and I eat a little bit, and there is something remarkable there, the idea of a powder that's a thousand years old, that's linked to centuries and centuries and centuries of not believing what we are told is there. And it's interesting because you eat the ash and it tastes like honey. And you get high and it cures illnesses. I've had people in my house who've had various illnesses, quite sick, and I've given them this powder and they go away apparently healed. I don't know how that works; all I know is that nothing is as it seems and that's a good thing.

Another good thing is to realize that none of us have any original thoughts at all. When we go somewhere like Nepal or Bali or somewhere in South America or wherever it might be, we suddenly discover these ancient cultures, and we see that we've been crawling back to something we should have known a long time ago. Somebody stole this from us. Somebody didn't tell us about this. And there is a reason they didn't tell us. The reason is, I think, that we can control what seems to be reality more than we expect. And interestingly enough we have people who learn physics now coming to the same conclusions; that time and space are actually energies, and the body and flesh are just that.

This person you can see now is called the Milk Baba – a remarkable man, who for more than 20 years only drinks tea and milk, has no solid food and he has dreadlocks like no one. Look at that! I've seen some dreadlocks but they ain't nothing on him. What is interesting though is to be in the presence of that level of command over one's universe; it is a very humbling experience and a very inspiring experience. We're really amateurs out here in the West, and certainly coming from England in the 50s, very ignorant, speaking of myself. And I wonder why we don't really have in our education the idea of spirit, of the divine. I don't know about you, maybe it's different in Sweden, but no one told me or discussed with me during my education philosophy, the divine creativity, reality, reasons to exist, the mystery of life… The most I got was Jesus. Bow down for Jesus, kneel down for Jesus… and I did, I knelt down and I got hit and kicked, beaten, insulted and humiliated… Ironically enough, all of the things that supposedly happened to Jesus, but it doesn't seem like that's what we should be doing.

One of the things that I found out as I was starting to make objects and rituals was that sometimes different things would happen that I wasn't supposed to expect. The most useful of those is one that I just touched upon, which was that it seems that one can quite literally change the human metabolism and heal illness. And so after a while I started to very quietly make pieces of art that had functions. So instead of them being made to be looked at or admired for their aesthetic value or because they were pretty, I would make them for a person that needed something… It might be that they needed money, or it might be that they had a blood disease and they wanted to be cured. I would use all these things that happened to me before; my own body and blood, my hair, my skin, my belief in the possibility of changing reality, and I would give this as a gift to those special people in just the same way that it's done in all these other places in the world.

One of the things that I would love to see happen with art is for it to return to its sacred purpose. If one really looks at where art came from, it was the process of the shaman and the healer; it was to speak to nature and the natural forces;

to intervene in what we think of as reality and alter it for the good of others. It was not meant to be a career, and it was not meant to be about celebrity. It was not meant to be about money and dealing and banking. It was sacred, holy work, and I believe art and creativity are only present in sacred, holy work. The body is a sacred, holy vehicle which allows the spirit to speak to others and meet them. Our body is a vehicle of mobility during a life. A life is central in art. Art is this body. Life=Body=Art... And so we are able to feel all these moments through our bundle of senses. Body and Creation are inseparable.

That is why something like this tonight is a blessing; because I am able to meet you and try, very quickly, to suggest that you really believe that you are able to be fabulous and special and powerful in this world. No one has the right to steal your joy in being yourself, and your self is what you make of yourself. There is really no difference between art and religion, between art and healing, between art and gods. Perhaps each of us are really just small parts of what was once God, and that God can only experience through all of us. Without us there is no experience, there is nothing. But with us there is a potential for everything and anything to happen. And it does.

In the end, all we do is build a series of experiences, and we make the choices that allow those to happen. So when I was talking before about that each of you is a series of choices, that's true, but those choices are made about experiences, and you have the right to any experience that you wish. But you have the right to wish experiences that others don't wish. And you have the right to experience anything that you can imagine. When your imagination is stuck, cut up your experience and build another imagination. And you will never run out of things to do, places to go, people to meet, drugs to take, sex to have, love to be, shrines to build, memories to hold. I hope you noticed I'm trying to encourage you. A lot. And of course I can't prove anything that I say except that I've been doing it for 35 years and it's a lot of fun.

All of us contain a lot of different people, different characcters in potentia, and it would be really silly to think that you're just one person. We are probably at least few dozen, and they all want to have their voice and they all want to have their moment living in the body that you have right now, sharing it with you, playing with it, playing with other people through your body. So another thing that I would like to remind you of is just to let all those people speak. Take time to listen to them. Look for the ones who shock you; listen to them harder. Look for the ones who surprise you and embrace them a bit more – because those people are trying to help you to make the most of the time that you have and they are trying to encourage you to really maximize the potential that you have in there inside. The genius factor that no one wants you to know about...

We've reached a point where these are the actual sigils; the magical works that I used to make during the 90s to make things happen. Mostly for healing illnesses. None of these have ever been seen before for obvious reasons that they were very personal to the people they were made for and I had to get their consent to show them.

In this one, down in the bottom right corner, is an old friend of mine from the 60s: Derek Jarman, the filmmaker. He was actually very ill at the time with AIDS, and had begun to go blind and wanted to keep his eyesight long enough to finish one of his last and most powerful movies: "Blue." So he asked me if I could do something for him, and this is the one that I made. A beautiful, beautiful man. Anyway, it worked. And he actually got to do quite a lot more of visual work before he lost his sight again. And by the time when he was to pass on, I was living in America, and I had this really strong feeling to find this picture. I found it in a box and took it out and felt compelled to write a letter to Derek, and I mailed it to the last address that I had. And it was months later I met somebody from London who worked with him, and I said "Did Derek ever get that letter?" And he replied, "Yes, it arrived on the day he died. And we read it to him. And he said to say, "thank you."

At the very least, it reminds me not to assume that the material world is as it seems and that's all I need to know – things can happen when we don't expect, and expectation is really a curse. One of the worst things that you can ever do is to have expectations. One should always assume that something you didn't expect is going to happen. So will it be different, want it to be different; don't want it to be the same, and don't want it to be what you expect. Take control of it; it's yours.

[Slideshow]

TOPY was an attempt to organize a very loose network of people just enough so that they could exchange ideas and information about some of the things we talked about before. That one could make a ritual or make a sigil and have something that you wanted to happen actually happen… There was no logic to it, science didn't agree, but it seemed to several of us that we still got good results and that was really interesting. So what better way to check than ask anyone who wants to play a game to play the game? So that's what we did. We said, here is what seems to happen. You take an idea of something that you really genuinely desire and you in some way write it down or turn it into something graphic and then at the moment of orgasm – whether by having sex with another being or masturbating – you try and post that message into the part of consciousness that we don't usually think we control.

Austin Osman Spare was definitely influential in extending these ideas in the way that I made some of the artworks that you're looking at. And so very gradually, through communication and post, people like Carl and some people

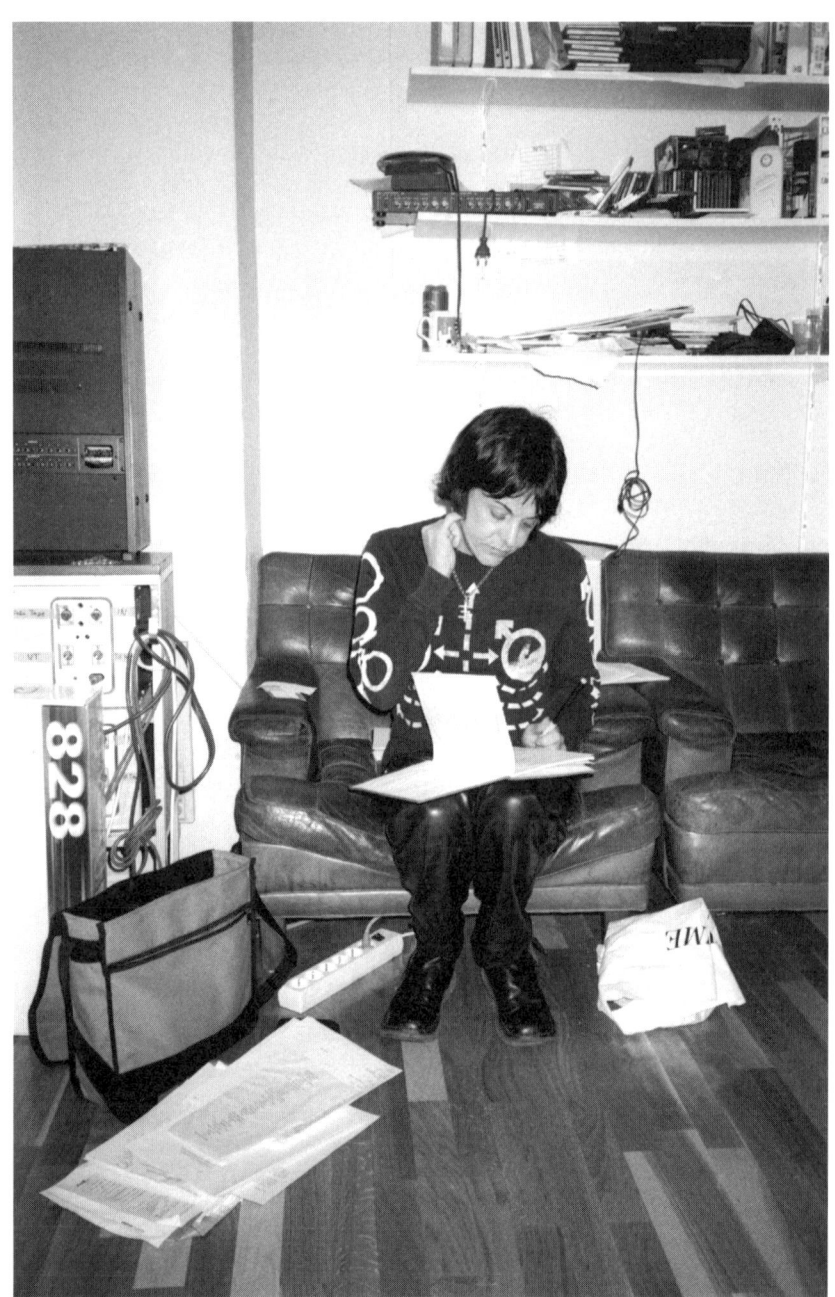

Stockholm, 2002

in America and people in England, we would meet or we would exchange letters and we would, on the 23rd of the month, at 2300 hours, experiment with sexual rituals. Sometimes just for our own personal desires and sometimes for group desires. And we did that for ten years, at which point the Queen and the British government decided I was the most evil man in Great Britain, and suddenly put my face on all these newspapers and said, "This evil man corrupts kids!" And I thought, yes, of course I do. What am I supposed to be doing if I'm not meant to corrupt kids? "Corrupting" being "change in the way that you think," right? And so Scotland Yard went to my house in England and took away all the photographs and videos that I had, and found nothing... I was in Kathmandhu, Nepal, subsidising and working for a soup kitchen for Tibetan refugees, lepers and beggar children, so it was a supremely ironic moment for me. Every morning I would get up at 6am and go and feed 300-600 beggars and lepers and Tibetan refugee families. One day afterwards I went back to our hotel to find a fax from TOPY HQ, or TOPYGLOBAL, that said "Big trouble. Call home asap!" And basically I've stayed away from the UK since then.

If you want to know more about TOPY what I can tell you is that the people who were really present at the beginning are still present in my life and they are all very creative people. They publish books and they write ideas and live the kind of lives we were talking about before. I would see that as evidence that whatever it was we did as an experiment in terms of ways to be was a fabulous experiment, and a very powerful one. And it drew to it people who genuinely wanted to change themselves and manifest their Will. People think they want to change; they say they want to change. Most people don't truly desire to change. Because it's scary. The unknown is scary for people. They want to keep telling you that they are radical, and they want to keep telling you that they experiment. They don't really do it for a lifetime. Most of you must have seen people drop away in life, maybe at school or university or whatever. They dropped away. And so you look around and there is only five or six left. It's not as easy as it sounds; it's very brutal and tough to genuinely want to change all the time. But that's what it was and that's what it does. TOPY is the process of trying to change.

The reason I do what I do is because it's a great way to live. And I'm blessed. And I have the best fucking life, I really have a great life and I just do what I want every day. I mean who can complain about that. Is it perfect? I doubt it. There are many people who think I'm a complete asshole. So what? One thing that I am is I'm authentic. I have integrity, I keep my word, and I'm very loyal. That's what matters. Not the stuff that gets made. The reason it gets made, that's important, but not what it is. Sometimes it's good too; sometimes I'm embarrassed, but so what? I'm honest. I live it as it happens and I don't pretend. What more can you expect from someone?

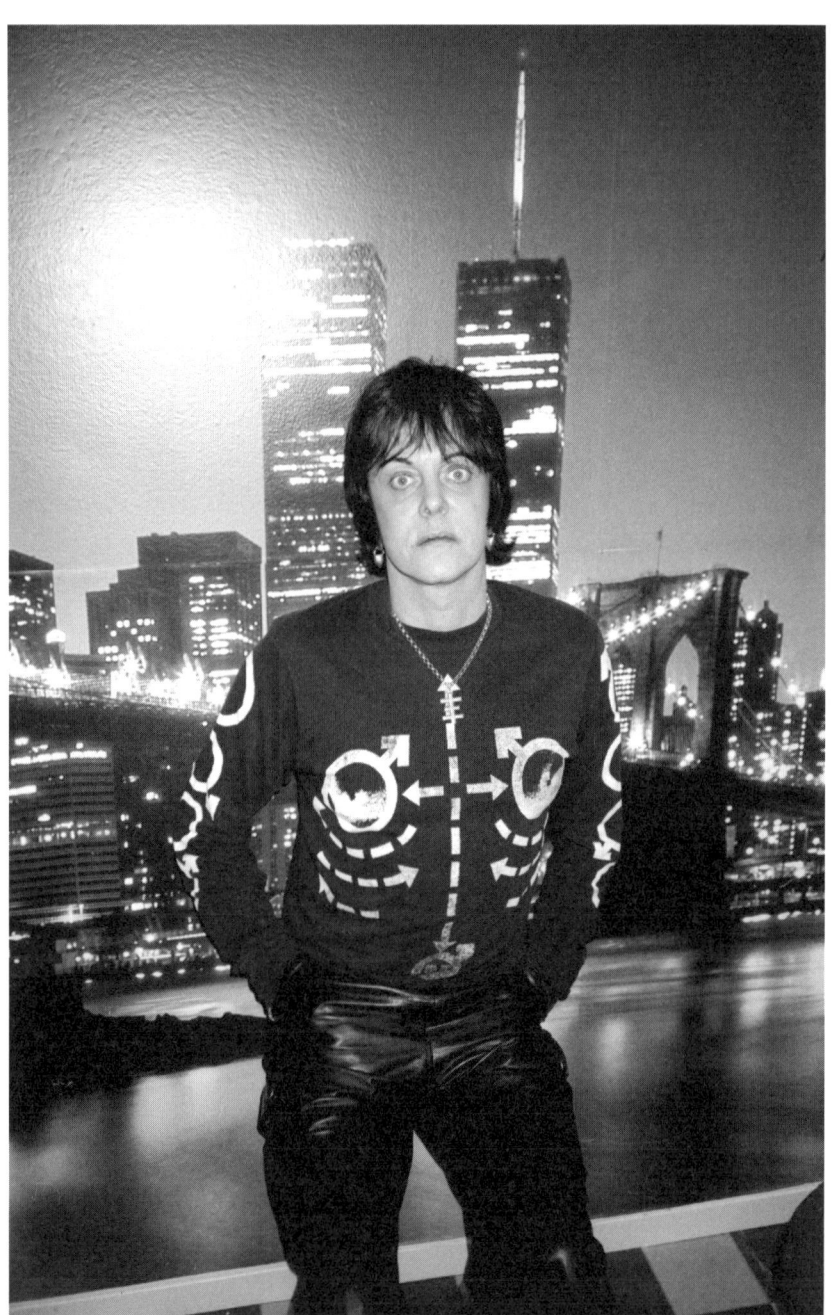

Stockholm, 2002

New York, February 14th, 2002

As we didn't have the time to do a proper interview during the Stockholm visit, I decided to follow up with one soon after this, to keep the continuity, and touch further upon subjects that were brought up during the lecture evening.

CA: One thing I found curious and interesting was that you finally found the slides and also the C.O.U.M. videos that you thought were lost.

GBPO: It's just very, very odd. When Scotland Yard came to our house in Brighton, they were escorted by Words.[1] He followed them around and wrote everything down. They took every slide, every photograph, every video and every piece of film. They're documented by ourselves and Scotland Yard as having been taken away and never seen again. Then I had everything that was left shipped from England about one and a half years later. I went through all the boxes and they weren't there. Then we moved to New York and went through all our belongings before we packed. We made a great box of everything we didn't want, and threw or gave it away. All the possessions, all the archives have been gone through three times, really thoroughly. It was unpacked here in New York, which was the fourth time. On none of these occasions did these slides appear. They were just assumed missing in action. Then suddenly, when the Soft Skull book[2] was in the process of manifesting, we were looking for images. I remember saying to Miss Jackie, "It's such a shame that nothing really exists from the early years. And there's nothing in colour." Some time after that, I came back from one of my trips. Miss Jackie says, "By the way, I found this cardboard box and when I opened it, it was full of strange cassette cases..." I opened the box and realised they weren't cassette cases; they were slide boxes. I pulled one out and opened it. Lo and behold, there were several hundred slides from the early 70s. They truly had not been there before. It's a very bizarre phenomenon.

CA: Perhaps they were just waiting for the book project?

---

1 Words = Paul Cecil, the owner of the TOPY-related publishing house Temple Press.
2 *Painful But Fabulous – The Lives & Art of Genesis P-Orridge*, Soft Skull Press, 2002.

GBPO: It looks like that for the people who don't believe in the symmetrical unfolding of the universe; they might find it odd. Luckily, I don't believe in coincidences. I do believe in that very thing that we use "23" to represent – the symmetrical unfolding of the universe. I can't speculate on the means or the process by which it happened. However, I can verify and confirm from my own personal experience that these slides were gone. Absolutely gone for years. When they were needed, they reappeared in my life. In this particular instance, Miss Jackie was the medium, literally, that helped them to manifest. And the invocation of the book itself. The heart of the book is really that the magical process is a more accurate picture of the world than the so called materialistic, scientific view of the Western world. Logic is actually something that constrains and restricts us. And something that probably prevents good fortune. The slides appeared in that manner: as a confirmation of the attitude that we represent. The C.O.U.M. videos were also gone. They'd not been seen for even longer. They vanished in England but suddenly reappeared in a cupboard. There's no explanation... It's as if there's a strange portal in the fabric of consensus reality. Perhaps it's like that with Sai Baba, who manifests objects. In this particular instance, the universe was kind. On behalf of its message, it ripped open the fabric for us and handed the videos back, knowing that we perhaps weren't skilled enough to do it on our own.

CA: I recently saw a TV program about some people in Malaysia, who walked in procession with strange constructs attached to their skins, consisting of threads and strings. They reminded me of some of the C.O.U.M. documentation.

GBPO: I really do believe that none of us is the owner of anything. Brion Gysin said, "Poets don't own words." For a long time, I thought that it was just a clever expression. It didn't really resonate with me at the time; it didn't elicit any kind of emotional response. It didn't seem important. Now, having had the experiences I've had, I realised that we don't really create unique words. At the very best, we recognise the inevitable. We are, in that moment, the voice of the people, of the tribe, of the chosen group or extended family or even the entire species. Depending on the importance and relevance of what we're trying to bring into being. That is inevitable. Someone will always be there and express the message that's necessary for us to evolve as a species. That's what the writer and the artist does. After realising that things are inevitable and that it's not one's genius or unique talent or ego that's so fabulous and superior, then you see things in a more intelligent and fantastic way. When you let go of that initial superior viewpoint, you see yourself as being devoted to, and happily surrendering to, what is supposed to happen for the better; for the healing and for the greater good of humanity. You also realise that it's not yours. You might make it; you might make the message; you might write it or put it on a canvas, and you do have the right to sign it because of your participation. Making it visible to everybody. But it's not yours. That's when I realised how powerful Brion's message was. It wasn't one of the less important things. In a way, it is very central to the path towards wisdom, where one becomes enlightened by growing older, through studying or through listening – preferably all three. You begin to realise that "Of course!" One realises how incredibly small one is in the universe; how incredibly unimportant and trivial. How superficial the things I invest so much energy in really are. If one gets more humble, the humility seeps into the ego of youth. It becomes more and more apparent that we are all blessed with the possibility of touching the message of the universe. But it's not our message. It really is a blessing to even notice and have some kind of comprehension of the higher level of possibilities.

CA: Could you tell me a little bit about the Frankfurt exhibition recently? What did it actually consist of?

GBPO: There was another artist there too, Rachel Lowther, who exhibited three sculptures and five little drawings. The one I was particularly interested in was a fibreglass goat with horns; very shiny and dark, life-size. She said that in a way my exhibition was a retrospective. It began with about ten sigils from the early 80s. They were created using Polaroids taken during the actual ritual act. Some of these actually took three or four, even up to ten years, to complete – if they're ever completed. There's a different aesthetic, in that they're done to make something happen rather than to conform to the limits of a flat surface or a normal fine art aesthetic. They can be out of balance, with colours that don't officially fit together. They have writing, bits of hair, blood, and they go off the edge of the picture into imagined space. They were also presented in an unorthodox way, in order to make people realise that they were sections of continuous time with intention, rather than just graphics.

It was actually Miss Jackie that came up with the way to display them. They were all in the same simple black frames with a white background; very close together, almost as if they're frames from a movie. Starting at eye height and then going down towards the floor. To look at everything, you had to actually crouch and lean over. What I particularly liked was that many of the people in the pictures are bending and crouching during sex magic rituals. They were being copied and mimicked unconsciously by the people who looked at them. They had to get in similar positions to see what was happening. As they did that, people coming into the gallery would see them do that but they couldn't see what they were looking at... There was also a column of concrete on which I had a series of five small photographic prints in gold frames, as a parody of old English miniatures. I had those right behind the column so you couldn't see them when you came in. But as you walked towards Rachel's goat on the shelf, you suddenly saw these little tiny frames. So you had to stop and peek at them to see what they were. They were actually a series of photos of two people making love in a cheap hotel room. It was very much like a little peep show. An intimate moment that you shouldn't see, like if you passed someone's apartment and the curtains were left open. A Peeping Tom-feeling. The first series were about being accidentally drawn into the images and the second was the forbidden, with guilt and excitement; seeing something that shouldn't be seen.

I tried all the way through the exhibition to play with the reactions, physically and mentally, of the people who would come and look. The next wall, the one that faced you as you came in, was a new piece: a series of five images. I'd taken Polaroids from rituals, recent ones, and blown the Polaroids to three-four foot squares and had them printed on canvas, stretched onto canvas like a painting. They're very beautiful and calm. In front of each one was a custom made white column. On the column, there would be something connected to or extended out from the picture that you saw. In this instance, it was manipulation of male genitals with ropes and somebody's fingers, with long silver extensions. Like they use in Thailand and India in ritual and religious dancing. On the column was another actual Polaroid from the same sequence. In the big picture, there was white rope used for tying up. On the column, it was black rope. Next to that was one which was the groin area of a woman, covered with white sugar. On the column was a cone of white sugar that spilled over onto another Polaroid from the same sequence. Another one looks opaque but when you get nearer you realise that it's fishnet tights over flesh. The actual tights from the picture were hanging on a hook next to it. And on the column were more objects connected to the image. There was also a set of things from the late 90s. Sigils made on wood in mahogany frames. Beneath each one was hanging a thing relating to the ritual. Basically, everything is very much about making it clear that you are being allowed to, and invited to, a sacred moment. It's very personal and intimate.

The art is documentation of ritual, made with sacred intent. It's time-based as well; it's not made to be finished when it's framed and displayed. It stays alive. It can be reactivated by your participation. Some of them are made for healing people. Some of them are made for more mundane purposes, like generating and multiplying money. Some of them are made to do something more general, like trigger a change in the species. They're obviously very pro-sexual, and there's a lot of ambiguous imagery in terms of gender. They're very much about breaking down a binary, dualistic system which I feel tends to limit and constrain all of us and our potential. Ultimately, everything is about releasing and encouraging people in terms of change and their embracing of their own genius factor. Everyone has the potential to express genius in some way. Everyone is capable of being everybody else in the best possible sense. Rising to their highest. I'm always challenged by the idea of taking something that would normally be seen as taboo or "pornographic" and revitalising it with a sense of devotion and holiness. Saying that this is an incredibly sacred and holy method; a way of working with the universe. You are blessed to witness this.

In order to get people, even unconsciously, to work with the idea of being sacred and holy and devotional, I put the things on the columns. When they came up to the columns, they would literally bow down, as in prayer. Someone looking from across the room would see these people standing before the images and bowing down and meditating as if they were praying. There was a wonderful, physical manipulation of people going through all the motions they usually go through in church, or in a Buddhist temple. They were going around the space giving physical signs of respect to the work. I thought that was very important. I'm not happy with anything being fixed on the canvas. In a way, a lot of pop art is about the surface and the framing. Warhol would use images screened onto canvas. I'm using the latest technology, but it's still similar. But he did it in order to flatten the image further, in order to dehumanise it and take away its emotions. I'm using it very much for the exact opposite reason. I want to invest it with goodness and respect. In order for it not to be trapped in the flat surface, I have these things falling out of the image and back into the space. The things happen in my room, in my sacred space. The gallery becomes, to an extent, a doorway. The room falls out of the painting. Like the mirrors in a Jean Cocteau film. My room is frozen on the flat canvas, but the other side is the gallery. They become the equivalent of mirrors.

CA: You've gone through various manifestations these past few years. The "Candy Factory"[3] show in the US and the UK, and now the exhibition in Frankfurt. The gallery work is distinctly connected to the art space, the art world, art institutions and art business. Have you consciously held yourself back from this world over the years? Why is this happening right now?

GBPO: I definitely withdrew from the art world in 1976 or thereabouts, after the ICA show,[4] which was a retrospective. My interest then was something immediately more dynamic. At that time, to see how we could manipulate and work within the music business. It was all about street level culture. We took the archetype of rock'n'roll and explored that. The idea was to see if it was ultimately possible to take something that normally has the ability of infinite content but is usually reduced just to gossip. We wanted to turn that around until it had content

---

3 "Candy Factory," an exhibition at Team Gallery in New York in 2001, made together with American artist Eric Heist.
4 "Prostitution," a retrospective exhibition held at the Institute for Contemporary Art (ICA) in London, October 1976.

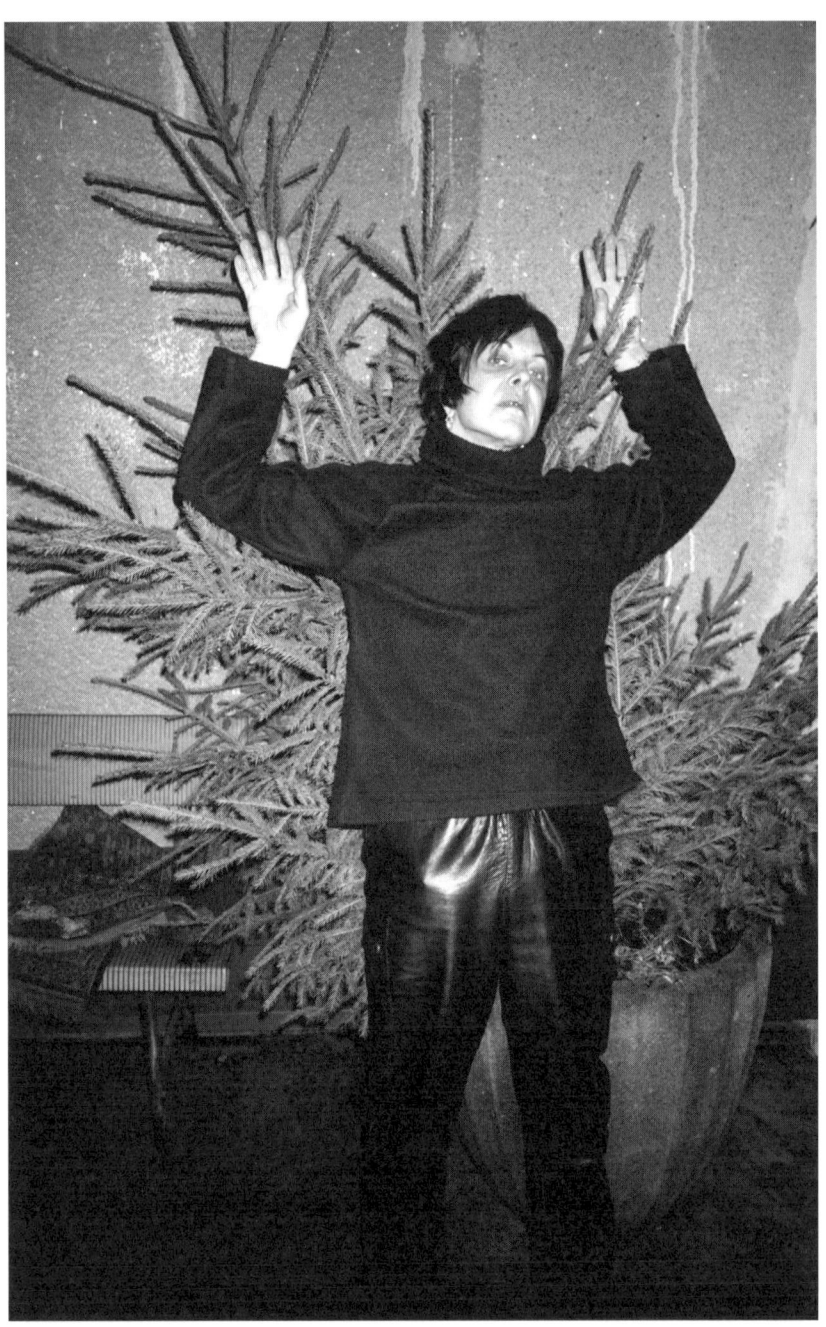

Stockholm, 2002

again. And even sensuality. I was also very, very disenchanted with the art world and the way that it commodifies and castrates the imagination of the determined artist.

For me, art is really a process of personal evolution on behalf of the species. The artist's job is to take risks. For me, to be prepared to sacrifice sanity and physical safety in order to find out what the possibilities and the joys and the evolutionary destiny of our incredible species might be. We're like the people who climbed Everest first. The people who fly faster than sound although the plane might fall apart. We're the reckless ones who are reckless on behalf of humanity and the greater good. Not for glory, and not for the adrenalin rush. Not for money, not for self-aggrandisement and ego, but truly because we want the human species to be at peace with itself. To love itself. We should be proud of ourselves. At the moment, we're rather shameful in the ways we behave. We're reactive and violent and primitive. For me, art is all about going from the state of primitive to the state of evolved and wonderful.

CA: With that noble purpose in mind, but still working with expressions that are fairly complicated for common people to assimilate, have you never felt disenchanted, or asked yourself why you're doing it?

GBPO: Almost all of the time. I dropped out of the formal art world for the reason of being disenchanted. For the hypocrisy, for the fact that people didn't really believe in art at all; they believed in business. They believed an artist should do the same thing all of the time: work with a formula. One should find a formula that appears to represent an idea and then repeat it forever and ever. That, for me, was anathema – the absolute opposite of what I was about. You're not supposed to do the same thing as you did last year. Whatever your job, even if you're sweeping the streets, you should sweep the streets differently every year. You should find new ways to sweep the streets. Life is about truly changing and truly challenging oneself. Every day! To break habits and try and understand if what you're doing is real activity or just learned activity. That relates to the last question. Yes, every morning I wake up and think to myself, "Am I waking up and making art today because I made art yesterday and am I being Genesis P-Orridge because that's just what I do and what I've always done? Is it worth it? What happened yesterday when I was an artist?" A lot of the time, it's grief. One gets attacked, criticized and ridiculed. But there are also those wonderful moments when someone you don't know walks up to you and says, "You don't know me, but I'd like to say 'Thank You,' because you changed my life. You inspired me to have the courage to do something that's made me feel satisfied and at peace."

It depends where one measures oneself. If you measure yourself against the commercial or established social reality, then it's very easy to feel disenchanted and hopeless and fed up and discouraged. Why should I expose my heart to these people? What we're all doing as artists... We're choosing to live our lives exposed. It's like having the skin peeled off. Everything that happens is incredibly sensitive. What might seem like a minor event to someone else can generate tremendous and real pain for someone who's trying to understand what we're all about and why we live and why we die and so on. Why love hurts and why love makes joy. Why the beautiful things can be destroyed by stupidity and ignorance. Why hypocrisy seems to be synonymous with control and power, and why integrity seems to be attacked and squashed and treated with some form of despising. If you measure yourself against what society expects and values, it's tremendously hard to continue. But if you step back and try and remember that you should love what you dreamt of in the beginning, it's fine. What you dreamt of in the beginning is usually what you're meant for; what your intended existence is supposed to be about. You love the small people and remember that a lot of this is about preventing isolation in others; that isolation and disconnection are some of the great enemies in this world. That's why people want to be in love, they want to be connected with someone outside themselves. They want to be validated and be alive. We all do.

That's why the simple path can be so difficult. To let go of an attachment to success and to only hold on to that which truly is given back from those who understand. That is a hard path. It's the classic Zen or oriental way of looking at it. It's easy and it's difficult to let go of needing anything, but it gives one a great liberation. There are times when one is living in a culture where needing things is the backbone of how it's supported. When one is revealed as having rejected the illusions upon which society is built, especially materialism – nothing is material anyway – you're very much exposed as a threat. The unknown and the pure are usually attacked. One only has to look at all the saints in history, in different religions, to see that that's the case. I'm not in any way trying to suggest that I'm a saint – far from it! – but what I am saying is that purity is seen as a curse. We've discussed this before between ourselves.

Ultimately, intention is the key. If one has clarity and purity of intent, I truly believe that the universe will protect you, in the essential ways. The ways in which one appears to be hurt at the time turn out to be the wisest and most useful lessons. When one thinks one is being attacked and hurt and losing something, you realise afterwards that it was absolutely necessary for you to be given something more fantastic. There are times when one has to have what the Christian Church calls Faith. You have to truly believe that the universe is kind. It's unfolding in its own symmetry. You don't control it. When you try and control it, that's when real pain happens and we can actually hurt ourselves and others. Over the years, I've just basically started to try and let go more and more every day. And accept that the great big "I.T." is looking after everybody. Far be it for me to do anything but just accept that and try and become more and more honest in how I express what I see. That's what I'm doing with the art now. I think I'm doing art galleries again because I have more control of the space now than I used to. It lasts longer. With music, it just happens and it's gone and it only exists in the memories of the people present. For a long time, that's why I liked it so much. I only wanted to do that, to exist in the memories of the people there. But I've started to feel differently.

I like the idea that I can set up a very site specific exhibition in Frankfurt. I didn't just go in with the same twelve paintings in the same style. I worked with the space; worked with what was there. There was a box with light switches and fuses, right in the middle of the wall. The gallery said they were sorry about it and tried to cover it with a wooden box. I said that it was OK as it was. I put a framed picture and two shoe sculptures on the front. On top, I put another sculpture, so it all looked as if it was intended. I made it work for the exhibition. I think there's a difference in how I look at exhibiting at galleries now. They're just flexible spaces that I improvise with in order to get a much longer time-based reaction from people. Each day as I'm doing some other work, that space is a place of a live performance as people walk in. Their bodies and their aesthetics and their emotional reactions are being consciously affected by me, without me being present. So I see it as a way to amplify and extend the work that I do and actually document the reaction and document the way in which things intersect. By having separated myself from the art world I don't have a gallery, I don't have a dealer, I don't have a manager, or an agent. I'm completely free. If I'm invited to a space, that's the universe saying, "Here's a space for you to work with."

CA: Something interesting that has taken place over the past few years is the work on the books. *Wreckers of Civilisation* put your work in a very distinct art perspective. That must have been an interesting experience for you.

GBPO: It was ironic, but also a tremendous vindication. I felt very vindicated. I took a path that everyone said was idiosyncratic. All of us were established in the art world as performance artists, exhibiting with Gilbert & George and other people. Then we turned our backs on it and walked in an entirely opposite direction. A lot of people thought we were bastardising ourselves and throwing away a potentially very lucrative and respected career. Anything connected with music was worthless. Having watched MTV, I can now see their point! All the more reason to explore and work with that medium, that challenge. All along, I've worked in a very renegade way. I've gone against all the established forms of accepting the path of recognition. It was nice to see things reassessed, in hindsight, and have people see some of the implications of importance and relevance.

And now, there's of course the new book, which is called *Painful but Fabu-*

lous. It sort of sums up what it's like to live life in this way. Again, what's exciting about that for me is that I actually have to reassess myself and my own life as a visual artist. I loved the visual arts so much in the beginning that I thought it was a sacred, holy calling – like being a priest. When I realised how corrupted it was, I was so upset and angry that I didn't want to ever have any part of it ever again. I think I suppressed an awful lot of my own self. I always made art, but I kept it hidden because I was worried it'd be violated if people knew about it. They would try and judge it or critique it in irrelevant ways because they wouldn't understand what I was trying to do in the bigger picture – no pun intended!

Now, to suddenly have to go back, I realise that way, way back in 1964, 1965, 1966, I was already dealing with some of the same things I'm dealing with now. I have a painting from 1966 called "Saint Margaret." It's painted on wood, just like the recent sigils. It's a silhouette in white of a top torso of a naked woman without a head. It's quite androgynous. It's textured on the actual surface and there's a separate piece of the same painting with the same silhouette in wood, painted white and with a psychedelic pattern painted on it. The whole painting is in those two pieces, so they could be moved around in the same room or be in two rooms or even two countries. Even then, in 1966, I was trying to make paintings that were outside time and space. I hadn't consciously realised how obsessed and single-minded I am in terms of some of the themes and content. Working on the book has really made me see the consistency in everything. Most artists work with a visual formula where it all looks the same and people can recognise it because it's always dots or it's always donkeys or whatever. With mine, it's always ideas, working with ideas in different ways. The styles I'm using are very contemporary in any given moment.

CA: What effects do you hope for, in terms of the new *Painful* book?

GBPO: In all honesty, I'd like to be taken a little bit more seriously. The reason for that is a hope that similar people, my extended family, even those I've not yet met, are also taken more seriously. I would like people to realise that art can still be about ideas, and it can be collaborative, and it can be a loose-knit family of people who use creativity in order to maximise their own personal vision and their own joy in life. Art is a trick by which we reach spiritual gold. It's the expression of the most important thing that consciousness makes possible. That's what I want it to be: a trigger. I'm so happy that different people are writing pieces in it. It's not mine. It's not a biography. It's a book triggered by my existence. This I do in order for other people to speak. That's why I think it'll be an interesting book. I'm really happy. The book has now become a piece of art instead of just a book. It validates our ideas about creativity. It has its own life and we don't own it. I don't own the book and I don't own the effects of my art. I make it and am blessed to get the chance to do what I do. It's a book for everyone to use in order to make something happen for them. It's an interesting dynamic. The point of it all is for the maximum number of people, who are sincerely interested in change and growth, to have an excuse to live that kind of life. You can live this life. You can live a bohemian life based on magic and sensuality and love and creativity and survive and have a jolly good adventure on the way. What more could we ask for?

CA: In all your experiments with shape-shifting and looks in general, and specifically the more recent gender-based experiments, what kinds of insights have they brought you?

GBPO: I'm surprised how right I was. It's surprising to me how malleable consensus reality is. I was asked to demonstrate the feasibility of determined magical actions. I don't normally try and flex but as it happened, it fit in with my own agenda. So I went along with it. For me, it's been incredibly liberating because now I'm finally able to be a being instead of just a man or a woman. As one could imagine, what's more liberating than to be able to be anybody you want? It appears that what we think we are when we look in a mirror is merely a recorded memory of what people have told us we are. We're not that at all. We can agree with the gnostics and mystics of all ages: the appearance is just an illusion. Nothing is fixed and nothing is really solid. In the same way, personality and identity are equally fluid and malleable and non-existent. We are only what we believe we are. That includes the apparent physical body and the gender. Obviously, one can maximise one's intentions and one's experiments by playing with the surface of what we appear to be – the body, the skin and so on – but it's surprising how it can be really subtle and tiny things that appear to be universal gender triggers. For example, I think one of the most powerful changes I've made was just shaping my eyebrows. For some reason, shaped eyebrows in almost all cultures are associated with femininity. In terms of tattoos, sometimes tattooing just one beauty spot in the face is more potent than a thousand inches of tribal patterns from Polynesia. It's the subtle and tiny details that people pick up in their peripheral cultural vision. The fact that hair is carefully groomed, the style of an earring, the darkness of eyelashes, fingernails, wearing a diamond ring on your wedding ring finger if you're a man... It's incredible how many people react to superficial details.

CA: You mentioned at the lecture in Stockholm that every individual consists of several selves and several identities. I found it a relief to hear that. Some schools of psychology would say that there is only one self. It's a simplified view of something that is truly multifaceted.

GBPO: I'm agreeing with you. To me, it seems ludicrous to assume that because we appear to have one physical body temporarily, that means we're limited to one very basic root personality. I can't imagine why anyone would want to assume that. I don't even want to insult animals by suggesting that they are only one-dimensional creatures. I tend to think that most of them are not. Primates, mammals, dolphins... Even ants seem to be very sophisticated. Even if we think that certain biological creatures are one-dimensional, consciousness is so clearly a holographic phenomenon that just happens to speak through various physical bodies. It's certainly not limited to the body. We dream and we hallucinate, and there are those of us who are able to access completely different voices and personalities – mediums, yogis, rinpoches, supposed schizophrenics and so on... The evidence is very, very clear and overwhelming. Lots of people live here! I've heard the argument given, in regard to reincarnation, that there aren't enough bodies to reincarnate in. So they share them. Hence we have multiple personalities. That's not really what I'm talking about though. I just know there are many different Genesis P-Orridges. There's the me who is gentle, kind, thoughtful and very feminine. Probably a woman. Then there's me who's an aggressive chimpanzee; territorial and beating its chest. Then I have conflicting ideas about life and reality and I have dialogues with other people in my head that are equally valid. I take all of their opinions very seriously. And I'm not unique. I'm not different to anyone else. One has to make the assumption that we're all the same.

CA: We are not alone.

GBPO: Exactly. We're not alone. At the very least, as an educational or spiritual discipline, it's very helpful and very healthy, as a kind of emotional and psychic hygiene, to assume there are many people in here. It's a blessing to be able to access them all and not just stick with the inherited version and the inherited archetype. That was probably just conveniently constructed for the convenience of others. The person you are told you are. "You are male... Your roles in life are these... These are the expectations... Your name is... Your social position is..." Who does that serve? As Burroughs used to say: "Always look for the vested interest and you'll probably get the right answer!" Those in control would love if we all believed we're limited to one person with no possibility of change. But it's not the case.

CA: Perhaps the insight about this comes as a result of the awareness of one's own purpose in life? If one works towards the insight about what one should do with one's life, one comes to realise one is in need of different kinds of forces in oneself.

GBPO: Yes, they're all in there, waiting to help and serve and emphasise and solidify and strengthen that which you should have happen.

CA: At the lecture you also brought up the touching speculation about the relationship between Neil and Genesis.

GBPO: A psychiatrist would say that's a very dangerous game. It's an important thing to have learnt and be able to see. Various different disciplines tell us, if we listen carefully, that the universe is holographic, and all consciousness is one. Whoever we think we are as a person, we still have access to all the rest. There's a thread that goes from every consciousness back into the rest. I guess Steiner would call it the Akashic record or whatever. I think it's quite clearly established through LSD, through Yoga, through trance states in Vodun, or whatever it might be in different cultures, that all will have some form of discipline or intellectual or spiritual exploration technique that relies upon and accepts and recognizes that all is one and all consciousness is ultimately it. We all have the right to access any part of it that we wish: our ancestors, our futures, etc. As His Holiness the Dalai Lama said, "Everybody has been everybody else's mother..." At some time in no time in this great amorphous something, we've all been everyone else and we've all given birth to everybody else. Everything is possible and everyone lives here. And they're all friendly if you just pay respect. It's a wonderful idea and phenomenon that one can actually access and befriend and collaborate with anyone and anything ever thought and lived.

As I was saying in Stockholm, wouldn't it be incredible if education was based upon consciousness instead of learning by repetition? If you went to school with a shamanic, spiritual, metaphysical view of the universe. That you went to school in order to understand how blessed you are to actually breathe every moment; that each minute of existence on the physical plane is a blessing and that no one has the right to take that blessing away from anyone else. And having said that, what can we do with it? What's the most useful, fabulous and exciting way to share this with each other? That's education. Education, creativity, spirituality become one. That, to me, is exactly as it should be. That's another reason why the art I'm making is without boundaries. Existence is without boundaries. Thinking is without boundaries. Loving is without boundaries.

CA: Living without boundaries... You've certainly lived a very nomadic life. Where do you think you'll go next?

GBPO: I'm waiting to find out. I'm waiting to see what I'm told next. I don't expect to be in the United States forever. I am prepared to do that, if that's what's expected of me. Ultimately I'm supposed to be where I'm the most useful. I accept that. That's my job. I'm supposed to be in the hot spot and improvise with that. The space of life and the gallery space and the space on a CD, they're all the same to me. I try to make the best of it all that I can, in the most creative and positive way I can. I honestly don't know what will come next, and that's pretty exciting. In this day and age, with the Internet and cell phones and everything, locations become less relevant. I think what might be happening is that, as Timothy Leary used to say, most technology in terms of communication is invented for the human body to travel at the maximum speed with the minimum inconvenience. The greatest thing with air flight was that you could take your brain somewhere else. Now we're almost in a situation where there's no need to physically move. To what extent that really is a good thing, I don't know. I suspect it leads to complacency, because all the information that's coming in is edited. Edited by vested interests.

CA: Not forgetting the actual radiation from cell phones and computer screens.

GBPO: My gut feeling is that actual physical travel will become even more vital the less it becomes necessary. My plan with Miss Jackie, as far as I have one, is to be ready to be very nomadic and mobile. To have no particular destinations or expectations in mind in advance. To almost be like a small well-trained commando unit, ready to go at a moment's notice. It's classic... As above, so below. The military has its special response units and so should we... If Control are building all these systems, you can bet there's a good reason. Control is giving certain templates to work with, and if you don't have a plan of your own, you can be sure they have a plan there for a good reason. So it's good to work with a reversal of that. One of my earliest "Old TOPI Proverb" sayings was "When in doubt, do the opposite to what you did last." I think that is still an excellent fall back strategy. Being flexible, effective, philanthropic, open-hearted, mobile and compassionate... Small creative units, small creative enclaves able to keep the flame of illumination alive. Preventing the extinguishing of intelligence by fundamentalists is probably the main task of the next 50 years. That's the job of all of us who have any kind of soul. It's like the clerics in the dark middle ages who copied books and manuscripts by hand. We're here to preserve and illuminate and at the very least to maintain the existence and presence of the highest ideals. It doesn't matter where we are as long as we keep the concept of knowledge alive. The forces of ignorance and darkness are utilising the most primitive of weapons: violence. It seems like their last stand in a way. They're trying to re-establish their power over consciousness. It's a very biblical, mythical moment in many ways. As usual, those who are trying to prevent this are the tiny voices of poetry and magic hidden away. It's been done before. Magic has survived. People, languages and cultures who have almost been extinguished have survived.

New York, 2002

I believe the entire planet is really a recording device. Everything has been recorded. From dinosaurs as fossils in geology to books. The good news is that everything that's been thought and everything that's lived and all the cultures that have gone have to some degree been preserved and recorded. This is why I believe books like yours are so incredibly important.

CA: One thing I find magically significant, at least on a symbolic level, is the fact that there is now, again, a huge library in Alexandria.

GBPO: The whole thing has become so epic. It's mind-boggling to think that all those books about the history of the world, like the Bible and the Koran, have suddenly become so significant. So many of the predictions are unfolding. I believe it has to do with with this apparent phenomenon that anything you do or write or have faith in will potentially manifest.

CA: A self-fulfilling prophecy?

GBPO: "Be careful what you say..." So the message to the world should be, "Start saying something more intelligent and compassionate, please!" So that something fabulous will manifest as a result of that in the future.

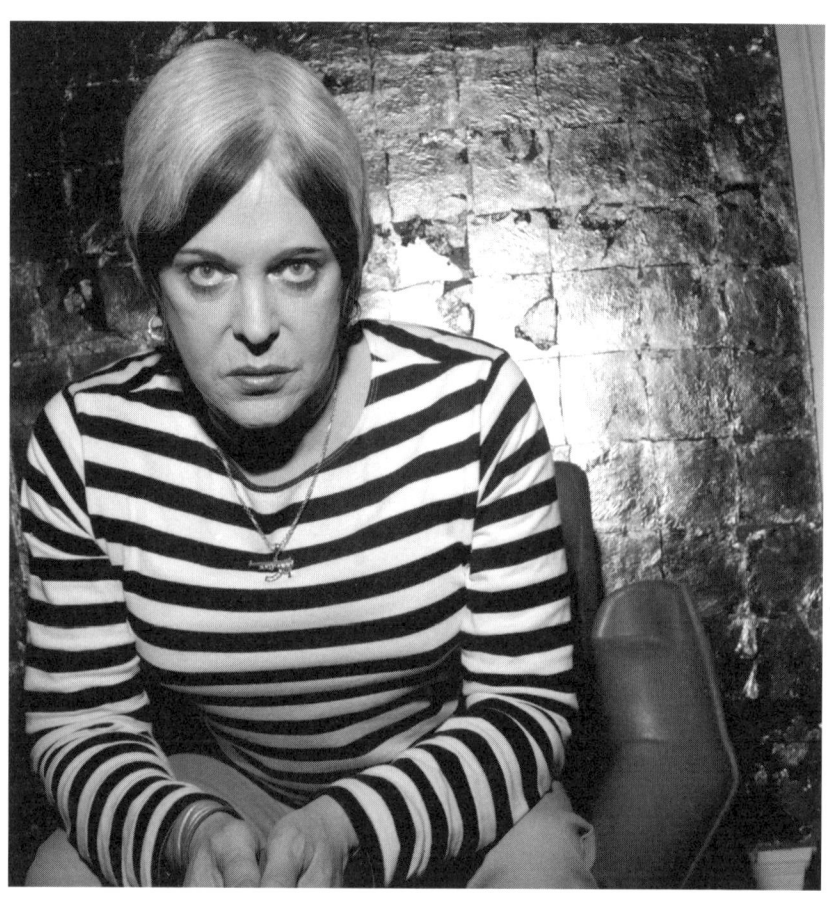

New York, 2004

New York, January 15th, 2004

As the Pandrogeny project was in full swing at this time, Breyer P-Orridge entered an inspired trajectory which included considerably more than making music with Psychic TV. A return to the art scene (specifically in New York City), a willingness to talk about the new concepts, and a colourful presence together with Jackie "Lady Jaye" Breyer, brought Genesis to new levels of creativity.

CA: Well, here we are in New York, and it's already January of 2004. It's been a while since we had our last discussion. So, we have a lot of catching up to do. But then again, we don't want to be too stiffly chronological, so I suggest that, as always, we jump back and forth, backwards and forwards, and in those directions that seem most appropriate and convenient.

GBPO: This is my life, this is my cross, this is my voice. It's very beautiful out there in the snow.

CA: It is. It's serene, that's what it is.

GBPO: It's interesting how the whole city just transforms from an innate surface of ugliness into a different surface... A uniform, white, sparkling surface, giving a completely different impression of what's there.

CA: Yeah.

GBPO: It's just another illusion. Just as the innate ugliness is an illusion due to the non-sentient matter of the buildings, and streets, and so on. The structure, itself, of the city is actually innately beautiful because it has life and achievement living through it. And in the same way that the apparent beauty of the snow is just as pretentious, in terms of what it hides. For example, today is garbage day, and all we see are beautiful, smooth, white mounds...

CA: Yes, crystals.

Sacred Intent

GBPO: Crystals. I think that's why one feels it is essentially poetry on an evening like this. Also, because the people usually disappear because it is too cold. So, you actually become more aware of being yourself, walking through the environment, rather than overwhelmed by the environment, and dodging and weaving like an ant in an ant colony. Suddenly, it is very different, more of a one on one, the city is one being and you are another being. So, it changes the conversation aesthetically and emotionally between the two.

CA: The philosophy of the city as an organic being and the city as being a framework for different things and directions has been touched upon in, for instance those three long poems or texts, where you read all three of them but we used two for the album and one is yet to be used.[1] Moving to New York must have spawned those kinds of ideas and philosophical speculations about the city as such.

GBPO: One reason I wanted to pin that idea down in the beginning was because I think it's been central, because we have our dialogues in the different places on the planet. It's surprising how much that metaphor, or that description of this being, and illusions and surfaces or so on, are very much a metaphor for my New York experience. And my eventual using of the New York experience to explore a different avenue of magic than we used before, certainly to heavily accentuate something that most people, observing previously, have seen as a minor diversion or topic of some of the writings, and so on. They were surprised that I should suddenly lend such weight to the whole pandrogeny concept... And the American experience, which for me is very much about the impregnation of mass culture from top to bottom. I don't think it's post-modernism, I don't like those words, I'm not sure what they mean. It's very post-Warholian. This is the most strikingly Warholian era imaginable. I just wanted to mention those thoughts and themes because I think they are central to what's happening.

CA: New York is a very special place, and a most flamboyant one. In this sense of flamboyance, in the sense that there are a lot of strange people, or people who are not afraid to show themselves as they feel they really are. Yet, in all of this, the greatness and the mere, large number of people who are here, there is also a sense of anonymity. You know, you can get away and be as flamboyant as you want, and you can be noticed, and you can also retract and disappear. I was thinking of this disappearance factor... Have you seen this stage as "larval?" Before coming out as a butterfly, in that sense, and starting actual physical transformations?

---

1 Refers to recording sessions in Stockholm in 2002, which manifested as the Thee Majesty & Cotton Ferox album "Wordship" in 2004, and contributions to compilation albums.

GBPO: Yes. You mean "pupa." The de-materialisation of identity is where I want to take it. When I was at University I wrote a poem. It's not a particularly good poem. A lot of the stuff I wrote back then in the 60s was difficult teenage poetry mixed with my somewhat awkward and mismatched attempts of adding in Kerouac and James Joyce – with a beatnik touch to it, of course. But the gist of it was that New York was the world's toilet, and it was where the rest of the world flushed away that which it shat out, like faeces. In that way, New York had this slight difference to most ports, without dwelling on it. The reason that we ended up with beat music in Liverpool and Manchester is because it was the nearest port to the United States, so the sailors would come over and sell Rhythm and Blues records to people they met in bars or put them on the jukeboxes. So they would bring over American music and that was it. They got there first. The other places they eventually got to, of course. But London because that was the other port where they would come in. So, usually, ports were culturally very much as a matrix and an accumulating interface between the cultures. Where one interprets the other and they exchange basic trade, you know it's a trade; an exchange basically.

New York isn't quite so much about exchange as it seems. It seems to be able to infinitely absorb everything that comes in, without any equal and opposite exchange. There's a near equality of what's absorbed and synthesized into what we call New York, and what comes back out from New York. New York is a very ephemeral and intangible thing; it's not really important at all. Which is what I was trying to say, way back then: it's a place things are taken and put, and left to its own devices. From all that supposed garbage, and sewage, and cast off raw material of humanity, usually because of a disaster somewhere else; it's traumatized raw material. All that is then jumbled up, mixed together, and as you say, very thickly crammed together on an island so it could only go up. So it really is like a pile. Then that becomes very much the breeding ground; rather than exchange, it becomes more of a compost heap. A breeding ground for something else which is almost viral, which is bacterial, which can then can go back out and exchange in the normal way which conflicts changes; it's a different process that happens. That was something that took a long time to really make any sense of or identify as part of what's different in the world. You will often find people here saying, "I don't like living in New York." I find myself saying this, it's incredibly common, all kinds of people say, "I don't like living in New York, but I can't think of anywhere else I could live, now that I've lived in New York." That's part of the difference of cultural processes.

CA: This is a small territory, a small area, with a lot of people confined there. They make the most of it, and perhaps that generates a unique tradition?

GBPO: I was thinking a bit more in terms of an accumulation of layer upon layer upon layer of outcasts. The people who are not wanted in other countries for different reasons; they simply can't be supported anymore. And then the mixing up of that into this matter, this material which you could call tradition at that point. But certainly into a phenomenon, really, where there are probably people from more countries in New York than any other city. There is somebody from everywhere, which is one of its uniquenesses. Of course all of those layers and that accumulation over such a short period of time is like a Petri dish or an alchemist's glass or vase with a flame under it. It is a very experimental situation in terms of humanity.

It's funny how people used to say how violent New York was and how much crime there was, but it's always struck me and Jaye as well, that it's incredible how little crime there is in New York given how much people are piled up upon each other, and how many apparently contradictory cultures there are. There is an amazing tolerance of the loss of cultural and physical space. First of all, most people think of New York and they really mean Manhattan. Then, when you think of Manhattan, it's an island. There's a boundary within which one has to work. I think that's another reason people have this idea of it being a finite, fixed space you are coming to and staying in, rather than travel through on your way to somewhere else. So although it's a nexus and a hope for going everywhere, it tends to be a place where people come from everywhere. That's an important difference, and has an impact on the way the place works, in the psyche of the people. You become a New Yorker very quickly by just being here, people will very quickly say, "I'm from New York." But, in most countries and most towns people will say, "Oh, the new people." And they will be someone who moved there 30 years ago. Especially in small countries and villages and such. So there's a deeply immediate acceptance of the new, and of strangeness, and surprise. Which is what you were touching on earlier, that people can be very visible and can also become very invisible. I think one of the characteristics that operates so well here is what Lady Jaye often talks about that I've been trying to describe. New york lends itself to a person living with a chameleonlike flexibity of image. That every morning allows you to choose variations of who you present to the outside world. Like Jaye says, there is no reason why you can't be a different person every day. Yet at the very same time I have certainly said to people that I've never been able to be so private since I've been in New York. Nobody bothers me, and I've had more privacy and more consideration of my privacy than anywhere else, which is also a very positive experience. These are all things that are attractive.

So you get two things here really: you get the people who are thrown out or thrown away by old cultures, old civilizations and old dynasties. Then you get the people who are the strange attractors. The people who are here by choice because they know that they can get that life of flexibility. They can be characters and create characters for themselves, explore costumes in every sense of the word, disguise themselves, be anonymous and be incredibly notorious. So it really is a unique, very potent environment.

CA: Had you consciously or unconsciously thought about moving to New York before it actually happened? Say, ten years ago? I can recall one of those dance tracks where the sample says, "In New York, in New York, in New York." Remember the one?

GBPO: I know the one you mean. No, far from it. I had always sworn that the one place I would never live was New York.

CA: Ha, there you go!

GBPO: Just for that sake of being obnoxious; perhaps a little bit because of fear of liking it. A bit like you might be afraid of trying cocaine in case you liked it and then you would be hooked, you know. So I think sometimes there's a certain immaturity in one aspect of my personality that it took me a long time to deal with, which was that sometimes there would be things I was really attracted to, and so I would act repelled and be very aggressive towards them. A simple example would be that when I was much, much younger, around five or six, I was allergic to cats. But don't forget too my first memory ever is being told by my mother that our cat "Sugar" was being put down because of me having asthma and my allergy to cats. So I used to tell everybody that I hated cats and make a big song and dance about how cats were stupid, horrible animals and so on. But really I was resentful of the fact that I couldn't choose. I was angry at the lack of choice and the fact that I wasn't able to have any, it seemed at least at that point, any control over whether or not I had a positive relationship with the cat colonies of the world. So, later on when I learned more about how to have some control over allergies and asthma, I got a cat, and then let go of all these pompous statements I had made about not having cats.

I think New York was a little bit like that: it was a combination of temptation, and also a certain desire not to do the obvious. The same reason I chose not to go to art college, because everybody expected me to. No, I never consciously expected to ever move to New York. It probably would be one of the places I would be quite adamant and confident of not going to. It's interesting that I should have ended up being here now for almost ten years. Which is the longest I have been anywhere. I came here to literally lick my wounds. I mean, that was the other thing: the anonymity aspect and being able to just disappear and not have to be Genesis P-Orridge, or anyone else. That was very appealing, and especially not living in Manhattan. Living in Ridgewood, which was then far more ghetto. Low key ghetto, but a ghetto never the less. So that was the only real appeal: we had the opportunity to get this far. Also, that we could vanish and I could actually try and get physically well.

I was so, so utterly disillusioned with music business, the spiritual and magical support systems that I assumed were as committed to me when I needed support that I'd been or was to them. That revelation of being far more truly alone, that really shocked me. It was probably as traumatic as when my actual physical body had been smashed; probably more traumatic really.

Often, when I was first here in New York, I felt like Turner in "Performance."[2] The character that Mick Jagger does. I felt a lot like that. I was this iconographic fictional character. The storyline had got out of control and was being written by a committee of people who were arguing and not always referring to me for what I might like to happen next. I felt a bit like that. I just needed space to see who was there. All of New York has been about this whole... Layers and identity and appearance and disappearance, in all kinds of interpretations; the substance of one's identity and the relevance of one's body of work. I guess a certain contemplation of mortality, the physical and then of course since being here, we've had 9/11, which is relevant. So, it's been a very, very intense time and yet to outward appearance, very, very quiet. And yet it's probably been one of the noisiest internally....

CA: Do you at times regard things through the matrix of active versus reactive? Because this process of transformation that the both of you have begun now is a very active thing.[3] You are doing this, it is your will to do this, but of course that affects things within you and between you, and of course, the outside world; by proxy, if you will. Whereas many of the things that led to your coming to New York had actually been reactive things. When you were away in Asia things happened to which you had to react. The breaking up with a long-time partner created a reaction, which you couldn't really be active in; you had to succumb and react to the situation.

GBPO: And the fire.[4]

CA: And the fire... What could you do? You could only react. It's like things beyond your control, in a way, and then you had to adapt. Whereas now, amidst all the chaos and hectic life of New York, you have taken control again.

---

2 The film from 1970 by Nicholas Roeg and Donald Cammell, starring Mick Jagger.
3 Refers to the actual physical transformations begun within the Pandrogeny project.
4 A reference to a house fire in California in 1995, from which P-Orridge had to jump out of a window, and seriously damaged an arm and other parts of the body.

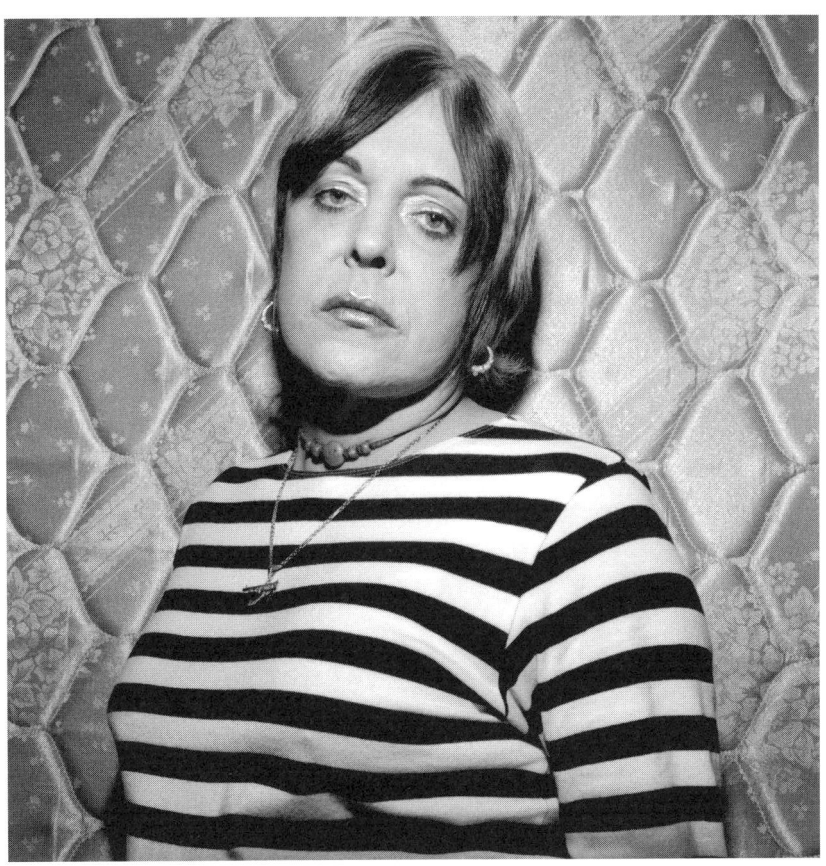

New York, 2004

GBPO: Yeah, I mean, that's true. I think that was probably it. I would say that is a very valid observation. It was a lot of my actual personality, as well, that was reactive. And that compounded the extremities of how I was responding to the outside events. I was basically taking things personally. But I was also getting these epiphanies too. So it was this two-edged sword. I was falling out of the burning building and lying in intensive care. But I was also having, probably partly morphine induced, but nevertheless, visions and epiphanies about dimensional portals, but primarily about karma, if you'd like to simplify it. And responsibility for one's actions, and time to contemplate what it was that, first of all... Who the hell I was. Because life had gotten to this point of acceleration that there was no time to stop and think. Do I still want to be Genesis P-Orridge? Who is Genesis P-Orridge? What should Genesis P-Orridge look like, and so on. What should be done next and does this need to keep being done because it was done before...?

CA: And at such a pace!

GBPO: All my usual markers for keeping a disciplined control over events, and hopefully a certain gradual maturing of my vision, wrestled their way out of my control and grasp. I remembered something... One of the most important early lessons that I ever had, in terms of doing life. Which was that, in a magical universe... That which one wills, that is a part of the positive evolution and development of the universe; that which one wills that has integrity and purity of intent does always happen. But it unfolds according to the time table of that person. I made that classic error that I even have written down many times in diaries and talked about which was, I know it is going to happen, so why can't it just happen right now? And of course, what I went up against was this brick wall. Nothing happens the way we want it; it happens the way it wants it. So, I was compelled, and I think rightly, by the universe. I had to be stopped in my tracks because I was just a part of an accelerator in the red zone, and I was just speeding faster and faster and faster. Having less and less time to contemplate or even develop my behavioural responses to what was going on around me and why.

CA: You were also reminded of that fact that you are a mortal via the fire and the related physical pain.

GBPO: And then of course you sit down, and in your mind you make a list: why am I glad I'm still alive? What is it and who am I, and all those things. And you have time to think about it. And of course loyalty... Well, who were the friends and the people who were still helping me? You basically begin the process of reduction, and one of the things that you notice is that there's a good reason why some people go off onto the mountain tops and into the desert to contemplate.

Because life is so noisy and busy. You just don't have time to process that which you are learning. And if you aren't processing, you aren't learning at all. You merely experience it.

CA: Or collect it.

GBPO: Or collect it. I was suddenly hit with a sense of great inner immaturity. So, I was very blessed because Jaye gave me an opportunity to step back and decide what it was I wanted to be. It was during that process that I started to do things that seemed weird to other people. I became an avid listener to American talk radio. I listened to all these right wing talk shows and left wing talk shows, where people phone in. I read the *National Enquirer* every week and I started to watch things like "Access Hollywood." I basically started to study the culture, anthropologically and so on. I took time off to find out where I was. What is this place I've ended up in? I was observing that, and I was looking at the ever increasing obsession with celebrity and the way that something had happened between the 60s and the present. From burning bras, to wearing bras on the covers of magazines... Not only okay again, but almost a prerequisite of a female celebrity. Suddenly, women celebrities were expected to play the sex card. From that you would look at things with Pamela Anderson, for example, and now Paris Hilton. So there's that whole plasticity and the celebrity, and somewhere the change or the return to, but in a much more exaggerated way, a very Warholian way: the celebration of money and excess and greed and riches; that is was actually OK to display one's wealth again. In fact, you were expected to. From the ghetto and up. Whether it was to have the right Nike sneakers to having your own private jet. Pretty much across the board in the United States, and this is really a contemporary situation; part of the social game that's played now is the display of wealth.

CA: And the height of entertainment is watching other people fighting for it on TV.

GBPO: And displaying more and more and more of it to a level of absurdity. But no one is laughing. You'll watch an MTV video of people parading around in amounts of platinum and diamonds that are ridiculous and unappealing aesthetically, and only stating a dollar sign, which, of course, was one of the first pendants. So there's been a huge shift from feeling guilty about having money, and supposedly selling out and being apart of the commercial process. Suddenly that is the ambition of the American. The American dream is bling bling, and it's to be on television. Preferably both. So there's that, and that goes with celebrity, goes with identity. What is identity? So that was one thing that began to seem very significant about the United States, the place that I was in. I'm a cultural engineer. I have to look at the raw material of the culture to see what it is that's going on. What are the dynamics? Are there any games I can play with this? Are there any things that I can do to readjust or realign slightly in order to reveal something I'm interested in? So, that was happening, and then with my personal microcosm as opposed to that macrocosm. It's dealt with of course with the *Painful but Fabulous* book; the whole thing of Neil Megson inventing Genesis P-Orridge as an artwork, basically. And Genesis P-Orridge succeeded as an artwork to the point that it didn't need the artist anymore. What does that mean when the artist has created an artwork that becomes the being that inhabits the planet? Where is Neil? And if we could go back to 1965, would Neil want to be parasitised by Genesis?

CA: And the answer is...?

GBPO: The answer is... We will never know; we would have to ask him. The answer is still a mystery. One has to assume the answer is yes. He would because each choice that was made was a conscious choice.

CA: But now we are also seeing a further shift in the sense that Genesis P-Orridge is in a stage of transformation and has become someone else. But only as a part of Breyer P-Orridge. You are already changed. Thereby inside also, you are changed. So it's like we are now two steps away from Neil.

GBPO: Absolutely. Well, there were two ways to go. One was not exactly to feel guilty, although we did half jokingly say, "Genesis murdered Neil so that he could stay." I was having a good time in his body. But I think what really happened was that I sort of concretised my thought processes, the malleability of what we think of as our self, our identity, the person we talk to in our mind. When I'm talking to myself, I'm talking to this "I," this holograph. Just telling you that sentence actually was almost like vertigo. I've considered this a lot and I have so truly realized how flimsy and transient and fragile our given identity is, or the idea of being is. How unsure I am of solidity or concrete reality of anything that I almost get nausea from extrapolating the implications of it.

I'm very aware that this space is arbitrary. Thank goodness, a part of physics is now agreeing with this, which is reassuring. Science is tending to vindicate a lot of visionary concepts. I had two choices. I could feel very guilty about it. One of the strategies that was considered was to maybe change my name back and say that that was it. I created Genesis P-Orridge, that was my artwork and I'm Neil Megson, the artist. I could claim that it was clever and ask if people really believed Genesis existed. I could claim it was all an artwork. Or I could dismiss the entire mystery and say it doesn't really matter because I'm living my life as Genesis now. Or we could look for a more interesting strategy and take time to think about what the implications are of a more magical way of looking at things. From all the disciplines that we've looked at, talked about... I can have any name, I can change my name, but that also changes you.

CA: What's in a name? A lot is in a name...

GBPO: Each time we build ourselves differently we make these choices. The old TOPY saying, "First change your bedroom, then change your house, then change your street, then you'll change your town..." Whatever you do, that's a flood effect; you really can have an impact far beyond that which you expect. That's something you should never forget. Everything we're doing really is having an impact on everything else. And so I did my checklist. The message I was receiving from outside in America was that medicine and surgery and science and bioengineering... and so on – all those different disciplines had become far more sophisticated, and give one the opportunity to explore physically sigilising with my body in a deeper way, even more than I had done previously. I mean, I've always included the physical body. And yet there also had to be a name change of some kind somehow. The physical surface of me became raw material again. Instead of just putting myself into the canvas as part of the picture, I've also included the internal. Every aspect of me, the entire hologram, is now a construct consciously built and capable of being built differently. That was something that came out of all these different experiences. I mean, who knows if the trauma of having my arm rebuilt has to do with it too? What I wanted to do was to integrate everything that had happened so far, and then actually self-consciously decide what should happen next.

The problem with the Neil-Genesis interface was that Neil didn't know what was going on. It was impulsive and, as you were saying, reactive, in a way. It was a simpler, less sophisticated approach. A kind of "phase one." Wouldn't it be interesting having stated to oneself that all identity is fiction and must be because I was a fiction. For example, everything I read in all the hundreds of magazines lying around is not really me. There is no way to record me. Likewise, with you or anyone else. If I was that malleable and that fictional and everybody else was fictional, then let's have a magical strategy: the old thing of turning shit into gold – or let's take the inherited physical body and the culturally created being behavioural person that is known as Genesis... Let's take this raw material, and let's consciously write and describe it, like a book.

So that was kind of like "step one" in the thinking. Like you were saying, I could re-take control over, not just my relationship with events, but I could also take control of my own physical body. Which probably has something to do with

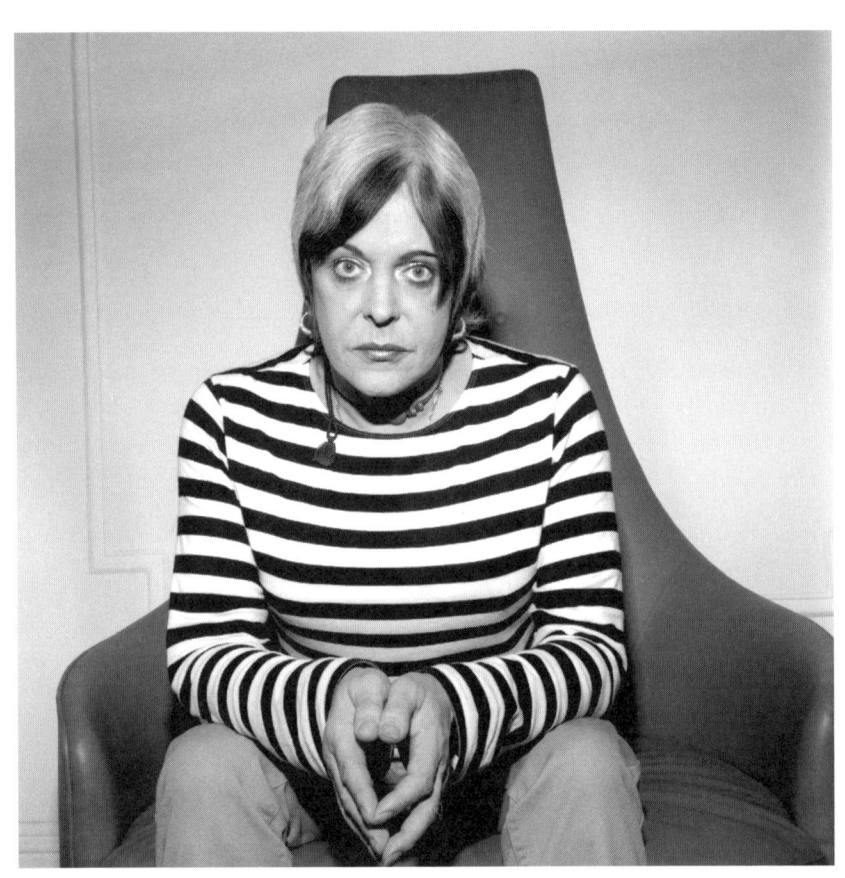
New York, 2004

having lost control over it too, in the sense of nearly dying and being broken after the fire. As a symbolic gesture, the first thing I did was to continue and finish the process of having gold teeth. It's true that I was watching Buñuel's film "Belle de jour"[5] a long time ago, when it first came out, and I saw Pierre Clementi with his gold teeth, and I was tripping on acid and I just thought, "One day I'm going to have gold teeth like that!" That is a true story; as true as it gets in terms of anecdotes. That's a very good example of not knowing how long it takes for the road to unfold. That was way, way back, 1969, early 70s. We're talking about a long, long time ago. It's very clear, that very pure intent, and remembering that intent just three years ago, and carrying it through, the universe made it possible through the insurance settlement because my body had been broken... The body wasn't necessarily me. All these epiphanies started to actually generate the new processes and strategies and changes. They had their source in things going back to the very beginning. It's funny, but I still forget about the teeth. I often smile at people to put them at ease but of course the gold teeth puts them far less at ease... They stare, shocked or slightly disturbed or curious. I do forget that! It happens all the time. People shrinking back slightly when I smile, which is an odd change to the usual response.

CA: The teeth are one thing. They're just a physical trait. But the other stuff you've done touches upon more complicated aspects, that have to do with gender and identity based in gender. Then we come to the bigger question of "uniting the opposites."

GBPO: That's right. It happened step by step. Having completed the teeth, I had some kind of basic breakthrough in terms of the completion of a very specific physical change of my body. It having resonance with and impact on other people every day. That's it! It's changed forever... I have gold teeth! That affects how people treat me. Sometimes hip-hop kids who would want to be rude will be absolutely fascinated and think I'm really cool, because of those teeth. And then somebody who might be really interested in me for instance will be so turned off that they won't listen to me anymore. So that changes dynamics. But what it did say was that there is this... "being area," in which I explore a lot more consciously than just the old, more traditional body modifications. It was because in my mind the gold teeth were very consciously to do with alchemy that I started thinking about alchemical archetypes and also about film. That's getting back to that thought...The impact of "Belle de Jour," how fascinating that was some 30 years later. Ironically, or interestingly, it's also Lady Jaye's favourite movie, for slightly different reasons.

5 "Belle de Jour," a film by Luis Buñuel from 1967, starring Catherine Deneuve as a young woman who becomes a high-end sex worker.

So I started looking around at stereotypes, examining types... The switching of archetypes. Just the idea of having an alchemical view of material reality was circulating; it was a swirling soup within which all the other ideas were taking place. Parallel to that soup of having de-constructed my identity, at least to the point of realising how fictitious it is, and having also taken control of my body again, I had this alchemical view back in the forefront. Parallel to that I get asked to do the book, *Painful but Fabulous*, the title for which just popped out from the cosmos. It wasn't my title. It just came. It was so appropriate it was uncanny. The thing that surprised me the most about the process of making that book was that I noticed all the differences; all the different ways I had looked. It was that book, and having to go back and observe 30 years... That was when it dawned on me much, much, much more directly and forcefully, that I'd really been dealing with identity but also, already back in the 60s, I'd been dealing with switching gender.

There were several performances even in the 60s that were about switching from male to female, back and forth. I was describing them in the things I was writing as being two parts of one, and not as two separate beings; an organ as two thought processes of one, if you like; or two aspects of one being. And so the book reinforced for me that identity is arbitrary, fictional and blank. There is an incredible magical reservoir that hasn't been fully explored or tapped – the energy in it – based upon that realisation. But also that the most consistent theme of everything that I'd done of placing my body physically into the work and being prepared to have my body be experimented upon – to be the guinea pig. It was this ongoing fascination with the hermaphrodite or the androgyne. And then my life-long quest for the soul-mate, my Cosmosis, the female Other, was more significant than trying to find a heterosexual lover. It was trying to find my other half. That, if you like, I was looking for my twin and I was trying to find this other piece of me! I think sometimes with hindsight I used the performances to try to conjure up and sigilise that up. That was a big breakthrough. I realised that the whole first section of my physical, biological work at this particular time – really, all of my research – had been dealing with isolating and then presenting this enigma, and this, to me, incredibly important issue... magical force... cultural need. The more I thought about it, the more I was convinced. It was a bit like you were saying: there was humanity as a species, as being in this larval or pupal stage, and it's now stuck as if it is trying to fight its way out. It's shouting, and it can't get out, and it's suffocating itself.

I guess I have to introduce this point Lady Jaye would make. We both know that the first step of each really important magical process would be naming something, and once it became clear to me, it dawned upon me and it also dawned upon Lady Jaye... Her role lies in the part that there will also be an intersection of the two of us, and that we'd met because of that. And that we'd be so overruled by the power of it. We were almost constantly facing other people not understanding exactly what we were. We chose to give birth to the being that we now explore in Breyer P-Orridge. It just came out, popped out, and there was nothing to say about it.

And then of course you have to break the thread of the "third mind."[6] We've always been trying to find ways since the 60s to extend the work of Brion and William, and keep them energized in a very contemporary context, and not look at them as arcane or just historical lineage but also practical magical techniques; living, working re-applicable magical techniques. And that could be adjusted and modernized and readjusted just like any other technique. So that was another of the epiphanies. Just as you can create a third mind by the collaboration of two people then surely one can create another being by collaboration of two beings. And so Breyer P-Orridge is the name of that being – as far as it's feasible – the physical androgyne of Breyer P-Orridge, the physical being. In a way, more importantly, just Breyer P-Orridge as a suggested prototype for how we extricate ourselves as a species from this binary predicament, which just got us stuck in the pupae stage. Yeah, so that's kind of brought it to where we are in New York.

CA: Would you say that the publication of *Wreckers of Civilisation* and *Painful but Fabulous* has made you feel that it's easier to move forward, now that your past has in many ways been "vindicated"?

GBPO: With *Wreckers of Civilisation* less so, although the feeling I had was, "Now I don't have to tell that story anymore."

CA: That's what I mean: you're free to move forward.

GBPO: I think it did a fantastic job, and hence I don't have to tell that story anymore. As far as I'm concerned anyway, it's close enough.

CA: It's a tangible book that puts things into an art perspective about history.

GBPO: *Painful but Fabulous* is life-altering. I'm still not sure what it is. Is it a manual? Because there's a lot of information that is very practical. Or, is it a historical journey like a biography? Or is it a cut-up? It's a jigsaw. And I've learned so much from it that I can only hope that other people will pick up useful tips. So I hope it stands as one example of it being possible to create a life. Now what's

---

6 Reference to the concept of the "third mind," as being born out of two minds in communication, and the application of this as a creative method or formula. Originally presented by William S. Burroughs and Brion Gysin, for instance in the book of the same name: *The Third Mind*, The Viking Press, New York, 1978.

interesting is that with Breyer P-Orridge, together we're creating another life form that's more complex and it is a direct attack upon the very foundation of Western society for sure. Western society's concepts of balance and structure. We only have to look at the conservative fear of the idea of gay marriage to remember the idea of just being male and female is keeping the things in their place... It's fundamental to most people, but even something to consider. And yet the physical body is, as Lady Jaye loves to describe it... It's just a suitcase, just an old suitcase that carries us round, and it's not such a precious item, it's packaging. It's functional, in that it's mobile. That we, each of us, are thoughts; consciousness is us, not the package. So if that is so arbitrary you can pack your suitcase with anything you want. This is quite a stunning epiphany; this is quite a shocking revelation even for me! I've been very blessed.

It's one thing to have these ideas and it's fine for me to say I'm going to follow through on these concepts, because I feel duty-bound. This is just how I work, how I feel; I always feel duty-bound. Once I have an idea that I believe in, to follow through and live it; just see if I'm right and also to see what happens. In order to report back and share that information if it's useful. But to find one's other half, and have them be able to truly be in the same state, and see what happens when we do this pandrogyne/androgyne thing. Desperate times calls for unusual measures, unusual strategies and unusual speculations.

CA: Do you feel like a utopian or dystopian?

GBPO: I don't think I was ever truly utopian, but I'm very sad. When the World Trade Center collapsed my optimism truly collapsed, and I don't think I'm in any way unique in this. To be in New York that day... We could see who were there, and then they are in the grips of something that isn't there, and I'm not talking about one culture and another culture. You can switch the speeches, wars and the Bush cabinet, and it might as well be the same. In just two years we have undone 500 years of renaissance. It's a tragedy, and that's how I feel about it. I feel like I'm witnessing a tragedy. And it's a bit baffling, this tragedy acted out by closed-minded bigots. Because their only concept of resolution is violent. On the other hand you have the most wonderful developments in science, and in tech... The communication of ideas, sharing of values, and the resolution – the re-solution – of differences in order to create something new.

We could resolve in ten years most of the problems, the physical problems. And an abundance would be left over. But it would be require thinking differently, and it would be requiring not being afraid that somebody else would cheat. So on the one hand you have this species that is mind-boggling in its ability to make sense of the dynamics of the universe. Send pictures back from Mars. Find hundreds of particles smaller than atoms and realize that there is no end to the wonders.

CA: But isn't that the entire problem, that any kind of "progress" that really matters has so far eventually always been used in negative ways. Like genetic research that could cure diseases, but instead turns into a product; a commodity in itself. And how the supposedly "liberating" aspects of technology actually enslave people. Everything turns into something to be bought and sold.

GBPO: Or into a weapon. You're asking me about utopia. I still see that beautiful picture. And the contribution that I feel we can make as Breyer P-Orridge. That is to say very clearly, by example physically, mentally, spiritually, to surrender to each other in an active absolute mutual passion and trust, and use the idea of pandrogeny and the pandrogyne to symbolize all those processes, all those options. Which are the options that could save us as a species – we believe we have a great right to be saved as a species – and that would give us the ability as a species to be proud of being human beings, and to have ability of spirit and ability of motive, and to stand and face any kind of being from any dimension and any aeon, and say, "these are human beings; they're worth it." That's what we should all try to represent in our lives in our own way.

This is two beings, resolving and going on to reunion. That's when we get back to what we miss. That must be the ultimate point of view. And that's what life energy is for: it is to first become self-aware as a species, and then as a species resolve the difference; let go of it. Ultimately just become beings with no gender. We both try and avoid saying it's about gender, because for all it's not really about gender; it's about identity and creating new beings. The next phase of being, and that we feel ultimately those beings don't have physical bodies. In a way physical bodies are a bit arbitrary; they are suitcases and we don't want to ever mistake that, because our dream ultimately would be to be free-flowing consciousness, yet still aware of itself. Outside time and space, but able to maintain this integrity of being individual enough, to continue to learn, to exchange information.

CA: Communication is also the foundation of human problems.

GBPO: I don't think it's a mistake that the first book of the *Bible* is the *Book of Creation*. We've talked about that before. As to all the strange symmetry in terms of my private personal life being Genesis and the creation of a hermaphrodite... Did we talk about the early pictures of hermaphrodites? We should mention that too, because that's something I'm always looking at. I came across a couple of pictures of a sexual hermaphrodite. It seems that in many – if not all, certainly the majority – of the early drawings and paintings that represented the Garden of Eden, Adam and Eve, Lilith, and even God sneaking a peek from behind a bush; all were painted as full hermaphrodites with male and female genitalia and breasts. And then at some point when the Holy Roman Empire was marauding around Europe, just as the Nazis went around stealing art, destroying other things they didn't like in terms of culture. They started destroying "decadent works." The Holy Roman Empire and its cohorts destroyed every picture they could find of Adam and Eve as hermaphrodites. There are now only maybe less than half a dozen – if that – anywhere in the world. But when I saw one of those pictures, it just, as they say, "defied mind." I was just so excited that it makes absolute sense. It's them in a state of grace before they are being cast out of the garden. It's inevitable in that they were both male and female, both sexes, because they were in a state of grace; they were perfect beings. The perfect human being is a hermaphrodite. So as Man was made in God's image, that would suggest that God is a hermaphrodite. I would say that God is a pandrogyne and was painted as Adam and Eve. Because the natural state of culture's perfection and beauty is beyond sex, which means beyond the need to replicate physically. That is the hermaphrodite/pandrogyne. So I assume this is a confirmation, a validation, of all of our theories and feelings and intuitions, and then I thought what happened before was the tree. There's the snake and whispering, and the snake is kind of wrapped around a tree; almost a double helix. The DNA is merely the motor that drives replication, as well as being a recording device. There is an interplay between the DNA and Self.

CA: DNA exists after death, so it has nothing to do with the life force itself. It's basically a store-house of information.

GBPO: It's a recording device. Having said that, we still have to figure out what was the form... Ask the real question, because the form created by resistant impulse to physically replicate, is it just a metaphorical and symbolical story?

CA: As with all mythic stories, there is a lot of wisdom in there. The problem always arises when proxy-people like corrupt churches decide they own the right to tell that story. But the actual truth of the myths are often stronger than temporary, rational superstructures.

GBPO: That was when it became fascinating, with the whole superficiality becoming so mainstream. Physical superficiality. If you think of that then, plastic surgery was a big secret. And now, in Hollywood, it's quite OK. Now it's kind of a sign of status. It's an interesting case where the people we've chosen to represent our ideas... You can now almost buy them off the shelf – their "suitcase" – and inhabit their body. Which is a very odd thought, because of course, that's not them; that's not the person they thought they would be. Their hologram of what they call "me" isn't them at all.

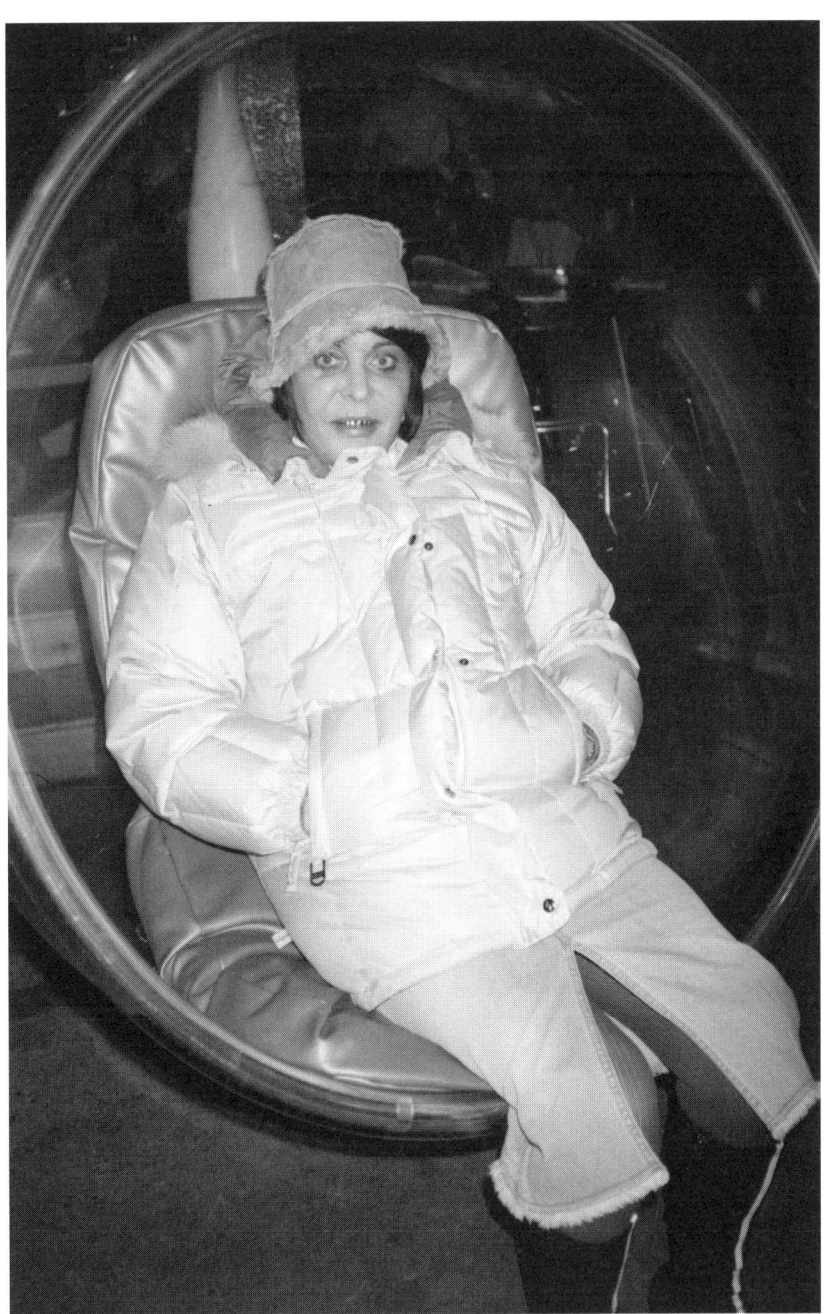

New York, 2004

CA: Most people seem to do that because of vanity. But then of course that leads to the realization that everything that goes on in their life eventually fades. But it can also give you insights.

GBPO: We are not doing it because of glamour. In fact, the interesting thing this time, with the most recent surgical procedure, was we went in and we saw the doctor and we explained the aim and the "pro" of the project we're doing as Breyer P-Orridge. He was really interested, and totally understood. Supports us in the project; obviously, it's a worthy project so we want it to work. Because he has a highly esteemed reputation, and he was just voted the best cosmetic surgeon in the whole North Eastern United States. He would not want to do anything negative to his incredible reputation. So we went in, and we sat and explained everything; that we want to make our faces look as much like each other as possible, within reason, because it's not that... It's not the be-all and end-all; it's important that we actually go through this process to some degree, to prove that we're serious. And then he said, "I can do this, and I can do this..." It doesn't really matter what we end up looking like, and he was so pleased and thrilled to hear someone say that! But also, it was so radical to have someone sitting there and the one thing that was not involved was trying to look better than they thought they looked. Trying to be more glamorous etc, but rather just saying, "I'm doing this because it's conceptual probing." And "I'm prepared to have my face done... Anything!" He said, "how would you like to be?" And I said, "Well, surprise me!" (laughs)

So he was very excited by the approach that we were both were sincerely prepared to sacrifice something, and it was interesting. I was thinking to myself, "I like the face I have, I really like it a lot, I'm comfortable with his face and don't I really want to change it. Well, I guess I have to. I do want to look more like Jaye, because that's part of the evolution process we're undergoing." It's a very different approach to the usual United States approach.

Somebody said something actually at a gig that had not occurred to me, which was, "wouldn't it be interesting with PTV3 performing if you got – or at least started to get – straight heterosexual boys and girls getting cosmetic surgery; especially say, straight boys with tits, because they were really into PTV? Like how people used to get piercings and scarifications. Would that be interesting? If there became a whole different reasoning?" And I was saying it's always good for people to copy the icon, but it would be kind of interesting as a social phenomenon because it would completely undermine the usual stereotypes. Like in the gay community for example... The only animosity I've experienced when it comes to having breasts is from gay transvestites. Because they don't think it's right that I actually have breasts and stuff like that. If we are really honest though, it seems there is resistance because we do not identify as "gay" for some reason.

Why would I wish to swap one identity tyranny for another? I don't identify as hetero- or homo-sexual; just *sexual.*

CA: What about actual effects so far? I can understand that the body aches and things like that, post-surgery, but what about new insights?

GBPO: Most of it is kind of residual change. I'm in a new territory. As you've noticed yourself it's simple for me to live with it 24/7. People assume now that I'm female. And on a day-to-day basis, that's fine. Because it's the art shows, the books and so on now that really contain the hard-core dialogue about the idea of this approach. And of course now touring as well... You see, the light show is also based around all the surgical procedures; it's all very psychedelic. (laughs) So, we're out there proselytising the pandrogyne. It's a very unique thing and it's territory that doesn't have a language. Yet. As you know, I worked for six months as a female dominatrix. And no-one realised... Remarkable!

CA: Did you do a good job?

GBPO: Did I do a good job? Yes and no. I've used ladies' bathrooms and I've been to gyms. When I go to the gym or I go to a sauna or wherever, I lose the masculine aura. Very discreetly I try to make sure that no one realizes so that no one feels uncomfortable, because I can get away with having breasts being in a women's changing room. I have realized there's no way I can get away with that in a men's changing room – they would notice the breasts. And that would be a whole different thing. There's an immediate fear of knee-jerk male violence. One is forced to be afraid. And as the fake christians get hysterical, those dangers increase. So primarily for reasons of convenience that's the way I choose to strategise daily life – it's the only way it works. I would like to be able to go to either side. But that wouldn't make any difference, because that's not the case. But it's early days. I mean, we only got the breasts for Valentine's Day, so February last year. I can't think of very many biological morals that have slipped, shape-shifted or slipped back or forth between genders. I've been very aware that it's a very complex and difficult situation. I don't want anyone to feel uncomfortable, I don't want anyone to see me and freak out, I don't want anyone to feel exploited. I have to go through an awful lot of moral considerations just to be able to decide which bathroom to go into. So my awareness of other people's physical comfort level, what they are most likely to assume, takes on a very important consideration.

You take your life in your own hands every time you leave the house if you're meet the wrong sort of insecure, heterosexual male. You could be in serious physical trouble. Someone decides you're female and then decides you're not female – whatever that means. Of course I realize now it doesn't mean anything.

Sacred Intent

CA: Alchemy is basically a supra-language for sexual magic, but also for the human being to be transformed. The hermaphrodite would be the prime symbol of course, of how you could make people see that.

GBPO: Not just in our society, but in any society. Although in India there is actually a caste for transsexuals.

CA: There is an old esoteric saying: "The greater thy trial, the greater thy triumph." Magical sacrifice shouldn't be disregarded either; you sacrifice a lot by giving up your previous identity; by giving up that safety.

GBPO: I see it as adding to and empowering what's already there. Not choosing. Not the opposite, not switching. I used to look in the back of *The Village Voice* and get to the sex-for-sale adverts part. And there are more she-males there now than ever before. And sometimes there are even more she-males than biological females. What does that mean? Most of the men who go to she-male prostitutes are heterosexual men; almost all. So what is it that's happened over the last X number of years, that's allowed men to feel comfortable with that? And even prefer the pandrogyne hermaphrodite. I always think that as a cultural engineer. I mean, that is more indication and confirmation of the theory that it's an evolutionary step; it's an inevitable step. These are manifestations, symptoms and evidence of something much bigger happening in the universe.

But what's also interesting is that women seem to find it very sexual as well. I see it as magical, because that's how it tends to be with everyone. There has been a shift. I see evidence of a shift to the pandrogyne; to a new expression of social, sexual magic. And I think it's a good thing. It's a great thing because it makes me feel more physically safe and secure. Or acceptable, really. The less I feel insecure, the less I want help in an ambiguous way. There is an underlying psychic drive, a psychic desire for the new being. It could be that we're so afraid of what we are as a binary species, the destructive species, that we want to erase that and create another one that is not threatening to each other's body or ego. I think that's part of what we represent as a species; that is, the non-threatening version of the species.

You were saying to me how my voice changes a lot during live gigs. There are a lot of people that live in here and they all want to talk. But why, as we develop as a species, should it be limited to only one person? We can be many different characters. And as the body lives longer physically, all the more reason to explore various people, various identities. It's a very liberating feeling to find that that which is reflected in a mirror isn't all there is. And that gets to be a bit Buddhist – the body is just this arbitrary suitcase, Lady Jaye's "suitcase," and that's not me.

I was debating with Lady Jaye, what should we call each other now? Do I call you my wife, do you call me your wife, you know, are you my husband or am I your husband? The language is failing us here because we're in a new territory. What am I? And it was Jaye that said, "Well, you're my other half." Which of course, as in that English joke, you know, "the other half" or "the better half." But it also is totally precise. And as soon as she said it, it just kind of went on, and on, and on... Of course, she's my other half. It's quite a commitment to donate one's body to another being, if you're going to have it reconstructed.

CA: But the other half is also doing that.

GBPO: Absolutely. She is next, because her eyes are different here so they would have to go in, which would be a really delicate work. And I think that a little bit I'm going to lift my chin here. And then she's going get more of me. And of course eventually, she needs to get gold teeth. Never ending! So much to do, so little time! So expensive! (laughs) It's a pity it's such an expensive project.

Lady Jaye, New York, January 16th, 2004

The development of the Pandrogeny project to a great degree emerged from the "third mind" of Genesis and Lady Jaye. There was a constant flow of ideas in-between them, which resulted not only in the physical changes but also in a deepening of the concepts as such. Ever since our first meeting in 1998, I realised that I needed to talk to Lady Jaye about this too.

CA: Does this kind of massive transformation change the romantic attraction? Does it make it stronger?

LJBPO: I can say I'm becoming more and more narcissistic all the time, as I fall more deeply in love with my partner. But I have to say that I've stopped looking in the mirror so much. I don't know how relevant this is. I don't bother with it. But when it comes to romance, what I think needs to be addressed first is that this project is made more complicated by working with someone in the public sphere. This individual that Genesis used to be is being regarded so specifically that the person that we are working on developing now is not getting accepted so readily.

CA: If you are diligent, the people will listen. What do you think of the journey so far? What do you think has been the most rewarding thing so far?

LJBPO: It's the experience I think, of having to surrender so much of the ego. Because in order to do this there has to be compromise. Everything is a compromise. Rather than have one of us, you know whichever one has the stronger personality, devour the other. And that one person would sort of be a mimic of the other. But to be very thoughtful and meaningful and useful we have to make a lot of decisions together, and it's hard to let go of the ego. I might have to come to that point again where I have to give more than I have. It was a real natural sort of instinct for me to resist giving up my individuality, even though intellectually I thought I was behind the project, I thought it was a good idea; that good things would come from it.

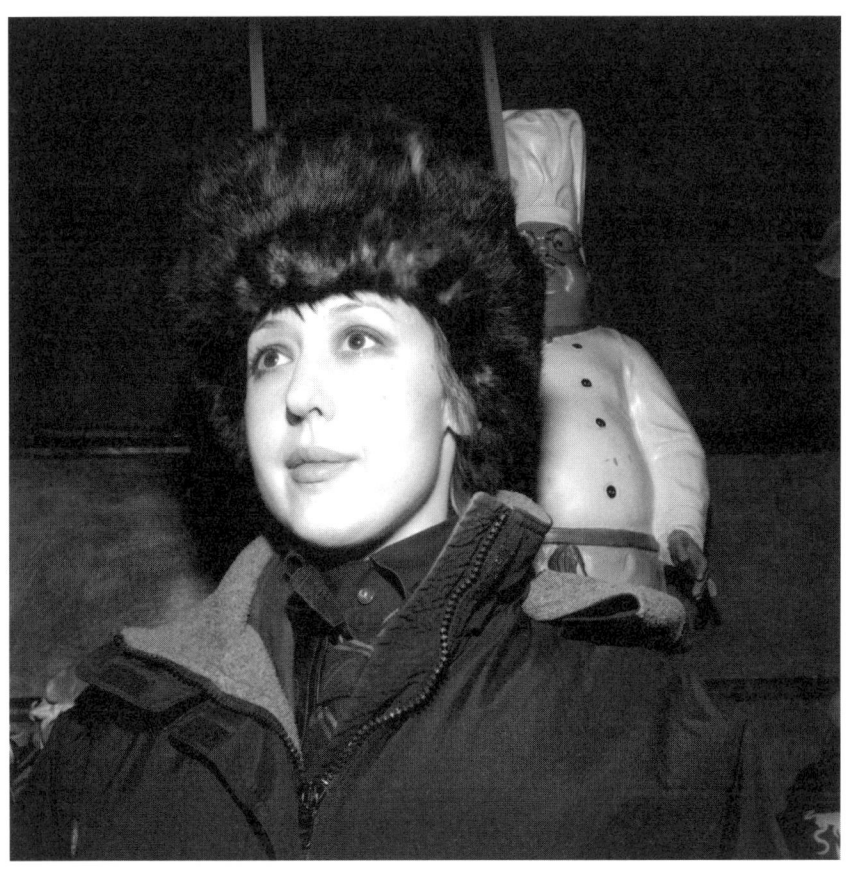

Lady Jaye Breyer P-Orridge, New York, 2004

CA: The ego is such an intelligent trickster, and one would assume that if major change takes place which opposes the ego, the ego would say, "I don't want to do this, I want to change back." Has that occurred?

LJBPO: It's tried, but not successfully. I mean we are both able to be objective enough to step back from our experiences and take a look at our arguments or the difficult parts and say, "OK, this is difficult, because there's something here that needs to be worked on." And rather than being too emotional about it, we think it through. That is supposed to be the idea of two people working towards the same goal. I couldn't do it alone. And it would be helpful even more to have the support from the people on the outside. There are a lot of friends who may be conceptually inclined, and they think that giving up your ego is submitting to another person, and that's unnatural and unhealthy. Yes, it is submitting to a degree, as if that's wrong and it's the same impulse on the outside. I was also feeling, "You can't give that up! That's you! That's special! That's unique. Who is this other person that you're willing to build this new person of?" Fortunately, I think that this other person is the finest person I've ever known and one of the most morally refined, so that makes it very comfortable. But I think if other people would support it a little bit more it would be easier to fall into, because part of the reason we want to look the same is not just to be like this cute couple that dresses in identical clothes. We want to use our exterior to get a certain response from the outside world, because we know that people react to you in a visual way – at least primarily. So we thought that if we look the same, strangers are looking at us and making decisions about who we are and then treating us in a certain way. And it's helpful in that way, because then we are both receiving some of the same sensory information from strangers wherever we go. So in terms of human interactions, it's useful. It only becomes tricky, as I said, when people that have known us for a long time will have certain expectations. So not only have we had to give up our expectations of ourselves. But the people who love us have to also do the same thing. So it's tricky all around.

CA: After an actual physical change, whether that would mean implants, or injections, do you get any kind of insights? You know, inner insights coming from all these physical alterations. Has that been the case?

LJBPO: Oh, absolutely. It has been very relaxing to feel as though my external appearance reflects my internal thoughts and desires. It's usually rewarding. I mean, it's only symbolic, but I've always felt uncomfortable in the body I inherited, you know, just by chance. You could argue that it was a perfectly fine body and there's nothing wrong with it, but I've never felt completely comfortable in my skin and a lot of people work on that in different ways. I feel as though the way I'm becoming when I say "I" (I mean myself and Gen), either the changing makes us feel as though this is close to us; the way our spiritual selves could manifest. It's more of a body that represents our thoughts and our desires towards perfection. Sometimes it's magical alchemy, sometimes it's chemical alchemy, sometimes it's spiritual alchemy, and this time it's physical. I mean, I felt like the old body was so imperfect, and was an imperfect representation of my spirit, and one that was more beautiful and more aesthetically pleasing was more accurate. I mean, I could follow the "judge a book by its cover," but there's a lot of very beautiful, very elevated people that are hindered in their spiritual growth because they are in these damn ugly bodies, and they are forced to see the uglier side of life and the uglier side of what human nature can serve up, because they're trapped. So I'm very pro-transformation of any kind. If you have thought about of using surgery of any kind of way you can embellish yourself to encourage free expression, that is a good thing. Or individuality... This is how I'm choosing to exercise my individuality: to join forces with another.

CA: This is a very active thing; it's an active step of transformation. Which sort of comes from you – from the inside out.

LJBPO: Exactly. We can't control all of it. We are working on controlling what we can, and seeing what happens.

CA: So, Breyer P-Orridge is a "Third Mind" in the classical sense of the word. In what direction would you like to see that mind go?

LJBPO: Well, it's already heading in a very good direction. We're able complete each other's sentences when we're alone together; we're becoming telepathic to a level that I'm really happy with but it is certainly more than coincidence. We are very in tune with each other.

CA: Do you get insights, ideas and epiphanies that are decidedly Third Mind-directed?

LJBPO: I think something is happening, and at this point it's getting me frustrated. Because in the past I've been contributing some wildly different perspectives. Now with me sitting at the table, I'm finding that I'm not bringing anything more to it. But since our perceptions of the world are so synched up, the Third Mind project has some drawbacks because we're becoming so much one that we're losing the third; the one and the two are losing the edge. So it's important for us to keep putting ourselves out there on our own. Because if not, it would be so easy to become lazy. But I didn't know that would happen.

CA: What is the greatest thing that P-Orridge brings to Breyer P-Orridge?

LJBPO: Discipline. Discipline and experience. It's so easy for me to be startled sometimes. All of the others have some accomplishments. Gen has a long history of experimenting, and because of that I've never met anyone else like her. But the discipline definitely attracted me. And also we are from different generations and that definitely put a slant on perception. Gen is able to notice things about pop culture – what will stand out, what changes will occur – that I'm not aware of. Not necessarily due to my shabby education but because more of a failure of journalism and of the media to record certain trends. So it's a very good question.

CA: What is the greatest thing that Breyer brings to Breyer P-Orridge?

LJBPO: I think probably my ability to sort through information and focus in on what is important. And to take a bunch of bulk and narrow it down, either information-wise or visual material. Let me use a metaphor: I will take a bunch of visual information and focus in on something great; very, very tightly and focus in on that. Gen will take that small piece and expand it again, and then decide what shape it's going to take in terms of media and the final expression of it.

CA: What was it like when you discussed the project initially? Did you come up with it, saying: "we should alter ourselves so that we look more like each other," or did it grow over time? Was it specifically inspired by alchemy or...?

LJBPO: It was definitely inspired by alchemy and the idea of a hermaphrodite, being in a full blur the original human, the original virus, and also an angelic representation of the humans. Some of them are just very sexy images; they even have little horns. I don't know where that comes from, but that image fascinated us because this was a being that was fruitful in every possible way as the artist's muse. The hermaphrodite is a symbol of creative potential. It has genitals of both genders so it had everything contained within itself. There's never been a pregnant hermaphrodite. Hermaphrodites don't breed; they just have that creative attention all the time. Especially when I listen to a lot of women talking about "the goddess" and fertility and creative potential, how the female body is sacred because it can make a baby... Of course the male body is sacred too, because it helps to make that baby. Just because one has a fine core and one has a gross core does not make them independent. But I saw more of my own creativity as a woman being the same as that of a hermaphrodite. I don't need to make a baby to prove that I'm creative. I'll choose to not express my creativity that way. I will choose to not make other humans. I will not have a baby and I will choose to more aggressively express my creativity with the works of my hands and my minds. Something more wilful because it was certain to create, you know. You make the baby, you know, you deliver the child and you feed it and then after a certain amount of time it's really crap what you're going to get back. So it didn't seem like it suited me. And it was fine; there was no conflict there because Genesis had already had the experience of fatherhood, and I've taken care of children. And when Gen's children were around seven or eight and eleven years old I helped with their parenting until they were through their teens, so I know I'm not missing anything. Lucky you; you could have such a good time.

CA: It's hard work.

LJBPO: If I'm going to have hard work I want to have something beautiful at the end. But the name change came up over and over again. Why should I change my name; why should I change my name to be ours and give up Breyer? Besides, P-Orridge is a much more interesting name in my opinion. Because I didn't want to surrender my ego, so we'll have to be, you know, Breyer P-Orridge. And I said "Okay, I don't care, I'll be P-Orridge," and Gen would just say, "No, no I don't care, I'll be Breyer! It's fine." And I said, "well you can't be Breyer because when it comes to you addressing the people with whom you work they'll be very confused. If you just change your name it will lead to all kinds of difficulties. And if you changed to Breyer it would be dull, and if I changed to P-Orridge then it would be hard to tell that there were two people working on that." It was a big mess. We kept changing it, and now we've just gotten to the point so that we don't care.

CA: Well, now it *is* established as one name.

LJBPO: We wanted to find another name that was interesting and represented the both of us. But it just didn't manifest itself, and we didn't want to push it. You know, I could come up with half a dozen cutesy little names but I think that after a time I'll get really sick of hearing them.

CA: In terms of now actively working together, what are the greatest similarities between the two of you?

LJBPO: That's a hard question because there is huge amount of similarities. I mean some of Gen's skills when it comes to details are rubbing off on me, and likewise Gen is developing some of my eye. Our perceptions are becoming very similar; it's hard to describe. If you were to be present when we are working on a project it'd be easier for me to point things out. What we'll do is we'll sit down together and this "we" can go in so many different directions. At first we'll sit down and say, "okay, what is it that we really want to address?" Because if we don't try to stick to that it can go out in too many directions. What Gen is really best at is that I can be too rational sometimes. I'd say, "if we represent this and this way, couldn't it be misunderstood," you know, "is this the best way of expressing an idea to get the point across?" And he is more like, "if that's what you felt first, go with your guts and if people don't get it – fuck them, it's not your problem. You keep telling me I can't worry about that too much, you express yourself the way you want to and leave it to them to figure it out. Tell them it's not my job to educate the public."

CA: What are the greatest differences between you?

LJBPO: I'm a little more practical when it comes to execution in a very mundane way. Gen is not interested, and I love this about Gen, in the budget. Gen would just go, "do it, run, 20ft high, and we'll put beautiful gem stones on your body, and a beautiful light above it, maybe on a pedestal that turns," which is great, you know. If we have the kind of backing that a lot of people do, there would be some truly fine art. But given that we work with limited resources – I mean we're not making it with selling it in mind – we make it to express an idea or to just make something we think is a thing of beauty. And if everybody liked what we did I guess we wouldn't be good artists, we wouldn't be good graphics designers. I'm always having to pull things back into the realm of reality and say, "okay, here you go buddy, this is the budget and we'll have to find another way to execute the same idea on a smaller scale."

CA: Do you consciously look upon yourself as part of Breyer P-Orridge as a living part of a living art history?

LJBPO: I haven't thought of that either. Good question! I suppose I am because of the fact that my other half has done so much that precedes us, and we carry that with us and into the future. For example there might be things that I've never done but Genesis has. A lot of the things that Gen was doing in his early twenties were a lot of the same things that I was trying to express. Maybe I did them a little differently but we were both feeling the same things emotionally at the same point of our development. And I might have not done certain things because I didn't have the venue. I didn't have the balls but I'm finding that I don't really need to be satisfied with hearing about how Gen's experiences played themselves out.

CA: I was thinking whether you specifically, consciously, regarded the work that you're doing as a part of the continuous flow of art history? We usually refer to

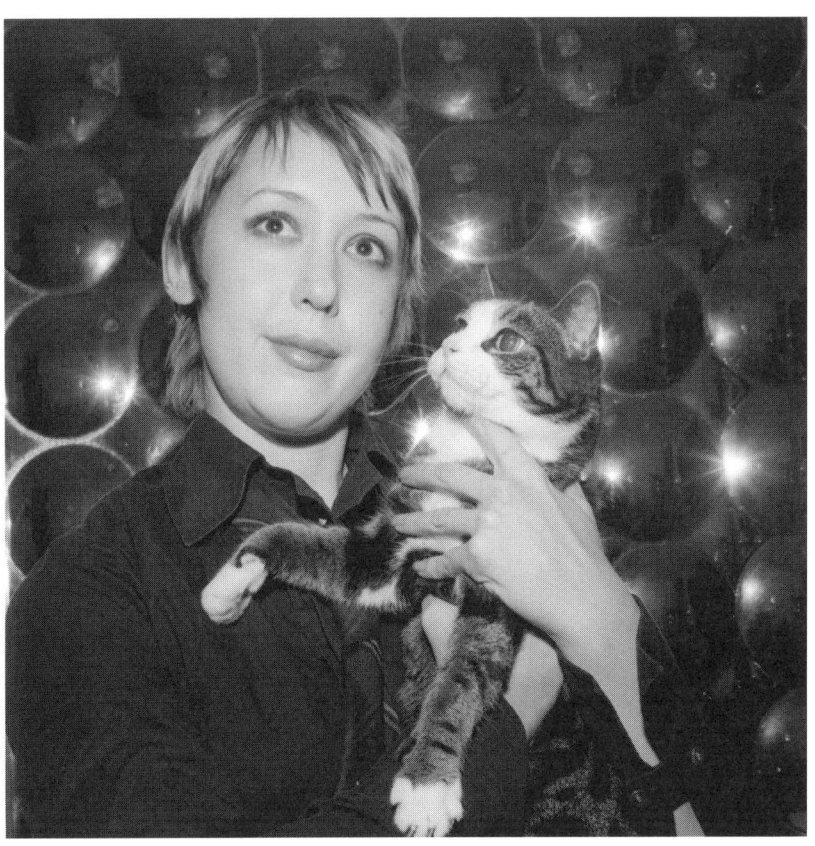

With Lucy Fur, New York, 2004.

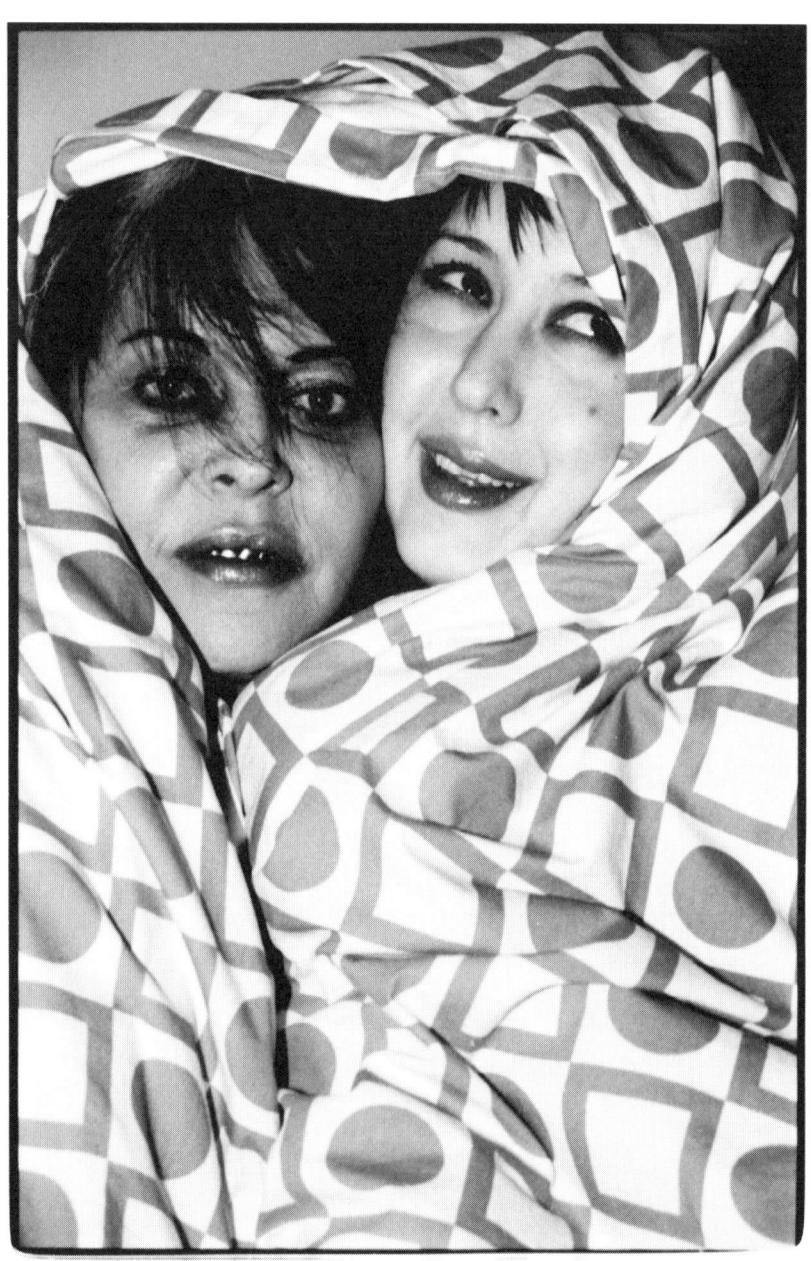

Breyer P-Orridge, New York, 2004

history as something that's already happened, but of course it's a continuous process which contains all art that's been made.

LJBPO: The people who were or are giants are only human beings with a creative urge and they've done things not out of whim but because they had the motivation to do these things. But you are doing exactly the same thing. So there is no difference. I am just one of those mythical people along with Gen, but on a low budget, so we have to look everyone in the eye. And once we have a big enough budget then we too can retire to Saint Tropez, and we'll be legendary; no one will ever see us anymore; just maybe read about us in *The National Enquirer* sometimes. I'm ready for that.

CA: How far would this go? Not so much in the production or conceptualization of art, but in terms of transformation of the body?

LJBPO: I think our goal, one of them, could be that we become siblings. At least to the outside world; to be perceived as siblings. For a very long time now we've been talking about a couple of characters that we'd like to grow into when we're older. They are a couple of Victorian type spinster sisters who are eccentric and live in the countryside and live a quiet and mysterious life, like two Miss Marples as artists... Elsie and Gladys Brown. Maybe if we have a couple of cocktails or take some of that wine that's left, we can do Elsie and Gladys Brown impersonations for you. But it's sort of inspired by a couple of Gen's aunts who were very Victorian. Gen remembers being a tiny boy, and Aunty Lily and Ethel were obviously a couple of ladies that chose not to marry or join the convent – like mine did. It was very unusual for those days because only one of them was actually not too pretty. Who knows, maybe they weren't aunties either. Maybe Ethel used to be uncle Eddie? Well, they say there's nothing new under the sun, don't they? Feels that way sometimes. But we'll see where it ends up. We could decide that we've become so much alike that neither of us is bringing anything unique to the table anymore. And if that happens we're just going to have to spend less time together, which will change the dynamic in different ways because that's the part that's allowing us to become so telepathic; to be able to spend so much time together. And we are receiving a lot of the same stimuli, you know. We talk to each other quite often if we have conversations with other people, so the same idea is being synthesized at the same time, using the same words, producing the same information, which so far has been really great but I could see how that can lead to problems later on. But right now I'm very happy to continue working with it and refining it as much as possible. I think once I age a bit more it's going to be easier. Right now Gen is perceived as being the older sister so I think as I age we'll be able to look even more alike.

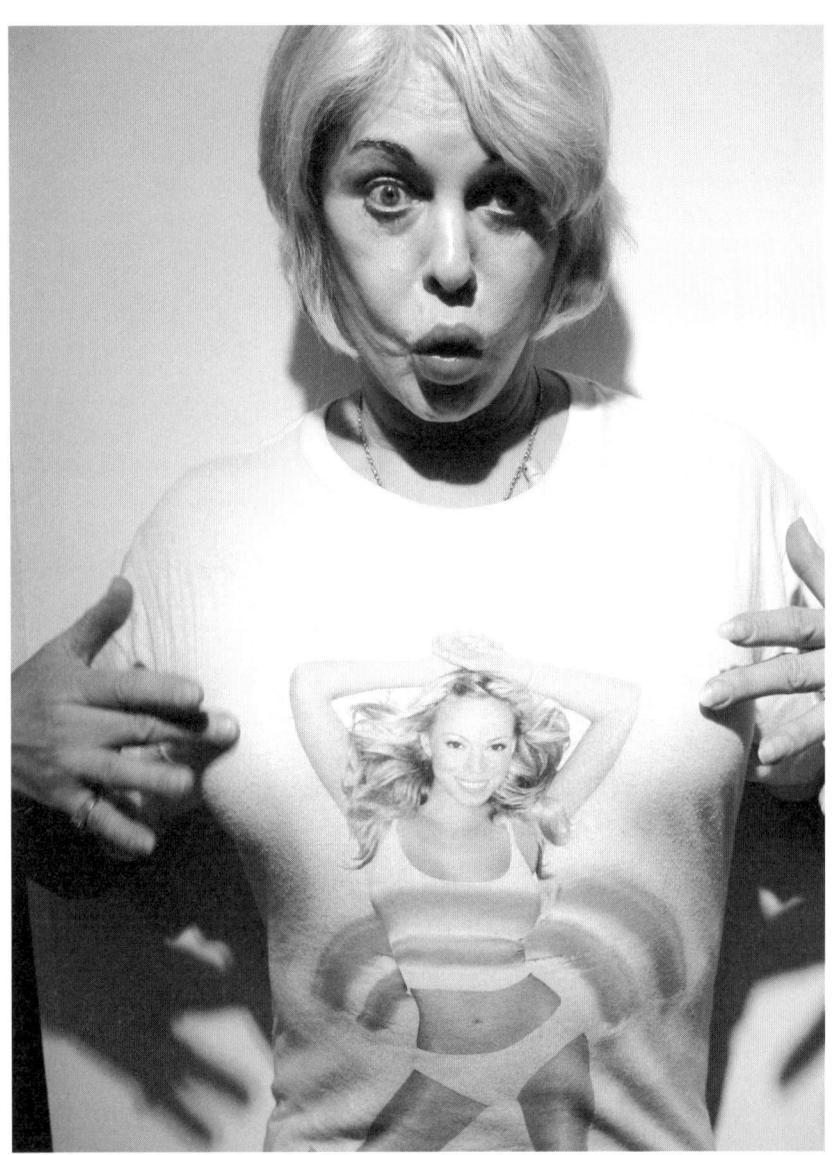

New York, 2005

New York, April 6th, 2005

The work of Breyer P-Orridge moved on relentlessly, and physical changes began to become visible in both Genesis and Lady Jaye. Cosmetic surgery and tandem styling became art experiments in the public sphere, as well as outer reaches of an inner drive striving for higher levels of consciousness.

CA: We have previously talked about she-males, and their seeming increased presence in the public sphere. And also the emergence of what used to be called sex-dolls but are now more like adjustable "companions"... A lot of creativity is used in the presentation of an ideal.

GBPO: It extends the malleability of things like cosmetics, accessories and hair-dos further, and includes the malleability of the flesh and the body itself as an accessory that can be manipulated and changed in order to fit. If you look in the back of magazines, in the private ads, the adult ads, a lot of them are for sexual favours. There used to be primarily pretty, biological girls. It seems now that two thirds of them are she-males. Which can only imply that supposedly or traditionally straight heterosexual males who frequent hookers are excited by the combination for some reason, and they don't feel belittled enough or insecure enough or whatever reason to avoid that. They are actually revelling in and immersing themselves in their attraction to an excitement by she-males, or pandrogynes. We could argue that actually it's probably better to be pandrogyne as these are magically aware of the alchemical implication. A trans-gendered person isn't necessarily interested in that iconography at all; that's one of the differences. But there's definitely something bubbling beneath the surface in the culture. One of the symptoms of whatever it is that's bubbling under the surface is the acceleration of interest in she-male transsexuals and body modification to neutralize the archetypes. I don't think it's anywhere near as clear cut as people used to assume. I know it's not. It was that classic thing where I'm a man trapped in a woman's body, or I'm a woman trapped in a man's body. We should know that a pandrogyne is simply just trapped in a body. And the body has to become a part of the dialogue in terms of control over the narrative of your life. No longer is it required to omit the physical biological body from one's inner dialogue in terms of what you want to become. The technology is now much more accessible.

CA: And also, paradoxically enough, made possible by a huge growth market that's very wrong and superficial in many ways: trying to make illusory Barbie dolls out of housewives who basically just want to have healthy relationships with their husbands.

GBPO: You want to be more subservient by becoming more artificial. When you watch those reality shows, they have their team of doctors and they advise them as experts, but if you turn away and just listen to what they say, they just go, "well, you need a face lift and you need your nose done and you need your lips or hands, new chin implant and cheek implants, then you need breast implants and liposuction and then your teeth fixed..." They go to the next one, and they say the same thing to all of them regardless of whether they are the same. Which is, in a way, the most important aspect of this show: it's not the concept of which a lot of people would be complaining about and be critical of. The actual concept would be giving people the opportunity to design their body to be exactly how they would like it to be; to fantasize an imaginary being and then become that as near as possible. That's great, but that is *not* what is happening. They are having a new stereotype, an idealized Hollywood stereotype imposed upon their body and they are still trapped, in my opinion. They haven't thought about their psychology; they haven't really looked at why they feel inadequate – most of them talk about feeling inadequate. They are somehow being tricked into feeling that they are the ones at fault, that there is a fault; they are not the same as the pictures that we see in the magazines. This is quite sad, really. We get these, I have to say really quite grotesque, spouses being mean-spirited towards their wives, and despite that they love them enough to risk everything. They don't actually engage in a deep dialogue with each other at all. I was happy with how I looked, and with Lady Jaye we felt blessed that we liked our looks and we were content with that. But in some ways my face is less of how I would like it to be than it was before, but that's not the issue. We're surrendering to possibilities far more than we are trying to be attractive to some abstract idealized status quo.

CA: You can apply many different kinds of explanation factors or matrices to things that are interesting to yourself, whether it be the cosmic aspects or the alchemical aspects or magical aspects, or simply the cultural, technological aspects. Could it be that the interest is somehow a cultural reaction to the homogenisation of looks, to perceptions of looks? Is it simply a reaction?

GBPO: My first thought on that is that they are being persuaded to accept homogeneisation itself as a pinnacle of beauty. My anthropological observation is that it's more to do with a build-up of cultural pressure, which instinctively is looking for change in evolution. I think that the human species is at a crossroads of potentiality. And often people who may not have access to the language and the ways to articulate, what they are feeling inside will still find an outlet for the impulses that are affecting them; by different means of expression which would be cosmetic surgery and the realization through all these different programs which are cross-advertising a homogenized, idealized form. Even though those programs are trying to almost reinforce a status quo by making all forms of femininity look the same, no matter how rebellious the reasoning behind the individual doing something. Those programs are still opening people's eyes; educating them to what is becoming possible and also familiarizing them with the language of biological, physical change. They watch Jerry Springer and even though people are screaming insults and saying "show us your tits" and every episode is basically exactly the same script with the screaming and the yelling and the secret affairs and, "I didn't know you're a man," and "I didn't know you are a woman," "I'm in love with your sister," all that stuff...

Bit by bit RuPaul tried television programming, including occasional references to trans-gendered people. The familiarity of just the topic is warming people to be more tolerant. Once they are tolerant and they've become comfortable with the fact it's a possibility they can start to sense and begin to include that possibility; that knowledge of what they could become into their daily imagination; their fantasy life. Some people will discover deeper resonance in the expected and find themselves excited, challenged or thrilled when they imagine either being with somebody who is not biologically formed, or imagining themselves in a new physical, biological shape. And that is the old story, that just by exposing people to a possibility, that possibility is increased. Because if millions of people know that they might become other than they were genetically predisposed to be, then more of them inevitably will choose that path, than if only a thousand know so that it becomes a self-fulfilling cycle, or at least self-perpetuating. Which I believe is healthy. I think that the reason all that is happening, is this drive in far more people than we expected, and it's not limited just to sexual orientation. It is actually something incredibly deep – for all of our airs and graces we're actually prehistoric. We're not really much more than clever ants, and our basic behavioural patterns are the same as they were when we were prehistoric. Our only real drive was to survive and replicate. One of the basic instincts, basic genetic tools we had when we were prehistoric that made us succeed in terms of survival as a species was "fight or flight." Adrenal of course. And that fight or flight was basically a genetic tool that was friendly towards us, because it helped us to stake out territories, and enough to kill any food, and fight and kill other tribes and clans in order to survive. That is how we've developed culturally. We never let go of those impulse behaviour patterns, those drives, and we are still driven by the same prehistoric patterns. We still have governments that fight and struggle over territory, whether it would be economic territory or cultural territory, or religious territory or literal physical land. The main fights that occur, the wars that occur with armies and money and ideas, occur over territory. And we still react with frustration if we don't get what we want, as a society... with violence. Basically the human species still uses prehistoric impulses and drives to own and control territory in all forms, even with information. And its way of keeping control is violence and intimidation. That was fine when we were struggling against a truly unfriendly environment and climate and there weren't that many others and there were dinosaurs and creatures around us that were going to eat us if we didn't get them first. But that's changed. We now have a relatively stable relationship with our environment; it's actually the other way around now. So what's happened is that we are still subservient to these prehistoric reactions and patterns of behaviour, but they are redundant. Where they were once our friend and helped us survive, they are now all funneled together and are our enemy, and threatening to bring annihilation. And yet those who run and control the various cultural zones on our planet at the moment, are reverting to even more primitive interpretations, fundamentalist interpretations of behaviour and becoming more and more violent, more and more entranced and less and less creative and imaginative in the ways of resolving issues.

So I think that's where the evolutionary impulse is: we're either going to revert to being slaves of intimidation and violence and fear, which are no longer of any positive use to us whatsoever, or we're going to stand up and revolt and say: "No, we have potential now, in our minds and in our technology to have a symbiotic relationship with the environment. The environment is no longer our enemy." If we only apply ourselves to creative, positive, new forms of behaviour and develop new patterns for how we respond to frustration and the alternatives, then we can become miraculous new beings. Basically there is no limit to what we're imagining. With nano-technology and some of the developments that are just around the corner; with computers, Artificial Intelligence, quantum physics, physics and biochemistry, we can literally sit down and decide what we want to be, and in which direction to go. Why on earth should we think that the biological body that was useful a hundred thousand years ago to go through the grass and hide in caves, is sacrosanct. The most important lesson that the human species has to learn and take to heart right now is that the human body is not sacred. And the next lesson they have to learn and accept is that there is absolutely no need to replicate biologically. But that isn't necessarily the most exciting alternative. I'm absolutely in favour of genetic engineering, cosmetic surgery, anything that adds to the list, the shopping list, of what you want to become.

The fact of the matter is, from my perspective, that each individual has a certain biological amount of time and that is their narrative, their story and they are, if you like, a character in this movie. But the movie is made day to day, moment for moment, by choices, and those choices should be made truly autonomously. Not because of conditioning, not because of peer pressure, not because of fear of repercussion by other beings that are afraid of change. So, to ask the initial question with that as the context, I think that the deepest reason for the manifestations we're seeing in Western culture certainly, are graspings towards evolutionary change. And that's the right way to put it. We have to evolve, otherwise it's not really counting as being here, and we're just filling a space and repeating ourselves over and over again. With these variations of "I don't like something different, I don't understand it, I'm afraid of it, I must hurt it." And that is basically all we've achieved so far, certainly *en masse*. The individual always has choices in terms of what they would like to do, and that's what is happening. These people are starting very slowly to realize that there are far more choices than they were told. And those choices are not just economic and political; they are far more fundamental than that. They are actually about being yourself, relating to the world, and understanding that the material world is malleable; everything is malleable, everything can be different.

What we thought we knew 20 years ago is laughable now. And if we know that that's always been the case, then we can also expect that in 20 years time, what I'm saying is laughable, because it would be accepted practice to decide whether or not to have a biological baby or whether to go to a replication bank and pick one. And then have a list of attributes that you think would be useful, and one of the courses at school would be, when you'll be 15 or when you'll be 18, who would you like to be? Would you like four arms, as we have found that a pilot of our new quantum space modules really need four arms because there are so many controls, switches and buttons to operate plus two or more computer interfaces. Or would you like to be a space explorer and have things like capsules of more oxygen or special nano-altered organs, which means that you can live in oxygen-limited environments and gravity-limited environments, or do you need legs at all? Sometimes we might live enclosed inside space vehicles, never leaving for years so we might not need legs at all that would eventually atrophy anyway, and just move around in strange contraptions outside a ship that are basically being designed for strength functions already by DARPA.[1] But then they will just use it to make super soldiers; of course they will. But all the technology that is used for control trickles down into the everyday life. It has to, because it's too expensive to do it otherwise. So we will still get those choices, whether we like it or not. We will still have those options. And it's time to start considering how to utilize them and accepting and embracing them; in fact being happy to have the most luxurious options than in any time in history. So I really think that's

1 Defense Advanced Research Projects Agency.

happening. I don't think everybody understands what's happening, but I think that people are feeling that something is happening, for sure.

CA: Your radar catches these things, and your antenna catches these signals. You yourself have become a pioneer, in the sense that you will try everything, and you will talk about it. Thereby you are by choice, and also perhaps to a greater extent than you've realized, a catalyst for all these things. Sometimes you are a component in the plan that makes all these things happen.

GBPO: As you give it terminology, as you start to develop a new language for the new ways of being, inevitably it becomes more possible and more of a choice to evolve. Because as we know, once you start to give names to phenomena, they root themselves in the culture, and that in itself has a potency, a power. It becomes a means. People mention it, they keep on saying it and that is basically the same as an invocation or a spell. And it gets to the point when you say "pandrogeny," people go, "oh, that's that topic that includes all these options that I can have." That word gives me freedom of choice and all kinds of stuff, including my body, and that is an incredibly powerful cultural engineering. And certainly, I work on impulse and intuition and observation, to feel the course and watch a serial phenomenon occur and try and understand what they might imply. But having watched them and decided to surrender to my leap to try and see if it is the truth. It's a point when that is given back to everybody and they've become their own experiment. As you say, I'm a catalyst; I watch the shadows of what's going on and I try to imagine what the implications might be. And if me and Lady Jaye have any skill at all, or gift, it is the courage to put our bodies where our minds are. We believe that the species has to evolve; we believe this is a symptom of its evolution or its optional evolution. Because we believe so strongly that we are correct in our observation we're going to do it first, and it may not do it correctly, and there may be better ways later on, but... We feel really strongly that someone has to state that this must happen. One way or another this must happen. Or we just give up and we're just a stupid bunch of clever chimpanzees. We should stop kidding ourselves. I love human beings. I just don't like the human species. That may well reverse as the social story unfolds. I hope so.

CA: You mentioned earlier about that when you were on a tour with PTV3[2] you were getting a lot of attention in French major media; specifically focusing on the pandrogeny thing. That's a pretty fast turnover for something that you started experimenting with visibly, physically, only a couple of years ago. Do you think that there needs to be a specific commercial market for things to really catch on?

---

2 The incarnation of Psychic TV from 2003 and onwards.

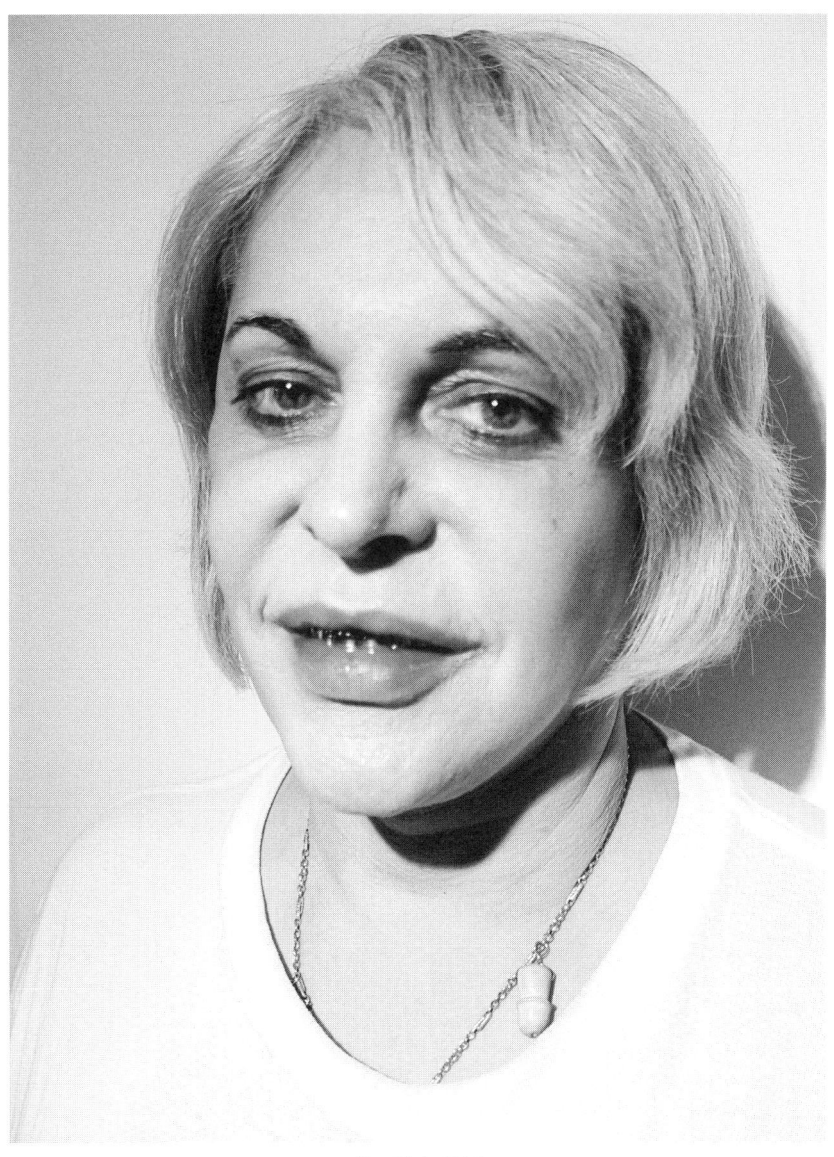

New York, 2005

GBPO: No, not at all. At the beginning no one knew we existed and hardly anyone was listening. Each time we predict something like "industrial music" and "modern primitivism," our credibility in terms of prophecy is increasing. So people take that into account and listen a little bit more carefully to what we say. So some of the speed of access to dialogue is simply having done good work in the past. It doesn't necessarily mean that culture is accelerated. However, that's a privilege that brings with it a lot of responsibility in terms of being ever more careful in terms of what we say and why we say it. And in a way I've been thinking about pandrogeny since 1969 when I was in the Gay Lib Street Theatre, and we were doing transvestitism as a political act. And when Lady Jaye and I got married in 1995, we switched gender roles to get married. So there's been a consistent thread throughout all my work. In a way going around or squirting around the edges of this issue. And it was a good thing. What made it fabulous, was that it made it clear that that was the underlying problem or issue that really needed to be addressed. I also realized that my obsession is to try and assist us as a species, as beings, to evolve. I don't really care where we get to or what we look like, and that's a part of the message: "it doesn't matter." Something should be happening and it should be moving away from violence and prejudice and bigotry and towards collaboration and compassion and change. It is that simple. The basic equations are incredibly simple but they are also incredibly hard to truly surrender to.

CA: Would you describe it as a social kind of Buddhism?

GBPO: Well, I've always found myself drawn to Buddhism more than any other belief system, and I can see why. I still find a lot of empathy in resonance with the great deal of the Buddhist perceptions. That's why I always say, "change the way to perceive, and change all memory!" And if you try and change the way we perceive ourselves and our place amongst things now, you will then with hindsight also re-evaluate all the things that might evolve. I live in a state of constant sadness, in the sense of Buddhist sadness. The waste of time and love and sharing creativity that goes on between our species. The lessons that we need to learn have already been learned over and over and over again. Can you think of a good reason to have a war? Or is it just a program you watched the other day; a documentary about the First World War? There is nothing glorious about that. And no one should be forced to make individual sacrifices which are in themselves noble. Individual acts may be noble, but war is never noble. And it's never clever; it's never worthwhile. To watch all these wonderful so called ordinary men and women, getting blown up. For what?! There's no justification of that. We should be proud of what we have achieved intellectually. And we should be looking for ways... Consciousness should be taught at school, mysticism should be taught at school, creation should be taught at school... I mean in terms of becoming an active creative individual.

I read a book about the crusades not long ago, and I was surprised that the rhetoric that they used, those popes, to motivate people to walk thousands of miles to be slaughtered; it was almost the same as what they're saying now. After a thousand years of saying garbage, people are still fond of it and marching up to be slaughtered. Someone has to say, "Stop, this is ridiculous, what kind of morons are you?!" There is no other animal that would keep doing this to itself. We're not the smartest creatures we could be, and certainly don't seem to be genetically listening to our species' past recordings in the way I would prefer as a Utopian. That's really what it all comes down to. What would you like your future to be; what would you like the future for the species to even be? What could you possibly do with the species to keep expanding? Societies behave like individuals. They have reactions, traumas, and behavioural patterns. And loops of behaviour that they go over and over again and do not appear to learn from, and at times they get hurt. We do have the wisdom, the knowledge, the information, the techniques, and the technologies to be the most beautiful science-fiction colony we could imagine. And we make amazing things. We take molecules and we take atoms apart and we build viruses. Stuff that is impossible to believe. And they are doing it as an everyday event. That I find inspiring, and I think that's what we should concentrate on: the inspirational skills we have as beings.

One of the motives for what I've been doing is to not want to be like other humans. To disconnect and distance my self from ordinary biological human beings because I'm so disenchanted with how they behave. And it's almost an aspect in itself: I don't want to be one of them; I feel as if I'm from a different minority species, and I don't want any part of that majority species, because I can't come up with a single reason why I should.

CA: That's a theme or concept that has been consistent in your existence, as well as in your art. Going all the way back from the concept of the "alien brain" over the proactive existentialism or the cruel nihilistic existentialism of TG, etc. That kind of an outsider-ship has always been there.

GBPO: I guess I was just very hurt by what I found when I supposedly grew up. The adult world really disappointed me. And the way that I saw people behaving *en masse*, I found it just despicable. And then the 60s came along and there was this sense of hope or optimism; that somehow consciousness was overruled by vicariousness. And that compassion and love would triumph over violence and stupidity and hypocrisy. And I still feel that's possible: that we are blessed with being born with potential. But the recent activities on this planet by those who have access to the mass media and access to organized violence tends to suggest that we really, really have to think now of what our future is, about ways to be different from that. It's not acceptable to be cruel. It's just not acceptable. It's not acceptable to lie to yourself. We've talked about that. At least symbolically voting to become the beginnings of a new species, which needs breathing space to consider what it is that it wants to become.

CA: The way I see it, the challenge should be to sow seeds that are more potent. However, not carelessly, because freedom is a very tough thing to deal with.

GBPO: Up until the 21st century, the big issue was control. How to short-circuit control. What and where was control... What's happened in a very subtle way is that it's shifted. The primary concern now is inertia. Control is almost secondary to an ever-deepening inertia. Privacy has become the last taboo. It's a simple thing that there's almost infinite information available now through the Internet. People say that eventually everything will be uploaded and we'll be able to find out everything that we've ever said... And we'll read about what people blog, so we'll be able to find out what everybody is doing in the most mundane ways, but that's actually a kind of creative inertia. It's such a glut though that things become blocked. And no one can tell what may or may not have long term value and longevity. As we get more globalised, these things become far more interdependent. That is the new weapon. Control may be the entity in some way, but now the process that Control utilizes to maintain its supremacy is an ever-widening and deepening inertia. And all the things that go under the myriad, umbrella or the banner of mass-culture are just ever-multiplied versions of emptiness. They simply distract the minds of the population from activity: fragmentation. And through that fragmentation you get paralysis. And that's why it does become a radical political act to champion the concept of choice again, and to say change in and of itself is radical. And choosing your narrative of the story you live becomes the most important thing you can ever do.

People are conceived in a womb and whilst they are still in the womb, people around the mother are discussing what name to give that person, and what they are going to be like, and what their expectations are of this person before they even become adult. And we all are to some degree guilty of that – myself included. And then you go on, and you give a name, and that name is already this hologram of all these expectations and demands and compromises that you are expected to accept without discussion. And that continues with the peer groups, with who you do and do not get to play with; where you go to school. Every single environment of people puts another layer of expectations, another layer of demands upon you – none of which you've chosen. It's not until you reach that stage you are describing as being like a teenager, the adolescent stage, when you even have the breathing space to say, "What? Who am I? Why am I here? Are these my parents? They don't feel like they're mine." They don't feel like it because they just molded you, and have these undiscussed demands that they've made, and expectations that they've put upon you, and you never had any choices. That's why, for me, it was such a powerful action to change my name legally. It was truly was a rejection of all those imprinted, conditioned preconceptions that were put upon me. And I was supposed to live and manifest for someone else, who I have not negotiated with. I made no negotiations at all with anyone in my life by the age of 18 now. They still haven't. I was supposed to then go to university and continue to be Neil, and then become an advertising executive or something. No one ever sat down with me and negotiated my rights to be something or someone different. So finally, reclaiming control for the first time of the story of your life is incredibly liberating. Also difficult, because no one gives you the tools to do it. Far from it; they try and hide or discourage whatever tools might help you decide or make choices as you wish to be. And if you want to be creative and you think that art in its widest sense and creativity and creation are some of the most wonderful gifts and explorations we're going to have, you're basically ridiculed. It's really seen as pretty much the cheapest and last option. However when you look at humans and their story, all the quantum leaps all the great applications of novelty and change have been made by artists and alternative thinkers. And yet to this day it is one of the least valued occupations. Meanwhile, museums are still revered. Basically dead thinkers are revered because they are out of the way and they can become copied or qualified. But I think one of the great tragedies of the 20th century was when artists began to collude in qualification. So there wasn't even clarity as to where inspiration began and trickery ended.

CA: Is that because there was merging and melting between planes? I mean PR, art, curatorship, gathering market qualifications? It's like there are no boundaries anymore; everything is just a blur. Celebrity is the currency, and entertainment is the language, but also it's *not* so clear-cut and distinct. Everything is fragmented into noise.

GBPO: Well, I had the good sense to stay away from cellphones. I find it disturbing, this idea of being available to people I may not even know, 24 hours a day. That's a form of slavery.

CA: It's good for the people who don't have integrity themselves. They panic when they can't be reached. Maybe a better slogan nowadays would be, "Turn off... tune in..."[3]

---

3 Reference to Timothy Leary's 1960s slogan "Turn on, tune in, drop out."

GBPO: Yeah, that's good, definitely I like, "turn off and drop out." We also talked before about privacy becoming the last taboo.

CA: Quietude is a prerequisite for a clear-minded thinking.

GBPO: I see what you mean: being accessible to normal people suggests that you're in demand. Which suggests that you have some sort of importance. And people have begun to measure whether or not they exist, their materiality, by whether or not people would want to contact them. Isn't that superficial?

No one has ever told me whether it is good for me to have millions and millions of phone conversations around me all the time. I don't want them talking to me. One of the most powerful political acts in America certainly breaches the turning off of a cell phone. Everything that always baffles me with that cell phone thing is how many people without questioning it, have decided to work longer hours for no extra pay by becoming available by cell phones all the time. And it doesn't seem to occur to them that it means that they're still at work while they shower; they're still at work in the evenings; they're still at work at the weekend, and no one is paying them anything extra. They think it makes them important; it gives them self esteem, but they're actually becoming slaves: non-paid workers. This always baffles me and amuses me that people are prepared to become advertising boards. It used to be the bums and the drunks and the homeless people who wore these sandwich boards with adverts on them, and that was a pathetic occupation to walk around with an advert on a board. And now people pay 300, 400 dollars for a pair of cheap shoes with somebody else's advert on them. They pay the companies to wear their adverts. What kind of craziness is that? To belong to a product, or to a group of people who have swallowed the fact that the commercial substance of this product is the best. The media obviously are controlled because what appears is disgusting. Over here certainly. Everything is just being swallowed without critical faculties.

Politicians have all these grand ideas, but they are not prepared to actually be honest about them. I would have a lot more respect for them if they did that. It's just salesmanship; they think that's a way to get ignorant people to vote for them. And they do it based on their belief that the people who vote are ignorant. And if only the people who are being thought of as ignorant would be insulted and refuse to play that game, everything would be a lot better.

CA: Concerning projects as reoccurring vehicles: the TG reunion[4] first didn't happen, but then it happened, and then happened again one more time.

---

4 In 2004, Throbbing Gristle decided to perform together again, for a few select festivals and venues.

GBPO: It's the re-re-re-TG. Originally we were being very purist about it. We especially said we didn't want to do it again. But we talked about it and came to a compromise solution really, in that there is a demand. There are lots of people who wish to see TG. Everybody is able to travel nowadays.

The TG thing's changed. The main difference is that with TG it hasn't got a future. It has a past but we are not trying to then create a new future. We have no interest in doing the whole band thing. It's really just a long farewell or a long resolution. But we're not intending in any way to record any more after the one that we already did; we're not intending to develop – it's already over. It just so happens that there are a few spasms left. At the beginning I was actually doing interviews in the context of TG. As time's gone by I've begun to withdraw and I do not want to be seen in that context anymore. That's gone. I don't mind it being a legacy – a respected legacy – but I don't really want to talk in that context. I prefer PTV3 or Thee Majesty or Breyer P-Orridge because to me those are still alive; they are not in the museum yet.

I'm fascinated with novelty and surprise, and there isn't really any left in TG. I guess I'm just really lucky that it seems that the media want to talk to me. There is a certain interest in what I'm thinking, which is fabulous; it's a responsibility but it's fantastic. It is exciting to think that we can get newspapers in Russia discussing very seriously the destruction of gender and the malleability of our identity and life as inherited, and all these phases they may never really have considered before.

That's what I always wanted: to try and create serious commentary about life. To me that's really what life is supposed to do. So I've simply arrived in this place where I can be that of which I dream. It's kind of nice! And I'm able to become the body that I dream. I too am learning the freedom of imagination in modern times. I feel very fortunate that I've lived long enough to experience all these procedures that were available to me.

CA: Do you ever feel that you have to go through these emotions, and dealing with concepts that you aren't familiar with simply because you know there's an audience that demands that or requests that? Do you feel the need of satisfying *their* needs?

GBPO: On the last PTV3 tour the journalists were told that they weren't allowed to even mention Throbbing Gristle.

CA: I was thinking more on the level of your commitment to such an extensive tour as PTV3 were just on. We talked shortly after the tour, and you were obviously so worn out that you became ill.

GBPO: That's my job. I think it has to be. I think a time is going to come when I have to just retreat to my books. I think it would be at the service of my own imagination. I'll try and record what I've been thinking about. So that'd be stuff from the last 30 or 40 years... I owe it to the world, whether or not they think it makes sense, to try and explain *why* Genesis P-Orridge was creative.

CA: The people who are perceptive enough will find your thoughts, whether it's during a concert or whether it's in a comic book or in another piece of writing or performance art or whatever. The process doesn't necessarily require you wearing yourself out on endless tours.

GBPO: But if anything that's just been a surprise: it is really fun playing on a tight rope. It's just really exciting and exhilarating to have this band that would just rock out and play for three hours and always be so hyper. It's a kind of organic creature that I haven't really experienced before. And that's interesting for me, to be immersed in that; it's fascinating. It's a good trigger to get new people to start to go look for the other things. A lot of really young people are hungry, and if that's the way to start looking for more nourishing information, then that's okay; I think I'm prepared to do that. I don't want to die for it though.

Russia was really interesting. There was this immense excitement and hunger for anything. It was all equal because they've never had a chance before to actually feel these things. It was the same with the media too. They were in a way almost naïve and vulnerable to my manipulation, because they were hungry to just have debates with people who haven't got the chance to access me.

I asked people, how do you know all of this stuff? How do you know about these weird and obscure things? And they said that sometimes one of them would get a visa and managed to get to Europe, or to England, and then they'd bring back records, tapes, books... And then they would have these meetings at different people's apartments; secret meetings where they had the new PTV album or the new TG album or somebody else. Then they would play them and then they would all make cassette tapes of it. They would sit down and work together on the translations of texts that I was writing, and made copies of those too. And they said that we'd be surprised how much the Utopian writings influenced the radicals who were really central to the disruption of the communist regime; that we were really important to their way of thinking. We represented certain types of radical libertarian thinking that inspired them. That was it. So, little did we know when we were doing all that stuff. You don't know who is listening. You don't know who is listening, or where it makes the most sense. That's why I like to use that scattered thing; just throw it everywhere and have faith that it's going to come to rest at some point.

It was a really humbling and inspiring experience to know that people could feel so reinforced by our privileged messages. You and I are very privileged with our education and access to all kinds of ideas and people that most Europeans wouldn't know of.

CA: Also, we never got stuck in stasis. I think that's the key: to just push a little bit further and see what happens. Most of the people I grew up with, or went to school with, they don't really exist anymore. I mean, not to me. They gave up along the way. What can you do? Keep on going.

GBPO: Keep on going, not surrendering. They've certainly tried to discourage me. They are not going to shut us up. You mentioned the "Great Beast"[5] at some point. As you know, I really like the Beast but I think we're more fabulous. We learned from what happened then, about how to integrate an ongoing evolution in our strategies. And not get sidetracked by pretension or celebrity or fame; to shrug that off, and to just keep going.

I often find myself doing the same thing, but slightly differently – like most artists do. It doesn't interest me, it doesn't get me excited. I have to feel excited. I get excited by something I didn't know before. By something I didn't feel before. And I'm not scared of that; I find that very appealing. But other people, as you said earlier, are afraid of new ideas. The trick is to see it all a bit like a roller-coaster. Some of it is slow, and it's just struggling up, and there is this plateau and this exhilaration, excitement, and then there's a thrilling dip. It's very much like that. But it would be awful just to be stuck at the top, and also at the bottom. It's the full range of emotions and experiences that make things worthwhile.

People are encouraged to remove any pain or any discomfort or any surprises and shock, and their thoughts are encouraged to desire similarity and familiarity. But I know how that's going to be already; how that feels. I want much more than that.

---

5 Reference to Aleister Crowley (1875-1947): British poet and occultist, whose philosophy of Thelema has been a source of inspiration for P-Orridge and Thee Temple Ov Psychick Youth.

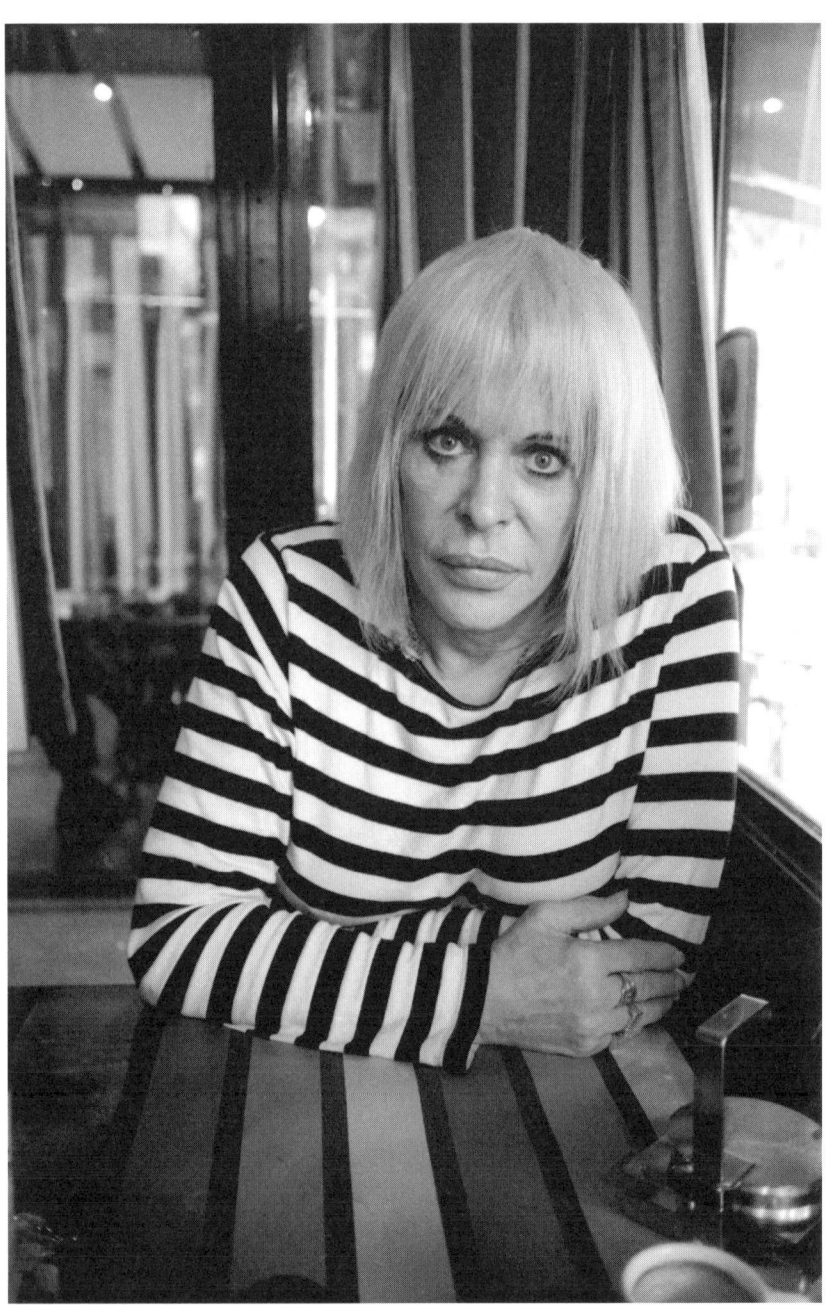

Paris, 2008

Paris, June 7th, 2008

On October 9th, 2007, Jackie "Lady Jaye" Breyer "dropped her body" in New York. This was shortly after her final concert with PTV3[1] (incidentally in Stockholm). This was of course an unfathomable loss to Genesis, who had not only lived and loved together with Lady Jaye since 1993, but had also in many ways merged with her.

CA: I think that it could be appropriate to start with a very negative thing that has happened since last we met: Jaye's passing. Is it even possible after these eight months to look back on such a long and fruitful relationship? What was Jaye's most important aspects for you and your work? What kind of catalyst was she?

GBPO: Jaye was very intuitive immediately, and on the very first day we met, that evening Terence Sellers[2] was planning to go out to a slave auction at a club. I never checked whether Terence realized there was a really strong chemistry between me and Lady Jaye, or Jaye decided to come along for some reason. But she basically took me under her wing and immediately started to put make-up on me and dress me in her clothes as a sort of androgynous boy-girl. Then we went to this amazing S&M club – very underground in a semi-derelict building – and needless to say I was thrilled to be standing next to this pretty, tall, very beautiful young woman. We were talking quietly to each other and basically saying how ridiculous the S&M scene was, and then I heard this growl and had to look down. All the time we had been talking she had had her heel on the back of a man's hand. He had crawled up without me noticing, and begged to be hurt by Jaye. I just thought it was so stylish; that without a word she'd been working him. I mean, grinding her heel into this guy's hand while we were just saying what a stupid place to be in, and maybe we should have stayed put? I just thought it was very classy.

The very first time that we went to her apartment, she immediately put me

---

1 During this tour, Lady Jaye was part of the band.
2 Terence Sellers (1952-2016): American author, dominatrix, and friend of P-Orridge's since the 1980s.

into a green velvet bodysuit and a leather mini skirt. She took me out, bought me these green leather goat boots that she loved, and then took me to a Tibetan shop in the East Village and bought all these solid silver and actual snake vertebra beads with bits of turquoise and started to weave them into my dreadlocks and make my face up... She instantly began to sort of manipulate our look; that we should become more like each other, and also to feminize me; instantly, from the first second she saw me. Which, when you only think about it with hindsight, is quite remarkable. Because she didn't know who I was at that point. All she knew was that there was this person staying with Terence who had done the collages for *The Correct Sadist*.[3] So in her mind I was just some English collage artist that knew Terence; that was it. She hadn't made the connection with TG or anything else. So this was pure intuition from nowhere. And we also started doing magic together pretty much straight away. Initially somewhat under the cover of using the dungeon as a location basically, but not using it in a traditional S&M way; we were beyond that.

We would be lighting candles and taking psychedelics and discussing things that we would like to have, and again she would be blending gender in terms of what we both were – right from the very beginning, too. She completely understood the idea of sensory deprivation in order to leave the body and retrieve information from other dimensions. When we talked about that early on, of course it became apparent that she'd been tremendously psychedelic from a very young age. Taking magic mushrooms at one point every day for months whilst working in the East Village, and also performing in the evenings. She actually used DMT more than Terence McKenna, and completely on her own, and had worked out how to control where she went by humming particular notes. Fearless, absolutely fearless in terms of psychedelic experiences. The idea of being afraid never even crossed her mind. She just wanted to explore.

So that was very exciting for me: to have someone like this powerful woman who is beautiful, and also very compassionate and caring; a professional dominatrix and a registered nurse. Very delicate in terms of looking after you and so on, and yet also powerful and able to have somebody grovel by just looking at them. We saw that many times. She would be somewhere and she would somehow in a room full of people know which person was the submissive, and she would do so and walk over and just put out a cigarette on his hand, and they would immediately follow like a puppy for the rest of the day. I mean, she was incredibly perceptive of people's psychology. I don't think I knew anyone who could hide something from her in terms of their true behaviour. Which is also a very inspiring quality. In many ways she had qualities far more developed,

---

3 Terence Sellers's most well-known book. The edition referred to here was published by TOPY-affiliated Temple Press in Brighton in 1989.

that I would have liked to have had, or I had been searching for within myself for many years. But she didn't contextualize them in the same way. To her, these were just how she was, and it was not really anybody else's business. She had no sense of self-congratulatory pride in her clearly exceptional skills, but she did nevertheless have skills that made her really remarkably adept. That humility is something that stays with me.

We did this song, "The Worm Waits Its Turn," for the last TG album. It is based on one of her poems; one of her stories actually. She'd been telling me this story that when she was about five or six years old she used to play at the railway line behind her house a lot, because the railway line and the cemetery were her playgrounds. One day she was wandering around the railway line, and she saw something in the distance that was glittering in white and she thought, "that looks really interesting; it looks like a giant of crystal or something." So she started to walk towards it, and as she got closer it wasn't just white and shiny; it seemed to be moving, like it was filled with atoms and it was just whirling, so she was even more fascinated and walked towards it a bit quicker. When she got close enough to see what it was, it was a dead dog that had been hit by a train and it was just all filled with maggots, and there was just this seething white blob. So in the various distances that she travelled towards it, her emotional responses and visual perceptions of it completely changed. But she wasn't horrified when she finally saw what it actually was. To her it was just yet another state of putrefaction of matter.

CA: That would be a very appropriate theme for a TG track.

GBPO: Absolutely. So we made that song. That was my solo track for the album "The Endless Knot."[4] She was able to pinpoint a story that would not only inspire me despite my reservation but would also be perfect. She said, "I don't care if I get credits or not; I did this with you." And that was the difference: this sophistication that she truly had, with no concerns about puerile things such as credit and the pretence of creativity. She was very much self-contained and confident in what she did. She didn't need any kind of recognition or reinforcement. That was very inspiring for me. It sort of liberated me from sometimes being vulnerable to other people's opinions. I just thought it was an amazingly advanced, wise position. And she was like that in everything, you know. From the very beginning.

There was another time when I came to New York, and I was going through this horrible divorce, which she knew about. I was really depressed, and without saying anything she just said, "just sit quietly don't worry about anything." Then without telling me she ran a bath and she went out and she got roses and

---

4 The album recorded by the temporarily re-united Throbbing Gristle in 2007.

she filled it with rose petals and scent and went and put candles around the tub. When everything was ready she just said, "come through," and then she undressed me as a beautiful sort of initiation ritual. Which it was, in a way. And then she just bathed me in the bath, and then she anointed me with oils, and then she brought both of us a pair of black silk Chinese pyjamas, and she put me into bed and just held me.

CA: During this period of grief that's lasted almost nine months now, can you find that when you go through this, and you're involved in this kind of emotion basically all of the time, that it has also on some level been creative for you?

GBPO: No. People keep saying it will get better every day, but it doesn't. It gets worse.

CA: You mentioned when we talked – I guess that was only about a week after she had passed – in an almost humorous way that she'd been around recently. I was curious about what exactly she was communicating... Was it like "keep up the good spirit," or was it something else? How did you interpret her?

GBPO: We actually talked about ways to signal each other, because both of us were obviously fascinated with other dimensions and states of reality. It was what we talked about all the time, really. So we sat down many times and thought about whichever of us goes first, how are we going to try and tell the other that we still exist in some form, and that we still have the personality of the Breyer P-Orridge pandrogyne, and that we are still coherent in terms of identity? Well, we could have special words like "rosebud," and that Orson Welles memetic thing, but that's just too easy to fudge. People would just say that "how do we know that you heard that? How do we know that it appeared in a letter?" Or whatever. It's a very vague and inconclusive means of communication; just as séances could be taken as subjective. So we thought about that a lot and decided there were certain things that would be more convincing. One of them had to be things that would be concrete; material objects; at the very least throw stuff around, but it should be things that were in some way significant to us. And the other was that there should always be witnesses. So there couldn't be any questions about what you thought had happened, but of course we know it was wishful thinking. There had to be other people there who preferably were sceptical. And these were the three things that we figured out to be most likely to be convincing.

On the day after the funeral there were at least six people there: Alice,[5] Caresse and Genesse, and others... We were sitting in the living room, by the kitchen, and

---

5 Alice Genese, bass player in PTV3.

we were sitting in a circle, and they were trying to get me to go to California with the girls for a month to adjust, and I was just refusing. At one point they nearly bullied me into saying yes. At the moment they nearly bullied me into saying yes I thought, "well, if I'm going to go away to California to be in some strange bedroom, I at least need a picture of me and Jaye together, which one should I take?" So I went into the bedroom where there's the kissing wall – the wall with all our kissing photos – and the one that jumped out was the one from Kathmandu when we were both wearing those red outfits; they were bright red cotton outfits and we had gold eye make up on us, and we were kissing in the garden of the hotel. And it was sort of with hindsight we realized how appropriate it was, because it was both of us wearing the red – it looked like one big red blob of a body with two heads kissing, which of course was a perfect pandrogyne.

It was in a frame, so we took it off the wall and took it through and then laid it flat like this, with the picture face down on the top of some 1960s orange and red plastic cupboards to one side of me. None of the windows were open, so there were no drafts from anywhere. And then I sat in an armchair, maybe six feet from there. I was saying that I want to stay here because I want to be near Jaye's spirit; that this is where she'll be. And somebody said, "how do you know that she's going to be here?" At that moment the photograph – we had laid it face down, flat, so it couldn't fall over – rose up from the cupboards and floated across slowly until it was in front of me and then turned over so the photo was now the top side just like that! Then it sank down to the floor in front of my feet. "I guess Jaye wants me to stay here with her spirit," we said. There were six people all saw this happen, and there was this deadly silence, and no one disagreed with me staying in the house after that. That's just one thing that happened.

That evening we realised that this event had included the three qualities we had agreed with Jaye would suggest strongly that the Other Half had communicated from beyond physical death as pure consciousness; that had succeeded in maintaining a state of fully individuated being. The event had witnesses; something physical took place by moving a solid picture frame; the event had special meaning to us – in this case we were pictured like an amorphous pandrogyne with our two heads kissing in the photograph and it was taken in Kathmandu, our special place.

Maybe two days later there was this woman, Miss Lucy. She's in her 50s, a local Latina woman that Jaye befriended because she was helping her with her pain management, and gave her nursing advice. They became good friends. Jaye must have heard of her through a mutual acquaintance. And so Miss Lucy started to come by a lot and really inevitably adored Jaye. So this particular day she came around to see me and said, "let's go to the diner." You know, get away from everyone. So she took me to the local diner and she got in first, in one of those booths, sat down, and I got in second and sat next to her. Then the waitress came and put a glass of water there for Lucy and one here for me, and then she put one there in front of Lucy. Lucy was saying, "I've been seeing Jaye a lot," and as she said it the glass moved. The waitress wasn't even touching it. It went across the table and off the other side on to the other chair. Miss Lucy just burst out laughing and said "Hi Jackie, how are you doing?" She said, "I told you she's around," and I replied "I know she's around."

PTV3 went away for the first tour since Jaye dropped her body, which was about three weeks ago. We just did five concerts and Ryan[6] – now nicknamed "Ryangelic" because he's such a good boy – looked after Big Boy,[7] by living in the apartment with him so he didn't have to change his routine. So he was there for ten days with Big Boy. He's very methodical and very organized, so every morning he would take Big Boy for a walk and then feed him breakfast and then make the bed, perfectly with the bed clothes pulled over the pillows just like in a hotel, and the day when we were due to come back he did exactly the same thing and then he went to work. Then he came back in the afternoon just to check that Big Boy was okay because my plane wouldn't land until about 9 o'clock. He went into the bedroom, which he had always kept locked with a padlock so Big Boy could not get in there while he was out. When we got home later, he said, "I'm so spooked, Gen, something really spooky happened." And I said, "what?" He told me a story about how he checked in the locked bedroom and looked. He had made the bed hotel style when he left that morning, with the bedclothes pulled up square and tucked tightly in, perfectly. But now the covers had been turned down on my side in a perfect triangle and two fluffy, rainbow striped bed socks he'd never seen before were now placed exactly parallel to each other in the triangular space below my pillow. And he just said, "I don't understand it, where the fuck did those socks come from? And how could that happen?" I told him that whenever I had to go away without Jaye, we had this whole routine about hotel rooms, where she would turn our bedclothes back exactly like that, making a triangle, with fresh sheets, including my favourite fluffy rainbow bedsocks placed the same exact way, to welcome me back home. And she'd say "Here's your best sexy hotel room," as she tucked me in bed. Nobody but Ryan had keys to my apartment so nobody could have come in and done, or known our routine! The fluffy socks had been in a drawer and Big Boy could not have picked a padlock or reached and opened the high up drawer.

Which was all very precise and specific and again fulfils our three criteria: a witness in Ryan that something happened, and it was material and significant to us. Amazing. Ryan was so genuinely freaked out that he took photographs as evidence.

---

6 Ryan Martin, P-Orridge's manager, and founder of the NYC based label Dais Records.
7 P-Orridge's dog at the time.

CA: What was the project that was imminent, if Jaye hadn't passed at this time? What were you working on?

GBPO: Well, we had reached the point where pandrogeny had become clearly about evolution – that there is this crossroads that the species has hit. Where the disconnect between technology and behaviour is so critical that the odds are incredibly high that the planet and the logistics and any other effect involved might only just reject us out of hand... As having failed to honour our place on the planet – through plague, through hunger, through war, through anything... That the planet will reject us as the clever rats that we are, and replace us eventually with some other form of life. Jaye and I, for our sins, our romantic sins, thought it would be really nice for the species to finally evolve and become a species to be proud of itself; one that's focused completely and utterly on physical and inter-dimensional evolution. So that was the biggest project of all, and our personal project was to find a way to be with each other after death and actually then become one entity made from two consciousnesses. Which is a thing that most people don't know about pandrogeny... That it actually started as a way to cheat death and bypass obliteration, and actually voluntarily be absorbed into each other.

CA: One could say that technically the project hasn't been aborted. It could still just go on.

GBPO: Exactly. She's even giving signals from the other half of the project to say it's viable. She is pretty remarkable. Which is not to say that it doesn't leave me physically lonely.

We were talking earlier about influences. You know that Jaye left home when she was 14, and ran away to Alphabet City, which in the early 80s was one of the most dangerous places in America – if not in the world! And lived there as a 14 year old cute girl in squats, which is immensely ridiculous, and put herself through nursing college at the same time as she was working at night in strange cabarets. Which means she hardly ever slept, and that in itself is an amazingly focused person. She became a nurse for two reasons: one was that when she was really young she was always in a hospital. She had a curvature of the spine so she had to wear a corset for two or three years, and that's one of the reasons she was so interested in corsets and bondage; she fetishised it rather than fought it. Allegedly, the very first word she ever spoke was "stockings." Isn't that amazing? Not "daddy" or "mummy," but... "stockings!" So anyway, that fascination she had with the human body that came from synthesising being sick as a young child and spending so much time ill, made her fascinated with the human body as a cheap suitcase, as she used to like to say, but also with the potential of biology. Her

189

favourite part of learning to be a nurse was the operating theatre. So that combination obviously had a significant effect and influence on the pathway of pandrogeny when we met and started to discuss ways to blend as an ultimate act of love – which is how it began. She inevitably saw it as a surgical, biological aspect as well as metaphysical one – all of that medical aspect came from her. People tend to assume that pandrogeny is something that's come from me, and that she kind of agreed to be part of. But in fact it's far more complex than that, which needed Lady Jaye to concretise, so she threw in her combination of medical fascination and knowledge and fearlessness, and took it to a level that I'd never have found otherwise. And who else would you imagine could sit with Genesis P-Orridge as he was before he was Genesis Breyer P-Orridge, and go YES to everything, "YES, LET'S DO IT!" Yes, let's jump off that cliff... Yes, let's meet in some other dimension, let's practice by taking ketamine 3000 times together – which is what we did. As you know, we were taking it huge numbers of times. We had a deal for about a year that whoever woke up first injected the other one before they even woke up. So we woke up high on ketamine, and usually having sex. You know, it was an incredibly intense alchemical exploration with no physical limits.

CA: Once you had started with the actual physical alterations, was it all good? In the sense that did you ever have second thoughts or doubts or even regrets once you were on the path?

GBPO: No, not once. It started out as a very romantic idea. We were just so madly in love and we were doing so many psychedelics that we'd become closer and closer deliberately. People often say, "oh god, I wish I could just be absorbed by you, I wish I didn't exist, I wish I would just subsume completely to you." It happens when you have a mutual orgasm; you both absorb into each other temporarily. When people have a baby and it's born of love, that's a pandrogyne because that's two people becoming one, which is something a lot of people miss. So the initial impetus was this massive romantic appetite for each other. To take the idea of total unconditional love to the "Nth" degree at all cost; even at the cost of sanity. We started to do that and explored so deeply with ritual and psychedelics, and just being with each other 24 hours a day, seven days a week; just constantly focusing on that... We started to look at the whole. First of all, as you know, she begun dressing me like her the minute we met, so we started to dress and buy two of everything and we were lucky that we had the same size shoes, so it wasn't as difficult as it might have been for other people. As we became more and more like twins we started to see the things that still irritated us in terms of not looking enough like each other; not feeling enough of the reflection of each other. That's when the surgical interventions began. We began with really tiny things. For instance, I had these two beauty marks tattooed here and had one

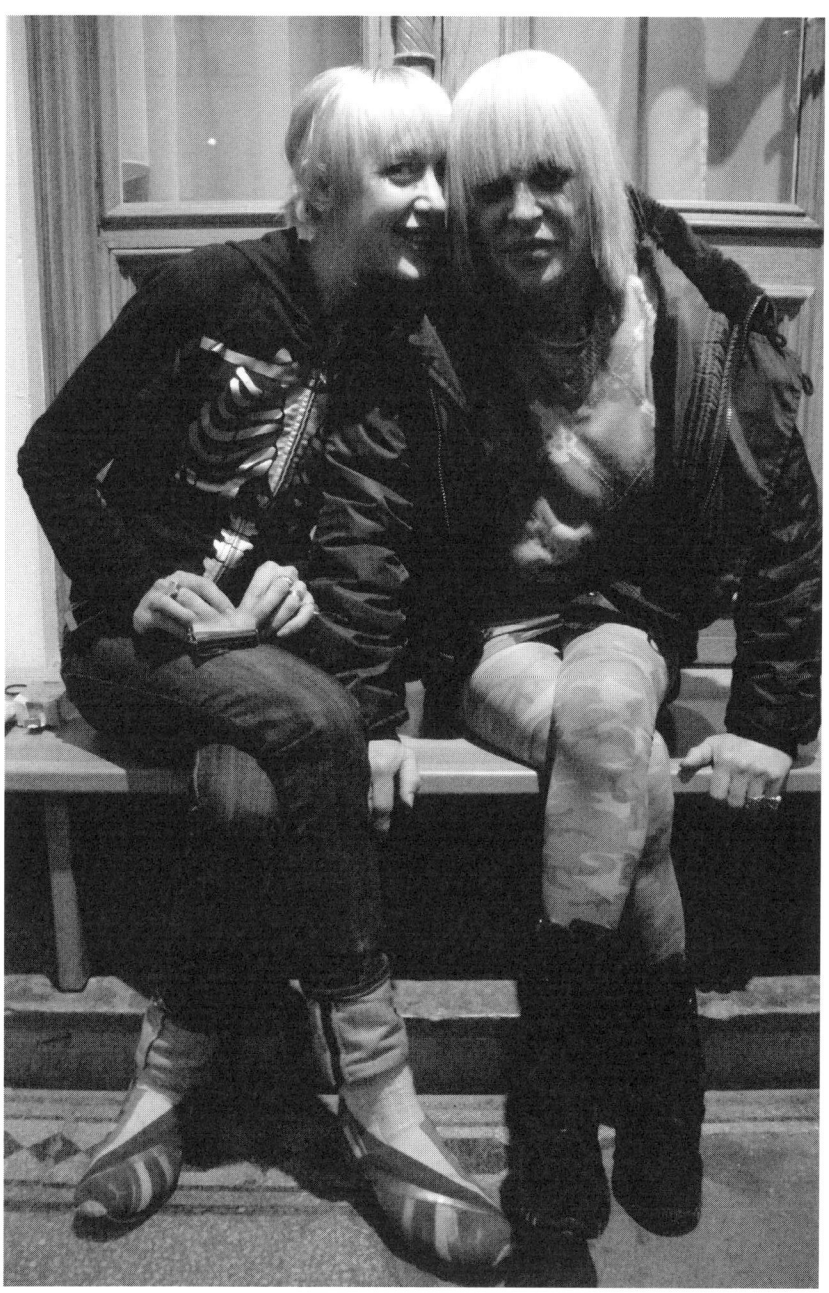

Breyer P-Orridge, Stockholm, September 30th, 2007.

taken off here, and that was the very first intervention that we did. Of course then we started doing our hair exactly the same, and our make up the same, and then Jaye would say, "I wish I had your nose, you've got such a pretty nose." I replied, "why don't you get one then?" So we went and found out; she got the nose and then she wanted the chin. And then we started talking about breasts because I was already wearing bras as a sort of symbolic statement of being pandrogynous. She was saying, "I used to have really nice breasts when we met and I'm not satisfied with the way they look now." I replied again, "so then, why don't you get what you want?" As I do – you know me – so we might as well do it then, right? That's my basic strategy for everything. And she said, "oh, alright then." So we went to see doctor Baker, a wonderful plastic surgeon, and sat and discussed Jaye getting breasts and how they would look and blah blah blah. We explained everything and then, just before we left the office, I blurted out, "and I want them too! But they have to be exactly the same size and same proportions because of this project that we are doing." And we explained all about pandrogeny and he went, "oh, okay, I can do that." Which was remarkable, because we've heard a lot of people that are more traditionally trans-gendered say that they had real problems getting breast implants, and had to see psychiatrists for three years and prove they'd lived as a woman for three years in society, and all these other restrictions. He just saw it for what it was, and thought it was wonderful. So it was a great art project, and very romantic, in that we were obviously sensible enough to know what we wanted. So that was that.

On Valentine's Day, February 14th, 2003, we both got to Doctor Baker's to get our breast implants together, and woke up next to each other in the recovery room holding hands. And grinned like hell to each other for a while – and from pain too, I assume; maybe that and from fun – because we were still coming off the anaesthetic. I looked down and said, "wow!" Because it is something quite radical to suddenly wake up with breasts. Especially when you're not trying to become a woman rather than a man, but when you're travelling a greater, much more conceptual path. So it was that as we looked down we turned towards Lady Jaye and blurted out with childlike glee, "These are our Angelic Bodies!" Which was yet another revelation that we had never considered before. It was a vital aspect of life to reconnect with our pure Angelic Being. So we started to look at this whole thing a Garden of Eden perspective and the Angelic Body. We quickly noticed that angels don't have belly buttons, because they are not biologically born.

We did research into the Garden of Eden and the *Book of Genesis,* and we discovered that all the original, extremely early paintings of the Garden of Eden represented God and Adam and Eve as hermaphrodites, and that that was the tradition for a long time until, of course, the Popes of the magnificent, infallible Holy Roman Empire started murdering all the pagan women, midwives and female healers as demonic, and destroying all the paintings of the original vision of that state of perfection – the divine perfection. Which inevitably had to be hermaphrodite because it had to be the best combination of everything. So obvious really, but it has been erased from our culture. So every time we found new bits of information they just reinforced our conclusions. What began as a love affair turned into something that was political and economic and spiritual and evolutionary and that needed to be addressed in terms of misguided and deliberate disassembling of the species imperative – which has to be the reclamation of divinity. There isn't anything else for human beings to be meant to do; no matter how they express that.

CA: Would you say that that insight in itself, and the concept as such, is a major motivation for you in your life now?

GBPO: Yes, absolutely.

CA: You must inevitably have been thinking about death a great deal since Jaye passed. Do you feel strong enough to carry on this project on your own – at least on this physical plane?

GBPO: She said that if I died first, she would just commit suicide because it wouldn't be worth being here without me. Because I was the only reason she stayed anyway. She had no addiction to being alive in and of itself. Knowledge was her only interest really, and evolution and exploration. But she was not in any way attached to the physical. Having seen that the human body is just a lump of meat that you can chop off and screw back together and stick bits of plastics in and inject in some... That it is just a piece of furniture that carries around the brain which has consciousness in it... She was absolutely enlightened in terms of that in a very sort of Buddhist way. Which was reinforced for her when she went to Nepal of course. You know how much she loved that... So yeah, she always said that she would just join me because she felt that would be the appropriate response, but the other way around. She said I had to stay because I had to write books. That it was my duty to finish the various books that we talked about before I could go and join her. She's given me my tasks, and the other reason of course is just to celebrate her, and make sure that people understand that her part in pandrogeny and Breyer P-Orridge and everything else that we do from here on is at the very least equal; in my opinion is actually more than equal. I feel that I have been learning from her far more than the other way around. Hopefully other people will gradually realize that through things like Marie's film,[8] and

---

8 "The Ballad Of Genesis and Lady Jaye," a documentary by French filmmaker Marie Losier, released in 2011.

your interviews, and things that I've been doing; they'll see that in fact she is one of the most remarkable human beings that's been around for a long time.

CA: Evolution doesn't only imply a direction that you're going somewhere – a trajectory – it also implies that you are coming from somewhere. In terms of the biology that you are trying to change, you're also coming from two specific parts – your parents. You've always been involved in fairly extreme expressions of art, culture and cultural engineering. What was the response from their side? Was it different when you started with pandrogeny than for instance when TG got a lot of bad press in the UK? How did your parents respond to this development?

GBPO: Well, my father is dead so we don't know what he knows yet. But my mother absolutely adored Jaye. She has many times said, "thank God you found the right person." She's never ever been critical of what we've been doing, but to her it all makes sense. Her basic explanation of things to people who are friends of hers now, is that, "they've always been ahead of their time." That's it. She said, "whatever they are doing now, people in 20 years will be doing the same thing." So based on her own observation, she's come to the conclusion that no matter how eccentric it seems somehow, Neil and Jaye know what they are doing and that's enough. She didn't lose a son; she gained two daughters and two sons – divine twins. So she's doing well; she's had her own epiphany.

CA: Has that actually been important for you, you think? To have that kind of support?

GBPO: Yeah, it's nice. It's nice to have that, definitely, and to see her feeling so self-confident. But then again, it's that classic thing that Jaye could do. She could just really inspire great love in people very quickly. And it was this innate generosity that she had, because she didn't give herself any specific value. And that was also from the work she used to do, which is the most difficult in a way. She was a paediatric nurse doing home visits for children that were chronically sick and incurable. Really chronically sick children, born with non-functioning brain and things like that, who to everybody else were just vegetables. But Jaye would work with them, and massage them, and talk to them, and sometimes get responses that didn't fit the medical diagnosis. The families that she took care of in that situation absolutely adored her. When she stopped doing that work to be more focused on our pandrogeny, they were ringing up all the time asking for advice and saying, "when you will be coming back," and "we really miss you, there's no one else like you," etc. She had a very remarkable effect on people. So for many people, there are anecdotes of some act of generosity that had changed their life for the better. And yet her archetype in our society is, "takes drugs, takes psychedelics, dominatrix, weird art, pandrogyne, very unorthodox." But her actual interaction with people was always very, very positive. I think it's one of those chicken and eggs situations: did the nurse come from the compassion or vice versa? It was a very important aspect of her personality. She really wanted to go back to university and become a doctor. That was one thing she was going to do for herself. But there you are... It didn't happen.

CA: Do you have any deterministic streaks, in the sense that you accept things because, "okay, this was something that was in a strange way meant to be. I may not understand it now but..." Brion Gysin often used the North African attitude of "Mekthoub." Meaning, everything has been written; this is the way it was written... Can find that way of thinking in yourself?

GBPO: I accept it, but not always willingly. There were some very strange things in that last week, very odd; the very last day was really strange. It was almost exactly like a mirror image of the very first day that we were together as lovers. So much so that we stayed up really late, as we did that time, and we made love in exactly the same positions, and at the same time that morning as when Chi-Chi Valenti snapped a Polaroid of us after we *first* made full love together at the Life Café in 1993. We made love together like we did that first time. It was like an out of body, out of time, out of mind, sensation re-experienced at the same time as that first morning. She had an incredible orgasm. Sometimes her body would freeze, her breathing would almost stop and she would have the weirdest enigmatic smile on her face. We would talk to her but she didn't respond. Didn't blink. As if she had died. We would sometimes panic and slap her body extremely hard. She still didn't blink. She was gone to what we call "Thee Absolute Elsewhere." After around seven minutes or so she would snap back into herself as if nothing at all had been strange, and carry on talking. It often scared me. We'd think she was dead. Maybe she was. But she experienced nothing odd, just a pure bliss without concerns of any kind. My experience was so intense we hadn't come yet. Suddenly she was back and she said with a beauty-filled giggle, "I'm just going to the bathroom to freshen up, then I'm going come back and suck you dry. What fabulous last words!

But she didn't come back. We must have drifted in half-sleep for a few minutes. When we woke up we immediately knew something had changed in the fabric of my current universe. Sheer terror gripped me. Something essential was missing from animate and inanimate surroundings. Everything was dead. Like when we once saw this world minus "god" on ketamine. She didn't come back. Life was stripped away.

But it was really specific – uncannily so – exactly like a film running backwards, and it was very much as if she had planned that day, in a very particular

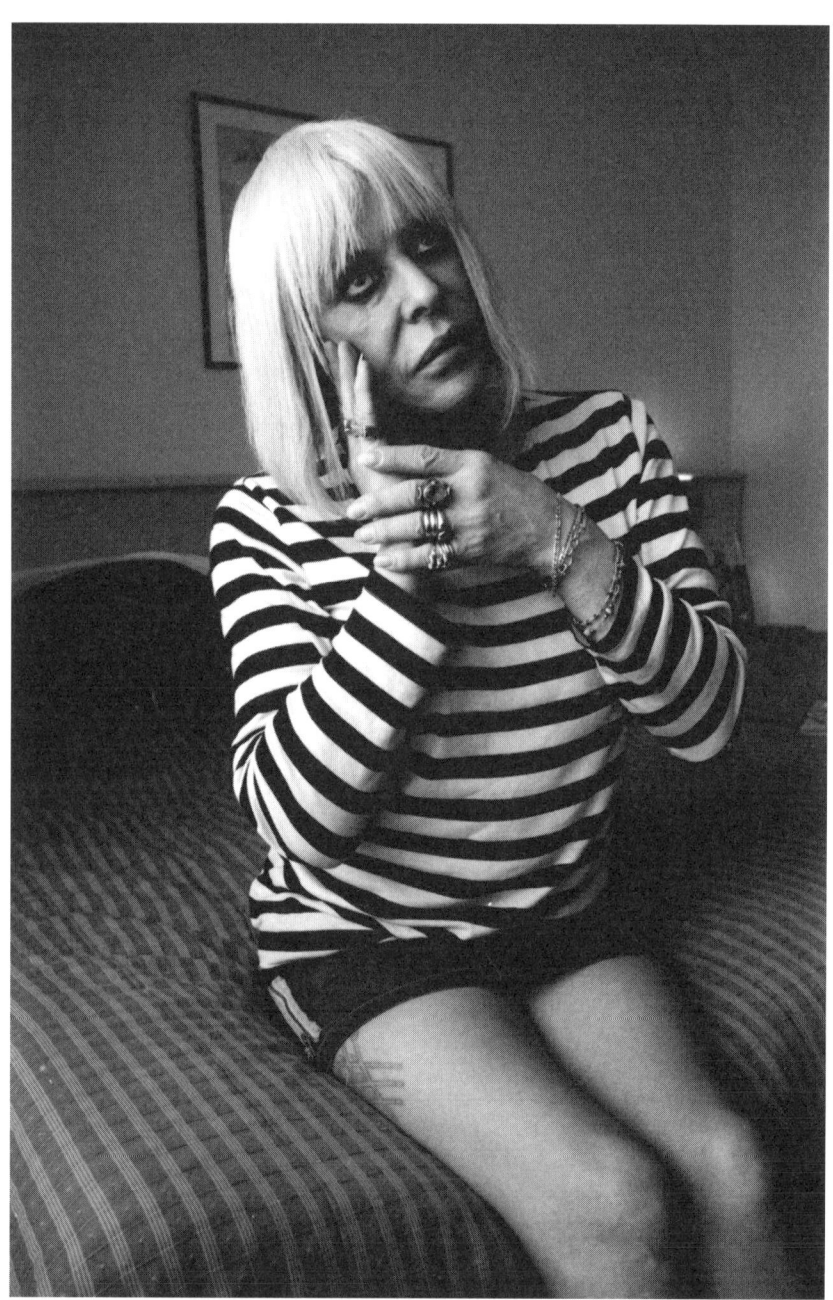

Paris, 2008

way. Some part of her knew, for sure. But there were other little things. Just before we went on tour a friend bought a lot of some kind of super 8 film that's not made any more. When he was mentioning to Jaye how he was he was excited to have found this film, she said to him – and he didn't tell me this until later – "You should save some of that for my funeral." And he did actually film some of her funeral. Isn't that weird? That was about eight weeks before. There are a few things like that.

CA: Maybe she couldn't articulate the feeling that she had; that something was wrong?

GBPO: So yeah, in that sense I guess, "Mekthoub."

CA: "Mekthoub" is certainly one way of dealing with the world; one way of looking at it...

GBPO: As long as you don't make it a form of laziness.

CA: You've always had a very collaborative creativity, whether it's working together with one person or several people in a band. With Jaye it became so incredibly intertwined. How do you cope with that void? Is it possible to in any way compensate?

GBPO: I read books to try and not have time to think. I read and watch TV until six in the morning. I have to wait until I'm exhausted to go to sleep. Because there's nothing in the day that wasn't part of what we did together. But we knew it was a risk; it was a voluntary risk.

CA: Is that in a sense why you continue quite actively to be involved in this kind of hectic lifestyle, with tours and events... Is it a form of therapy?

GBPO: No. Because there were six months when I didn't do anything. Sometimes I didn't go out of the house for weeks. This is just stuff that happens anyway, and of course the need to pay bills. Although we really like doing the poetry because that's more specifically about Jaye. With Psychic TV the light shows are still all about Jaye, so that's a way of maintaining that celebration and insisting that people understand that connection. When it's TG that's not there.

We didn't know when we met that Jaye was so involved in Yoruba, the Yoruba tradition, and that she was a sort of priestess; that was something that only came out later. So there were these amazing parallels in our lives. We were both really sick with asthma as children, and therefore very isolated from our peer group and bullied, and both skinny and both made fun of being skinny. The parallels were remarkable. One of us would mention an anecdote, and it would be uncanny that the other one had been through the same thing. The more we got to know each other the more that was true.

CA: In terms of the psychology of an artist – regardless of what kind of art the person is making – would you say that it's an over-simplification with the classical psychoanalytical theory that the artist is an unacknowledged child; albeit a creative one? A child that is unacknowledged and creates a compensatory creative drive?

GBPO: Possibly. I'm always happy to say that I'm infantile.

CA: The stronger expression you have as an artist, could it possibly have to do with that you have felt failed, neglected or unacknowledged?

GBPO: Well, my father was very much an absent father. Also the family, whilst they were happy to discuss politics and ideas and read books, didn't talk about feelings and emotions at all. We don't remember ever being cuddled by our father. Maybe kissed... I don't remember it, but maybe. We might have been terrified of him, and I remember being physically abused by my mother many times, like beaten up and thrown into doors and stuff. So yeah... possibly. Jaye was told from a very early age that she was an accident; they didn't really want her. Then she finally left home at around age 14. She'd escape from the house, just sneak out the window; just like in a classic teenage way and go off to a club and then come home right back through the window so that she was in bed when they got up. There was one particular moment when she was fast asleep, and she suddenly heard all this yelling and she felt wet, and she woke up from this deep sleep and there was her mother and her mother's best friend chanting an exorcism from the Catholic whatever; squirting holy water around her, exorcising some evil demons. The remains of that holy bottle with some water still in it are actually at the Shiva statue in the bedroom; she gave it to me as a gift. She just took it with her when she left home to remind her of why she left home.

CA: We all carry a lot of heavy baggage with us to some extent.

GBPO: Because my father moved in jobs I never had an ongoing group of friends. I had to be very independent. Jaye likewise didn't have any group of friends because she was sick, so she didn't get to know anybody when she went to school. She was a stranger and they made fun of her. She was never included in her peer group, so she was very much an outsider. But she did tell me that when she was very young, maybe five years old, that when she was really, really upset and alone and she would be hiding in the cemetery, and she would hear this very calm voice with an odd accent; it was a disembodied voice that *she* could hear, clearly telling her that she was going to be okay and the person from her future whose voice so reassured her was her spiritual protector. When she finally met me in the dungeon years later she realised it had been my voice speaking to her. So there was a weird time distortion.

That was something she discovered and then forgot again for several years. She told me that she remembered this voice, that she viewed as her protective angel, but was so shocked and taken aback by the precision of it crossing time, scared really, that she didn't tell me and tried to forget about it. Eventually, several years later, she said, "It was you, Gen. Thank you. It helped me survive." Apparently it helped a lot. When she told me she said she would always sit, sometimes with a picnic, at the grave of Harry Houdini in Glendale. Her family's house backed onto a railway and a huge cemetery.

CA: You mentioned yesterday that because we're in Paris now, you wanted to talk about how William S. Burroughs tried to intervene when you wanted to meet Brion Gysin.

GBPO: Yeah, because Paris to me is synonymous with Brion Gysin. Absolutely. I met Burroughs in 1971. When I went to London I stared sending him bits of my art, and he wrote me a postcard saying, "if you come to London, ring this number." So we became friends and he was very supportive from then on. But not long after we met and got to know each other, we kept noticing these references to Brion Gysin. "Who is this Brion Gysin guy? Tell me more about Brion…" And Burroughs was very reluctant to talk about Brion. He always tried not exactly to change the subject but it just wouldn't develop. It took years of asking him, "where is Brion and why can't I write to Brion? Why won't you let me have his address?" "But he's in Paris, he's not feeling very well," he replied. "Well, I can still send him something nice in the post you know." This went on and off for years.

In 1975 we started working on co-editing (with Colin Naylor) the big book *Contemporary Artists*. One of the conditions that I gave to the publisher was that I would only work on the book if they would guarantee that Brion Gysin and Pierre Molinier[9] were included; which they agreed to do. And that gave me my "in" with William. "I've got to have Brion's address because he's going to be in the book." And that's when he finally gave me the address. First of all there was the correspondence: "could you just answer all these questions, where were you

9 Pierre Moliner (1900-1976), a French artist working with explorations of gender, mainly in collage form.

born and blah blah blah" Brion's first letter back to me at the publisher, Macmillan's, started with the lines, "Even the CIA don't know this much about me, Genesis. Who are you?" But it was kind of light-hearted, and so outside that job we started writing to each other. At some point I said, "I'd love to come and meet you." And he said, "sure, just come on over." So I saved up a bit of money and went over to Paris, rang him up, got a taxi, went around to see where his place was at, and went up with the elevator to his door, his apartment, and there was a little note saying, "Genesis, gone out but back in 30 minutes," which we took a Polaroid photo of – and I still have some photos – and I said, "so typical that he's not in. Wonder if he's playing games like William?"

I went downstairs, had a coffee, and after 30 minutes he came back and spotted me. From then on I would go to Paris absolutely whenever I could afford the fare and stay either with Laurence Dupré who did the TG uniforms or at a cheap hotel, and every morning go to Brion's at eleven, after he'd done his colostomy bag. He'd make breakfast and peppermint tea, we'd sit down, and he always had a beautiful fresh flower arrangement... And I'd get my tape recorder out and we'd start to talk, and we'd talk till eleven o'clock at night. Sometimes he'd make a meal for us. At that time my favourite biscuits were Cadbury's Chocolate Fingers. And after that first week of going to see him every day for a week, from then on he always had at least two packets of Cadbury's Chocolate Fingers in his cupboard that he wouldn't let anyone else have. I thought that was so amazingly generous and thoughtful. "Those are Gen's biscuits, you can't have those!"

CA: Some of those conversations must have been used for the *RE/Search* issue on Throbbing Gristle, William S. Burroughs, and Brion Gysin.[10]

GBPO: Not much.

CA: So you must have a lot of material?

GBPO: Several hundred pages.

CA: Well, that's another interesting book.[11]

GBPO: But it would be a memento; it wouldn't be a biography or anything. Who he was to me. What it was like to me. My impressions. And of course that's an ongoing story because of the documentary film that was made, utilizing a lot of

---

10 *RE/Search* no 4/5, published in 1982 in San Francisco.
11 This eventually became the book *Brion Gysin: His Name Was Master*, Trapart Books, Stockholm, 2018.

our archives with Brion. It was just shown at a Documentary Film Festival in Toronto about two months ago. It took three years to finish. It was based on *Chapel of Extreme Experience*, about the Dreamachine, by John Geiger.[12] "Flicker – The Story of Brion Gysin and the Dreamachine" won Best Documentary of the Year. That was this year. For me, it was a really happy moment because we promised Brion in 1986 that we'd do everything we could to maintain people's awareness of the Dreamachine, and also of him and his influence and work as an artist and thinker, so that was a very special moment.

CA: Gysin was aware of the importance of being included in various contexts and collections; some of them frustratingly superficial. Right now, there's the massive "Traces de Sacré" exhibition at the Pompidou here in town, focussing on esoteric subjects in art, but you're not included. Do things like that concern you?

GBPO: We're aware of it, but it's not a particularly high priority because it's inevitable anyway. In terms of strategy it would be simpler sometimes for me if people were a little more honest about my place in things, and later on it would be the Breyer P-Orridge place. But perhaps that's why it's had to wait? You know, this is sort of the reconciliation of the threads that create the rope to hang yourself with. The Candy Factory exhibition was just ignored, even though it was the biggest opening in years. And those works, in a way, are the beginnings of the Breyer P-Orridge collaboration too, because the images are either by Jaye or of Jaye. So the art people are catching up. And those works are now part of the art market. So it's getting closer.

CA: I don't see that market as a negative or evil place at all; it's just what you do with it.

GBPO: As you know, the TATE has been making noises about wanting to purchase our archives for years, and earlier this year they even sent a woman over just to look at the archive. So she could go back and actually say what it looked like and how it felt, not just the list, but to get a much better picture of it. Since then we've not heard anything else, so they are very slow. But just the fact that they are sniffing around on that level, that's a huge shift in terms of what they are prepared to recognize.

CA: I think that started with *Wreckers of Civilization*; that sort of reintegration into a more highbrow sphere, or whatever you want to call it.

---

12 John Geiger, *Chapel of Extreme Experience*, Create Space, 2003.

GBPO: Perhaps, but they are also just trying to make sense of the 70s, because they've always obviously had this obsession with that decade, which to me is way overrated. But there was always a lot of performance art and actionist art, there were always mixed media or alternative media, but it was not gallery oriented; these were artists who were not trying to have careers, and were off making their living by being a photographer or a musician or something else. Gilbert and George also started out being very "non-object." So that whole era is being problematic in terms of how you integrate it into the art-historical story. But recently there have been three major exhibitions that have all made attempts to integrate the 70s into the story so... They are working on it.

CA: If someone asked me what you are in terms of art I would say that you're essentially a poet, but that your expressions take on many forms. That means that you are simply a very creative individual, but you have a collaborative psychology; you've often worked together with other people. Can you feel at times that the mere force of habit in having different bands or different projects can be stifling for you? That you would actually like to specifically write more? That you are more or less forced by habit to do all these things together with other people?

GBPO: Oh, not habit, but financial restraint. Jaye always wanted me to just focus on writing. And that's why she was so keen to encourage Thee Majesty after the fire in California. Strangely enough, or an "Of Course Factor" in "Jaye speak," that fire happened in Harry Houdini's old mansion in Laurel Canyon! But the sad thing of the economics of this world is that last month we were selling off some furniture just to pay the bills. So if we got offered a TG gig that would make me five times that amount in three days it would be ludicrous not to do that; it would be self-defeating. It's not because of habit.

CA: What makes you think that your writing couldn't be potentially equally as financially rewarding?

GBPO: My own experience. 58 years of writing for magazines and books and not getting paid, I guess. And also being deliberately marginalised by people who feel threatened by me in different ways. Whether threatened by the exposé of their derivativeness or threatened because the requirements of thought would have to be increased.

CA: I'm sure you've thought of this many times... You know what kind of books actually sell? Autobiographies. You've led a colourful life, to say the least; you've met a lot of interesting people. You could tell your own story.

GBPO: But that seems so egocentric. That's the truth: that's what blocks me. Jaye sent a message after she dropped her body. She said that's what I'm supposed to do. "Sell the house, get out of New York, write your book." And we actually will, because we had a vision many years ago, of waking up and having left this body; waking up on maybe just a slab in a morgue, and Lady Jaye stood at the end grinning, and the last words I spoke were, "did I finish the book?" And she said, "It's alright, I finished it for you." It is very possible that it's an accurate vision. So the sooner we get it done, the sooner I can be with Jaye.

CA: Let's drag out that process; let's go slow.

GBPO: Isn't that what you wished for? We are very interested to see if that's exactly what's going to happen.

CA: In a way this interview and project could be like a stepping stone that will put you on the market again, so to speak; as being someone who exists in a book.

GBPO: Books last longer than most things. If you look at the history of this species on this planet, it's remarkable how many books, manuscripts and myths are being preserved through writing, against all odds.

CA: I think your biography will be part of history; it's certainly colourful enough. I think they should do it like a comic book: a psychedelic manga thing.

GBPO: It would have to be very psychedelic. Me and Jaye on ketamine.

CA: Eternal science fiction.

GBPO: That was an amazing phase, that ketamine phase.

CA: I can imagine.

GBPO: Because it takes a lot of time to learn how to retrieve the information. But it was also that part that really reinforced the pandrogeny project, as a sort of necessary final phase.

CA: Is there is something that you would like to add to this specific session, regarding Paris, or anything having to do with your own experiences in Paris, or Gysin?

GBPO: Anthony Fawcett gave me a copy of *Black Sun*, the Harry Crosby[13] book, because he thought somehow that I was a very Harry Crosby figure, and that's how Caresse got her name: Crosby's wife's name was Caresse. So we came over here, having made a list of different places mentioned in Harry Crosby's diaries, to try and visit them all, and we brought a really heavy old portable video. He used to live in this apartment with Caresse Crosby, and in the mornings they would have a strawberries and champagne breakfast, and have various friends come around. They would all sit on this four-poster bed. So we thought we need to have a champagne and strawberry breakfast, and we went to look for the apartment, to see if it was still there. We found it, knocked on the door, and some little lady opened the door, and just behind her was her husband. It was actually Max Ernst and his wife!

That was a very specific moment. We asked, "is this Harry Crosby's apartment?" And they said, "yes, it was actually." I was staring at Max Ernst... "Wow, that's Max Ernst." They wouldn't let us in though. We were trying to get us in and film inside; they probably thought that we were crazy and insulting them because we didn't know better then. "Is this where Harry and Caresse used to fuck themselves stupid?" That was a funny moment.

Ian Curtis[14] and myself had been talking for a while about how alienated we were from the other members of our appointed bands. He felt completely and utterly isolated from the ones that became New Order. Monte[15] basically reinforced my position that Chris and Cosey and Sleazy were hoping that I'd die on stage. So they'd be on a gravy train forever... And basically Ian had the same feeling: that the others wanted him to die. So we cooked up a plan with Jean Pierre Turmel from the label Sordide Sentimentale, who had issued first the TG single, "We hate you little girls" / "Five knuckle Shuffle," and then the Joy Division single "Atmosphere," which was their first real form of the exploration of the more electronic keyboard sound. The idea was to do a joint gig, with Joy Division and Throbbing Gristle at La Palace, where a booker, Patrick, was really into that double bill. Jean-Pierre Turmel[16] would support it too, Rob Gretton[17] had agreed. Ian and I just left out the last "quitting to form a new band scenario." That was the main part, and then do a jam with "Sister Ray" with whoever in the two bands wanted to play. And at the end of that encore Ian and I would go back out and announce that he was quitting Joy Division and I was quitting Throbbing Gristle,

---

13 Harry Crosby (1898-1929), American poet and founder of Black Sun Press, which published many of the avant garde poets and writers of the day.
14 Ian Curtis (1956-1980), a British singer with the band Joy Division.
15 Monte Cazazza, American artist, instigator of the "industrial" music and arts scenes, and a long-time friend of Breyer P-Orridge's.
16 Jean-Pierre Turmel, director of the French label Sordide Sentimentale.
17 Rob Gretton, manager of Joy Division, and later of New Order.

and that we were going to form a band together. That was the plan. It was all set up. I'd be making secret trips to Paris and arranging this concert, making sure it could happen, and that it would only be announced at the last minute because it would be so packed.

Then this whole thing came of Tony Wilson[18] trying to insist that Joy Division go to America so that they could make more money, which always struck me as a stupid idea. Ian said absolutely categorically that he'd rather be dead than go to America. Meaning it quite literally. And no-one else realized that he meant it literally, except me, so he did kill himself, as we know. That's the only reason it didn't happen, which is a shame. I had a very strong feeling that it could have been a very interesting experiment, even if short-lived. And he wasn't a particularly sort of egocentric front person. Contrary to some peoples' opinions neither am I, so it could have been quite fascinating. We had already checked; our voices went together really well. I was the last person he spoke to. And he was saying, "I'm not going to go," because it was either the next day or the day after he was supposed to go to America. He said, "they think I'm going to go but I'm not going to fucking come, I'm going to kill myself." And he sang "Weeping" all the way through, which was the song I wrote after trying to kill myself.[19] So although we already knew it was his favourite song, the way he sang it had this particular feeling that made me realize that he was very serious.

We rang up some other people in Manchester who were connected to Joy Division and Factory and said, "someone has got to get inside Ian's house." You have to remember no-one had cell phones then. Not everybody even had a phone either. It was new that he had a phone, and people we did speak to just laughed and said, "he always says stuff like that, he doesn't mean it." And I said, "no, no he means it, he's going to kill himself, you've got to go and do something." Because I was in London, I was 300 miles away. And no-one would do anything. So he died. I'm still convinced that if someone had gone around he'd have got through it. It would have given him enough time to just say, "I'll just fucking leave and go and live with Annik,"[20] you know. She came a couple of times. She's become not exactly a good friend but a friend. That was a strange moment, wasn't it, in Brussels? We were playing with Peaches two years ago. Jaye came around and said there's someone I think you really would like to meet. I said, "who is it?" and then she said, "it's Annik." We just looked at each other, Annik and I, and we just started crying. But there is an example of Jaye's intuition. I mean, she just knew straight away exactly the right thing to do.

18 Tony Wilson (1950-2007), director and impressario of Factory Records.
19 "Weeping" is included on the Throbbing Gristle album "D.o.A. – The Third and Final Report."
20 Annik Honoré (1957-2014) was Ian Curtis's girlfriend during the last years of Curtis's life.

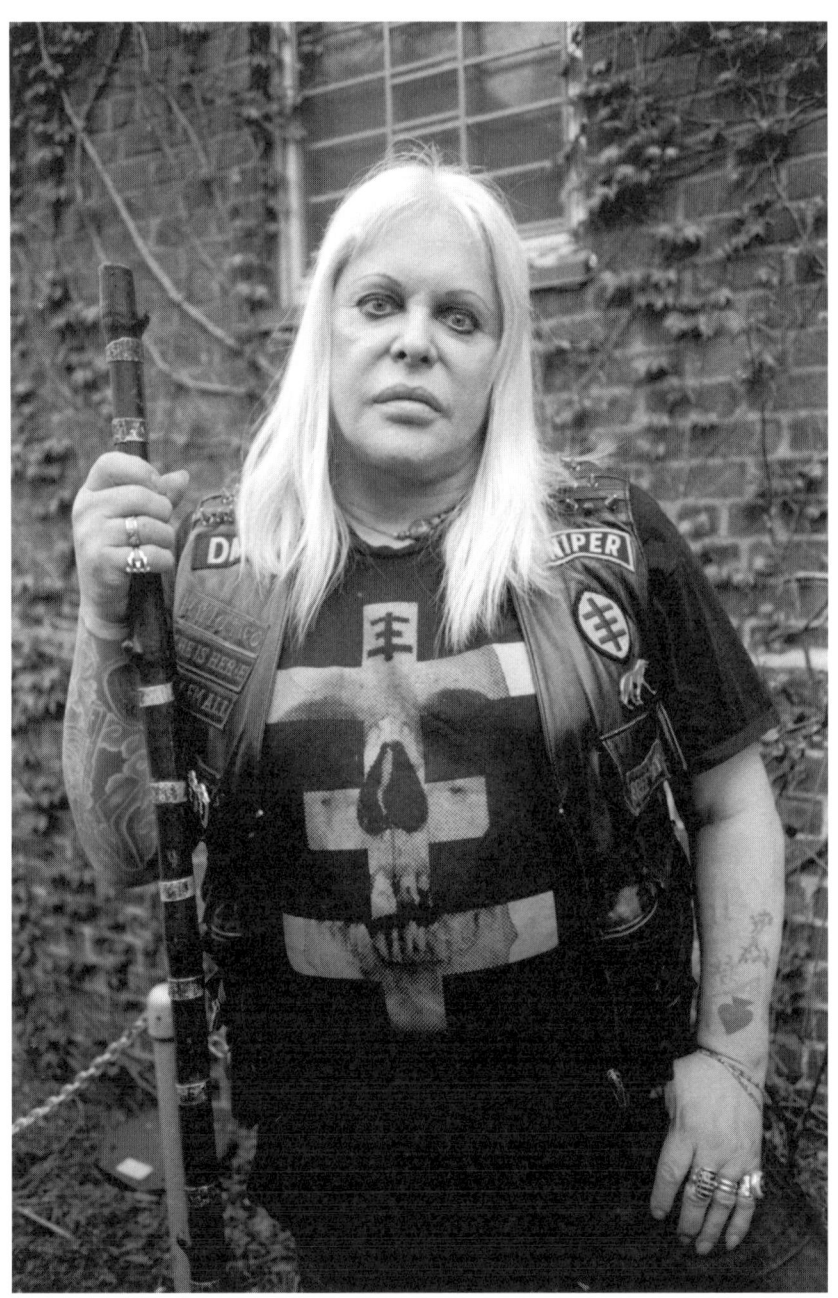

New York, 2012

New York, April 10th, 2012

The early 2010s saw an increase in presence on the New York art scene, as well as successes for PTV3. In 2011, French filmmaker Marie Losier made a film about Breyer P-Orridge and Pandrogeny called "The Ballad of Genesis & Lady Jaye" which created a new platform for discussions about the work – past, present and future.

CA: I think we have to take in consideration that there's an entirely new generation that is waking up to new and interesting things, and of course they haven't read all the interviews, they haven't seen all the interviews. Everything starts anew, afresh. Of all the things that you do or create, what you do the very best are the interviews.

GBPO: Used to be, but we are not so sure anymore. Lately we've been feeling inarticulate. It might just be from doing so many.

CA: Yes, I think so. Also, one can't always compare with oneself but has to compare with what's going on in general.

GBPO: It's a useful self-critical tool. That is always good. We did this lecture at MOMA about a year or so ago, and it was what they call "Modern Mondays." They get the most important contemporary artists to talk about their work, because on a Monday night in New York nothing much is going on; it's a quiet time. So they invited me to talk about C.O.U.M. Transmissions. It was really the first time we've actually given a lecture just on C.O.U.M. Ever!

CA: And in a nice context too.

GBPO: Beautiful theatre... So, I might be wrong, but there were maybe 500 seats in the theatre. Usually they get 60 people; 100 is incredible. The average is 30. Two days before we got to speak it was sold out, and they had 300 people on the waiting list for cancelled tickets. On the night we actually spoke there was this massive line of people hoping to get in. There were ticket scalpers outside, like for rock bands. People were selling tickets for sort of triple, quadruple the price to see somebody talk about art. It's unheard of. We were amazed as well. The woman who organized it told me afterwards that they had a real struggle to get the people at the top to agree to let me speak. They were like, "No one has heard of Genesis Breyer P-Orridge." Of course she was really pleased because they were staggered to think that someone could get that many people to come and listen to Avant-garde art from the 70s. As a test, before we actually really began talking, we showed one of the C.O.U.M. videos from 1974 – the one that we made at the Royal College of Art with Sleazy, and that in itself was a lecture in the media department. But instead of talking we did an actual performance video, and edited it with them, and we took the section of where we are sitting on the floor with long hair and makeup and beard, and we start to play with our trousers and eventually take off the trousers, and masturbating and sticking things in the bottle… So we showed that section first. We said, "Before we begin we want to show you this video, it's very rare…" After it finished five people left. And we said, "Everyone who is still here, if you have been able to cope with that, then you should be here." And after that, no-one else left... It was a nice test... So of all those people only five were outraged at watching me masturbating...

CA: I think you're absolutely right in being proud of having achieved something that is viable and worth something such a long time afterwards. Yet at the same time you do seem a bit surprised at the success of it! Isn't that a strange kind of a psychological dichotomy in a way? A paradox?

GBPO: Of course. Of course it's a paradox. We've been so used to being criticized and attacked for what we do. I mean even from childhood... One of my earliest childhood memories is of being punished for what somebody else did; maybe I was three years old, maybe less. My mother reminded me of this; I kind of re-member... We went out playing with the boy next door, messing around. It was raining in Manchester, so we played with puddles and made dams with the mud; we had a really great time. I went home, my mother was giving me dinner and there was a knock on the door; it's the mother of the boy next door, and she said, "Your son is a monster!" And my mother said, "What?!" And the woman was kind of going, "Neil got my little boy messing with mud and playing in it; you've completely ruined his clothes! Neil's ruined his clothes! Look! Look! Look at him! Look at his socks!" My mother said, "What's wrong with them? They look fine for a pair of grey socks." And the woman goes, "Yes, but they were white!"

That's how it all began. From then on we learned to deflect and box up and put aside attacks and criticism and negative opinions and blame and all the other things we'd been accused of. So that's become easy to deal with. As Jaye would say, "Fuck 'em all!" It's not fun; it used to hurt sometimes because we were very sincere all the time, but we learned to deal with it, psychologically. But we never learned to deal with praise, because we simply didn't get much. And when we did, it was from a small group of people who became sort of aware of what we were doing and why. They were similar people, a "tribe" – unrecognised but similar people. That's always been there, so when you struggle for 45 years in public to try and reveal things, and take risks, and be really stubborn about what you believe, it's still somewhat of a shock to suddenly have to be vindicated on such a level so fast. So yeah, it's still confusing. We don't ever want to relax our guard, because we know how fickle success, if you call it that, or appreciation, can be. Especially in the art world – it can be very fickle. Which is the norm? 44 years of being despised? Or one year of being vindicated and appreciated? It's hard to know. But we're glad.

CA: It can also become a trap, I guess? Being too successful or getting too much praise.

GBPO: Of course, which we're very aware of. So we try and remain within our chosen environment of people, friends, etc. And ignore as far as we can the value judgments that are going around. We do more exhibitions these days; we just did one recently. When it was opening night you couldn't get in, quite literally. It was so packed that we had people protecting the images on the walls because they were about to be knocked off, because people couldn't avoid pushing against the wall. And then there was a big huge crowd outside. People come in and they go, "look, it's fantastic! Oh, this is a brilliant exhibition!" But as Monte used to say, "don't send fan mail – send cheques." You know... "It's brilliant, but are you going to offer us a show in your gallery?! Are you going to put on something in your museum?! Are you going to buy something for your collection?!" There is still a big barrier there. Part of the barrier might be that the content is too radical, and part of it is probably their awareness that if they encourage us too much, what would we do next? Because we've been so difficult for so long; refusing to play the game. They know we're not going to play the game. It's on our terms, and that worries them. To what degree can they buy into this, in case we suddenly cause another great scandal or whatever, and they have to run away?

CA: But people *can* get away with really rough and radical stuff, as long as they are commodified artists, and accepted on the inside. I'm thinking specifically of Gilbert & George that we talked about before.

GBPO: Or Damien Hirst... That's a good point.

CA: Although I can understand it can be frustrating in terms of the outer re-

sponse, your radical stance is also something that proves that you're right in terms of protecting your own integrity.

GBPO: Definitely. The most satisfying part for us is still not so much our Breyer P-Orridge success or whatever it might be, or the change in attitude towards what we've always said, which is to try and push that door open, and if we can get the door opened a little bit, then we are happy to be the wedge to let lots of other people through. That is also something that we think we're aware of. That it doesn't stop with this. That we just try and blow a hole in the atrophy of the art world, and actually in most of the creative worlds; in culture in general. So when you have a reputation as a sort of cultural anarchist, and it's deserved, there is always going to be a little nervousness until people can decide how to explain you. What is happening at the moment is probably a transition into the realisation and affirmation of us being truly serious. Not just sensational and difficult, but actually proposing really serious ideas. And that is beginning to come together. Because despite saying, "when are you're going to buy things?" and so on, some people actually have bought stuff. Somebody bought "Snowflakes," which is a big 7x5 ft. plexi piece with myself and Lady Jaye, both of us naked except in silver slippers from Chinatown; it's sort of like a spiral, a DNA spiral, in the blue sky with clouds; it's beautiful. Apparently, it now resides in this very rich collector's penthouse in between a de Kooning and a Warhol. I just thought, "oh, that's just so fucking cool!" Let's be honest, we got a buzz from that. The woman who is very high up, if not in charge, at Christie's in New York bought "Mum and Dad."[1] In fact, several collectors tried to buy it, because they'd become aware of that being a key piece.

The first important exhibition was "30 Years Of Being Cut Up"[2] That was interesting because it was the first time that a serious art world, the New York art world, had seen that there was a continuity in my work; in fact we had been making collages for 30 years. And that they were high quality, and that there was definitely a methodology, and there are ideas and attitudes in them; they weren't just decorative, they weren't just fashionable. At any given time, they were very individual. That really made a big difference.

CA: A lot of the visual stuff has been subservient to record covers; it's been sort of underneath the musical stuff or the musical items.

---

1 "Mum and Dad", by Genesis P-Orridge, 1971. A seminal GPO artwork displaying a meticulous collage attitude, a surrealist approach, and a very early signaling of ideas about gender and (gender) perception.
2 An exhibition of P-Orridge's collages and magical sigils at Invisible Exports in New York in 2009.

GBPO: That was actually a hard one for me, because as you know, collages were my secret pleasure. We had quite a psychological issue with making them public domain. Because it was taking away one of the only things we had that was just ours. That certainly has a value in itself. The financial value as well. We never ever made them for that reason. They were made purely and simply for the pleasure of making them.

CA: And let's not forget, they also very much integrated your magical language in the terms of the sigilising.

GBPO: That's an interesting point. Because the ones that were almost impossible to sell were actually the sigils. People were finding it really hard to understand what they were, when they don't know about Austin Spare. Most of them don't know anything about Crowley except that he was a bad man. So there is a complete confusion of information in terms of the references within the magical pieces.

CA: When there is something else there than the mere aesthetics, you can subconsciously feel it somehow. I think that scares people a little bit. That it's not just art for art's sake.

GBPO: Right. It's functional. And also, the aesthetic considerations are completely different. It has nothing to do with what looks right, or what goes with what, or anything else. It's about the content. It's totally about content and function. The thing that sort of disappointed me was that they couldn't see that those are the closest to the origins of art. You go back to prehistoric times, and paintings in the caves are not for decorations to make their home look nice; they are to help make hunting successful, to make sure the sun comes back after the winter, and to in some way encapsulate the story of the people. That goes on to that Tibetan mandalas are made in coloured sand; also native American sand paintings. They were made and then destroyed. I mean, that is so alien to the art world. There is no profit. Which is why we have always been really attracted to the Tibetan idea. You make something incredibly beautiful for a particular reason, for a particular period of time, and on a particular date, and then it's not usable any more because it's done... It's like you make a machine to drill a hole and when the hole is drilled you don't need to keep drilling the hole.

CA: Here we come to something that I've intended to ask you, because many of your projects are also long term projects. Have you ever felt that maybe the best thing is to make a burst and then just leave it? I'm thinking of the sort of original TG burst that again resurfaced, and resurfaced and resurfaced, and actually created a lot of problems for you instead of whatever it was that you were after originally. Do you feel that the long term projects are almost as "albatrosses" once in a while?

GBPO: No, because we've always worked from the position of the day that we are dying. Everything we've always done has been based on looking back from death... And feeling justified, and satisfied, and as far as it's possible, that we'd been sincere all the way through. It's the Sufi idea that you make things and you live each day as if it's the last day, and that day is the one you'd be judged on. We work like that with everything we do. That we make it to the best of our possibilities with what we have available in terms of resources. And then we let go of it. Because that's the day, if you like, that was the conceptual death. It's done. Which is why we can let go of projects so easily. Because it's not about attachment; it's about making things happen. And then it's gone. Or is a kind of documentation of the process. It's a very different approach than trying to make an object to be revered and seen to be valuable. So when we look back, what we'd like to be able to say is that we did build a community; all the rest is just to try and make that practical, when we're trying to set up a community that will be very different in terms of its value systems to the social structures that we live within. An alternative community, with some kind of glue; that glue would be creativity and some basic perceptions about how life is.

CA: I think that sort of answered the question, but I don't know... It was this thing that we were talking about: the mandala aspect of creating something for a specific purpose and then wham, it's gone! But in some cases, when the mandalas strangely resurface, and when that sometimes creates more problems for you, perhaps on a personal level... Perhaps the original idea even gets lost when it resurfaces and takes on new shape?

GBPO: That's true. In that sense, TG is a very good example. As you know, whatever anyone else says, in 1981 it was actually me that decided to quit TG. Because we could see, and the others could see it too. I spoke first but there was no disagreement. We could see that we had reached a point where we were being accepted, and the only way it could go was to "be TG" and have this reputation. Basically, to just become another band. Because of that popularity, you get casual observers – people who just go for the sensory excitement, or because it is hip and cool. But they are not actually attached to the ideas and the concepts; they are merely enjoying the moment. Which is fine. But if that overwhelms the intent, then you can lose the value of the intent. As time goes by, it can become swamped by becoming so ordinary. When TG regrouped there was a lot of discussion about how it could work and not damage the legacy. Because TG had, for better or worse, become mythological. The value of being mythological is so immense in terms of cultural engineering that anything that damages that is tragic and could really make the whole pack of cards start to shake – if not fall down.

CA: I think the TG myth will stay pristine, and that example of the C.O.U.M. lecture shows that the myth, the early myth, is pretty solid. People are undoubtedly interested in what Genesis P-Orridge created.

GBPO: We hope so, because there is a *débâcle*. And again, as you know, it was triggered simply by me saying, "hang on, we need to talk about this." In response to the idea of becoming four laptops and turning up to a concert and there's three laptops and the proposal is no more songs, no more guitars, no more violins... In other words: no more Gen. That's a very different thing, and that can definitely damage the myth. Because then the idea that this was a unified radical band with four people against the world starts to fall apart. For example, we were really shocked, probably around 2008. Early on in the regrouping, we were doing an interview and the journalist asked, "Can you each say what you expected?" or "What drove you to make TG?" And to my surprise all three went, "to make really good music." I was really puzzled by that. What happened to, "to change the world?" And propose new ideas, and change the structure of what people imagined music was? Breaking down preconceptions, breaking down habitual patterns, and using that as a reflection to change the world outside. It was very confusing because the only motive we could think of, for them, was to be accepted. And we don't need to be accepted. TG is accepted on such a deep level – as we said: a mythological level – that there is no need to pander or compromise anything. Maybe making nice music is not pandering... Who knows? But to me that wasn't TG, and whether everybody else wants to accept it or not, we believe that the theoretical part of TG was Monte Cazazza, myself and then later Sleazy. And now Sleazy is dead. We've been sort of thrown in jail in a sense. The other two people are in a sense trying to appropriate the mythological aspect of TG, and then trying to stitch it onto their own project. And turn their own project into appearing to be TG. Without saying that. And so there is this sort of underlying conflict that is irresolvable, in terms of ideas. And that could, in my opinion, really damage TG.

CA: It isn't the same thing though, and it never could be.

GBPO: I'm not worried. We've let go of it. We don't even play TG; we don't want anything to do with TG; we took the patch off our jacket, because at the moment, what is being presented is the residue of TG. It's disappointing and misleading, at best. We don't want anything to do with that. It's not TG.

CA: Is it possible to pinpoint in your life today what actually triggers a creative impulse?

GBPO: That's a really good question. Emotionally, we really do care about TG. We know that Cosey will disagree, but I came up with the name and the idea; she never even wanted to play music while we were together. And Chris came along later, and he was invited in. Sleazy was always interested in the set. But the concept, and the strategies especially of making TG what it was, were coming from myself, and later from myself and Sleazy. Then of course, once it glued together, all of us... But the origin of it was basically myself. And Monte Cazazza. Monte really should get much more credit, because there wouldn't be TG without Monte. When he was living with me those were six months of bouncing ideas back and forth. "How can we do this? How can we create something that really fucks music? And strips it away and says it's a whole new way of doing this?" It was these long dialogues which are relevant to the question you asked.

My first proposal is to Monte. "Something is wrong with the state of music." And then he'd try and look and say, "*What* is it that's wrong? *What* is it that isn't satisfying? *What* is not happening that should be? What did music do that we enjoyed or found positive?" If we're useful in terms of cultural engineering, we isolate the pros and the cons of your idea of perfect music, and then you see if there is a way... The first thing that comes to mind is, "what resources do we have? What are we capable of?" And then you think, "okay, we're not trained in art, we haven't been to art college, but we can assemble things through a series of cut-ups right now in a way that we feel is effective." Or in music... "We can't play, so let's make music where it's not necessary, and find a new way to create this."

That is one way it starts, but really deep down for me most of them start with a long process of thinking. And that goes right back to being eight years old or so. And the other part which is really important is inevitability. We observe the culture. And in a sense we are incredibly ordinary. That is part of the system. Because it is either very arrogant or it's very humble the way it works. Which is that we assume if we are feeling that way about music, art, literature, whatever, then probably a lot of other people are, too. We are like a lot of other people. So if we think that makes sense and looks exciting, we assume other people will too. That is always there. Either the world has to agree with me or it already does.

CA: That point of view has proven to be very right over the decades, because TG, as a phenomenon, was a very unlikely success. I'm not talking specifically about sales, but about the response you've received. The same goes for TOPY and C.O.U.M.; a lot of the things that you've been involved in have caught on, and it's not because you're a great musician, but because of the fact that it is very right time-wise. It's always happening at the right moment.

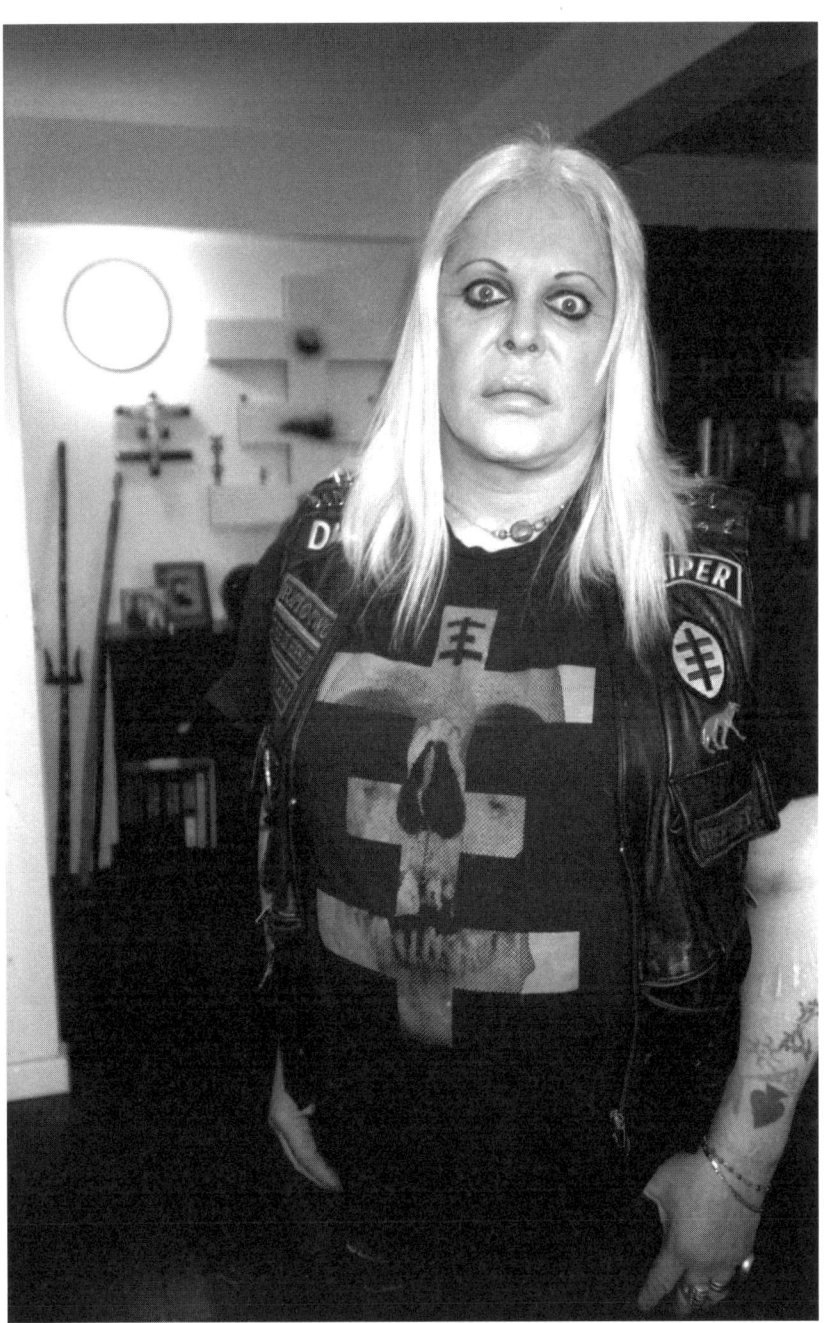

New York, 2012

GBPO: Well, that's simply by watching the culture. However that happens, my entire metabolism acts, not like an aerial exactly, but like it is plugged in to the actual core of culture. And we can feel the vibration... That's a horrible word, but we can feel the shifts and the sort of circle of changes that are happening, and we can sense attitudes, dissonances, all these different things. And we start to hone in on an aspect of the culture that seems to be in a state of turmoil or flexibility or mutability. A really good example is the pandrogyne. We were going through diaries and things last year, and it turned out we find the word "pandrogyne" in one of them from about the late 80s. And so the word was there, floating around but it wasn't the right moment. It was there, and it was put in the box of the future. Future, we'll come back to this one! And there it was. Within everything we've done, was the shifting between male and female stereotypes. In C.O.U.M., we had the orange and blue which was basically male in orange, and the woman in blue, and gradually shifting until they wore each others' clothes, and that's the actual piece. So, we feel that there is something to look at in this particular instance. As you know, myself and Lady Jaye had intuitively and instinctively started to mirror each other. The next step is to think about why this is so satisfying; on a plane outside just our personal relationship. Does this have any relevance? Because most people, no matter how much they don't think so, are actually responding to, and are affected by, the environment outside. What's going on in the media especially. So we started to think about just anything that sort of felt relevant to the way we were exploring our lives together. And one of the things that cropped up was probably through Bryin Dall,[3] because he used to do all the sex ads at the back of *The Village Voice*. He worked for a company that would put all the adverts in for massages and personal services. When we first came to New York in 1996, the sex ads at the back of *The Village Voice* were almost entirely biological women giving services to heterosexual men. And there was a small section of gay men for gay men. As we stayed in New York we noticed that a shift had happened, and that the majority of adverts for heterosexual men were now transsexuals: "she-males." That is really a fascinating shift, because these are the same heterosexual men who are now knowingly comfortable with having sex with hermaphrodites, hermaphrodite-like beings; pandrogynes if you like; unawakened pandrogynes. Because pandrogyne is a way of thinking, a consciousness. That's a huge social phenomenon. It baffles me it's not being remarked upon more. It's a massive psychological shift in the society.

Parallel to that was the talk shows. People come on there with things like "I slept with my boyfriend's daughter." So suddenly it's okay to have people on these shows. We had goths first, and then piercing and tattooing; that was the first

---

3 Bryin Dall, an American artist and friend of P-Orridge's. They have worked together in the band/ project Thee Majesty, from 1998 and onwards.

stage, and then the trannies. And so bit by bit, the redneck population of America are being inoculated against prejudice; they are actually getting more comfortable with, or at least more used to seeing, these alternative lifestyles. Once upon a time they would have just killed those people, on sight. Some of them still would, but the fact that they are more tolerable and acceptable is another huge shift. Especially in a country as bigoted as the United States. I mean this is a country where black people only got the vote a short time ago. Unbelievable...

We saw the fact that these people were on TV; their characters were used in films. There was the shift, quite clear shift, in terms of acceptability and visibility. That seemed significant to us. Lady Jaye was a nurse, and her fascination with the human body, and its limitations, and its ability to accept physical change and stress and recuperate, etc... All of that really interested her. She always saw the human body as an almost mechanical, biological machine. Which is why she was a nurse as well as a dominatrix. Those were the two areas in which she was both equipped and able to explore her fascination with the human body, and its malleability; both physically and mentally. Also the limits and people's different ways of perceiving their body; that the imagination, combined with sexuality, could reveal and explore untold of variations that go completely against people's normal acceptability of what's acceptable. All of those things, if you like, emphasize and illuminate this topic. Primarily its focus is *identity*, which includes gender roles, people's sexuality, malleability of roles and body presentation; genetic engineering even comes in because of the human body's cells programming... and cosmetic surgery and body modification.

We noticed that not that long ago, Hollywood stars and famous people would deny having ever had any plastic surgery. But that changed. That certainly almost became fashionable to boast about. And then you get Pamela Anderson appearing on TV, and becoming a massive media star; at the same time the men are having sex with she-males, TV is letting people be on television in roles and on talk shows. So all of those were combining at once. We found that had a relationship with what we were thinking or feeling.

When we're starting on a project, all those facets are part of the decision to then say, "What can we do with this? What does it mean? Why are we curious? Why does it seem potent? And what does it imply about the unfolding of society?" Because the ultimate point of everything for us is, "are human beings even capable of behavioural change?" And that is why we got interested in ritual and magic as well; one of the main reasons. And why we were so fascinated with the cut-up. All of those signals that we were getting, combined with the tools we already had, which are thinking, cut-ups, ritual... We decided to start really, really exploring this one. And of course there is also a personal, if you like, micro-reason, which is we wanted to extend ourselves as far as we could. That's our nature.

That's why we were such a perfect couple, because Jaye was fearless; more fearless than me. We both had the attitude that we summed up as, "see a cliff – jump off." So for once, we didn't have to pull anyone along and explain what we were thinking and why; we had someone who was bouncing equally enthusiastically... "What about this? What about that? Let's just do it!" So we had this amazing amplification together with Lady Jaye that we've never had before. We decided that if we're going to do this, we're going to have to think it through very deeply, because the psychological implications were vague at that point. And at that time we met Timothy Wyllie[4] and that's where the wild card comes in so. There's always a wild card as well. And those are the chaos things. So Timothy Wyllie turns up and says, "you both should really try ketamine." And we're not talking about sniffing it; we're talking about pure ketamine injected in the muscle... We were both very dubious about this, you know. However, Lady Jaye was a very experienced psychonaut. Another reason ours was such a perfect union was her motivation for using psychedelics. It was the same as mine, which was to try and find ways to travel outside what we call "non-census reality," and not just leave linear space-time, but be able to retrieve the information in an intelligible way – documented. Because most people will know that when you take acid and other strong psychedelics you can write an entire notebook of stuff and the next day you're all, "this is gibberish..." The best one in the world? Even though these were at the time of the experience the revelations that explained everything... And then you look, and it goes... "tea pot?" So the hardest part of that process is absolutely the retrieval. Magical ritual was a really good foundation in this sense. And we have used psychedelics in contexts of magical ritual with success. So Timothy said to us, "you should try ketamine." Because we'd been discussing psychedelics and travelling that way. And then he said something really important, which was, "You've got to do it 300 times before you get it." Very enigmatic... Also, it initially sounded like, "I've got bigger muscles than you... I can do 300 of this!" But for whatever reason it lodged in our minds that we should take that statement really seriously, so we decided to do just that. We started to use ketamine every single day. And Timothy was totally right. After around 300 times we certainly found we could be really gone and still speak to each other, and even tape record or write down things, often also to make sigils. We made a lot of sigils that way. We used Polaroid cameras; we had every possible way of recording. Before we began, sometimes we did it within the context of TOPY style rituals: a blend of the dungeon and magic. That's the way we've always done it. What was interesting was that Timothy worked with John Lilly for a while – the person that Ken Russell's film "Altered States" is based on – and Lilly did all the research

---

4 Timothy Wyllie (1940-2017), a British architect and designer who was involved in The Process Church of the Final Judgement and became an advocate of higher states of consciousness and communications.

on dolphin language and intelligence, and he did ketamine every day, for years, and eventually started to become a cross-dresser. Timothy told us that John Lilly got into having a female persona and cross-dressing. And then actually started to try and grow breasts by inserting foam rubber under his pecs to try and make it look more like breasts. But of course that was unsuccessful and made a big mess. But the important part was that he became male/female. Timothy Wyllie also developed a female persona, Georgia, that still continues to this day. The more we did ketamine, the more my female persona came through as well until it became a matter of some urgency for both of us to become more hermaphroditic. We became convinced that all this evidence was pointing towards that this was the time to really investigate the pandrogyne.

CA: Do you think there is a reason why certain chemicals pop up in our culture at certain given times or phases? Like LSD showing up in the very midst of the second World War, and the development of the atomic bomb... And ketamine showing up when we obviously need this kind of extra super- or supra-communication; when human beings are really thrashing the planet.

GBPO: We've thought about that. I mean, it dawned on us, as obviously it did with you, that the splitting of the atom pretty much coincided with the splitting of the mind with LSD. Both of them were these radical explosions of possibility and destruction. The whole tool/weapon argument became critical. Because LSD was being investigated, as we all know, as a weapon – *not* as a revelatory transcendent.

CA: Recently, we have seen a lot of downgrading in terms of drugs via-à-vis the justice system for other reasons – mainly financial ones. Taxing legal drugs is highly profitable whereas the draconian approach seems to cost more than it delivers.

GBPO: In terms of the financial balancing of the books the "war on drugs" is a disaster beyond belief. And has completely failed as well. Then you have the prison system here, where a huge percentage are in there for minor drug offenses. And all that money is being spent on keeping them incarcerated and lawyers and courts... It's ludicrous! It's totally ludicrous. Tobacco and alcohol are the most dangerous and destructive of all of the drugs. And yet those are the only two that are fully legal. It's a disaster. It's clouded by the fact that there are great powers that are behind the bureaucracy. They also utilize drugs in general to try and short-circuit rebellion. When acid was making this sort of counter-culture really vibrant, they introduced speed and heroin. So there is actually not a war on drugs, but a war *of* drugs. And it's obviously significant that the drugs that invite new ideas and spiritual ideas and peaceful ideas are attacked. Now we know why that is: it's because society is built on this whole *either/or* binary system that allows for something different or other; whether it's a nation or religion, or a way of life, to be attacked, and thereby give a false unity to the society. Oh, we have this common enemy; we must all do what we have to just to stop it from overwhelming us. And that's how it's controlled. And they use the army, the military and the police to physically intimidate people into agreeing. Now that is how all our societies work; especially in the West, but now, pretty much everywhere. Really, all our societies are only still holding themselves together by intimidation and violence from above. So of course, when something is as useful a tool as psychedelics, even if it's only for a minority of thinkers, it is a real threat to the status quo. As self-proclaimed enemies of the status quo, it's not really surprising that those are tools that we've used.

Certainly Wyllie believed that Ecstasy and "K"[5] appeared as gifts from certain powers in the universe, in order to enable at least the radical minority to affect change. And also not just affect change but slow down the destruction of civilization and the species. Which is why the end part of the consideration for pandrogeny for myself and Lady Jaye, which surprised us, was that we were dealing with the evolution of the human species. That's where we reconnect with Timothy and everyone, and we came to the conclusion that, if you like, with TOPY in that era, we pushed out the 60s. But when you get to the TOPY era, it was about accelerating the reconnection of people with their individual self, and giving them ways of thinking, and certain ritual tools that would enable them to write their own narrative of their life, instead of having their narrative written for them. So that was where the individual had the potential through those systems to be liberated, and to find and write their own character. But what we were surprised at after that was that it's not enough. When you get to that point, you have a sense of duty and responsibility that comes with it, because the way you perceive things has changed. And now you actually are obliged to return to the species as one organism, and one community. And it becomes imperative to try and heal and encourage change in everyone. So it becomes a very altruistic situation. You could just have rested on your laurels and be glad to have started to be the one empowered to take care of your own existence, but it doesn't work that way. Certainly not for those who have approached it the way we have. We came to realise that we have to view everything in terms of being one organism, one cell of the "humane"[6] species, and that we all start to move beyond expanding just our self to always think in terms of this humane species, bypassing the impositions of families, the dogma of religions and rules of nations with their de-

---

5 Ketamine.
6 Breyer P-Orridge actually spells this word "humanE," in line with an entire life of re-spelling and

structive reliance upon boundaries and languages to define their unique territories. Then, once perceived as this Single Organism, all constituent "cells" are programmed to apply *any* appropriate resources they might have, nutrients, healing or balance to that place in the Single Organism that requires them the most, to heal things that are wounded, to feed and nurture parts of the organism that need to grow, regardless of geographic location, ethnicity, primary belief system and culture. And that if it was a humane species, then any resources would be given to the place most needy, inevitably, and that would be a complete shift in terms of the species' mindset – and a necessary one. And that is something that we feel has been just echoed and revealed in a more vibrant and vivid way, especially by Ketamine and Ecstasy. Those two. So in that sense they've arrived at a really critical time. There is no doubt in our minds that all the economies, all the different economic systems on the planet, are teetering on collapse. In a sense they are already collapsed but people keep saying there's nothing wrong. But it's just a matter of when it collapses; when the banks give up. The only system that's really flourishing is totalitarian capitalism. China is the perfect model. You can see that people are very quietly trying to shift everything towards there. If you look at the American Republican agenda, that's basically the same thing. They would love to be able to have a totalitarian state; that people had to do as they were told, or they would punished. And basically almost all leaders of any nation secretly have to admit that they would much rather make everybody just do what they want, and a lot of them do that too. It's rather the norm to have a dictatorship, and it's the exception to even pretend to be democratic.

That's where we ended up with pandrogeny. These binary systems – either/or, black/white, Muslim/Christian, etc – are vindicating the current failed violent system. By having an inclusive new vision where everybody is part of one, which is the two becoming one on a grand scale, the divine hermaphrodite is actually the alchemical symbol of our future. That's why it represents wisdom, and the balance of everything, and the philosopher's stone. To us the pandrogyne is actually the philosopher's stone. And by being, of course literally but also philosophically, male/female, one becomes unified, and there is no longer this friction and violence and enmity that we have at the moment. So on a very real level we would prefer the species to eventually become just humane, and within that would be everybody accepting being both male and female, but also being able then to then have a choice to continue and redesign themselves. Because by having redesigned the species, you'd have so much more time and so many more visionaries and so many more resources that you could actually finally focus on the transcendent evolution of the whole species to its full potential, and not just that of the individual. That ultimately has to be the whole point of existing, no matter

re-structuring words and sentences to re-contexualise meanings and look for new perspectives.

how long it takes and how many loops. That's why we are always fascinated with the Tibetan culture and the Himalayan culture; it's because Tibet was a country where 60 or 70% of the population for thousands of years have just meditated on knowledge, and as a result they are able, some of them, to reincarnate at will. I mean, this is incredible! And we could all move towards that. Possibly faster than we imagine through the combination of the various things we've investigated.

So that's where we've ended up. As for our projects, that came from looking at those ads in the *The Village Voice*. And also from wearing each other's clothes. There is the inevitable path, which is the one we choose in terms of cultural engineering, and then there's the contrived artificial path which is the established status quo. And we are really at a point where the species has to choose. Because like it or not, the current economic systems in particular are going against the laws of nature. They talk about productivity increasing every year as much as possible – which means consumption increasing every year as much as possible. And yet, we have limited resources. That is just a fact. Those two don't go together. You can't have infinite growth forever. As we've populated the earth and gone more and more technologically advanced, we've also accelerated the crisis point to where it collapses because there isn't any more. A lot of people we tell about this go, "oh, but we've always been able to come up with new inventions, it will be fine!" Maybe. But that's not really a dynamic answer. That's a surrender to the hope of something. And even if that would happen anyway, isn't it better to be engaged in creating a much more visionary and healthy, healing future?

CA: The only hopeful agenda would be if that point of view, somehow, could become profitable. That's what's changed things so far.

GBPO: Yes, but that's what has to go. The whole idea of profit is now anathema to survival. There's a good sense to the reasoning. But profit comes from this idea of constant growth, and it's simply not viable. Everybody knows that money doesn't exist. It's just an agreement; it's a complete illusion. It won't take much to crumble the illusion. It's going to crumble by itself. What we're already thinking about is how can we change that. It's almost an impossibility, because of the way things are so entrenched… So then you come to what else can we do, and that's when we come back to the "One True TOPI Tribe."[7] Small communities, small groups of people presenting the best possible alternative they can, given the situation and saying, "what are you going to do when it goes down?" Best to be prepared... Not in a survivalist way, but just as we used to say in TOPY: just because we don't like Christian churches, the bureaucratic Christian churches, that doesn't mean they

---

7 OTTT, the "One True TOPI Tribe," a fluid development of sorts from the original TOPY concept, in which the Y of "Youth" has been exchanged for the I of "Individual."

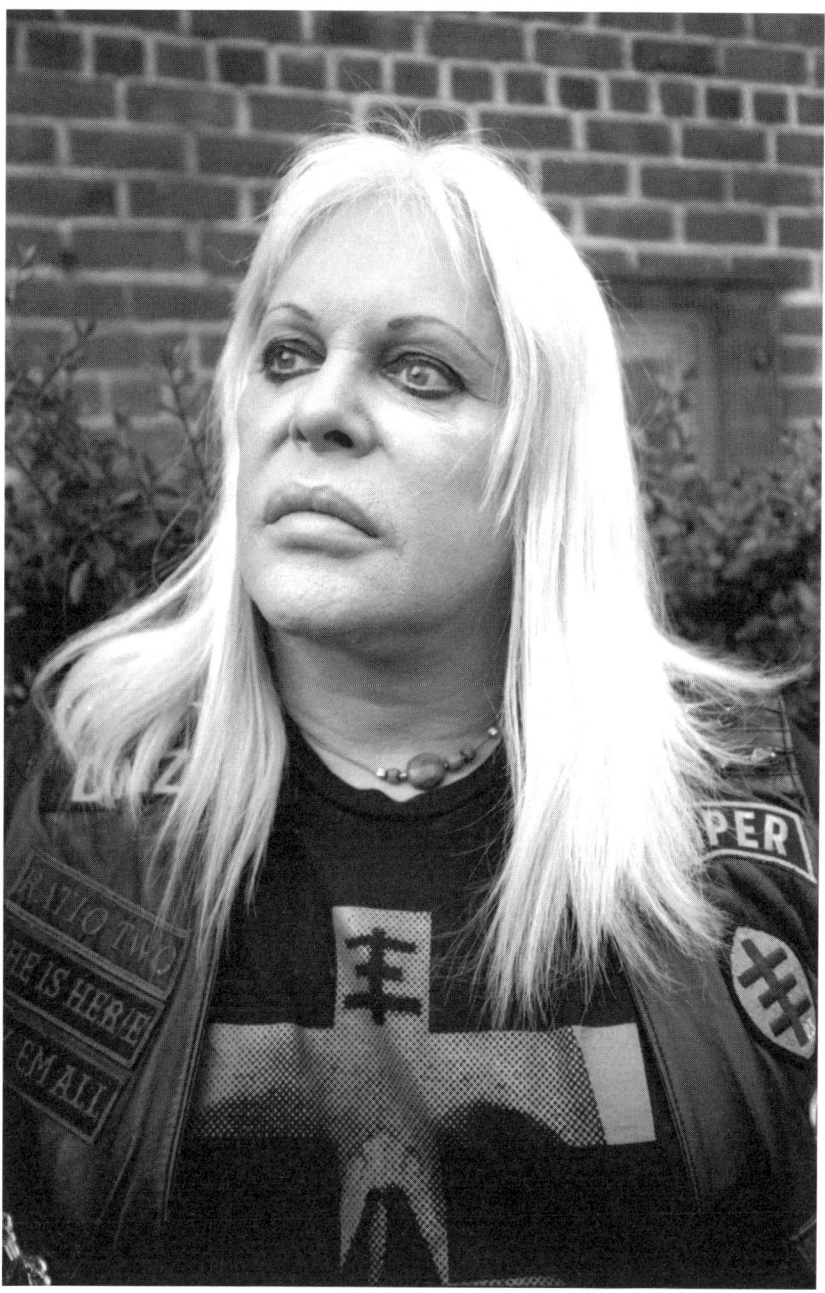

New York, 2012

don't have some great strategies. They have coffee mornings, and thrift stores, and they make a lot of money to survive. So just because we don't like survivalists – who are usually right-wing radicals – that doesn't mean they don't have some really good ways of organizing themselves and building communities. So we demystify the options, the strategies, we take away any political agenda, and we look at what is practical and useful. Forget about the symbols and all that other stuff; the same as we did with magic: take away the mystification and the need to have read all these other books. What is there that we can all use now to make this a slightly better world?

CA: Essentially, you're a poet who has worked in many different media. The writing doesn't necessarily need to be poetic or social commentary; it can also be "programmatic" via fiction. We have talked before about Brion Gysin's integration of the "Mekthoub" concept: you can write your own script. Someone needs to write the script, and it should preferably be yourself.

GBPO: Sure, we have come to that conclusion. Actually, we were thinking about it last night. Usually each night we talk to Lady Jaye as a kind of continuum. We were actually saying to her that people haven't realised yet what a dramatic influence she's had on me, in terms of focusing me and assisting me in learning to be more analytical in a more effective way. And she kept on at me, over and over, saying, "you should forget about Throbbing Gristle; it's done, it was great, leave it alone. You've done plenty of work with music, you don't need to do that anymore, you've done more than enough. Focus on making art because it can have a really profound effect for a long time." And also writing. She said, "you've got to start writing books." And that was her main message to me: "write, write!" We sat down and thought about exactly that: a strategy of writing a so-called "fictional book" that was actually a propaganda piece on at least one or two levels. It would be a really wonderful cultural tool to reach and inspire people almost unwittingly.

CA: It's still a highly potent form of magic.

GBPO: I mean, how much effect William S. Burroughs has had through his work on the novel form. What interested me is that the novels that are almost the most impenetrable are those that have had the most influence.

CA: Because they have a stronger magical appeal, perhaps...

GBPO: So we have begun on one... It's just a bit daunting, and it requires more space. Which is the main reason Jaye said, "stop touring." Which we have, in terms of long tours. Working on the film "The Ballad of Genesis and Lady Jaye"[8] was actually eating up loads of days and time. But we're still aiming for a space where we can actually sit down and each day continue the writing process without interruption, so that we remember what everything is doing. As research we've been reading lots and lots of "airport novels" and best-sellers, to try and figure out how they work; what is the structure that makes them so appealing to read; why they are entertaining? How does it all work? But the book we want to write... One way of explaining it would be like *Naked Lunch*[9] but written on Ketamine.

CA: It's good to analyse what works commercially. But then again that's not really the kind of novel you want to write. You need to write a novel like the ones that used to inspire you.

GBPO: Exactly. So it would be *Ulysses* and *Naked Lunch* through the magnifying glass of Ketamine. It's called *The Howler*. Should we tell you about it or not? Probably not too much.

CA: No, please don't do that. Write it instead. I look forward to reading it.

GBPO: Suffice it to say it's complex, and hopefully funny as well. What we're trying to do with it is to have a whole series of subliminal clues in it; not literal clues like in a competition, but certain things within it. There is a second book which is more of a manual that goes with it. If you really relate to and resonate with certain aspects of the first book, then the second book will make a lot more sense to you, and you'll go to it only because you've received the message.

CA: And what about an autobiography?

GBPO: I knew you're going to say that. (starts to sing) "Where do I begin, to tell the story of this funny love affair..."

CA: You should cut it up, start writing it.

GBPO: Just start writing it. We have started writing it. Funnily enough, we have two journals over there. One of them is my actual journal, and the other one contains things we remember from the past. So we've actually started writing that book.

---

8 The documentary film by Marie Losier, 2011. See earlier note.
9 The highly influential experimental novel by William S Burroughs, originally published in 1959.

CA: I think it's very hard to see any life make chronological sense, because that's not how life works. We work in circles, peaks, dips and loops. To sum up a life in a book is in itself incredibly difficult, but I think it could be doable once you just get cracking. Because the first things that will appear will be the most important ones.

GBPO: You think so?

CA: Yeah, I think so. It's just a matter of getting into the flow and structure it later. You can't structure something that's not there.

GBPO: We're not going to bother with structure; we're just going to write down what comes. Certain things that we've written as essays can be just dropped in. But it's a big task. We have to start soon because we're getting on in years. It would be frustrating to drop dead before we did it.

CA: Just think about it like this: you've led an interesting, eventful life, to say the least; a record of a life needs a lot of thinking about and also formulation. We'll never know when it ends. The main thing is to try and to get it done.

GBPO: Did you ever see "The Big Blue"?[10] That's just from two years... But it's useful because we can go and look and say, "oh, we forgot about that."

CA: It's a big help. I've been writing diaries since 1987. If I hadn't, I would have forgotten so many things. Photography is also really interesting. Now that I've done this *Lollipop*[11] thing, so much stuff comes back just from looking at one picture; one freeze frame of that moment. If I hadn't taken that photo the memories would just be gone.

GBPO: How old are you now?

CA: 46.

GBPO: A baby!

CA: I don't really feel like a baby, but I know what you mean.

---

10 Reference to an oversize notebook filled with P-Orridge's diary entries, philosophical musings and collages.
11 Reference to Carl Abrahamsson: *Fanzinera – Photographs 1985-1988*, Trapart Books, Stockholm, 2012. *Lollipop* was Abrahamsson's fanzine between 1985 and 1987. See the introduction of *Sacred Intent* for more information.

GBPO: All the close friends have said we really need to write it down. The other problem we have is that we don't feel like we're important enough to bother. But that's back so far... not wanting to seem important.

CA: How about saying, "I'm actually very important, I actually have a lot of things to do and a lot of things to say and a lot of things to explain." It's not a matter of self-aggrandisement or self-importance of the petty kind; it's just a different kind of approach. I think one of your strongest qualities lies in the formulation of words. The projects in themselves are parts of a totality, but you're very direct in your communication; in talking and writing. So why not work with that and say you're really good at that? "I'm really good at this! So that's why I'm going to do it!"

GBPO: We should consider this.

CA: I think you should. But also don't forget this thing with *The Howler* because fiction is a mighty, mighty, magical thing.

GBPO: I have to say the idea of the autobiography makes sense, but it's so daunting. When we look back we just say, "where do we begin?" People have told me, "you've lived about the equivalent of ten lives already, packed into a few years..." And it's true. Yet we feel like we've been really lazy. I've not done by any means enough work, so that's probably the creative drive right there, isn't it? You're never satisfied; you've never done enough; especially if you're not being creative as a career, but you're being creative as a calling – like being a priest or a doctor, or that you're serving the species, or as Brion Gysin used to say, "taking care of the psychic hygiene."

But anyway, on to Kathmandu, November 2011. We had a really busy year, and a lot of stress with the film[12] coming out. People forget that every time we watch the film and do a Q&A we go through the emotion of losing Jaye. Also, Big Boy[13] died of cancer a year and a half later, and as a result of not having Jaye's money we lost the house. So everything in that film is something that is a loss, and a grievous loss; it was really taking its toll on me, physically and mentally. Without a break, it was just constantly going through that over and over and over. So we decided we just had to get away. And we decided to go to Kathmandu again. So we thought okay, we want go, we want have time alone, but we don't want to be alone the whole time, because we'll be there for a month. So we in-

---

12 "The Ballad of Genesis and Lady Jaye," see earlier note.
13 Big Boy was P-Orridge's dog in the mid-00s. See earlier note.

vited Hazel Hill McCarthy III, who designed *Thee Psychick Bible*.[14] I asked her if she liked to go, and we said we'd buy her a ticket because we'd really like the company, and also it's fun to show somebody around, as you've been finding out with Sofia.[15] So we agreed that she would come about after a week or so after we got there. Stay two weeks, leave and so on.

So we arrived first in Kathmandu and went to the hotel, the Nirvana Gardens, where we always stay, and the porter took my bags to the room and we're thinking, "it's midday here and don't really feel tired so we go and have a cold drink in the garden." We went down to the garden, and the split second when we went from the concrete to the soil, like this, with my foot there, the ground started to undulate right there. We thought, "is this exhaustion? Are we just hallucinating from tiredness?" Then we realised, "no, it's really going up and down… Shit, it's an earthquake!" And because we've been in earthquakes in Los Angeles and San Francisco we realised it quickly. So we shouted "it's an earthquake!" And then nothing really happened. We found out afterwards that was the first earthquake on record in decades in Kathmandu. The split second we touched the ground… We thought, "this is going to be intense…"

The other reason we went, apart from getting rid of the New York toxins, was to see our friend Trilochan. He had had five strokes. That's not good. That was in a way the most important reason we chose to go when we did: to see him. He was living out in the jungle. We went to sleep after the earthquake, and decided that we'd go to see him the next day, in the jungle; in "paradise" as he likes to call it. One of his many friends came to pick me up and drove me out to the house. Trilochan was his usually perky self but you could tell that he'd been ill, and he had a piece of bamboo, about 5 ft. tall, that he got from the jungle and that he was using as a staff. He said that the biggest side effect was he was still suffering was loss of balance, so he was using that to keep his balance. So we had this great chat, we wandered around the ground and it's all grown beautifully now. Then we had some beautiful food as usual, and then we had another sort of walk in the garden before we went to sleep. At some point when we went back to the house he passed me his stick, that bamboo stick. The minute we touched it we had this impression, vision, whatever it was… It was like ectoplasm is described: liquid but solid, and its quality visually was like an octopus squirting ink… This jet of black ectoplasm came out, and enveloped me, and we let go of the stick like we'd had an electric shock and thought, "that was nasty!"

We can't really control when it happens, but we have been able to do healing sometimes, and the way it's always worked is that we take the illness into us,

14 Genesis Breyer P-Orridge et al, *Thee Psychick Bible*, Feral House, Port Townsend, 2009.
15 Sofia Lindström-Abrahamsson (b 1999), daughter of Carl Abrahamsson, and P-Orridge's god-child.

which is obviously a very dangerous way. It's not something we develop deliberately or consciously; it's just the only way that my consciousness knows to heal people: to take it away into me and then process it out. So my guess is that that's what happened: that a big jolt of his illness came into me, or it was a negative force of some kind that was part of the problem; a spiritual force that was evil and black.

Then we went to bed and slept fine and the next day we chatted some more and eventually Trilochan took me back to the hotel, and he said that he would see me in a couple of days. He only came into Kathmandu once a week, to see doctors, etc. We hung out at the hotel a bit, and the next morning we started to get this pain in my belly, and we thought it must be that food we ate or something, but it just got worse. And the next two or three days it got progressively worse and worse, until it was the most painful thing that we'd ever experienced. And we've fallen out of buildings and shattered the arm... As you know, we've had many traumatic, voluntary and involuntary, painful experiences; this was by far the worst. This was a pain that was delirium. It ended up so that after about four or five days there we were just lying in the bed in agony with the "do not disturb" on the door of the room. Fortunately, after about six days or a week, Hazel was due to arrive, and somehow we forced ourselves to get up and meet her at the airport. The minute she saw me she said, "you're really sick," and we went "yeah, we know; we're not really sure what it is but we've got this really bad pain." We went back to the hotel and we were sharing a room. At some point that evening she said to me, "Gen, you've got to go to the hospital; you're really, really ill. I've never seen you like this." And we just went, "no, no, no, it will be fine, it will go away."

Around midnight she called a taxi and made me go to the hospital, to the emergency. Luckily there was a doctor who was either English or American, and he said, "what's the pain like, can you describe the pain?" We said, "well, it's like a creature that's part crab, part centipede made out of obsidian and it's trying to eat its way out of me..." They did X-rays and sonograms and all this stuff, and came back and said, "you know you're lucky you came in when you did; another 24 hours and you'd be dead..." So Hazel saved my life. And then the doctor showed me the sonograms and said, "that's your gallbladder and it's more than twice its normal size, and there are white areas as if it's been eaten away. My advice to you as your doctor is, you change your ticket and you go back to New York tomorrow and have your gallbladder removed immediately, or we can't be responsible..." And we said, "no, we're not going back to New York; we've waited too long for this trip; we'd rather be here and die than go back to New York and lose this trip. We really have to be here."

Hazel took me back to the hotel somewhat reluctantly, and the doctors said come back in a week for check-up, see how it's going. They were kind of pissed off that we wouldn't go home. We had this feeling, this urgency, out of the blue,

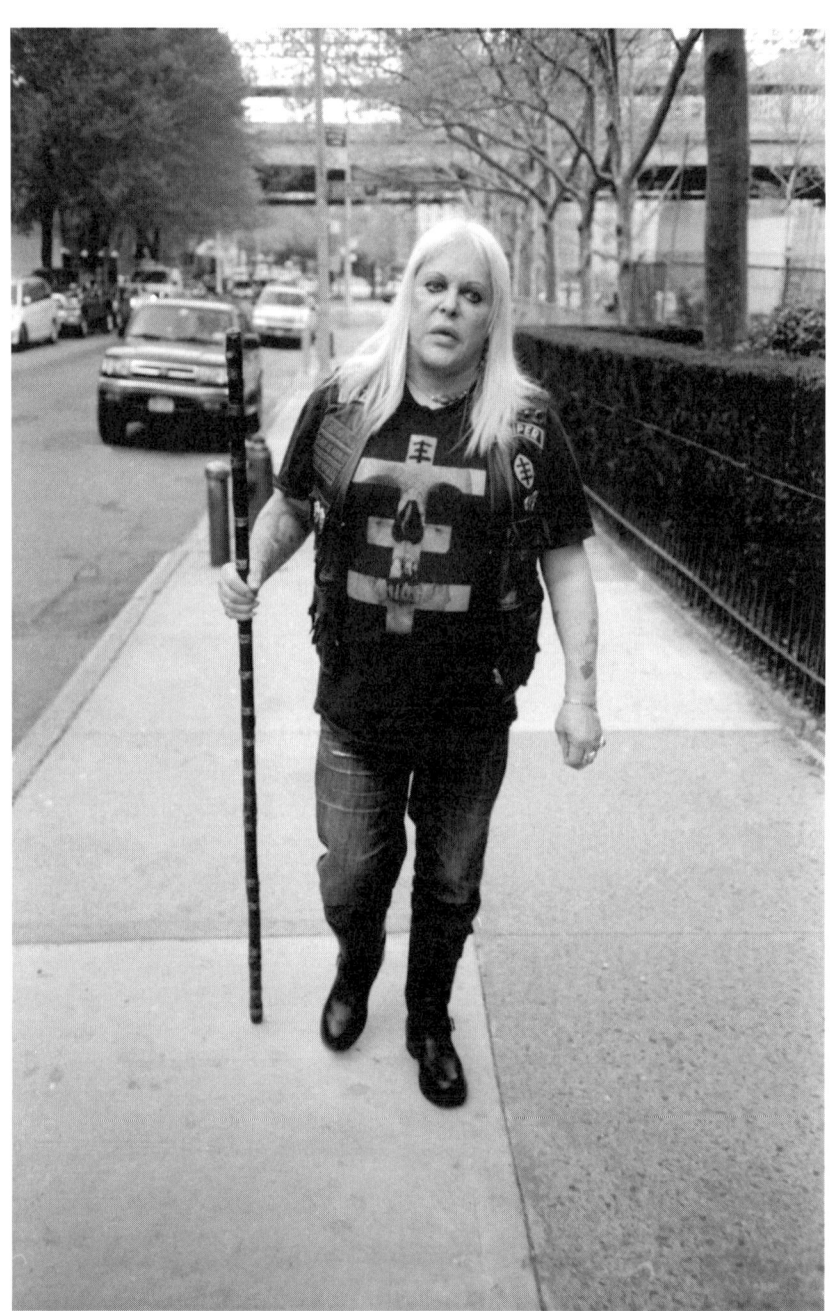

New York, 2012

that we had to deal with it on our own, in our own way: a magical way. So we went and bought all orange clothing: orange trousers, orange shirt; and then we went to the special shop... We call it the "secret shop" that Jaye and myself found, and this guy is the only one that doesn't have light-bulbs but if it does, it has just one, and it's really dark; everything is dusty, there are no big signs, and you don't notice it because it's so laid back. He's not really trying to sell anything; it's one of those places... But what he does have is museum quality stuff. We went in and we said, "look, we need to get some Naga healing talismans... Do you have anything?" He remembered me, so we got this one (shows it) which is really interesting as it's got a vagina on it... Fascinating! It's a little bit like those pictographs in the four corners, and also a bit like an alien but with breasts... And then also this one (shows it). So we got those, and we got this Naga bracelet of stones, and we also asked, "have you got any healing sticks?" He said, "yes!" One of them was about 6 ft. high dark wood, and it was carved all the way down with symbols and deities and figures; beautiful, really beautiful... The other one was the one which we took photos with, which is the long staff with the iron rings. That was basically our strategy: to just immerse ourselves in the local spiritual culture and trust that to heal me. We went to see Trilochan again, and decided he should have the tall carved staff, because he'd been much more sick. So we gave it to him as a gift.

At the end of the lane that led to Nirvana Gardens was a tiny pharmacy. Lots of people could not afford doctors or formal treatment so would get advise from the pharmacist who had great flexibility in what they could supply. Our man's inventory included morphine syrettes, valium and bottles of liquid ketamine plus syringes. On instinct, following my visions, we bought a supply of liquid ketamine and needles – or "noodles" as Lady Jaye would call them. Back in the hotel room we would inject around a 30-40 milliliter does into my muscle and then quietly meditate. I would travel to a white, very ancient, ruined city, covered in a thick dust. Once there I followed my mind towards the source of the pain and wrapped it in warmth and sunlight; swaddling it like a newborn baby. Sometimes the injection site would bleed a little, so I would dab the blood off on a primitive handmade paper toilet roll. As the days passed these rolls became scrolls of my blood marking healing.[16]

The next week we wandered around Kathmandu, still really weak, but in the spiritual bubble. And then we had to go to the hospital for more tests. They did X-rays and sonograms again, and the doctor said, "that's really strange; there's nothing there. Your gallbladder, that was falling apart and swollen so large is now totally normal, as good as new, and there is no evidence of anything ever having been wrong with it. This does not make any sense." He gave us both scans

---

16 These were later included in the Breyer P-Orridge exhibition "I'M/MORTALITY" at Invisible-Exports Gallery, along with other documentations of this mix of medicine, media and mortality.

as xeroxes and it was clearly mysterious. "I have absolutely no explanation as to how you aren't dead, and how your gallbladder is totally healthy without any medical treatment."

All we could say to him was we believed it was the magic of Kathmandu and my surrender to that spiritual realm. Hazel too was flabbergasted. It took a lot of trust and will power to witness me be so seemingly reckless.

CA: Maybe the Nepalis are more used to it?

GBPO: We just felt that was a good example of trust in our way of thinking. And that's what has to happen with all that magic; you really have to believe. It sounds corny, but it has to be absolutely without any hesitation, and you must just accept the instinct, and not question it in any way. During the days we were in the hospital, we saw Jaye physically for the first time since she dropped her body. We were in the bed sleeping, resting, and then we suddenly woke up, and we were definitely awake, and we looked across the room, and there on a sofa that wasn't there before was Lady Jaye, reclining on this love seat thing, wearing a nurse's outfit. But it was really skin tight and short and she was flipping through a fashion magazine like *VOGUE*, with a cigarette of course. She saw that we woke up, and she looked up and smiled this radiant beautiful smile. "Hi bunny, don't worry, everything is going to be fine." And that's the first time we've seen her. That was really amazing. That convinced me of course that we were using or doing things the right way. That was just before we went orange. That reinforced my feeling. When we came back to New York at the end of the trip we saw my own doctor and told him what happened. We didn't tell him about the orange and the sticks; we just said we'd been sick but it seemed to be okay, and so he sent me not just for X-rays but also for an MRI. It's a scan of every part all the way down the body. So they MRI-ed the whole body, the torso, and he said, "there's nothing wrong with you. Gallbladder is fine." He compared them to the original ones in Kathmandu and went, "that's really strange, can't explain it. But there is one thing... At some point you must have had a really bad fall, because one of the disks in your spine is ruptured, and the liquids have come out and it's ground down to nothing." So between my spine and my tail bone basically there is no disk. And that explains all these pains in the hips I've been getting, because if we fall or anything in the wrong way, it's absolutely ruining the spinal cord.

CA: That happened during the trip?

GBPO: No. This is just an injury they discovered from doing the MRI, that they'd never seen before because they never had to look at that part. Which is interesting. So now we've got to do physical therapy to build up the muscles around that.

So we got a positive extra piece of information as well. Interesting. So the doctors are completely baffled but we certainly believe that that was the example of magic in practice; not just theory. It was all spontaneous; there was no thought process. "No, I'm not going to go home, I'm going to wear orange as action." None of it was a dialogue in a normal way, as if we were speaking alone and something was just saying this. So that was our Kathmandu experience. And we kept wearing orange, and the talismans and walking with the stick for several weeks after we got back.

CA: That's an amazing story.

GBPO: Even so, apparently everyone now tells me they were really worried about me because they've never seen me look so ill. It was really close call. But we made it! And Jaye was there looking after me. So that's the story. There have been a few little things that are very specific, and always there's been a witness as well. In this case is even evidence; we have the pictures.

CA: Basically, your European working phase was 23 years, sort of from 1968 to 1991. Since then you've more or less been here for almost 23 years. Do you look forward to perhaps relocating to another region, or do you feel very set here?

GBPO: In a perfect world we'd keep this apartment as a base in New York, and also have somewhere else. And that somewhere else ideally would be in Nepal. And that would be what we've talked about before; that would be a sort of artist retreat where there would be several small but nice bedrooms and a couple of communal bathrooms and then a large room for talks, yoga, whatever... Space for people... The rooms would be big enough for people to do books or whatever; a studio space, and a nice garden... And food every evening. If somebody wanted to write a book, and needed to get away completely, then they would say, "we want to go to the retreat." They would buy their own air ticket and then pay a very nominal fee for being there. In return for that they'll have a space, they'll have food without having to worry about it, etc. They'd be looked after. So it will be a retreat that will allow them to get their work done. Maybe six to eight people at a time, maximum. And have a Nepali family living there all the time with their own space, who cooked and drove people. That's one idea that's always been around.

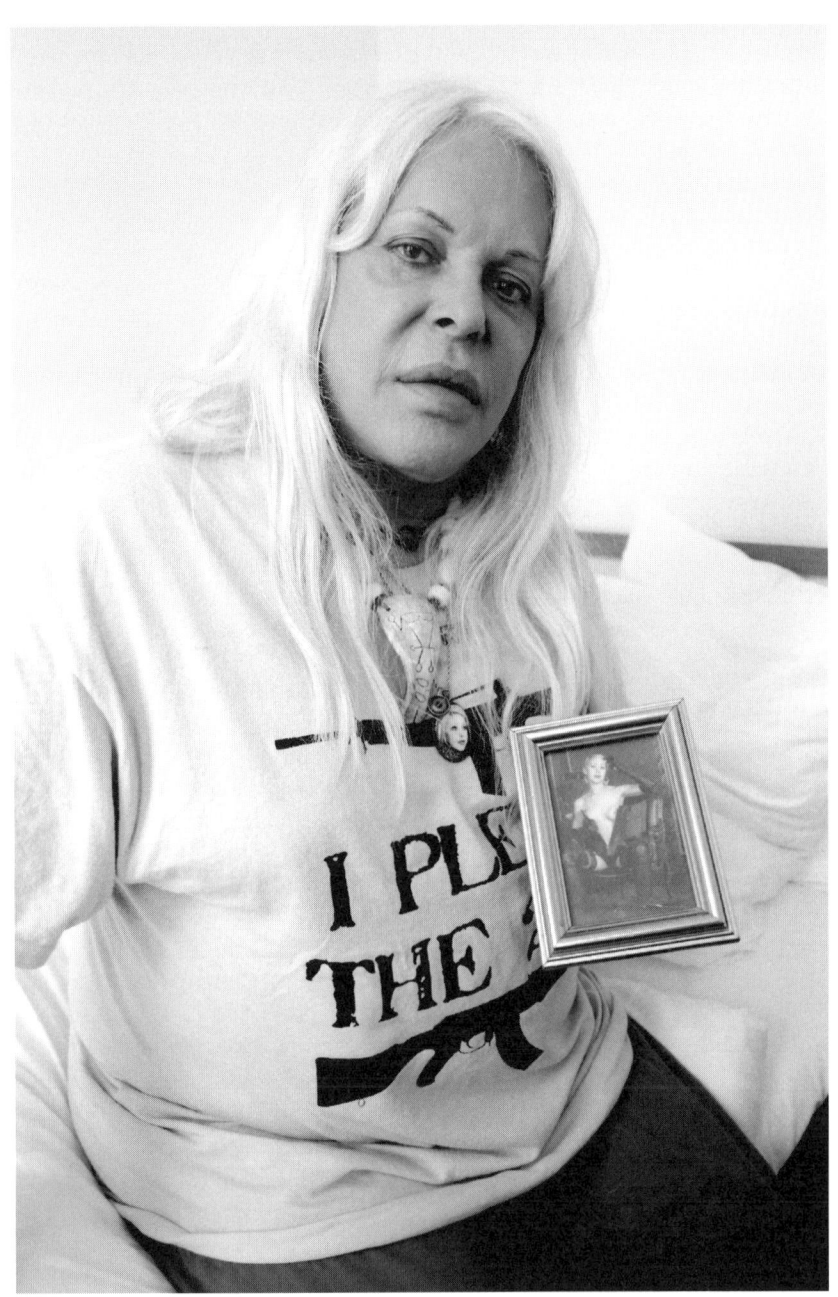

Stockholm, 2013

Stockholm, June 28th, 2013

I was working on a series of documentary films about artists called "An Art Apart" and definitely wanted to include Genesis in this endeavour. In the summer of 2013, Genesis and manager Ryan Martin came over to Sweden for a conference and performance in Gothenburg. But before that, we started filming in Stockholm.

CA: Is it possible to, in a short way or a long way, define what are you about?

GBPO: As you're probably very aware, it changes as you go on. What you're about changes. I guess one of the main themes is change itself. The question that completely obsesses me all the time, is whether human beings are capable of actually changing their behaviour. If they are not, then obviously we're doomed as a species and, as Brion Gysin would say, "we're just clever rats." But there is so much evidence that we are better than clever rats; that we keep on having this – who knows what motivates it – but some kind of optimism that is worth trying to look for, in methodologies, tools, examples... Anything – even just a brick with a sharp edge – anything that might just get people to stop living lives of behavioural loops and thoughtless activities. And that they finally say, as most of us do, but in a really sincere way: what the hell am I doing here? Is this real? What is happening and what is this thing we call existence? And what is the rest of this species doing to itself? So those are one of the main themes. But over the years it has become more spiritual and less aggressive if you like. Back in the 1960s and 1970s it was different. The basic strategy was just to attack everything; smash anything that smelled of hypocrisy; expose people who were lying to the rest of the world; and try by shock to cause them to think. But now it is much more complex than that. Culture changes, politics change culture, economics change, all the great ups and falls of what we call civilisation change, and as they do so, so do the strategies of what we've come to believe is the job of what we might call an artist. We prefer to say "kreator." Not with a big K, but with a little k.

CA: You've been at it for a long time. Is it possible to separate yourself from your art?

GBPO: Not anymore. One of the things we say most often when we give talks at universities and so on, is that we stress over and over and over again that there is no difference between life and art. And when we say art, we include mysticism and so on in there. The means of perception and the day-to-day activities of people are inextricably and totally linked. We worked for a while with a Cheyenne-Apache shaman called Nomad. In their language there is no word for "death," but they substitute it with the word "separation." That is a really profound way of thinking of things. Because when you look at the world outside, at this moment, we are separated from the earth itself – there is concrete here, there is glass here. We're separated from people in other places in the world, we're separated from the weather. All of those things are little deaths. Most of us spend our lives in a downpour of various forms of death; separation from even those we love. One of the great jobs of anyone who's trying to think and share ideas, is to become inclusive instead of exclusive. To include other people; to include daily objects; to take everything that's potentially significant.

In the exhibition at the Andy Warhol Museum, one of the works is called "Shoehorn." It's a gold high-heeled shoe with an animal horn attached to where the heel would be. These were just two things laying around in the house one night when Lady Jaye's niece was asking me how does art work and how do you come up with ideas? We said that art is everywhere – all the time. It's just putting things together in unexpected ways and having a surprise. We grabbed the shoe and the horn, and we stuck them together, and now we have a sculpture. What is that? It's a Shoehorn! But now you think about that phrase differently too, and all these reverberations happen. The action, the object, the meanings, all shift and change in such a simple way. Art is just everywhere. Maybe all of the things in that art exhibition were things that were laying around the house. It's true to say not everybody has wolf heads laying around the house and things like that. But, then again, that's another part of seeing the world; of seeing things that have some kind of resonance and power. We're great believers that you can find objects that already have power in them through their use, through the way they have been seen. Whether in a religion or a tribal situation, or even a very obsessive personal situation. But also you can *create* that power in things like this for example (shows walking stick), which by its use, by its being carried around, by its being seen in pictures, by its constantly being touched by my skin and absorbing my sweat, is gradually developing some kind of life of its own that represents part of what we are.

It was actually originally given to me in 1977 by Sandy Robertson who was writing for *Sounds*, the music magazine. One day he said, "I've got a gift for you, for Christmas," and it was this walking stick. And we said, "we don't really need a walking stick right now, Sandy." He replied, "one day you will." His father had been working in Scotland in the docks, shipbuilding, and actually working on building nuclear submarines so that they could send them secretly under the water with missiles and if necessary blast another country to smithereens. But then he got made redundant and decided that rather than just sit around unhappy or just watching TV that he'd develop a hobby. So he began making walking sticks. This metal is actually the metal they've used in nuclear submarines to contain radioactivity from a nuclear engine, and this we assume was an attempt at a skull, that he must have somehow picked up from Sandy had something to do with the cosmology, and that of course is our symbol, the "psychick cross."

So what is this... A prophesy? Is this a gift from the future that was made in the past? What other stories link with this as a part of this web of connection? Everything is connected. That's another of the things we tend to do: believe. And also while we look at art, talking of art, the first question we usually ask is, "what is the story; what is this telling me?" Most of the time it is not telling me anything, and that's what Brion Gysin called "deceptual art." That is something else that is very deeply engrained: what is the story, and what are we learning from this? The Native Americans used to say there are three questions when you look at something: is this giving me something I didn't have before? Is this giving my community, my tribe, my family something that they didn't have before? Is this giving the world something that it didn't have before? If it's not doing those things it has no value.

Another way of putting it is that Marilyn... The golden Marilyn that Andy Warhol was silk-screening when he was shot, and was hit by one of the bullets and sold for 23 million dollars. Now, is it worth 23 million? Is it worth more because there is a morbid connection? Am I way off telling people about what the value of art is? Take it into New Guinea; take it into the jungles of the Amazon and give it to them. In the West, with its "art market" and highly priced "art-works," it could be valued for a hundred million dollars. But what is it actually? A wooden or steel frame, canvas, oil paint... an "artspeak" essay of meanings. They may well quite like the image but when push comes to shove will see its primary value as being very waterproof. So their likely practical use for it will be to use it on their roof, and use the frame as part of a pig run or something. Maybe it will be repurposed as a golden item of clothing? A ceremonial hat or skirt, but any intrinsic value is in its being canvas and waterproof.

Certain tribes might not be able to recognise an image at all, because in the past, when people showed them films they couldn't see anything on the screen. Certain isolated tribes saw nothing in a mirror. So, value... What is value? Value is something very abstract. But to me value is sharing, generosity, kindness, love, sincerely hoping to improve the state of the world, things like that... Those are value. Money is just some distraction that somebody invented in order to keep people confused and suppressed in terms of their daily life.

CA: With that definition in mind then, is it possible for you to pinpoint or pick out a process or a product that has been very, very valuable to you?

GBPO: Obviously, the most important tool we've used are the cut-ups. Those pretty much go through everything we do, and have never failed us yet. Do you want to know more about the cut-ups? At school we were in the English class and my teacher called me after one of these boring classes about Shakespeare and he said, "you know, you seem to have a very different kind of cultural reference from most of the people I know. Here is the name of a book that I think you might really enjoy reading if you can find it." And he'd written down *On the Road* by Jack Kerouac, which at that time we had never heard of. A few weeks later my father brought it home. He'd found it in a motorway café, in a sort of cheap bin of bargain books, and that led me into the whole beatnik ethos. We'd already discovered Dada and Surrealism, and come to the conclusion that art wasn't really what we were fascinated by but the people who made it. The lives of the artists were at least equally exciting as any other object they made or book they published. So that was in fact what drew me to certain things. Most of what Andy Warhol made I don't really enjoy at all, but the fact that he set up The Factory and had all the interesting people coming through and keeping a constant state of stimulation – that's interesting. Who were they, where did they go later, and where did they come from, and who interacted with who? That's fascinating. But silk-screening an Olympic athlete? Not interesting.

So it has always been very much about the way the artist lives life; the way the creative person lives it. That is far more significant than what they leave behind in terms of objects. And the beatnik scene really epitomized that. They travelled around, they got jobs when they needed money, they looked for kicks, they looked out for new kinds of music, they looked for new kinds of philosophy, they looked for Eastern religions, they took it all very seriously, and travelled all over the world. They basically invented the "hippy trail" to the Far East. After reading some of those books we just thought, "that's what we want to be." A constantly evolving person who creates things, who writes things, who makes music – but that's *not* as important as just being a bohemian that is just open to the next possibility; open to the next surprise.

While we were looking at those people, the beatniks, we came across William S. Burroughs and Brion Gysin, and read about their experiments with cut-ups, which began purely as a sort of accident. Brion Gysin was cutting through some images, photographs, in order to use them for something, and then noticed underneath he had sliced up a magazine or a newspaper. When he started just idly moving the bits around and then reading across he found that the words and phrases and sentences were just fascinating, and really unusual and stimulating and surprising collisions were happening. There was a sense almost of a meaning that couldn't be found any other way; something was going on. There was something there that was very profound. And so he told Burroughs about it and Burroughs started to experiment with it too; mainly with writing. He also felt that this is one of the only ways to break down linear thinking; to break down conditioned thinking; to break down inherited ways of thinking. Once you start to chop things up and just assemble them apparently randomly, you've removed the element of conscious direction. And so you get things happening; you get things interacting: words, images, sounds that could never, ever meet each other any other way. If you are opened up to that, you start to see the world that way too. You realise that it is happening constantly; that as you are sitting here talking there is somebody in the background drilling, there are birds outside twittering, there are cars, people breathing, somebody over there is fucking, somebody over there is dying... Who knows? Nothing is as it seems. And if nothing is as it seems, then this is all potentially just a hallucination. So cut-ups became really central to the way of seeing the world, and became absorbed into everything that we did. What you find happens is that your brain starts to accelerate its comfort with cut-ups; it becomes more and more opened up to seeing these collisions in the most unlikely places.

We also came across Max Ernst's collages, and those books that he did: *The Hundred Headless Woman* and *A Little Girl Dreams of Taking the Veil*. And I started to collage too, which of course is a form of cut-up. Once you start to collage with different images from different places, you're actually, literally, creating worlds that did not exist before. That's a god-like gift – it's amazing! And as you start to look at all of those things in the beginning, it's very much about just wanting to be creative; wanting to be the bohemian world traveller, experimental artist, writer, thinker... It leads you to some interesting places. If we're all living bound by whatever the opposite of cut-ups is – Burroughs called it "Control" – if we're bound by Control from birth, can we ever escape it? Are we actually dealing with some of the details? What's the really central thing that's going on here? And that's when you start to think about philosophy and the human state.

We often talk about this too in lectures that we give. We say, "don't kid yourself, you're being conditioned before you were even born." Because assuming the parents want to create a child, the minute that they find out that they are pregnant there is, "is it going to be a boy or a girl? How will we define it? If it's one we could call it this, if it's the other we could call it this." And then relatives come around and friends from next door and they are going, "ah, you're having a baby?! What is he going to be?" Everybody discusses all of these different things, and you're inside and you can actually hear that. Sound passes through skin and through every part of the body. So even at the very beginning, everybody is starting to try and direct you into their expectations of what you should and can be.

The other thing that we found out that fascinated me was the theory of evolution that says that at some point on this planet there was single-celled slime mold in the sea, and slowly but surely it became clusters, and eventually the clusters passed chemical messages back and forth which supposedly increased their ability to exist and continue to exist... And bit by bit they became these tiny little squidgy creatures; then they became like fish, and then they became amphibians, and then they became reptiles, and they crawled out of the sea and eventually became like monkeys and blah, blah, blah... until they looked like us. In the nine months that people are pregnant the baby goes through every single piece of that story quite literally. It's a recording device. There is something so deeply significant about that: that pregnancy is in fact a three-dimensional reiteration of evolution so far. It obviously tells you that it can continue. If the story went through that many changes physically, then it is supposed to continue to go through physical changes, and any other changes too. But it seems to have stopped. People seem to be satisfied with the bodies they've got. They even talk about the body being sacred. We say that the fucking Vatican should be put on trial for crimes against humanity, for murdering more millions than any other insane dictator ever has. And as we speak children are being born into hopeless poverty and death, because of their rules and regulations. How dare they? That really annoys me. And the amount of culture that's been lost because of them burning alternative histories, alternative cultures, alternative groups... All the Aztec and Mayan codices that they burned, and now they are saying, "what did it mean? Why can't we find out what it meant?" Because the fucking priests destroyed it. That is a crime against everything; it is a crime against existence.

Meanwhile, back at the pregnancy, what happens first is you get named and you get nurtured as male or female, and your peer groups start to also push you towards what you're supposed to be; and society does the same and then education does the same, and where are "you" in all of that? Where is the flag flying? Where is the, "what do I want to be? Hello, is somebody saying that I'm free to become whatever I want?" There are a few people doing that but they are usually the people who are suppressed by the powers we all know.

We started to do performance art in the 1970s as C.O.U.M. Transmissions and as that went on, it went from being pretty much a street theatre and just provocation; just surprise things happening in unlikely situations... But as we went on it got more and more fascinating for me thinking about why are people surprised, and why is it so powerful to suddenly be naked in the middle of a theatre piece, performance or an action; who decides? It still makes me laugh to see people in the street... It happened today: we saw some young girl in a very short skirt constantly pulling it down. Even though she was wearing long johns underneath, she was pulling the skirt down. So there was this contradiction: she wanted to reveal as much as possible but not reveal anything. And yet that same person, on a beach, with the permission of being on a beach, would wear the most minimal possible clothing and feel totally okay about it. And all the men who she was so afraid would be seeing their underwear when they were pulling their skirt down are now just dismissed as irrelevant. There is a strange disconnect there.

Who makes the rules? Where are these lines drawn, and who draws them, about what is appropriate, and what is not appropriate? What is decent, what is indecent? As you start to grow up and see the world and possibly travel if you can, you'll notice that the rules are different everywhere. You go to Afghanistan and the women wear a great blue tent with a little tiny opening here to look out of, and are subject to the most totalitarian rules and regulations. But on Venice Beach it's quite different. And then in New Guinea the men wear bird's beaks over their penises but nothing else, and the women wear nothing at all. So all that matters is to extend and focus on the penis and so on. Therefore there are no universal rules and regulations about the human body: it's completely arbitrary. And yet it controls societies, both small and large, in such a deep way. That became really obsessive to me. How come that I can masturbate in my bed, but I can't masturbate on the bus? Who makes the rules and regulations, and where are the lines? Even when you are awake and when you are asleep... There isn't a specific point; it's a gradual shift of states but there is no line at all. Everything in fact is a gradual shifts of states. So all those different restrictions are there for some other reason. What is the reason they are there? It is to instil fear. Because once you've got boundaries and rules and regulations and options that are possible, and then also options that are punished, you live in a state of fear. If you are in a state of fear, you are not going to explore because you are going to get hurt. All the world societies – all of them – maintain discipline by intimidation and violence. And it goes right back to the origins in prehistoric times, or, as we prefer to call it, "astoric" times.

There was a certain animalistic point when the male of the species became the aggressive protector of the clan or the family or the small unit that was trying to survive. Who knows what it must have been like in the ice age? Women were magical creatures. Nobody understood where the babies came from; they didn't know that that strange short, sharp, electrical, little discharge they sometimes did with each other had anything to do with making babies, because they didn't even have linear time yet. So the idea was that babies just appeared out of women around them. So women were both incredible and to be feared, because only they knew how to make babies appear. The men would be afraid of that but they protected them because they needed more beings to continue the clan. And what would they do if they met another clan? They would have slightly different rules and regulations; they might not use bird beaks on their penises; they might have some feathers sticking out of their hair or something else... So it's different; it's something other. And if it's something other, then it's a threat because they've

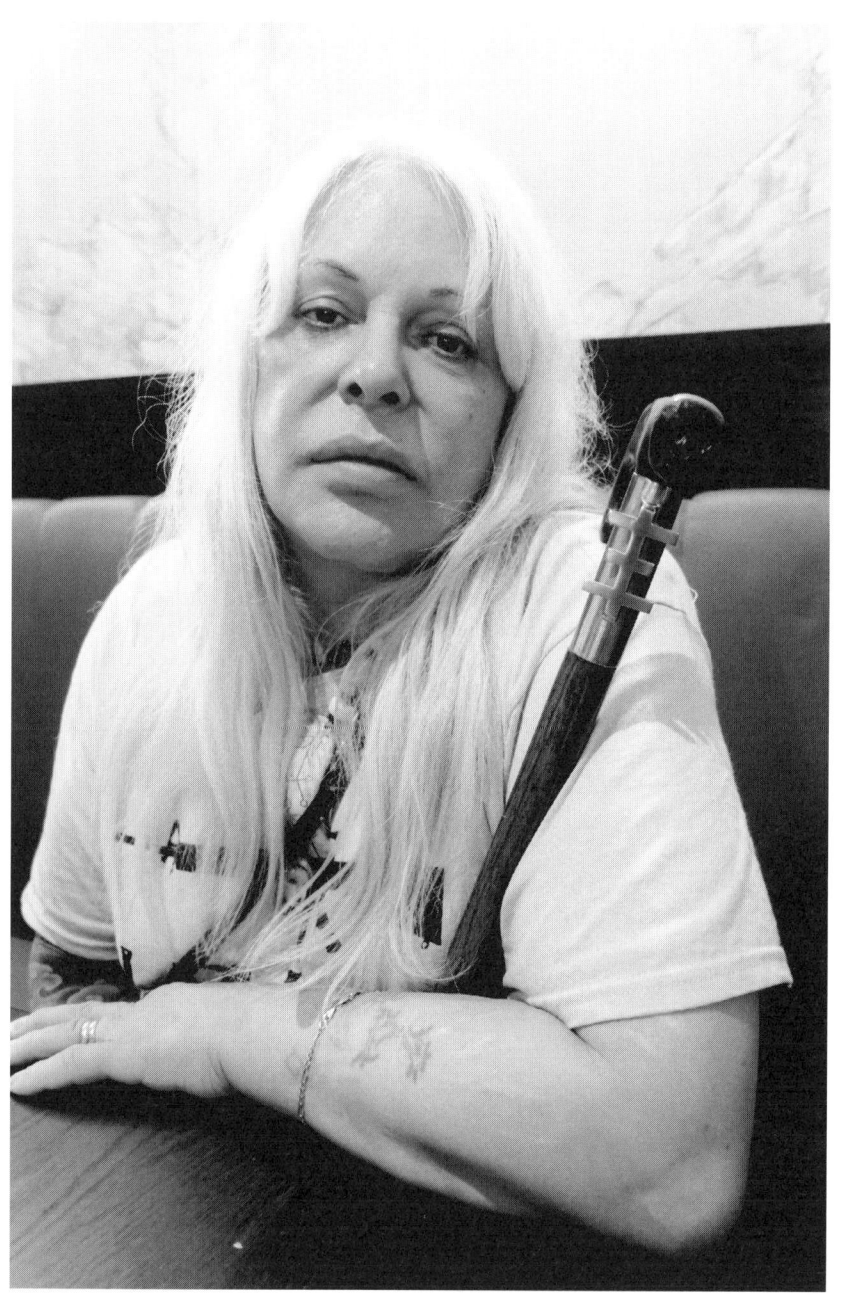

Stockholm, 2013

learned that women can make babies wherever they go, but men can't. So they have to protect their brood, and so they attack whatever is "other." Very early on that is what happened. It is different, it is other, it is not like us – hence we attack it. That is exactly the same dynamic that is going on right now. With the Islamists, with the Christians, the Communists, whoever it might be. They are different, we attack them. Rednecks in America: they are different, we attack them. Although the great irony with rednecks is now they've all got long hair, which is hilarious to me.

So there is one of the crucial issues; one of the crucial problems that faces us as a species. This is so deeply implanted after thousands and thousands and thousands of years – this idea of "it's different, it's other, we should be afraid of it, we should attack it." How do we change ourselves from something that is that in-grained within every different culture? How do we find the unifying factors, and how do we let go of the fear of the differences, and start looking for the things that are similar without staying afraid? "What if we are trying to be nice and they are secretly going to attack us anyway?" Aaaah, paranoia!

One of the things that came up was that during some of the more extreme things that we did towards the end of C.O.U.M., personally we found ourselves going into altered states. Mental altered states that were out of body experiences; talking and speaking in tongues; finding it impossible to feel pain; swallowing things that are poisonous and not being damaged by them; different things that we'd read about in so called primitive cultures. We thought there is something really interesting happening here, and it has something to do with putting pressure on the body; of stressing the body in certain ways. Exhaustion. Lots of exhausted people will notice that they can dream while they are still awake, because the brain will just force itself to dream because it is part of its way of staying healthy. And they will sometimes hallucinate and so on.

Those things were happening to me enough, and intensely enough, that we thought we needed to investigate this more. Because it somehow occurred to me that perhaps the way to adjust behaviour is to cut that up too. How would you cut it up? You can cut it up with ritual sometimes; repetition to the point of exhaustion, and to the point of not thinking so that something else comes through. You can use different items; it doesn't matter what they are. If this is always present in rituals, whether it is being touched and used or is just there inherently, we really believe that objects do absorb energy; they do have a memory. If people think that sounds ridiculous what do we use for memory in computers? Silicone and quartz. So, rocks can remember. And now they are working on computers that use water, and just change the direction of molecules. Liquid memory. So everything actually can remember. This is really important.

CA: What was it like meeting William S. Burroughs for the first time, given that he had been such a great source of inspiration for you?

GBPO: When we met Burroughs in 1971, we were very intimidated by him as a character. We were 21, and he was this mythical creature who was blowing apart linearity and culture in such an amazing way with his books and his ideas. And right from the beginning, although we enjoyed the books, it was publications like *The Job* and *The Third Mind* that were really inspiring. Where he was actually explaining different exercises that could be used.

He said to me, "how would you short circuit Control?" That was it. Basically we left, and that was left with me as this thought that has gone off; it continues to do so to this day. But while we were with him he was showing me his notebooks which we'd never seen before, and the pages were bits from newspapers, bits of writing and typing, images, bits of paint... Every single one was like an illuminated manuscript, almost like an alternative, illuminated Bible filled with all of these apparently unconnected bits of information. One constant between all of them was the number 23. We were talking about magic because we asked him, "do you utilize magical techniques?" or something like that. And he said, "well, of course, what do you think cut-ups are?" And then we went, "really?!" The other thing he told me, or sort of demonstrated, was how he went to this restaurant not far away. They had treated him really badly, and the food was terrible, and he was so pissed off. He thought, "I'm going to close them down." So he went home and got his camera. He took photos of the street, and he showed me this in his book; and then he'd cut out the restaurant, and burned that part of the photo, and joined the pictures of the streets together minus this restaurant. Then he'd also gone and recorded the sound of the street outside as he walked up and down. He also had the first TV we ever saw with a remote, so that he could flip through the channels all the time. And all of the time he was talking, he was chopping the channels together. On a tape that he had with the sounds of the street, he added in what he called "trouble noises:" police cars going past, ambulances, gunfire, bombs going off and people screaming. And then for a week, he walked up and down outside this restaurant playing these tapes over and over and over, and within a couple of weeks the restaurant was closed and never reopened again. We thought, "of course!"

In the renaissance the alchemists were using the best possible scientific equipment they had access to, which was beautiful glass jars, flames, different chemicals and powders; very simple things but top of the range for that era. Why do people try to mimic alchemy in our day and age with those objects, when they should be using tape recorders and cameras and Polaroids and anything else that is available now. That was a really important lesson to learn: alchemy is actually a growing phenomenon; it is almost a parallel culture to the culture of Control.

And one of the great things about the military industrial complex is that the only reason we have got Polaroids was because they had spent so much on research in order to create ID cards for the CIA, so they decided to sell the cameras to the public because they are so cheap. They simply tried to get their money back, which immediately gave all of us access to this object that cost billions to invent. It is the same with small tape recorders, and so much of the technology that we all get our hands on. It is their mean-spirited financial thinking that actually gives us the chance to have access to the same tools that they are using to control us. Something about that always really amuses or pleases me. That is something people need to remember.

Whatever people are using – even if it's just sticks and stones and shiny objects; maybe a mirror, maybe a metal blade that they have discovered or been given – they are also looking for the most powerful technology that they can get their hands on. All the objects that have been used ritually to try and make things happen, or to influence the way things happen, have this lineage going right back to pre-linguistic humans. That is a hell of a big reservoir of magical faith and belief and effectiveness that we can still tap into, and we can add to it; like you are doing right now with the equipment you are using. We talk to people and we sometimes say they should think back to the time when people were living in their caves, and try and remember that they didn't know the sun would come back ever. So what would they do? They would try and think of a way to ask it to come back – which might be to build a fire because the fire is like the light of the sun, and they would maybe sing some kind of chant or what might be called in our days a song which would be saying, "please, come back sun, please come back!" And perhaps whoever came up with the song and suggested the big fire was lauded... "My god you were right, you made the sun come back! You must be really powerful! You're a magician, you're a shaman, you're a wise person!"

That is the tradition of art and magic as it began to develop. They would draw things in the earth, they would arrange objects and shells, they would make necklaces, they would gradually develop a technology that was always about making things happen. And so my interest in art to this day is *can it still and will it still make things happen?* We believe it can and will. Maybe not the things themselves, but they are just the tip of the iceberg of the way of thinking. They represent the means of perception, and that is what we are changing. How people perceive the world; how people perceive the interactions of the world between power and ignorance; between fear of the unknown and exploration of the unknown. The great artists, the great thinkers, the great magicians, the great leaders of tribes are the ones who were not afraid to move into the unknown. On behalf of who? Their people.

In this day and age with a world that is unified with the internet and computers and god knows what, that means that the artist is there to represent and pull

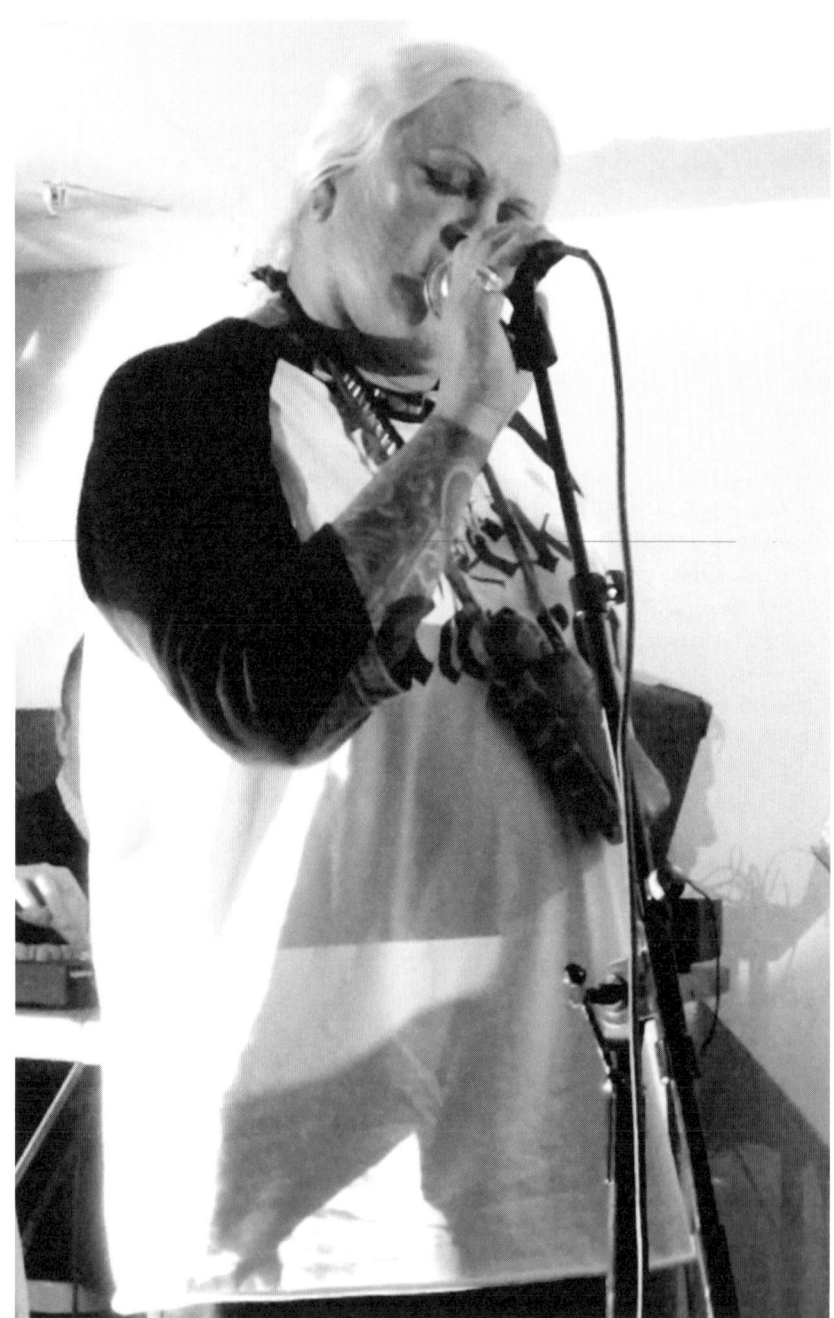

New York, 2016

all people into a new world. It is a huge, huge responsibility and it is also the most exciting game in town. That is for sure.

CA: In what ways would you say that the pandrogeny project has changed your mind? Is it possible to tell?

GBPO: The simple answer about the effect of pandrogeny on me is that it is absolutely inextricable from Lady Jaye. As you know, we've worked with some amazing people. Dr. Timothy Leary, Derek Jarman, Dr. Timothy Poston, William S. Burroughs, David Medalla, Gerald Fitzgerald, Colin Naylor and Brion Gysin to name a few; sadly all bio-males. However, without hesitation we can say that Lady Jaye Breyer P-Orridge is by far the most fearless person and thinker we've ever met. Just in simple things... She used to smoke DMT every weekend and call it "the sparkle." We smoked it once and it fucking terrified me. It was so overwhelming, but it still left me with this message which was that time is meaningless. Because while we were gone for ten minutes in Lady Jaye's apartment, we watched two galaxies be formed, all civilizations come and go, and big wars and fights and arguments, and then another galaxy, and then we came back here. And yet only ten earth minutes had gone by here! How is that possible? Only if time is meaningless. We usually tend to prefix anything these days with, "assuming that this exists;" then we try and explain what is going on. But don't think it exists for sure because there is no way of knowing. I don't know how it is for you, but for me, my dreams are equally as real as this. There is no way of saying what is supposedly real, and it is not really that important. What is really important is thinking about what people's minds are doing. That is one of the things that Jaye really clarified for me. She used to refer to the human body as a "cheap suitcase," and Timothy Leary used to say that the body is just here to move the brain around and give it mobility. Nikola Tesla called it a meat machine. So Jaye was in good company with her conclusions about that. If the body is a cheap suitcase, what is there of value in the being? Of course... it is consciousness.

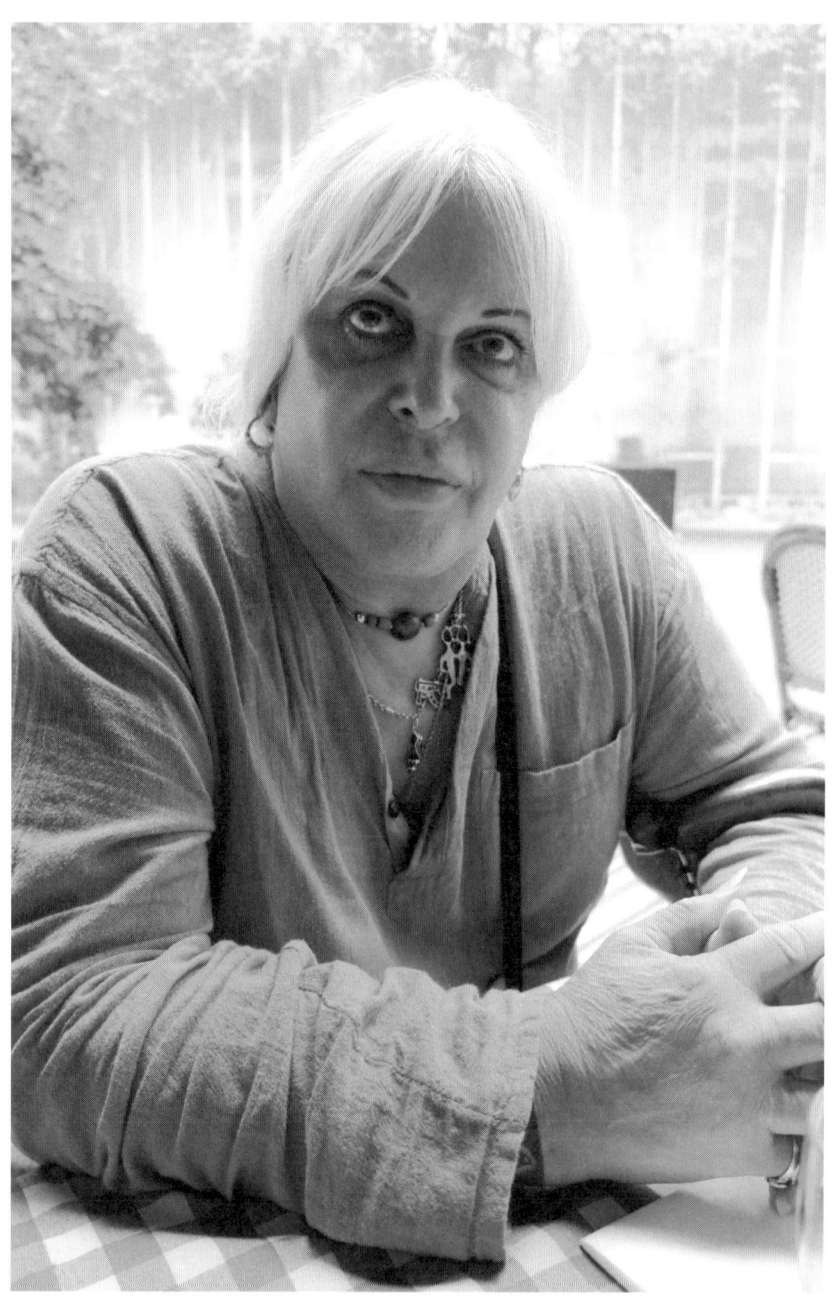

Stockholm, 2013

Gothenburg, June 29th, 2013

In 2013, Genesis was invited to talk at the ESSWE[1] Conference at Gothenburg University. The following chapter is an edited transcript of what was said.

GBPO: I guess I've always been a rebel by nature. We had come across things like Crowley's books. Not many, because it was quite hard to find them back then. Luckily we found Atlantis Bookshop on Museum Street in London, and got to be friends with the proprietors there: Geraldine Beskin, and her mother was still alive then too... So we started just always going in while we were in that area, and saying, "have you got anything else by Crowley? Who else is interesting?" She asked, "have you heard of Austin Osman Spare?" We said, "no, but if you recommend it I'll buy something." So she pointed to the wall above the books and there were all these incredible paintings. And she said, "you'd better buy one quick because Jimmy Page buys everything when he comes here!" So we asked, "how much are they?" "Sixty pounds," she said. That was two months of unemployment money, so that was a problem. But we did it anyway; we bought one with the dole money. That got me interested in Austin Spare.

My father introduced me to Tibetan ideas around 1961-62. He gave me the Heinrich Harrer book *Seven Years in Tibet*, and something about the culture there to this day absolutely fascinates me. Western occult ideas, and Austin Spare's sigilising sexual ideas, turned around with Tibetan instruments and shamanism. It just percolated over the years until one day we were just talking to somebody and said, "what would happen if we started a paramilitary occult organization now and made it really visible? If we all dress the same we'd really freak people out." We would have to have a special idea, a tool, to share; we'd have to have some information people didn't already know, to attract them. We started to bounce ideas around for a year or so and tape-record everything. We reduced it down to what became known as *Thee Grey Book*.[2] As the years went by, we got more and more serious. There was this great gaping hole between the "Victorian

---

1 The European Society for the Study of Western Esotericism.
2 Genesis P-Orridge et al, *Thee Grey Book*, privately published in London and elsewhere, ca 1981 and onwards.

Museum of Magic"³ and the present day. And there is no bridge. So why don't we be the bridge, and just say there is all this stuff you haven't heard about? We've been experimenting, and we are surprised how well it worked. Why don't you check it out too? I am not saying you might get anything from it, but, then again, you might. And if you do, isn't that great?

So we started to make records with Psychic TV in that spirit. On the first record we were wearing priests' collars, and we shaved our heads, and we were actually burning our own hair in a Catholic censer. We just said on the back of the first record, "if you want to know more about Thee Temple Ov Psychick Youth, write to this P.O. Box." Much to our surprise, lots of people started writing in. So we sent out statements and flyers, and talked about sigilisation, and then came up with this idea... Because we like the number 23 – something which we sort of inherited from William S. Burroughs – why not, on the 23rd of every month at 2300 hours, all of us do a sigil, and try and have an orgasm at the same time? No one has ever done that before. What would happen? So that is what we started to do. To this day, that is probably the only time that has ever been done on that scale. Eventually, globally, literally thousands of TOPY Individuals might sigilise similtaneously.

It had its effects. It appeared to be greater than it was, in terms of numbers, and it started to influence other people; they started to use magical ideas. Mostly people who grew out of the TOPY phenomenon and were living around our house or were working with us sometimes when we were trying to catch up with mail and so on. It just spread very organically, and showed that there was this hunger for something much more emotional and much more magical – to use the word that is so difficult to use. People also really got a great deal out of the network itself, of being in direct contact. Because in those days there was no internet; we were still using letters, postage stamps, postcards and all of that. We would have meetings and people would travel. Once a year we would rent a farm in Yorkshire called Arbor Low, which had its own stone circle inside the grounds. They would let us camp out there for three or four days every year. And we would just all meet. It was called "TOPY Global" and anyone from anywhere in the world could come. And we had a section for babies and mothers, and we all took turns doing different roles so that males could take care of kids and women had freedom and so on. We kept trying to constantly just reverse the different archetypes, just to see what would happen.

Amazing projects took place. To this day, the hardcore hundred or so people who became really involved and, like Carl, started their own networks – their own access points – we are still in touch with them. All of them are doing amazing thing: running book publishing, record labels, all kinds of things. It's like

---

3 A reference to the occult revival during the late 19th century, in England and elsewhere.

a secret masonic order that happened. The basic idea was that all we have in common really is the symbol.[4] And when you see that you think that that is somebody probably I can get on with. I could probably talk to them and they'd know what I was talking about. Or at least they'd be open-minded enough to listen. That was part of it too. So that is how it happened. We decided it would be a ten year project, 1981-1991, and then we stopped. The only hate mail we ever received during the whole time with TOPY was, "how dare you stop this?!" But we did. So then we sent out a postcard that said, "changed priorities ahead." Which was actually a street sign that we had seen. So it was a very sort of spontaneous reaction to things as we went along. There was no master plan except to try and keep things egalitarian, non-elitist and non-gender stereotyped. But in the beginning biological women were just called "Kali" because we wanted them to be as strong as they could, and then a number; biological males were called "Eden." We very quickly realized that people were starting to say, "what's your number? Oh, I am Eden 2 2 2. Oh, I am only Eden 1 3 1." The next year we just jumbled all the numbers around so nobody knew who was what, and what year they had got involved, or hadn't. And then we jumbled around the genders as well. So every time people tried to turn it into something fixed we tried to come up with a way to confound it. There was never a number 1, 2 or 3, and there were 23 number 23s.

Audience Question: You said something about creativity. I get the impression that a lot of what was happening was to create something in music, in art, in literature.

GBPO: We've always had this belief, ever since we joined a commune in 1968 in London called The Exploding Galaxy... The thing we took away the most, apart from the joy of sharing everything, was this idea that we received that everybody has a "genius factor." Everybody. And that if you can just encourage people to believe in themselves, and if you can give them the skills to start to explore different ways of expressing themselves, then no matter what it is – whether they are just the best person sweeping the floor or the greatest artist – it doesn't matter except they are a genius. We still believe in that until this day.

That is something we've always tried to encourage. And, of course, that leads to creativity. People would say things like, "why is there no magazine?!" Because we've not got time! "Well there should be a magazine!" Then you do it! And people would do it. People like Carl. "How come there is nothing Scandinavia?" And we said because nobody has asked. So it begun with TOPYSCAN, which eventually became TOPY EUROPE, and grew and grew and grew because of his

---

4 Reference to the "Psychick Cross."

influence. We didn't give them any instructions. We just said, *you do it*!

Ryan[5] was working with us in New York a long time after the TOPY ex-periment, and he came across a box of tapes; reel-to-reel tapes. And he said, "what are these?" Because he was going through the archives trying to catalogue everything in our basement, and we went, "ah, I don't know what they are!" "Well one of them says 'Early Worm,'" he said. "That's the first record we made in 1967." And he said, "well, why haven't you released it?" "Didn't have time." "Well you should; people would be interested." "Nah... no, no, no, it's crap, crap..." He said, "no really, people would like to know, they'd like to know how it went from wher-ever this is to where it is now." So then we said, "okay, you do it." He now has his own record label which has spread into all kinds of places worldwide with many, many different artists. All because we said *you do it*. It is an amazing response. It is amazing when you give people the confidence. You don't say it in a patronizing way, but just "why don't you do it?" You can. You can make things happen. Isn't that what magic is all about? That is how we've always worked. There is no linear system at all. It's just, "that seems useful."

Since we went, if you like, underground, people assumed it just stopped, but what has been surprising is that it continued. It got to the point where there was so much interest in what we'd been doing, that together with Jason Louv we even-tually compiled what is known as *Thee Psychick Bible*, which was originally like 120 pages in the early 1990s, but now is 540 pages. It was first published by Feral House Press in English. It is now also translated into Russian and French and is currently being translated into Spanish. It's been through its third or fourth edition, and it is still going strong and we've never advertised it or told anyone anything about it. It has its own life, which is the way we prefer. Those who want and those who know will find so... Now you've been told; you've got the option. We would recommend it; it is interesting.

At the end, when we got to the early 1990s, we were still experimenting; im-provising as we went. We ended up in Brighton in the South of England, and eventually there were five houses that were just all TOPY people, all TOPY indi-viduals, and each house was trying in its own way to create a TOPY way of living. Every Monday one house would cook for everybody else, and one house would clean for everybody else, and then one person would tell their life story. But they could only tell it if they promised to put *everything* that happened in. One of the things that shocked us was that over 80% of the people living in those houses had been sexually abused; males as well as females. That was one of the things none of us realized, but by telling our life stories and trusting each other that way, there was this incredibly deep loyalty that was being built.

Some of you might not know this, but in 1991 Scotland Yard and the British

---

5 Reference to Ryan Martin, P-Orridge's manager.

Government raided my house in Brighton because they considered me to be a "wrecker of civilization" and destroying the British way of life. They couldn't find a single person to say anything negative about me, and they offered bribes to people in TOPY, and no one said anything negative. That came from that same trust. So, where does it all end? It doesn't end. It's about opening the heart more and more to everything that is possible, and believing that everything is possible. The techniques you use, and the ways you focus yourself; work them out yourselves, take them from anywhere, invent new ones, use old ones; it doesn't matter.

Before all of this, we went to what is called a "public" school in England, which is actually a private school. They even had their own church, which was paid for by the Queen of England. So we went from Manchester down to the middle of England to go this school. The very first day that we went to that school, a bell went off and everybody disappeared, and we had no idea where everyone went. So we started walking around the buildings, looking for someone and eventually found a teacher and said, "where is everybody, Sir?" He grabbed me by my ear and hair, and he dragged me along and he said, "don't you know?!" I said "no, this is my first day..." He just dragged me through the school and into the church. Everybody in the school was there – all the teachers, all the pupils – and he dragged me down the middle of the church to the altar, threw me to the floor and said, "what class are you in?" And we said, "lower 5-2, Sir." And he said "no, you are not, you are in the class with all the six year olds, aren't you?!" And he shut me in with the six year olds, basically giving everyone permission to torment me for the next four years. Because I was under a huge painting of Jesus at the time, it made me think that there is something wrong with the forgiveness and love as part of this story. So we just started looking at it differently, and we decided to say the "Christ" instead of "Jesus" because the Christ can be just a way of life to me.

We are incredibly, almost pathologically curious, and so as time went by we started to read other things; partly by Crowley, partly by other people. We said, "hang on, this story is complete bullshit! The library in Alexandria; they destroyed all this stuff; how dare they?!" We just started to look for what might be the real story, and what might be the truth, and where it might really reside. It certainly seemed like one of the possibilities; that this could be at the very least purgatory or limbo; that this world was a sort of testing place. Lately we've come to the conclusion that we live in loops; in the way that they talk about string theory: there are infinite loops of our lives going on at the same time, and you can skip across them; a bit like a record, like with the grooves. So we suspect we skipped a few grooves but we don't know which direction they went. It's just one area of fascination.

Lady Jaye, who was my other half for a long time, was fascinated with Gnostic and Sumerian myths, and was really well read in those. She gave me a lot of interest in that, and told me all these stories of ancient myths. I have to be hon-

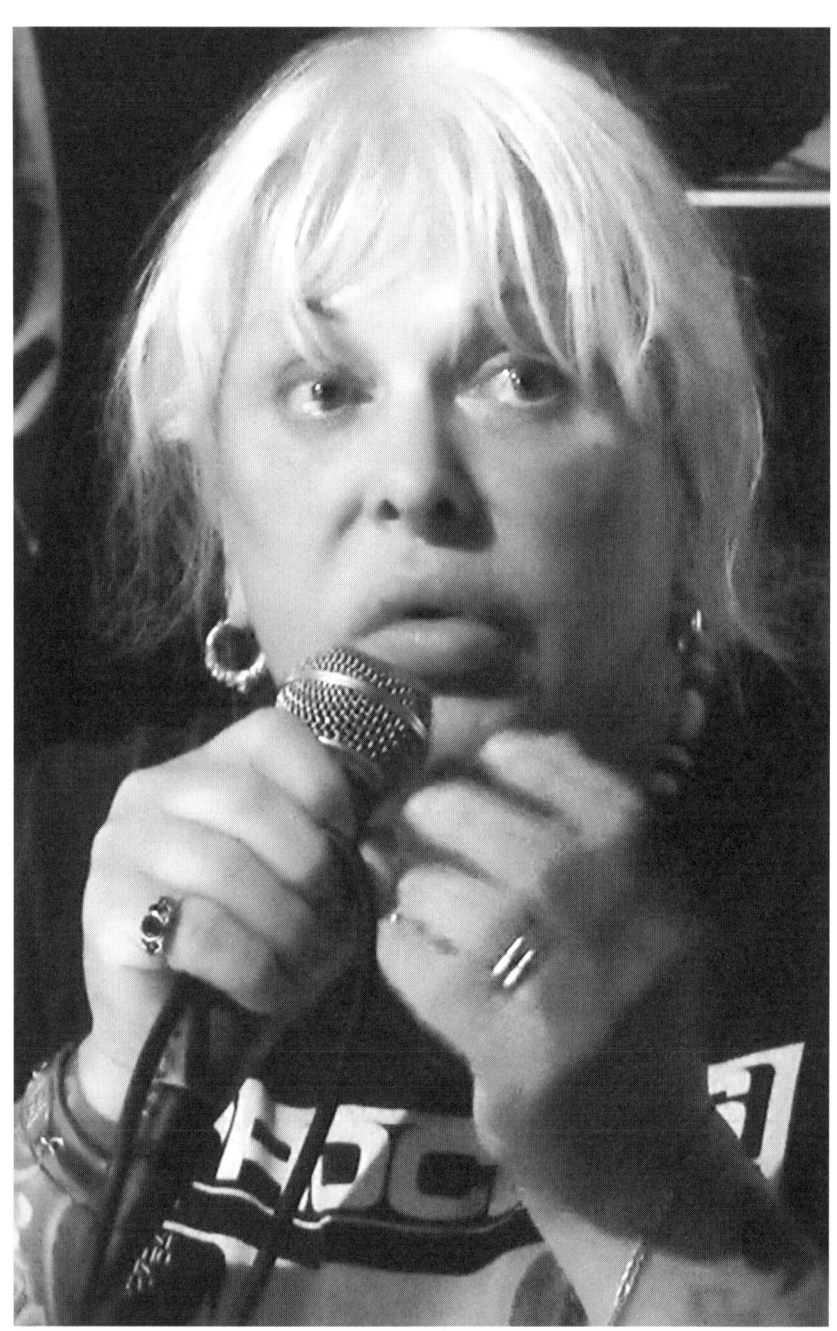

Live in Gothenburg together with White Stains, 2013. Video still by Patrik Lager.

est, you know... "Ancient Aliens" is really good too; that TV show they have in America. It has a really massive rating, and a whole mass of people are starting to question this story of what they've been told happened to human beings. There is a massive percentage that believe in the ancient aliens or extraterrestrials or the "panspermia of the creativerse," and not just a sudden flux; that we weren't just created by this Father Christmas thing. So, interesting things are happening in the culture. It is actually building up, like a pressure, that people are just really beginning to question those really deeply held, deeply entrenched control systems – which is what they are. When we see control systems, we try and see how they function. As Burroughs said, "always look for the vested interests."

Audience Question: When one reads things about you one often meets the word "pessimism," and a dark vision of the future; the idea that humanity is heading towards disaster. Is this something that has defined your vision?

GBPO: Well, we'd have to be optimistic to bother and do anything. If we were just pessimistic, there would be no point. We certainly think that humanity is at a crisis point; what's happened is that the prehistoric dynamic – which was quite useful at the time as a survival technique, if you like to simplify it – that the clan would try to survive, and there would be X number of children and females and males, and the males would try and keep the clan in existence through adversity and ice age and predators and so on... So the aggression of the male of the species was actually what kept our species on the planet. There was this basic moral, which is if it's something else, if it's something we've not seen before, if it's something we can't control, if it's the "other," then it's our enemy and we have to defend ourselves against it. While we have completely technologically advanced, we have left our behaviour behind. We've left it in a prehistoric state. It's other, it's different... Let's kill it. It's other, it's different... let's beat them up. That is still basically the formula of power on the planet. We have to completely rethink ourselves as a species and that is one of the reasons we came up with the idea of pandrogeny: the merging of the two. The ending of difference. When people say, "oh, the end of the world..." No, the world isn't going to end. But our species very easily could. Look at the arrogance there. Conflating this earth, this "world" with the survival of our species!

This planet may be very wounded by our obsession with unlimited consumption but it will recover and mutate, just as it did after the dinosaurs went extinct. So we *do* think the odds are very high that our species will refuse to fundamentally change and destroy itself, bar a few pockets, and return to a new stone age. But this beautiful "World" will replenish, mutate, and evolve. Perhaps even try yet another species to attempt to live in harmony with.

Audience Question: What if it doesn't happen?

GBPO: What if it doesn't happen? Then we'll all be happy, won't we? But you know what? We still think people should share; we still think they should think that way; we still think that that is the path to get to: the path where we are all part of one beautiful, forward-thinking organism, because we do believe, as Burroughs and Gysin said, that we're "here to go;" we're here to colonise space; we have amazing things that we are capable of doing that we've not done yet. And it would be such a tragedy not to do those. So in the end we'd rather do anything that forces us towards that direction that reminds us to keep on being inventive and amazing, because that is one of our great skills as beings.

Audience Question: What would you say are the most interesting things are going on in terms of magic and the occult?

GBPO: No idea... I'm sorry; we don't really have anything to do with it now. We go to Kathmandu. We have a little saying: "all you have to do is go to Kathmandu." That is the place where you see magic and devotion and the integration of every level of life, birth, death, sacrifice – all happening at the same time and happening without any friction. That is a really wonderful example, and it also includes Tibetan Buddhism. There is so much wisdom in Tibet; they have thousands of years of meditating. They are the only kind on this planet right now who have devoted themselves to thinking about peace. And what we have let happen to them... It's disquieting what has been allowed to happen. And we are letting it be destroyed in front of us.

Audience Question: How do you stay positive?

GBPO: Travel. When anyone says, "what can we do?" Travel. Go and see poverty, go and see different countries, go and see people who all they do is try and eat. Go and give food, as we did in Kathmandu. That year when we couldn't go home, we were doing a soup kitchen for beggars and refugees and lepers. And my children were helping, and they were nine and six years old, and they were giving food and clean water to lepers who had no fingers and were blind, but who smiled! And that is worth learning; seeing that face in there. It is all in the head and in consciousness, and it is in living the way that you believe as best as you can – whatever society you are in. Whenever you can go and see other places and see what is happening, you should. Because most of the ignorance is ignorance itself.

Gothenburg, 2013

Panel Question: As you know, this event is part of a conference organised by a society for the study of western esotericism. We have been thinking about that a lot: what is western esotericism? What would you say it is? If you would just try to put some words to it, because it's a very difficult concept.

GBPO: Well, we try not to put words to things too much. We use lots of words but we try to avoid definitions of anything. We keep hinting at things... To live a life that gets more generous, more kind and more open-hearted every day. To believe that things can be changed, both individually and in groups, and eventually in terms of the species. To have no limit to what you imagine. We imagined that DNA is a recording device that is just as likely to be the primary life force on this planet as Earth itself. We could just be the equivalent of cattle; just keeping DNA alive. That is a weird thought but it is true. DNA is continuous while we are not; we are individual. So we have thought about that, and we've thought that if we could start to forget that the human body is sacred, and instead say that it's not sacred because it's not. The human body is just a means of moving consciousness around. It's a temporary home for the consciousness. Once you start to look at what is possible, you could engineer this. We do believe that the end result would be to go into space; to colonize and go outwards both physically and mentally. Why not learn to hibernate? If little tiny creatures and bears can do it, surely we could do it too. And if we could hibernate, why not go further? Why not have gills and live under the sea? In other words, have no limit to what you imagine. And if you can imagine it, then try and make it happen. That, to me, is Western esotericism.

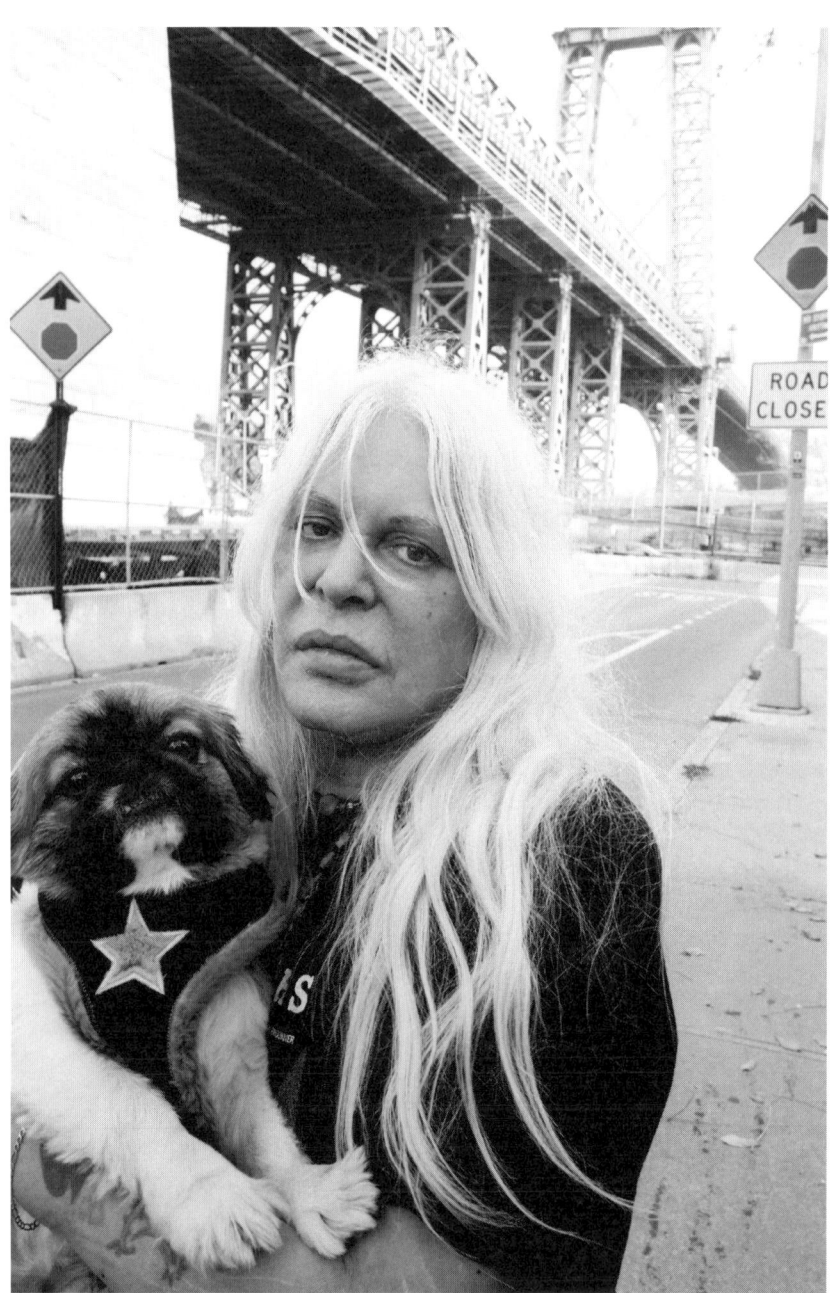

With Musty Dagger, New York, 2013

New York, October 29th, 2013

This time around, I brought the video camera to New York to continue the work on the "Change Itself" film that we had begun in Sweden during the summer of 2013.

CA: When you look back now at all the stuff that you've done, could you say that you have found yourself working in a specific tradition? Is there one term that could fit everything?

GBPO: Basically the tradition that we're interested in is "shamanic magical art." We came out of performance art, and noticed in performance that people would ritually dance, no matter how they looked to the other people, and that sometimes you are having out-of-body experiences, psychedelic repercussions, and so on. That was what made me go private in 1976 after the LAICA[1] performance by C.O.U.M., where we just decided to go for broke... I had blood enemas, and milk and piss enemas, and vomited and licked it up, and sliced my arm etc, etc... It was that classic, "where else can you go?" moment. You can go fine art, like Chris Burden, and say it wasn't gratuitous and that it was all very considered. Or you can die. Or you can look for why that drive is in you. What is it that drives you, over and over again, to do expression of any kind? The word that we would immediately use would be "ritual." We thought back to prehistoric times. How did art begin; what was the real origin of art? It was magical. The wise person or the oldest person of a clan would remember all the stories to pass on. They were a librarian in a sense, and also they were doing things visually, and with sound and costume and sand paintings and shrines. Literally to make the sun come back again. Because for tens of thousands of years proto-humans didn't know that the sun would come back. How could they? They would develop rituals to bring the sun back, and of course the shaman would always bring the sun back, so therefore the shaman must be greatly empowered, and got a lot of kudos for that; for bringing mornings. It was functional. Why did you need to even do that? Because you didn't know that the seasons would come back. You had no concept of human linear time. So everything, every single morning when you

---

1 Los Angeles Institute of Contemporary Arts.

awoke, was about trying to maintain continuity in order to survive. And it was also a spectacle that unified a clan. It could be a part of initiations after puberty. All these different aspects of biological life and geographical life, and the linearity of time; they all played into the origins of art.

Our passage began when we first came across Dada and Surrealism. It's funny to think back, but it was to avoid being beaten up at school. If you are a librarian in the school you could stay in the library all lunch time, and that would mean no-one would come in and attack you. To avoid being attacked every day we joined the librarians of the school, and really got into putting things in exact alphabetical order. Neat, tidy, easy to be found... All that stuff which we do to this day. Then we came across a book on Dada and Surrealism, and there's Max Ernst's collages, using old engravings. It was one of those Eureka moments... "Oh God, it doesn't have to look like anything you've seen or experienced!" You can create worlds, intentions, characters, archetypes, and include them in the work.

We were also fascinated by the lives of the artists. We found over the decades that the biographies and autobiographies of the artists that we admire or did admire are crucial to whether or not we can appreciate the work. So that was the path we chose. We thought art has to be about your life; your life has to be about art and the act of creation. Comprehension by others is the least important aspect. You do things that touch you and that feel symbolically powerful to you. You look for potency and the reclamation of your right to create and dream and reassess and adjust and rebuild consensus reality as you see fit. It is your absolute right. And of course that eventually unwound until it became, "it's also your absolute right as an artist to unfold the body." As the body is always included in the rituals, then there should be no separation. Somehow those must go together. How do they go together? What makes this form of creation potent and powerful and able to literally generate cultural engineering? You know it took Hitler and 30 guys to nearly take over the world. It took the Christ and supposedly 13 disciples to mess up spirituality on the planet for thousands of years, and in turn leading to the destruction of tens of millions of people who were killed for disagreeing.

So the whole thing was really clearly knitted together for me: spirituality and mysticism. The absolute right of any and all individuals to create. The malleability of everything we've been told; that whatever society says is the story is not the story. Therefore it is our job as an artist, as a performer, whatever it might be, to create miracles in a sense; to take even the most mundane things and recast them in such a way that they create this jolt in other people; and the jolt will hopefully make them hesitate before they fall back into the sequence of loops and habits and acceptance of the norm. So that jolt is incredibly important. You know, my jolt was discovering these artists. But we think we were really fortunate to realize that if their lives weren't interesting, if it was more of a careerist form of art, then it didn't have the same soul; the same depth of being and the same longevity.

There is a really regressive trait in humanity at the moment, and it disturbs me. The whole disconnection from the process of thinking of learning and hearing stories and allowing into your life the unexpected as a matter of principle. When we do lectures, we have a lot of young students in their early 20s, and they all say how much they love their laptops and they do digital this and digital that. We usually tell them that when we were 15 or 16 we were living in Birmingham. If we wanted to try and get a book by William S. Burroughs or Jack Kerouac or Jean Genet or Henry Miller they were banned. They were banned as obscene. Not because anyone had read them, but because they'd heard it. *Lady Chatterley's Lover* being obscene? But it was; it was banned. So we would have to choose to lie to our parents, and say we were visiting friends or relatives, and then save the train money we got from them, which meant we had to hitch-hike to London. During the hitch-hiking, there was a whole experience of physical discomfort – it's cold, you get rained on, you could be robbed... Once we counted it was over 17 hours before someone stopped, and it was snowing. One reason most people pick you up is to stay awake. They want you to talk, and they tell you all about their lives; they tell you really intimate secrets because they know they won't see you again, and you don't know who they are. So you get this beautiful sharing without any boundaries or censorship. That happened several times just on the way to London. Then you get to London and you know that if you go to Piccadilly Circus there will be people with long hair, and they'll know what's going on, where to get some hash, and usually one of them would say, "oh, you can crash at my place," and let you sleep on the floor. Then the next day we would go all around Soho to the porno shops, knowing that the only place to find these books at all was in dirty bookshops. And so we would have these conversations with the owners in the bookshops that showed us the secret envelopes of pornography and tried to sell those, and we would go, "No, no, no we want *Naked Lunch*!" And bit by bit we would find the books, and then we'd have to hitch-hike all the way back home and lie again to our parents about what we'd done, and sort of sneak the books in and not mention them, in the hope that they wouldn't notice that our library was growing. And now the process is almost an instinct or an impulse to get something and go to Amazon.com or the equivalent and see if it's available, press a button and it's sent. 30 seconds, instead of three days of unexpected meetings, of generosity from strangers. All of that is lost; that richness... Storytelling is one of the great activities of the human species.

CA: When the will and the effort unite, magical things will happen – synchronicities! – whereas today it's very much a causal handling of commodities dealing with or containing information. It is of course not the same thing. You have to make an effort to get something extra out of it.

GBPO: And you don't know what it's going to be. It's not predictable.

CA: It's an adventure.

GBPO: And that's one of the other differences. Clicking on Amazon is predictable, and there is very little chance of adventure involved. But when you let loose and jump off the cliff into the unknown, then incredible, unlikely, very enriching sensations and stories and alternate views of what we see as reality... Those are all there. In that leap of faith. Hence, "see a cliff and jump off!" One of our slogans which is crucial in terms of our approach to doing life and everything else. To me, nothing is worse than inertia.

CA: You have done so many different things, worked with so many different modes of expressions, but still I'd say that you are a poet. You are a poet and you filter reality and basically what comes out are words, and then those are used for different media, and different collaborations. Very often you find yourself in collaborations. Would you say that you are dependent on the "third mind experience?" Or could you consider working strictly in a "first mind" way?

GBPO: The third mind way, the third being, is essential. Yesterday, we were doing this panel, and it was about feminism and collage, and its relation to identity; partly regressive politics, and partly reassessment of the value of collage. Because for generations collage was seen as a not "real" art; it was something peripheral like a quick sketch. That's been changing.

There is a moment when you step over all the things you've created and made: the objects, the items, and so on, and think, what real value does this have? If we don't make use of it in some way to benefit the human species? Is there a way? If there is a way, what is the way? Over and over again, the answer we find is to share it with other people, to pool your resources, to move towards the idea of a community, to set up experimental and potentially imploding but to me essential new ways with small but like-minded groups. People pooling their mental, physical, magical, material resources, so that everybody suddenly has this excessive support in every possible way that they could never have alone. You can live like a millionaire if everybody trusted each other enough to give each other the key. If you know different people with houses in different countries you can have six houses and go there whenever you want. There is an amazing resistance to that idea; more so in the United States than anywhere else we've been. Not a commune, but a community; like a village but a village inhabited by people who believe in creation, who believe in looking for ways to expand our knowledge of spirit, soul, intelligence, everything... And that's sad. You know, there's always people who have cars and motorbikes, and when they are not using them they are locked up. When they could be used to make so many more things happen. So we always view that long term it has to be about community. Has to be. One of the other things that's really struck home is trying to explain pandrogeny. People think it's about gender. It's not about gender. It's about unification, it's about ending opposites, ending opposing binary systems and surrendering a huge amount of ego into a true faith in this idea of enrichment through sharing.

CA: Recently, you had a retrospective exhibition at the Warhol Museum in Pittsburgh.[2] There was also the big photo book with photos from your entire life.[3] When you look back at these things in this concrete way, very hands on, is there some phase in your career or your life that you're not satisfied with in terms of the art, or with what you were doing?

GBPO: We kept most of the art activity hidden for 30 years. To make collages, to paint, to create objects was my relaxation time. And it was a really big emotional wrench to make the collages available. A lot of them are very intimate; a lot of them are obscure British or Genesis in-jokes that a lot of people probably miss completely. So we were concerned about the language of our collages; the references, the very obscure and oblique aspects of them, and what they meant to me in terms of certain places in life. Some of them were just aesthetic experiments but a lot of them were the exploration of the self again... Take the body out of the body, put it in Polaroid, reassemble it, and discover that it looks like an alien baby's head. Those moments are the moments you live for: when something grows and it's almost instantaneous. One minute it's just stuff and then suddenly we see it!

We talked to Burroughs once about cut-ups. This was around about the time of his *Cities of the Red Night*. "Do you still do cut-ups?" I asked. He said, "almost never. My brain is mutated and does them automatically." And we thought it made sense. If you do something long enough, you are literally re-programming the various neuro-pathways. And we found the same thing with collage and connecting unlikely objects to create something funny or strange and provoking, whichever it might be. The longer we've done it, which now is 40 odd years, the more it happens without any conscious thought.

You're being told stories all the time. There are all these little stories and narratives going on, and some people unfortunately have been trained by peer groups, family, education, society, to only see a gold shoe and a horn. But they would never put the two together. And that is where the shift between a surrendered life – a life that's been surrendered to just live out the expectations of that

2 "S/he Is Her/e", June 15-September 15, 2013. A major retrospective of P-Orridge's work.
3 *S/he Is (Still) Her/e*, First Third Books, London, 2013.

particular norm, which might be Africa, India, New York, Moscow – and the people who either instinctively, or through a lot of thinking or through good fortune, see that everything really is raw material, and that you have an absolute right to reassemble anything and everything in new ways. That is always positive.

CA: You can say that that's a method that you inherited, and that you developed, and which is now completely integrated into your creative system. I'm curious if there are any areas of research or attraction where you haven't yet applied this method, but you feel that you would like to? Some kind of new technology, some kind of new medium?

GBPO: We would like to work with scientists. One thing myself and Jaye always wanted to do, if it was ever possible, was to have male and female genitals. And also to get rid of our bellybuttons. When we woke up from the breast implants, the matching breast implants on Valentine's Day 2003, the first words that came out from being under a heavy anaesthetic were, "these are our angelic bodies." And when we looked in books we realized that angels don't have bellybuttons because they are not born of woman. We thought that that would be so brilliant. Not so much to say we're angels, but to say we are not from your species, we are removing ourselves as absolutely as possible from your species in the hope that it might kickstart the evolutionary step that might not otherwise happen, by causing a dialogue, a debate, a provocation. So that is something we would like to do: work with a very friendly scientist who could propose things. We would love to have gills so we could live under water. Jaye wanted to have fur and horns like a deer. She said she had wanted horns since she could remember. So really what we're saying is we'd like to find genetic engineering and experimental science that opens up new options and vistas of other beings to be physically; to push it forward and say a) the human body is not finished; b) it's not sacred – it's just stuff. What matters is the mind. The mind is who you are. And really push everybody's concept of what a human body might be; especially as we do believe that it's our right and our destiny as a species to move into space, just like Brion Gysin said. At first we were sceptical, but having gone through 20 years of really rigorous debate with Lady Jaye, it became apparent that they were absolutely right. There is no point in being here to just repeat ourselves and just create more and more problems through lack of resources, or greed for resources, fake economic systems; totalitarian capitalism as we call it... We have to move out! Out into the other apparent universes; not necessarily even to colonize, but to explore. Very much just like "Star Trek." Just to go and see what's there! To experience different forms of being, existence, whatever you might call it.

CA: Isn't that actually quite a good summing up of your life and your art?

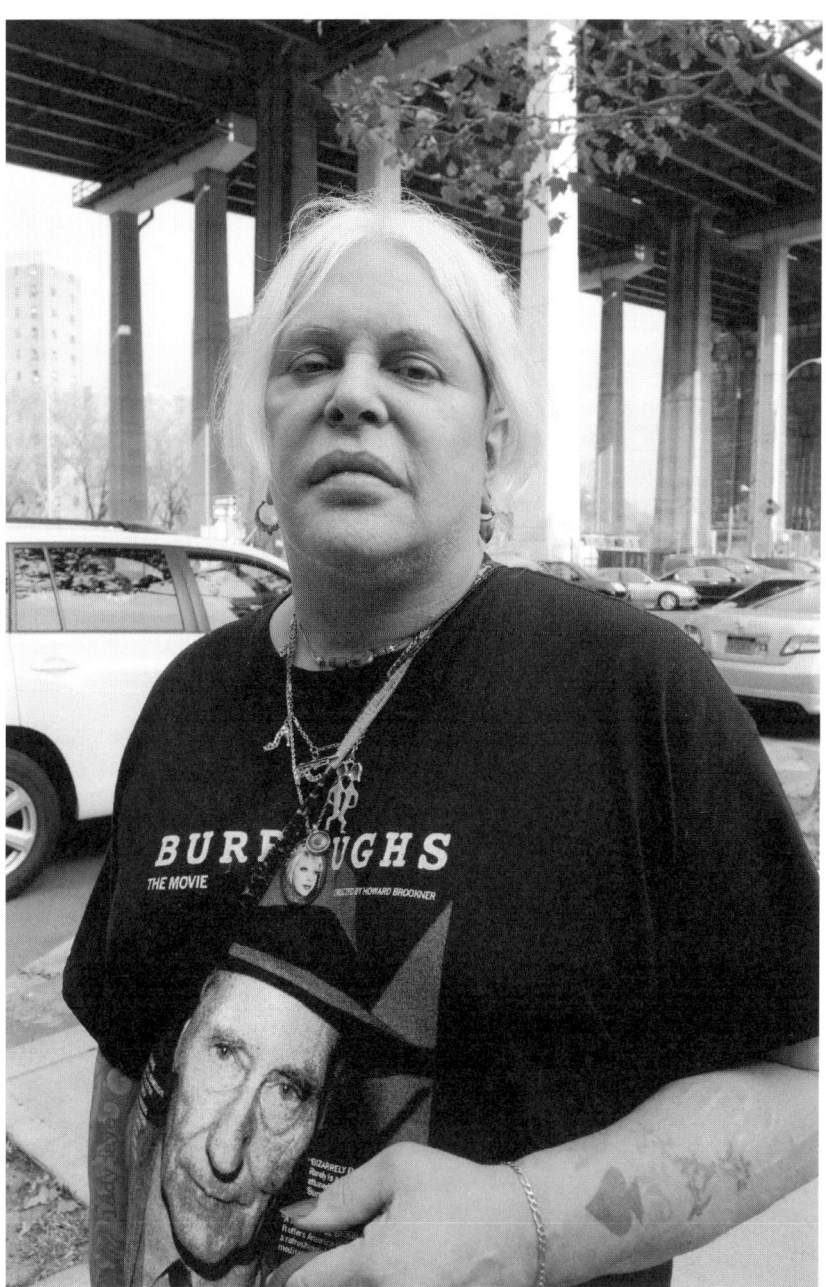

New York, 2013

GBPO: In a sense. You know, we have no limitations on the imagination and how it could adjust and reconfigure the human body and/or mind. The body is disposable; it has a very limited shelf life. But the mind can become more and more acute as time goes by, and continue learning and thinking and hopefully getting slightly more wise.

CA: But couldn't you say, just for art's sake, that a limited time frame is a fantastic incentive?

GBPO: It is, if people would become truly aware of its limitations in terms of time. Most people that we meet secretly think that somehow they'll always be alive. It's pretty much impossible for most people to truly conceive of being dead. It's even hard for me, and we've been dead... So that's one of the great interrupters of progress. That's why we had that thing painted. One of the first things we did at the Death Factory,[4] was to get some paint and put "WE ALL DIE" on the wall near the sink. Cosey objected, saying it was morbi; as did many visitors. Yet to me it is an essential code we must all confront. And when you have died, and you've lost people, you realise that truly every second is precious. How you deal with that idea that no matter how healthily you live, you don't know how long your body will be here. To put things off and say, "oh well, what did my parents want me to do? They wanted me to finish University, get a degree and then be an avant-garde artist..." And we said, "why wait four years? We can't do that," because we'd just been dead a year ago... We know that we have no idea how many seconds, minutes, days, years we have. That's been an amazingly positive incentive: live every day as if it is the last day that you live. Your entire life will be based on judging that day, and the same with work. One should always try and make work as complex, deep and strong as possible, because it could be the last thing you say.

It's amazing, much more so in Western societies, that people have somehow hypnotised themselves into the idea that they are not the one that is going to die. In places like Nepal and India, and so on, they have a much more integrated concept of death. It is part of daily life. If you live in Kathmandu, you see all the people's bodies burning and being swept out into the river, and it really comes home: you're just stuff. It's burnt, swept away like dirt and that's it… So who are you? Who were you? Where are you now? Are you anywhere? It was going to Nepal and meeting the Tibetans that convinced me and Jaye that existentialism is not enough. There are too many other phenomena that contradict it; just like Darwinism is a very, very deeply flawed concept. There is so much it does not

---

4 The "Death Factory" was the nickname of Industrial Records' studio/work space at 10, Martello Street, in London.

explain and can't explain. So, yeah, that's being alive. Trying to learn how to make every second precious.

CA: Now, the most difficult question ever: what makes you happy?

GBPO: What makes me happy? Very little since Lady Jaye dropped her body, to be honest. Truly happy. We get a small amount of happiness out of being vindicated. The TATE Britain have now bought two pieces of ours, and sent a letter saying that they are being put into their national collection of important modern art... Which is amazing. Robert Wilson, who did "Einstein on the Beach," the famous eight or 24 hour opera or whatever it was, finally bought "Boaz," which is three Plexiglass photographs of my teeth, going from normal teeth to gold in a column, relating to the freemasonic column. The Louvre in Paris have dedicated a room to articles from his art collection, and so our piece is in the Louvre. We have a piece of art in the Louvre! We have art in the TATE Britain and we also have an art installation in the Pompidou in Paris. So it's not so much exactly happiness, but it's nice to feel that you were right and that what you were trying to say and do has finally sunk in. Of course they've only got to the 1970s; that means they are still forty-five years behind in terms of concepts. But... it's a beginning.

CA: You have to take into consideration that some artists simply don't make it while they are alive. And yet you have.

GBPO: Yeah, it's pretty amazing, it's quite funny really... Old tampons[5] in the TATE. Musty Dagger,[6] she makes me happy. We can literally just lie on the bed for hours and play, and she'll attack the toys and they'll squeak, and when she grabs one of the squeakers she'll just do it over and over... She'd lie for hours being stroked on her belly and we talk, and she talks back. It's nice to have something that's living to touch. That's what we miss the most; having someone to hold or touch... Now we always have her there, so we can fall asleep with my left hand on her...

What else? Coming up with ideas makes me happy. Certainly putting together those Polaroids of Jaye's panties and going, "oh my god, that's brilliant!" That gives me a moment of real happiness; just to see that the process that we began so long ago not only still works but it's getting, in a sense to me, more and more accurate, more and more seamless... We talked yesterday at the Brooklyn Museum. We were showing collages, and we actually stopped and said, "by the way, just

5 Reference to the artwork "Tampax Romana," originally exhibited at the ICA, London, in 1976, and now in the collection of TATE Britain.
6 Musty Dagger was P-Orridge's dog at the time of this conversation.

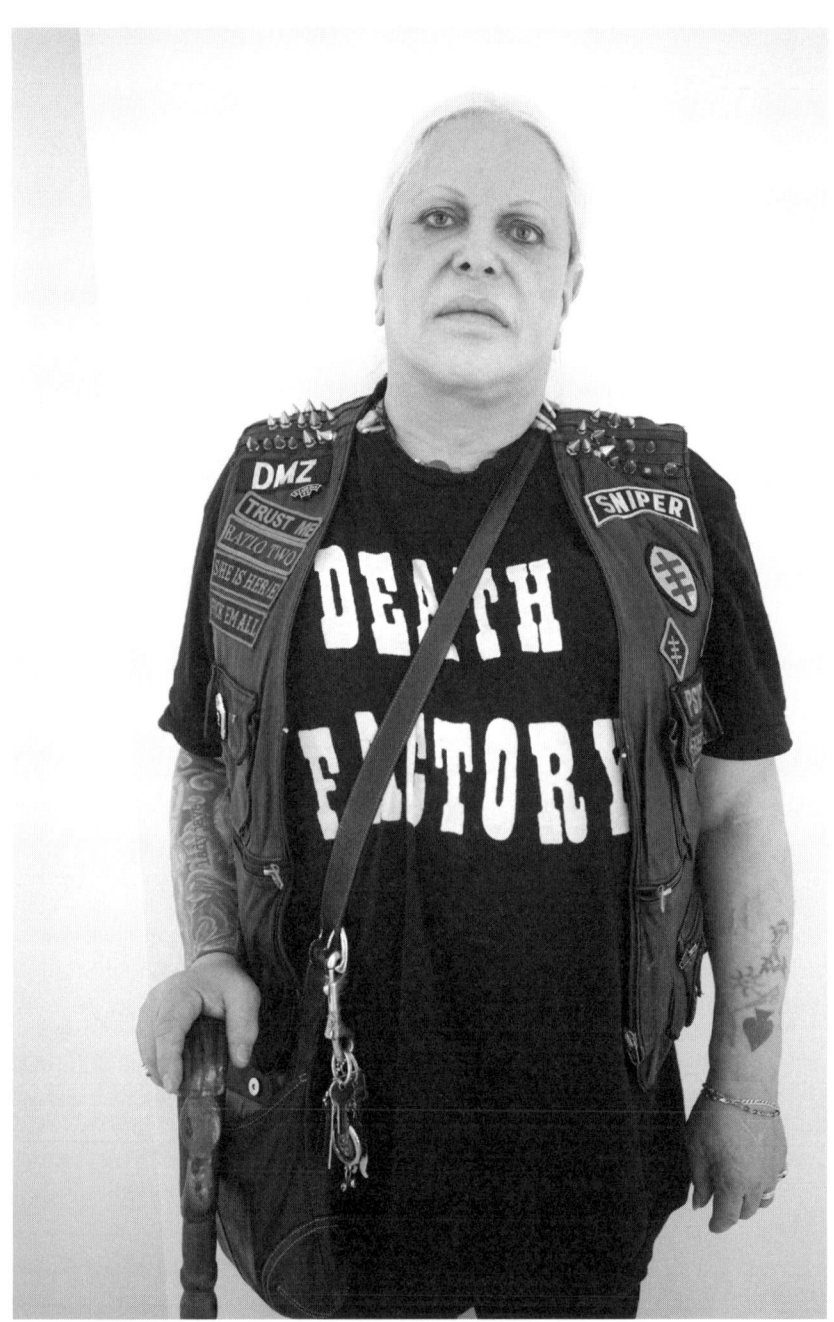

New York, 2016

so you know, we only use scissors and glue, scissors and stick-glue." Somebody went "really?" We said, "yes, we know, you will ask me what software do I use and the answer is *we don't.* It's all done with scissors and glue, and we have no reason to change." Because it's a skill that we've mastered, and just like it takes painters decades to feel they've got their painting working correctly, it's been like that with collages for me.

So we get happiness out of completing artworks, of seeing something and making it materialized. And when some museum or private collector buys something, that's nice. But these are all very fleeting things, compared to every minute filled with happiness and love by Jaye. There are still huge sections of emptiness…

CA: You have been what one could call a "serial monogamist," involved in very long relationships. Can't you see that you might enter a new relationship?

GBPO: People always ask me that. From a young age we believed that we were supposed to find the ultimate woman for me. That somewhere out there was the ultimate woman, and we found her. And now she can't be here twice. Well, we could go into reincarnation and so on but we believe that she is just waiting. People have expressed romantic interest in me, or sensual, sexual interest in me, but I don't feel anything. Nothing happens. So that actually doesn't bother me really. We have a lot of good friends that are that close, but no, we've not felt any interest really. We look at it like Jaye has left me to complete a lot of projects here, in this "non-census" reality, and we've been blessed by having a most amazing relationship in a physical form. Why be greedy, you know? You can't find the ultimate woman twice. You can think you have, but when you actually find her, you know there's no one else.

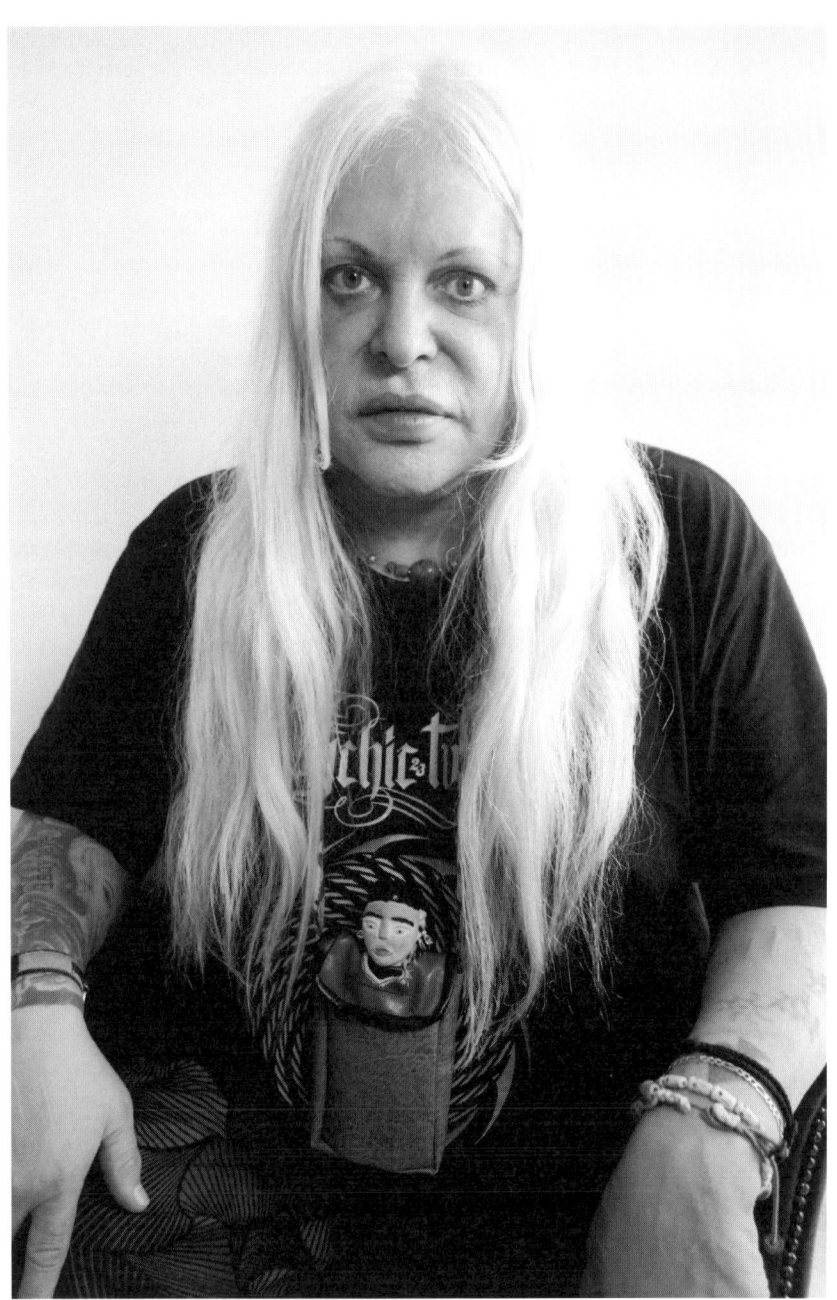

Oslo, 2014

Oslo, February 21st, 2014

PTV3 were on a European tour but didn't come to Stockholm. So I went over to Oslo instead to talk some more. Experience had taught us that tour life is not conducive to long and substantial interviews, but at least we got to shoot some material for the "Change Itself" film, and also recorded some poetry readings at Gen's hotel.

CA: You seem to be more or less always 30 years ahead of your time. Do you ever think about that perspective?

GBPO: Sometimes, but when we think about it, it's frustrating. We don't like the idea of being trapped in that little bubble of the 1970s. We're aware that there's always been, until recently, a huge error in art history, where the 1970s were basically ignored. Mail art and Fluxus, and even Joseph Beuys talking, were basically ignored because they couldn't fit them into the "isms." It's only in the last four years that they've actually started going back and filling in that gap. They did a big show at the Barbican, and had C.O.U.M. in it, and they had Gilbert & George, and so on. A lot of these people used to have spaces at 10, Martello Street, which is interesting.[1] So they have started to reassess the 1970s. We see it as a vindication. But you know the way we work: it's always what's next, what's in the future, how do we do something further along. Having them threading on the tail is a mixture of the pleasure of being accepted on some level, even tiny level. It's nice that we got a letter from Nick Serota[2] saying, "after meeting with the directors of the Tate, we are very happy to say that your works have been moved from the archives to the national collection of fine art and we hope to increase all this as years go by." So they intend to collect more, which is good. I mea, that's quite a breakthrough.

CA: Can you see yourself as having been, and being, influential?

---

1 This was the office and workspace of Throbbing Gristle and others. See earlier note.
2 Sir Nicholas Serota (b 1946), an art historian and curator, who served as the Director of the Tate from 1988 to 2017.

GBPO: There is no question. I mean, it could sound egocentric but the evidence is such. Somebody came up to me at the airport when we arrived here, and said "are you Genesis?" I said yes, and then they said, "you've influenced what I do, and you've changed my life, and thank you." People say that a lot. And other artists too; young artists in New York also say that I have been a big influence. Interesting. Recently, one person we know very well said that they were in love with someone, and that the reason for them being able to really, truly be in love for the first time was through the example of Jaye and myself of being 100% committed, regardless of the fear of failure; and they said, "it was you that made me feel that I should just surrender and give myself to what I really felt, and as a result my sex life is being incredible compared to anything before, and my life is happier than it's ever been, and that was because of you." That is as good as it gets.

CA: That's being quite influential!

GBPO: It's out there, and it's one of the best rewards you can get. We just hope there are enough opportunities for anybody who we might be useful to. That is why we try and do anything we can. Whether it's a book or a film or anything or whatever. My ongoing motivation for that is to try and reach who we're supposed to. That's a sense of duty as much as anything else; it's a responsibility to share what you feel you've learned, in case it's helpful. You don't know whether it will be, but just in case. That's why we've done so many interviews over the years, most of which disappear into archives and recycling... But sometimes it touches. And obviously with music, there is no question. There's a whole world with DJs and music labels and bands and t-shirt manufacturers and shops; all of which exist as a result of us coming up with the concept of "industrial" music. Even though it's mutated in so many directions – just like jazz or something. So that is where cultural engineering came in. There is no question. Times have changed with technology, and it's harder to have such specific leverage on the culture; and we're quite sure that that's deliberate: that a lot of the technology is a distraction that stops people from action. In my generation it was pot and hash, and thousands of people had great ideas and thought about what could happen and what they could do, and only a few were actually awake afterwards to actually put it into practice. Which is true even of me. It wasn't until after we had totally stopped smoking hash at University that we became truly pro-active. In 1969. Soon after that we had started C.O.U.M., and within five more years we had started industrial music. Technology has been working the same way. To me it's almost terrifying... When you go into restaurants in New York, and a group of people have come together for somebody's birthday, and they all sit down around a table and they all have fun and then they all start with their phones. They don't even talk to each other while they are having dinner together. That's pretty terrifying.

CA: In terms of the collages, and more specifically the sigils, you've done so much over the years. And of course they all have this "meta-programmatic" or magical aspect. Is that always consciously present even when you do other stuff, like sculptures that you know will end up in an exhibition? Is there always that sort of magical programming in it?

GBPO: Always. But interestingly, when we do an exhibition of collages, like "30 Years Of Being Cut Up," the sigils are the ones that don't sell. The ones that are actually clearly sigils. Nobody has bought any of them.

CA: Why do you think that is?

GBPO: They don't understand them, and they are probably a little afraid of them, and they don't fit any existing art aesthetic. They are not meant to look pretty, they are not meant to be finished, they are not made to be inside a frame, which is frightening to a lot of people. They don't know the language; it's an alien language; it's an alien landscape. That is something we have noticed, and it's obviously significant. They can follow us to the point of political satire – collages of the Queen and so on – but when it gets to direct magic, they shut off. That's interesting.

CA: Magic protects itself?

GBPO: Possibly. I mean, they were never really made to be sold so we're not really bothered about it on a commercial level. There is something in them that scares people, or intimidates them in some way.

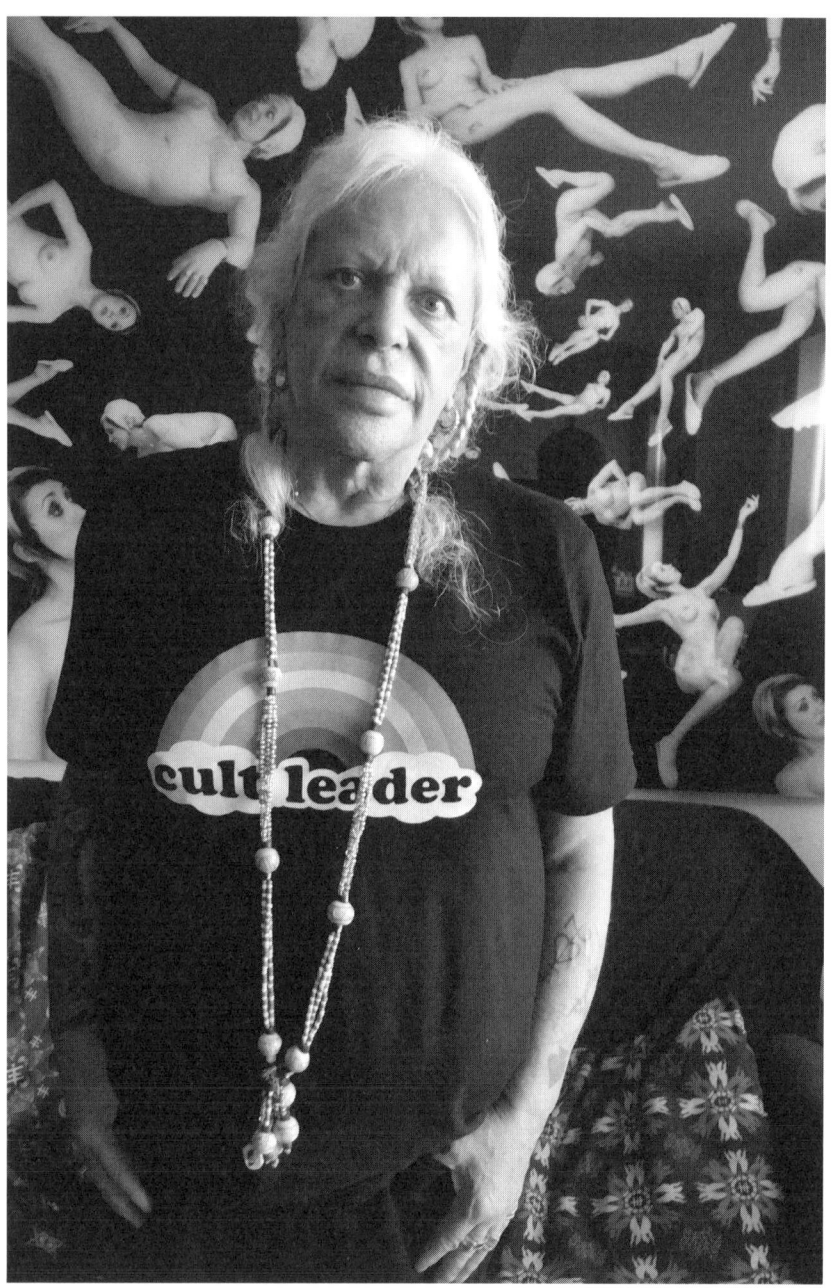

New York, 2018

New York, August 4th, 2018

Although I was spending a lot of time in New York between 2016 and 2018, we didn't get around to making a formal interview again until the summer of 2018. At that time, many interesting things were going on in Gen's life and career. Good things, such as an increase of exhibitions and exposure, and also a new relationship (with Spanish artist Susana Vico Valero). But also less good things, such as being diagnosed with leukaemia and beginning active cancer treatments.

CA: There was the thing at the Warhol Museum, there was the Rubin,[1] and there have been two or three shows at the Invisible Exports gallery. Within a fairly short period of time, there was a lot of exposure and success. How did that make you feel?

GBPO: It was an exponential movement. There was more and more exposure faster and faster, closer and closer to mainstream media. Actually into mainstream media. We've even ended up in fashion, which is about the lowest priority on my list. What's the question though? What do I feel about all of that happening?

CA: I was thinking mostly of the emotional aspects of crossing that hurdle. After having done things successfully but not on that integrated level on a larger scale, then suddenly you were there on that level.

GBPO: There isn't a clear formula, and there isn't that horrible repetition of formula that most people do when they have a piece that's successful. We change according to what we need to say, and as the world changes, and as society changes, and culture changes and mutates, and as we, hopefully, sometimes discover a little more wisdom, or have a new emotional experience that we can learn from, or meet somebody that we can be stimulated by... All of that goes into the work, always. Everything that ever happens to you is an influence. Everyone you meet,

---

1 "Try To Altar Everything", a Breyer P-Orridge exhibition at the Rubin Museum in New York, 2016. In re: the Warhol Museum exhibition in 2013, please see earlier notes.

that you've ever met, every person that's ever been a lover, every book you've ever read, every film you've ever seen, every time you've got on a bus; everything influences what you make if you're doing creation the way we do, which is that it truly is inseparable from life itself. Life is about seeking wisdom, and it's devotional, and if you succeed at all to start to speak, the reason you speak is to hopefully, in some way, inspire change in others. Otherwise it's got no value. Art never has intrinsic value; its only value is the story it tells, and whether that story gives something to other people. Not gives in terms of entertainment, but gives in terms of stimulation and information that they can then cherry pick for what's relevant in their context. It's all about giving and making available anything you feel you've learned or been confused by or spiritually re-energized by, revolted by, whatever it is. If it's affected you in some way maybe it can do the same, or the opposite, for someone else. So you present those special moments when something happened, and all you say is, "I'm humane, you're humane, this may be of use. If it's not, fine, but if it is, you're welcome." That's the value of creation.

CA: That said, the expansion into these so-called higher spheres of attention and exposure gives a greater potential platform to spread these ideas and to spread this information.

GBPO: It does if the ideas are still in it.

CA: In your case they are. The Rubin exhibition was like stepping into your psyche.

GBPO: Beth[2] came to me and said that she wanted to do an exhibition. She came to visit me here in the "nest" and talked about things, and she certainly seemed to get what we were doing. She saw it as more related to shamanic and occultural views of so-called reality; that our means of perception were closer to their traditional exhibitions than we'd ever thought. Because, as you know, their speciality and their sort of flagship reason for being there is that they collect and exhibit Himalayan and Nepalese art: artworks, relics and shamanic tools, and all the trappings of belief systems. Thangkas and altars, everything, but all to do with worship, spiritual journeys, the desire to have revelation, to get off the karmic wheel; all of that. Many of the items and sculptures are beautiful anyway, which is how we got drawn to so much of that when we were young. She knew that we'd been interested in Tibetan beliefs, culture, and Buddhism since we were ten years old, when my father gave me my copy of *Seven Years in Tibet*. She knew about that, which is also incredibly productive and liberating, and saves so much

---

2 Beth Citron, the curator of the exhibition "Try To Altar Everything," 2016.

time; you don't have to try and justify why you exist, and why they should be interested. There's nothing worse than when they come and say, "we're interested in doing an exhibition," and then they go, "prove to us that it's worth doing an exhibition." You shouldn't have to; you should be there because they've already decided. Anyway, she did something really, really constructive and that left a lasting impression on me in terms of subtleties and perceptions about how to curate a show. This was her first solo curated show at the museum. She took me there to look at the museum and see the space that we would be using. The exhibition that was on was about shamanic tools and relics from Nepal and Tibet and... what's the other place?

CA: Bhutan?

GBPO: Bhutan, thank you. We were walking around, and we actually said to her out loud, "these look like things we made with Jaye. This is just like what we make; our stuff would look totally at home in here." She said, "Yes, that's why I think it connects." That was the moment when we just let go of the doubts. It became a true collaboration with her. How long did we take? At least two years to get it together.

CA: Then you also travelled to Nepal again.

GBPO: When we made the deal that we would definitely do an exhibition, my only condition, apart from that I had to be there as much as possible, was to have a month in Nepal. They were fine with that. They needed a title. So we said "well, we'll go home and we'll send you 23 different possible titles and see if that works." We came home and we'd go and open a diary at random and look for a phrase that looked interesting. Notebooks, poems, collages, everything we had... Then we sent the list off, and they rang up a few days later and they said, "everyone agrees that title of yours, 'Try to Altar Everything,' is brilliant, that's exactly the one we want." We went, "what? What? Where did you get that from?" They said, "it was on your list, it was number 23." Apparently, I'd actually sent 40 titles, which we couldn't remember because we must have just been on autopilot here, and number 23 was "Try to Altar Everything," which was from the title of a collage which was on the altar at the "Gates Institute;"[3] in mine and Lady Jaye's special, magical space. As soon as she said that we realized it was a great title, and it was exactly what we do, you know? It was brilliant but we'd never consciously recognized it. "They're spotting it faster than we are; this is amazing, right?"

---

3 "The Gates Institute" was the name of the home and workspace of Breyer P-Orridge in Brooklyn, New York.

It was fantastic, I was so excited. They asked about audience participation. We went, "what if people are invited to bring in something small that for them has really potent significance of some kind; no matter how banal it looks to anyone else?" You know, it could be a bus ticket, but that could be the bus ticket that when you were on the bus you got a message that your parents died, or it could be the bus ticket from when you went to meet your ultimate lover, or anything. Anyone else would go, "it's just a piece of paper with a ticket on it." But it's not. It's just that you don't know that story. When you get that story, it's not a ticket anymore; it's this huge hologram of information which in turn is touching other holograms of information. In a sense, you're accessing the oracle. The oracle is everything in this amorphous, infinite, flowing cloud. Not the cloud like they talk about now – that's why we wanted to avoid the word – but that's how we imagine it: the Akashic record; whatever. We believe that when you do the oracular nuts or shells in Africa – in Vodun – it's the same oracle that you get from the *I Ching,* and it's the same oracle that you get from the Tibetan oracle going into a trance, and so on. All of them are the same one.

So we suggested that everyone at the opening could be invited, and during the show, to bring something – not too big, just for logistical reasons – that we would then display in some way to demonstrate this concept of trying to "altar" everything; and that everybody, probably most of the time unconsciously, is always a part of that process. You know, the way that people keep bits of jewellery they never wear, and things from their parents or grandparents, or a stone off a beach and so on. People do that all the time but they don't necessarily stand back and contextualize it and conceptualize it.

Then we thought about how to display them? We came up with jars, little glass circular jars with a screw-on lid, and then they made false walls all the way around, and drilled holes so you could put the jars in. There was a glass front, so we could just put the items into the jars and put them into the walls and gradually it would fill up into this massive magical battery – like when we used to collect all the sigils – and there were about a thousand or so of these jars in the walls.

Then they were saying that it would be nice if it's an exchange, so we said, "well, why don't we give everybody a little psychick cross pendant." Because to me, that represents everything we do at this point. That's the ultimate hologram of what we're doing. And it's also the thing that's easily recognized; it's like being a Freemason. It's the non-verbal key; a non-verbal signal that this is a person that probably has common interests with you, or at least has a lot of common information. Therefore, if you're in a room and there's five people and one is wearing a psychick cross, there are certainly higher odds in my opinion that they'll be the one you relate to quicker. And so they thought, "great, where should we get them made?" I said, "Kathmandu." Why not? When we went before we got the books made there,[4] and that got money for the Tibetan refugees, so let's do that again. That way we're not just making, doing and giving, but we're actually helping as well. Helping the place that you source everything from. We're taking something back instead of bringing it all out; isn't that a nice thought?

So Beth and I went to Kathmandu. We were there a month, she stayed about a week and Trilochan helped out, of course. We said we also want a carpet made because we had another thought. We'd been thinking for ages, for years, that we'd like to do a piece called "See Hear," where we'd just have a dedicated phone line. We're on one end in the gallery, and anyone who wants to, in the rest of the world, can phone up and ask questions or just talk. We wanted it to be with Lady Jaye's big red chair, but it also needed a rug, like a little living room.

A friend of Ryan's is a tattoo artist, and he only does Hindu style tattoos. We asked him if he would make me a pandrogyne Hindu deity design, created out of me and Jaye – as far as you can in a rug! – with a psychick cross and 23 etc. So he did. And the rug was made in Kathmandu. Every time we were there at the Rubin, twice a week, we would announce through Facebook and Instagram and on their website and so on: "Gen will be available between 2pm and 6pm on Thursday the so and so, and here's the number." We would go and sit with Musty at my feet on the rug, and we would just answer the phone. And of course people would come in to the museum and be wandering around and see me sitting there with the dog, talking on the phone. "Is that you, Genesis?" It became this point of exchange, of friendship and curiosity and ideas, and technology, old and new, mixed together. It was amazingly... perfect. Just positive reviews. People really took time to get it. The title was really helpful, they did a great job choosing that one.

CA: That was undoubtedly a great success, and makes me think about a word that you used when we shot the film.[5] We talked about the TATE. You used the word "vindication." I assume that the Rubin was a similar thing: a vindication process.

GBPO: It was also a revelation for me. We saw what we do; especially the work with Lady Jaye. We saw it as far more resonant and potent than we'd realized, because we were so wrapped up in being in it. Stepping back and seeing just how much it affected people in positive ways was amazing. That was a real revelation for me to see and to experience and realize that we really are doing what we thought we were doing, you know? We weren't just kidding and tricking our-

4 Reference to Genesis P-Orridge, *S/HE IS HER/E: Poems for Thee Majesty*, New Way On Press, Kathmandu & New York City, 2000.
5 Carl Abrahamsson (dir), "Change Itself – An Art Apart: Genesis Breyer P-Orridge," 2016.

selves. We've really been doing what we said, and finally people are starting to feel it and see it and at least a certain percentage will remember it. Which is what we've always thought it was about, and still do. You can't convert people; you can only present it; explain it the best you can, and say it's just an option you've got now, which is just on offer. All we can do is gift it to you, but we can't tell you that you have to do any of it. We can't persuade; we're not persuading. In the end it's a diary. All of it's a fucking diary. It's what we do; it's our lives; it's intimate; it's our struggle to make any kind of sense of apparently having a physical existence.

CA: Throughout your decades of hard labour as an artist, have you ever had doubts about that aspect? Whether people will fully understand or even attempt to understand as you would like them to?

GBPO: There often needs to be some kind of text to lead you in, and say this is why it's doing things, or constructed the way it is, because it's trying to take you here, or it's offering to take you there. But this particular exhibition also gave us the chance to finally make the Brion Gysin sculpture, "The Touching of Hands." We thought of that possibly a decade ago. Brion had said to me, "wisdom can only be passed on by the touching of hands." That was equally as central to one of my mutations as the Burroughs one: "how do you short circuit control?" Those are the two key phrases; they gave me one each.

Brion also asked, "do you know your real name?" In the book[6] we argue about that one. That concept was one of my two kind of bumper stickers of "what we are trying to do." Between myself and Ben,[7] we'd come up with this idea: we'd always wanted to make a bronze sculpture that got shiny from being touched. So it started to all gel into one piece with that. My right forearm, shaking hands position, and a plaque under it that just said, "wisdom can only be passed on by the touching of hands, Brion Gysin." It also said, "please touch the sculpture" next to it. People did, and they loved it; being allowed to touch the sculpture. They didn't do it to the inappropriate ones; they really respected the difference when they were going through the show.

It was beautiful; it was like a real temple experience. You went up the stairs and there was a white neon psychic cross hanging and then off go these different chapels, if you like, to the sides; each one with its own sort of specific emphasis. On all the walls were all these objects. Amazing. There was nothing that wasn't how we wanted it. It was scarily exactly how we wanted it. We just thought, "well,

6 Genesis Breyer P-Orridge et al, *Brion Gysin: His Name Was Master*, Trapart Books, Stockholm, 2018.
7 Benjamin Tischer, owner of P-Orridge's main gallery, Invisible Exports, together with Risa Needleman.

if they can do it, and they don't usually do this kind of shit, why can't other places do that; places that usually do this kind of shit?"

CA: I think the art world looks at you as a brand. They are interested in the brand "Genesis P-Orridge," but maybe they don't have the personal commitment to what it actually is that you're doing.

GBPO: And what I'm saying. We get in a lot of group shows now, so that's good. There's one now called "Black Light," in Barcelona. So that's been happening much more. We'll be in there with gilt-edged artists, and there will be something by Breyer P-Orridge; which at least shows it's being considered as valid as these other people in some way. It's still not respected the same way, and it certainly isn't valued the same way, but it's seen, at the very least, as curious and unusual enough that they feel they can't ignore it. So that's the progress that we've made, I think.

CA: Also, your art has been exposed enough in these different contexts during this past decade that it can never be rubbed out. It will just continue, and it will expand, too, I think.

GBPO: It's gradually like dominoes; they're like very slowly falling dominoes. Things have shifted. Part of it is probably that younger men and women are becoming curators in more prestigious venues, and they always knew about us from when they were teenagers. They've always valued what we've been saying, and our approach, and our... As Lady Jaye used to say: one of my most frustrating but most wonderful qualities is integrity. She said, "Gen'll turn down a fucking record deal because he doesn't believe in the way they do something – even when Gen's broke." It's from a really a good interview, and she spends a whole page talking about how my integrity used to really annoy her at the beginning because we wouldn't make decisions based on practical things or money. But she began to really love me for it, and thought how wonderful it was that somebody would do that. So there are people who've definitely grown up with this. Even my literary agent said he used to play TG and Psychic TV when he was, you know, a teenager and in his 20s.

CA: There's another positive thing that's going on right now, or for the past years, and that's the documentary film about TOPY: "Message from the Temple."[8] It'll be about the philosophy and history of TOPY, so that's a very nice development too.

---

8 "A Message from the Temple", a film by Jacqueline Castel, Aldona Watts, Ryan Martin and Caleb Braaten; forthcoming.

GBPO: That's why we love "Change Itself," because it's actually a film about what we're thinking, and we went, "thank goodness, it's not about fucking TG!" I almost vomit when I see TG things now. Some people can't leave that era alone, and they're stuck in it, so…

CA: But this will bring a completely different kind of exposure; one focussed on ideas, magical concepts and philosophy. People know about it, and they associate it with you. But not to any greater extent, I think.

GBPO: We're not saying we're on the same plane in any way, but we really love Marcel Duchamp for that: the books where he's just talking about fucking ideas, in depth – I love those books. The concept that ideas are an important aspect, that's not been fully integrated by some people. But when it is, it should all start to make more sense. Everything is interconnected, as you know. Interconnected, international and interesting. We gave up art and did TG and music for a while and Duchamp gave up art and played chess. Well, he may not have given up art, but he said he did. We never really did either. I mean, when we stopped doing C.O.U.M. we did rituals for TOPY, and made them more discrete. They weren't for the public per se. It became more anthropological.

CA: How do you think that this film will be received, and who will be receiving it?

GBPO: That's a really good question. About a year ago we would have been able to answer it more easily. About a year ago, in New York anyway, there was a real upsurge of young artists, young musicians, young everythings that try and do more than just live; becoming involved with, interested in, referencing the occult and magic and so on; with their symbols for clothing, with their drawings. Whatever they were doing they were starting to integrate occult symbolism. You could see it even in mainstream pop videos.

Of course those wonderful people who spread conspiracy theories think it's just proof that the Illuminati are taking over and are trying to brainwash us with their MK-Ultra, which they never stopped doing! And there were several smaller group shows in New York with occult themes, and there was the Marjorie Cameron[9] little upsurge, and so on. That's gone quiet again as far as we can tell. That doesn't mean it's stopped. Whether that will sustain, or whether it was more of an accessory, it's hard to say. But it still would have laid the ground for what we do

9 Marjorie Cameron (1922-1995), American artist and occultist most often associated with the vibrant Los Angeles art scene of the 1940s-1960s, and with her marriage to Aleister Crowley disciple John Whiteside "Jack" Parsons (1914-1952).

to be slightly easier to digest, for sure. The TOPY film will obviously go to those people. When they did the crowdfunder for the film it raised $60,000 or something. More than they asked for. That showed a really widespread fascination, and a hunger for more knowledge about that era because, again, people have grown up, they are older, and they want to go back and reassess, relive, re-contextualize what they were getting out of it back then. And there's loads of young people who want to know what were they were doing. A bit like the Process were, you know?[10] Everyone knew about the Process, but not what they were and what they really did. There were all these myths. That has kind of happened to TOPY because of that documentary. It's left it as this mysterious phenomenon that they just missed, which was from the pre-digital age; therefore they can't research it like they're used to. They go up against a brick wall except for some bits and bobs here and there; not all of which is accurate or even authentic. My hope is that there'll be a big surge of interest in finding out what TOPY was all about, and that that will inspire them to realize that the subjugation of their ego is essential to success. Most of them say, "I wish we could do that now; how would we do that now?" We usually go, "well, you have to stop being narcissistic and you have to stop wanting a career; you have to stop wanting to get rich, and you have to start sharing everything, fucker, or you won't be able to do it! You have to improvise, and it has to be relevant now. You have to look at what's going on now, and then debate what's wrong with it; and is there a way for you to rearrange what you've got, to get closer to what you'd like to have happen?" And then just live it, and hope that by example people say that it seems interesting, and they get drawn to it, and so on and so on, which is all that happened to us. We didn't know it would spread like it did; we didn't know what it would become; we just improvised. They seem really dissatisfied with me saying that all the time.

The women started saying it didn't seem to give them as much voice in TOPY, in Brighton, so we started something called Thee Kali Circle. We wouldn't have started it unless they'd said something, and then we all talked about it. "How can we do it? What would you like to have happen? What would make you happy? Let's do that, see if it works. If it doesn't work, change it." It was always just improvising, around and around, and loads of discussion and common sense. You all talk about it and bit by bit strategies appear and then everyone has to do it.

CA: I think that if the film turns out well, which I think it will, it can generate interest like wildfire because of the fact that it's coming out in an environment and time that is increasingly draconian.

---

10 Reference to The Process Church of the Final Judgement, a group influenced by ideas stemming from Scientology and occultism.

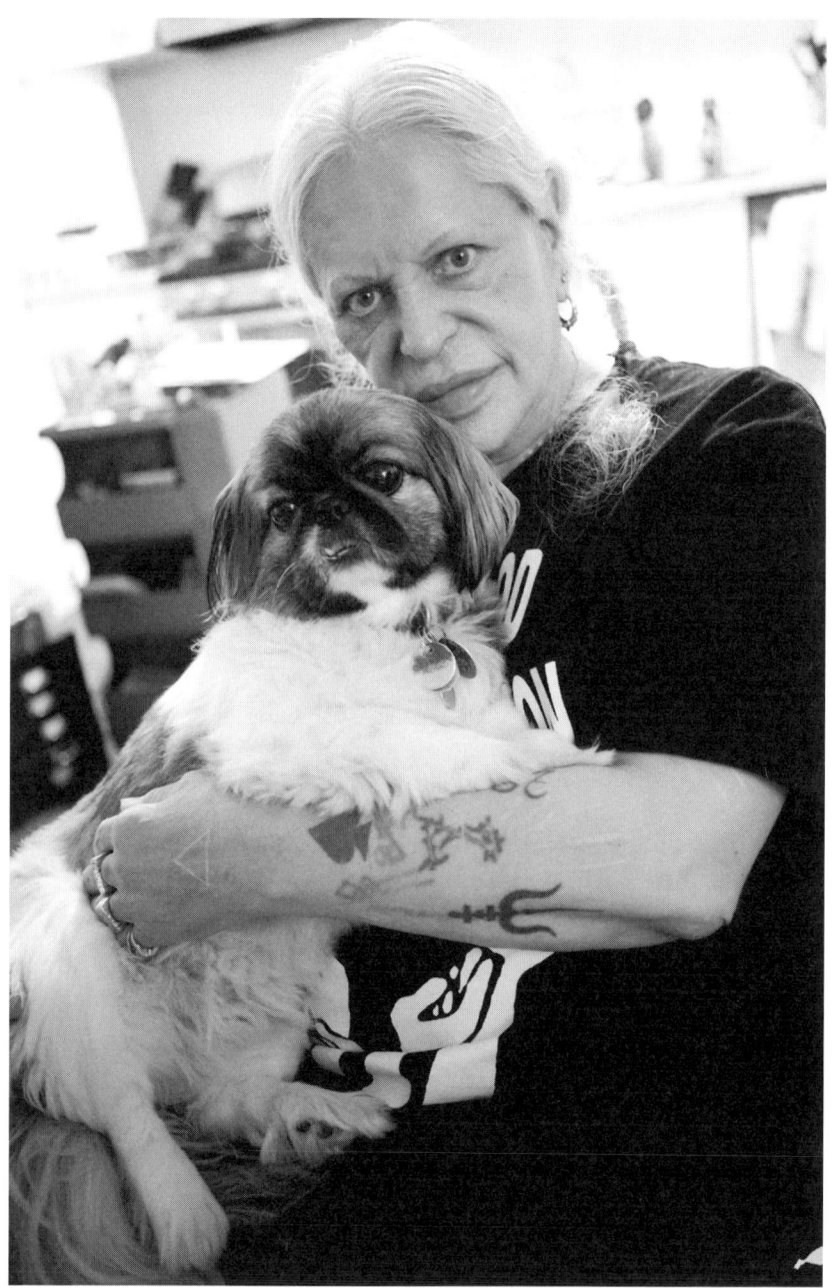

With Musty Dagger, New York, 2018

GBPO: Just like it was then.

CA: People are more fragmented today than they were back then, so maybe it will give them something to, at least, move through, or via.

GBPO: What do you think the internet is going to do in terms of the change in that environment? There's a certain innate laziness involved with the use of the internet. I don't write many real letters anymore, which really upsets me. The days seem too short now.

CA: Reading texts online is not the same sort of investment. Books? Most young people seem to get it from the screen or else they don't take it in.

GBPO: Some of these books, we buy them because otherwise they'll disappear. We're buying them to preserve them for the future. Not even necessarily to read them, but to keep these alternative viewpoints available in case they're useful. And the odds are they probably will be, because they're from an era where the situation was pretty dire, and somebody needed to break it open and come up with alternatives.

CA: Yeah, and just create a little watering hole. Speaking of film, there was also the Benin film recently.

GBPO: Oh yeah: "Bight of the Twin."[11]

CA: That not only takes us into the world and relationship with Jaye, but also to magical traditions stemming from Africa. That was quite an ambitious film project, and I think the film was very good. What was it like for you to not only be part of this process, but to have a film team along and have it presented on the big screen for strangers?

GBPO: Well, it wasn't meant to be a film like that when we went to Africa the first time. The first time we went, Hazel was visiting me here in New York, and one day she came up to the computer, and said, "hey, Gen, I found these incredible photos online. You're going to really love them." We're a little bit prejudiced at this point with the online thing, but we went, "oh, okay, show me." She pulled up these incredible images of the "ghosts," as they're called, in Benin. They're Vodun priests and also some priestesses in these costumes that were like Leigh

---

11 "Bight of the Twin," directed by Hazel Hill McCarthy III, USA, 2016.

Bowery[12] on DMT. Really strange, with no sense of Western design logic to them whatsoever. One of them looked like a medieval jester, but a really twisted interpretation. It seemed pretty obvious to me that uniforms and costumes worn by invading slave traders had been the initial inspiration for this "jester" in particular, but aspects of patterned fabric layering, core silhouettes. But how local people assimilated those sources into costumes to be worn by a Vodun priesthood whose beliefs and ceremonies were anathema to Catholic christianity was inspired genius. Examples of fabulous subversion by mutated imitation. Another one looked identical to a Punch and Judy square tent. None of these "ghosts" could show their hands or faces because they're ghosts, so there's no one in there, and they were just fabulously irrational. We loved it because they were built to function; *not* for any aesthetic reason, really. I mean, there is an aesthetic but that's not the primary reason. Things are there for what they represent or what they make happen. If they seem to go together as well, that's just a bonus, but that's not the reason they're done. They're not made to look nice or have a particular contextual reference to a certain era or anything like that, and they're certainly not "couture." They're totally functional and mysterious and devotional, and we looked at them and went, "those are great; those are just the weirdest things we've seen anyone wear." Hazel said, "there's a Vodun festival every year in Ouidah, Benin where these costumes are worn. You took me to Kathmandu and paid for it, so how about I take you to Benin and pay for it?" I just went, "okay! See a cliff, jump off, alright, let's do it!"

So we went with that in mind – just to go. She found out there was this festival coming up, which happens only every four years. We arranged to go there for that, and basically thought we'd just take photographs and, if we were really lucky, we might meet one of them or get them to sort of pose for a portrait or something. But because she's a filmmaker, Hazel always takes her cameras along. I think at the back of her mind she was thinking of it; not as a movie, but that she would document it; more than just a vacation home movie.

We arrived in Benin at Cotonou Airport, and it was just like you might expect when you think about a poor nation in West Africa. We had to get a taxi from there to Ouidah, which was on the coast; at least a three hour drive, if not more. Once you get out of the main town there's no tarmac. It's just orange earth with lots of holes. Bouncy, with no A/C and hardly any suspension. It is wonderful, because you do want it to be like that; you want it to be *not* like here. We arrived in Ouidah in the evening. We'd been met at the airport by our two guides, Sardou and Hypolite, who Hazel had found online. They arranged for the taxis to take us to Ouidah and they'd found a half finished house where the upstairs

---

12 Leigh Bowery (1961-1994), Australian performance artist known for outrageous and fanciful costumes.

was still just the walls without windows or anything, and the downstairs had windows but no kitchen, and one shower faucet that was only cold water and a toilet with no seat, but it did flush.

We arrived, and then we thought, "oh, let's go into the little town square and get a beer and just realise we're here, you know, we're in Africa, wow." So we did and we went into the little town square. There was a tiny little shop that sold beer, and it was next to the tailor's who ended up making the clothes we got, and a ba-obab tree that was huge, with a couple of old tables surrounded by rickety chairs under it. We sat around this table drinking our beers and feeling pretty excited. On the left was the Catholic church, and on the right was the Python Temple, and then there were the little shops. There were no street lights so it's really dark; there's this shadowy light. As everyone was talking a bit and winding down, my eyes just started to sort of stare idly off into the farthest unlit side of the square. The voices around me faded into ambience. Then I thought I saw a person in long blue, flowing robes who seemed to be just smoothly floating as if they were a few inches above the ground along the far wall; I had an impression of a really tall, thin figure who about half way along the wall suddenly disappeared, just as I blurted out loud, "I bet that's a high priest!" A lot like when we first ever saw Lady Jaye in Terence Seller's dungeon and went, "Dear Universe, if I can be with that woman for the rest of my life, that's all I ever want forever."

We got up the next day and we farted around a bit, getting our bearings, and then Sardou said, "I'd really like you to come and meet my family this evening and have a little something to eat." Around seven o'clock he came and got us and we came out of the corner by the Python Cult. We're walking along the wall and suddenly he stops, and set back in the shadows is a gate with "Gbédjinon" on it, which is his surname. Now we could make sense of who we saw last night and how he seemed to vanish. We went in, and he took us into this room, the family room, and there's Dah,[13] in blue robes, nearly seven foot tall and thin. So it was obviously him that I'd seen the night before. Now he was sitting in this big chair, which is his equivalent of the throne, with one of his acolytes next to him.

Sardou was translating as Dah looked at me, really intently, and then he whispered to Sardou, who said, "my father says you had a twin, but she died and you're wearing her gold earrings under your hair." He continued, "you need a Jumeau."[14] They tried to explain and we didn't understand a word they said about what it was; just vaguely that it was some kind of doll. The next day we went back to Dah, and he was so sweet. He started explaining that we needed certain things,

---

13 Dah Gbédjinon, Vodun high priest of the Python Cult in Ouijah, Benin.
14 "Les Jumeaux" signify a concept in Vodun about divine twins that are neither male nor female. Although looked upon as childlike spirits, they are usually regarded as older than the other Loa (spirits). Often revered through effigies like dolls, or "jumeaux."

like a couple of chickens and hooch, you know, bootleg spirits, and cigarettes. Certain herbs and this and that and water, and that we would start that evening with the initiation and the creation of the Jumeau. Hazel started filming. She realised that something's really going to happen.

It was very minimal and really had the feeling of some H.P. Lovecraft ancient powers. Sometimes they told me, very incoherently, to do things like say what I want. I think that we just said something like, "I want to bring my sister home..." Something weird like that just came out. And every time anything happened they threw the Cola nuts, the oracle, to check if we're doing it right, or if the entities are unhappy or say no or yes. There's this constant interrogation the whole way through, almost every few seconds, and the acolyte and Dah, every so often they really smile and go, "yeah, the spirit says yes, a hundred percent, that's the best answer you could get." We could feel Dah warming to me as he began to be able to read me. He never asked for money; he's not interested in trying to get money, which is the other thing that was really impressive. It was just, "you need this, we'll make it." Then they brought out the little wooden doll with a bit of cloth around it, and she had black hair then because all their dolls have black hair. But they put pale skin on it, and that became Jaye.

It's a bit of a blur because we were just so overwhelmed, and we were getting entranced by everything. We weren't really fully present in that world but we could feel other worlds opening up around me. There's this sense of these things shifting and dropping and moving. We thought we heard all these insects making a noise but there weren't any when we checked later. It was very interesting. We felt really stupid and inept because we kept blurting out gibberish when they asked me questions, but obviously it didn't bother them. The entities were fine.

Bit by bit, that was the first night's ceremony: to create the basic doll, which is carved out of the baobab tree, the sacred tree. Dah asked through Sardou, "do you really want this, because once you've got this, it's a huge responsibility because you have to take care of her for the rest of her life and your life." That the doll represents Jaye here and also *is* Jaye; she's the transmitter/receiver to the Jaye spirit that's in the immaterial world. She can call Jaye, she can travel to wherever Jaye is, and bring back messages and information and take messages.

I found that I just adored Dah. He's just such an open, totally unpretentious, genuine man. We got into this little routine where we would sit at Dah's favourite bar that was on a corner, just a street's width across from the Catholic Church, and drink beer together, slowly. There was another Dah, the "Dah of Wood," who was this hilarious little old guy with a trilby hat. He didn't speak any English but would just grin and laugh. We realized after about a week or so that we would sit with Dah all afternoon and we had these really long, deep conversations about spiritual matters and vodun and philosophy and belief and the origins of all of this. We didn't speak each other's language, but I know we had those conversations. God knows how he did it but it was pretty remarkable. He was the high priest of the Python Cult and the high priest of that area, which is considered the place that vodun originated from. So we went to the source, which we've always wanted to do.

Having been initiated in Santeria, we thought, "how different is the earlier form?" It's very, very different. Vodun in Benin, particularly in Ouidah, is a nature religion. It has two primary functions: one is balance with nature, which includes not over-farming and so on, and the other is healing; going back thousands of years. It still fulfils those two basic functions. The locals still go to the Vodun priests and priestesses. That's what they still do. We didn't come across anything dark or violent or negative, you know, like curses, and we were thinking a lot about that afterwards. Ouidah, where we were, is where they estimate up to 15 million slaves went through to the rest of the world; none of whom knew there was anything beyond the horizon. So when they were put in ships they thought they were going to go over the edge or just into hell or whatever. They were petrified. The beach where they used to be lined up to go is still as it was, except in the middle there's an archway, and it's called the "Arch of No Hope." That's the monument to the slaves, and theoretically, their spirits are still going through and leaving, in this endless loop.

On one side there are a couple of low buildings, and we asked Sardou, "what are these?" We went and looked and they're very low ceilings and very dark inside, and he answered, "that's where they would chain them." The women would always be chained face up so they could be raped, but the idea was mainly that they would get used to being in the hold of the ship, in the dark; unable to move for weeks, and just live in their own shit and piss. Revolting. To one side of that were these concrete effigies of little cottages that were all abandoned. Apparently some person from the main city, an investor, decided to build a resort there. The local people went crazy, of course, and they did curse it. It never got finished and it's now rotting, thank goodness.

Everywhere you go in the town there are these beautiful, kind of outsider art style statues of different deities and entities, and outside the Python Temple, which is about an acre that's just trees basically. All the pythons live in there. If they find one anywhere in the town they bring it and set it free in the Python Temple, so it's full of pythons. There's a room where they can go and get water and sleep and it's full of 20 or so pythons. Dah took us in one day and somebody was with him. We're sure that they were testing me; that they thought, being a westerner, that we'd be scared of pythons. But they didn't know that we used to have a boa constrictor that was nearly twelve foot long. So they draped a couple of these pythons on me and we loved it, and we were stroking them and one went to sleep round my neck. They were kind of impressed that the pythons loved me.

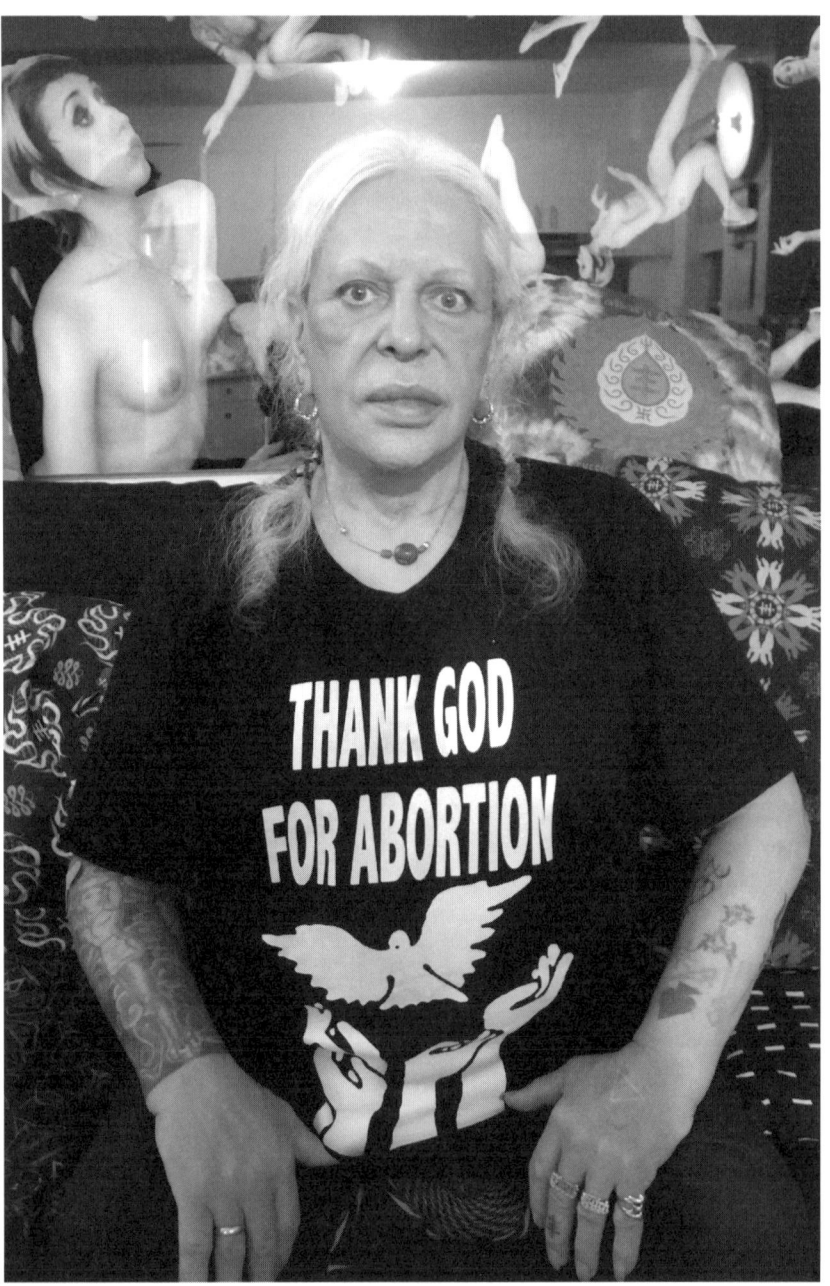

New York, 2018

New York, August 15th, 2018

A continuation of the previous session, some days later.

CA: Let's go back to Africa, because that's where we left off. We talked about the filming process, and you felt that you had more things you wanted to convey and say about the Benin experience.

GBPO: In the pandrogeny project we came to certain conclusions over a period of a few years. Originally there was no either/or, or male/female; there were just cells, just a species of slime mould. That's the sort of neo-scientific view. Then there is the spiritual view, which is that there is something else: we call it "I.T." – "imaginary time." It might be an energy, it might be consciousness of some unknown form, it might be a super species, it might be that there are infinite mirror types of consciousness, and that we're just one of many. But that one's a slightly more romantic vision of our place in everything. We decided that, either way, the origin usually explained in Western, Judeo-Christian mythologies and Islam, is that there was once this place, the "Garden of Eden," a perfect place, that had beings in it. Those original beings were neither male nor female. In the very first paintings that were done of the Garden of Eden – way, way back in the early times in Europe – God, Adam and Eve and Lilith are all depicted with breasts, penises and vaginas; they're all natural hermaphrodites. The only difference is that the theoretically male ones had longer hair and beards in the pictures. Naturally, the Vatican and the early despots of the Christian faith tried to destroy all those paintings when they turned it into a parable that suited *their* version of authority and totalitarianism. But that really intrigued us, you know, that that was the original vision even in the Western sources of ideology.

Then we went to Africa, being initiated in Santeria, and also knowing that Africa is still considered the place where we came from. We wondered, "what's going to be their creation story?" You know, we've been getting more and more interested into everybody's creation stories, like the Sumerian Anunnaki version. They all have this moment where there's this perfection, and it's non-gender related; it's just divine perfection, and that is always a hermaphrodite. So we go, "what about Africa?" Vodun is the oldest continuous religion, more or less, not the only one, there's probably aboriginal ones too. We thought, "we're going to a source, so what's their story?" And my guess, in advance, was that "I bet they have a hermaphrodite at the beginning," but we really had no idea. So when we got there the first time we kept asking all the different high priests and priestesses... My obsessive question to them all was, "what's your creation story, please?" None of them would answer until we were in this sacred grove, which had a sort of ramshackle hut in it where they would do certain rituals and prepare for rituals, and then the grove would be where they actually took place: a place for possessions and initiations. And we had the "grandfather of the sea," we had the Dah... Well, we had Dah, our Dah of Python Cult; we had the Dah of Trees and Wood... What was the other one? There were four plus Dah, and they were all threads of nature: one's the rivers and the seas, and one is the trees, and another one is the earth, even a Dah of Yams, because that's their staple food for a long time. They sat there and, again, we tried to ask and the other four, apart from our Dah, pretended they didn't speak any English. But I could tell that at least one of them did because of the way that their face changed at certain questions, and that was the grandfather of the sea. And just near the end we said, "look, I'm pretty sure that you know what I'm talking about. What's your creation myth or story?" And he went, "oh, everything comes from the sea" in perfect English, and that was it. I mean yeah, it all supposedly comes from the sea, and becomes amphibians and reptiles and blah blah blah... That's it, that's a throwaway, that's a distraction. So the first time we got nothing, but you know me: we wouldn't give up.

By the second time we went, we had discovered that there was a twin cult, through that whole thing with Dah and the Jumeau doll. We didn't know about the Twin Cult before. That was actually a bonus, on top. These are probably not a hundred percent accurate but they're the right ratios. Globally, it's something like between four and eight multiple births, usually twins, per one thousand births. In Benin, it's 32%, which is an insane statistical difference, and they've checked and it's not genetic; there's no genetic reason for it whatsoever. That became the other thread that we became fascinated with. There's this twin cult, and that's the one they keep quiet about? Why do they keep quiet about the Twin Cult? So we went back and I think by then Dah had a hundred percent decided to trust me, and all of us. We had these weird long conversations in the afternoon together, him and me, but he didn't speak English and we didn't speak very good French. We would get into these philosophical discussions, and afterwards we just went, "how the fuck did we do that?" So obviously he was doing something and we were communicating perfectly in complex ideas like these, you know. It never even dawned on me at the time because it was so relaxed and natural. We got to meet the high priestess of the Twin Cult through Dah. He started to introduce us to them and, with his guarantee, they actually opened up. In the end the priestess did the very first ever interview with anyone about the Twin Cult. One of the very first pictures that Hazel took of me, on the second or third day, in the market area, was me looking into this building that was just a cube of pink concrete with these interesting bricks in it that had holes in a pattern. It was locked with a padlock and had a weird symbol on it, and we were staring into it even though it was empty, and she took a picture from the other side. Months later, when we went back, we found out that that was the temple of the Twin Cult. It drew me to it, and that's just one of the things about Benin that's, you know, incredible. The "of course" factor is rampant out there.

We got to about halfway or so through the second visit and we were starting to talk about the twins. They have a festival once every four years for the twins. The first week of it is for those that have died, and the second week is for the ones that still live. That's when all the Jumeaux come out. All these women had a special costume just for the festival each time, and this particular year it was pink and white – a really horrible pink and white – and we all had to get costumes made. We asked the high priestess, "why pink and white?" She said, "well, we used to just have one design of a really nice multi-coloured fabric, but all the other houses started to copy it because they liked it so much, and then it became a fashion. So now we change it every time so that they can't copy it." That was the only reason. Nothing to do with aesthetics or ancient traditions and secret codes, but just to prevent stylistic plagiarism. And I thought that reasoning was hilariously great.

They did a beautiful ceremony in the town square against the wall of the Python Cult temple, and then we all went through the town to that little temple and, respectfully, myself and Hazel and the camera person stopped outside. But the little old lady who was the high priestess came out and dragged me and Hazel inside, which was really sweet and an incredible honour. Then they did a whole prayer and chant for Lady Jaye and, because it's twins, and they're perceived as still babies that didn't survive; they give them cookies and orange juice and all these nice things, and it's just this trough filled with years and years and years of biscuits and chocolate and fizzy drinks and so, it's just this kind of sea of dark, earthy stuff. It's very different to what you would think of as a representation of a divine entity anywhere else. It's not a statue or an image at all; it's just this place, so that the divinity, the entity, is actually the relationship with it, and that's just where the offerings go. Much more interesting, we thought; very different. About three days before we were going to leave, Dah suddenly got very active; with me as well. We had these long conversations, as we were saying, and then he took me aside and started doing this ritual, including sacrificing chickens, which is in Hazel's film. He put water from Ouidah, Benin, and earth from Ouidah, Benin, in a fetish-decorated bottle and said to me, "take this back to America, back to New York, and tell people the truth about our religion, Vodun." I solemnly promised that I would whenever an opportunity arose for me. A little later we thought, perhaps, at last this is a good moment to try one last time. So we piped up... "Dah, what *is* your creation story?" And he didn't answer, but the next day his son Sardou brought us a piece of paper in French... It basically says, "in the beginning, before there was anything, there was Mahu-Lissa, and Mahu-Lissa is one being, both female and male." To represent Mahu-Lissa, they used the chameleon and the python. One is the python and is male, and one is the chameleon and is female, but they are not separate; they are one, unity, one entity. Yet again the original of life is genderless, a pandrogyne, a positive androgyne. Waiting for our flight home we joyfully cried out loud, "Yes! We knew it, Lady Jaye and we were right... a fucking hermaphrodite!"

Everything comes from that. So we started applying that to humanity, myself and Jaye, and this issue of the either/or that creates all the basic friction, and is manipulated by those who have systems to maintain power, fear and guilt. The either/or is used to focus that. So we thought the whole point of existing is to somehow find ways to erode, and eventually erase, the either/or and the concept of male and female being separate, because we began as one. The whole point of existing is to find ways to reunify. No matter how long it takes, the whole point of having a human species is for it to recognize this in itself and finally remove the either/or and become hermaphrodites again, but with self-knowledge. From our point of view, it seems like a very long term way of discovering what we already knew and what our origin was; doing it through our own senses and choices. But the point is always to reconnect and be absorbed into the other to become one. We were thinking about why the human species hasn't really woken up to that, and the problem is people don't think about humanity as one species, one entity, in which each being is, if you like, a cell or a particle of that, and that it's already, always has been just one being, one organism.

If only we started to visualize everything that's going on politically, economically, socially, in that perspective – that it's about one species – what does one organism do if it's damaged? If it's damaged it takes whatever resources it has and heals the damage, because it's in the interest of the entire organism. If one part of the organism isn't getting enough nutrient the same thing happens; it supplies nutrient from everywhere, because it's in the best interest of the organism. What's wrong with the picture that people have of being here, is that they don't realize we are one organism. If only that picture was the picture that people are given from the beginning as they're educated, the way choices are being made would be completely different. It wouldn't matter where on the planet it was; it wouldn't matter what kind of people it was; if there was an issue or damage you would heal it, because it's always in the interest of the organism. So all of those other things, going right back to the 1960s, really just lead to this very simple conclusion that the only message that's really important to give, is that we are that one organism.

Without recognizing that and then perceiving everything that happens in that context, we are fucked, because we are going against the natural order of what we are. That's why we think we can control nature, and that we can use resources indefinitely, because we're not thinking in that other way. We are basically, in different forms, all part of societies that are based on the addiction to consumption, and it has an inevitable flaw: you can't take a planet with a certain amount of resources and keep on increasing what you take. There is a natural, inevitable limit when it stops. All these economic systems are built on the idea of growing productivity and growing consumption, and that absolutely goes against nature, and it also is why populations are out of control, because people aren't using that perspective to see how they use what's here. Those are the two issues that we're left with at this point, and that's why the only solution we could think of as a next step: to try and set up some form of community as an example on a small scale, of units that are based on that idea that that little community is an organism that represents the large one, and by sharing its resources and by taking care of what happens to each other, we demonstrate the alternative to what's going on right now. That's the only thing we wish we could get done before we go: to help set up a little community.

CA: You've done a good job so far, I think.

GBPO: So that's what Benin was all about, and all those incredible "of course" moments everywhere.

CA: Yeah, it's interesting also that those phenomena, or synchronicities, or whatever you wish to call them, can exist so much more or less, depending on the culture they're in.

GBPO: Exactly.

CA: It goes beyond the individual human mind.

G: The Tibetans and the Dalai Lama have an oracle. Tim Poston, from C.O.U.M., the physics and math genius, used the *I Ching* all the time, and said it worked perfectly as mathematics. The Africans throw the nuts, the shells, and so, are there lots of different oracles? There can't be. There's only one, and that oracle must be all of consciousness combined, outside the material sphere. The Akashic record is another name for it. Those are the questions that become really important when you're trying to think, "how do we not only save the species, but give it an enhanced future that's based on positive actions that are for the greater good, and the individual good?" When people stop being about the me me me, and look at what we've got. Just when the 1960s were going into new age, and all these philosophies were beginning to blend, and ideas like this were becoming more and more profound and more and more obvious, they inject the fucking phone, and make people narcissistic and self-centred and blind and unable to remember anything. Susana[1] just sent me a little link to a Spanish TV program where they go out in the street in New York and ask New Yorkers, "do you know where Spain is? What do you know about Spain?" The Latin ones from Mexico and Puerto Rico and so on, they all know that they speak Spanish there but they don't really know that Spanish is the original language. They think Spain just copied them; they don't even know anymore. We said to her, "maybe they're just so used to looking things up on their phones they don't bother to remember anything." They don't even learn how to remember. That's really dangerous. Burroughs always said, "when you consider any issue, look for the vested interest; who does it serve?" To have evermore ignorant, ill-informed people relying on an instantly removable network... They could close it anytime, and then everything people think they've got stored – their photos, their ideas, everything – is just gone. It doesn't exist.

CA: You had your notions confirmed that there is a recurring theme in so many creation stories, and that it was imbued with hermaphroditic theory. But there's also this thing that I remember after the African trip: that you came back with the effigy, with the Jumeau doll, and you were dressed in a similar way as it (and vice versa). Through this particular mythology and magical system, you could be in contact with Jaye in a new way. What was that like on an inner emotional level; this kind of externalization?

GBPO: Oh, wow. Obviously it's comforting, but you don't want to think that you're comforted just because it's nice to imagine. But there are so many times since we've had the Jumeau that we consult with it; we talk to it. Dah said, "this is a being, this isn't Lady Jaye; this is a transmitter/receiver. You've got to look after it, you can't ignore it, don't get lazy, remember to feed her, if not she can get very angry and pissed off, you know, it's a big responsibility, it's like having a child." We still take her almost everywhere, any important trips, and we refer to her, we feed her every day; she just got some steak. It has solidified a connection that we already felt. We don't feel that we have to be thinking about her all the time because we know she's there, and there's this object that reminds me of that. Every night we take her from in here to the bedroom and put her in a special place and we feed her; we play the Tibetan bells to her; we do everything in numbers of five because she liked five. Sometimes having that just focuses my mind on what

---

1 Susana Vico Valero, P-Orridge's girlfriend.

would be a normal conversation with Jaye about something. It seems to strip away a lot of subjectivity and emotion, and say, "Jaye would think this and you think that." One part of you is imagining her – her side of it, or it feels like that. But sometimes it doesn't; sometimes it's actually like she's there, advising, so we don't ever get lonely about her at all, because she's always there. People who know us and come here, they all seem to say that she's still around. They feel that quite strongly. So it's really good as a portal that is working; not just for me, but for all those who think in other ways. We wouldn't have expected that in advance. And you really do feel like you have to be aware of her emotions sometimes, you know? Can she see what's going on, and does she want to, and does she want a different outfit on? It's a hell of a responsibility. We hadn't really extrapolated all of those aspects of it when we said yes. We wanted it. But they've all been positive. Then Susana repainted it for me, because she, like many women, really admires what Lady Jaye represents in her mind. It always bothered me that Jumeau had black hair, you know, so now she's got blonde hair. And red nipples, like her lipstick, because she used to that: put lipstick on her nipples. She's more accurate now. She needed a change. We're thinking of making her a wig out of her own hair, because we have got quite a lot still. We're trying to figure out the right way to make a tiny wig.

CA: In all of your explorations of systems, whether they be magical or religious or philosophical, have you ever had one that you felt like a primary connection with? It sounds like these African trips were really a "game changer," but I also had that impression with Santeria when that was going on.

GBPO: My way of explaining it would be that Santeria is the corrupted daughter of Vodun. With Santeria there's a lot more emphasis on money. A lot of the houses[2] will ask for quite large amounts of money to do different things; to get the warriors,[3] you know, they'll charge… Some of them will charge a couple hundred dollars; some will charge five, six thousand for exactly the same thing. And it seems that they charge more if you're white. There's a lot of racism involved in the pricing, which is probably also to check that you're not just doing it as an accessory.

What we noticed in Benin was that there was very little darkness. It wasn't, you know, the Hollywood version of Vodun at all, with lots of it being about cursing and zombies and so on. It's a nature religion, and that's primarily what

---

2 A Santeria "house" is the place where rituals and initiations take place, but also refers to a distinct embodiment of a Santeria lineage.
3 A "warrior" is a magically charged effigy. Receiving the warriors is an important part of the initiation process, in which a deeper relationship with the Orishas is established.

it is: it's about a relationship and balance with nature, and about healing and midwifery. It's probably the most prevalent of the ancient religions. It goes back 10-12,000 years, that they know of. It comes from the more animal instinct of relationship with the environment, and it gradually got formalized. In Santeria there's a lot more emphasis on possession and gaining superiority in situations, whether it be to get money, or to succeed over somebody else, or to steal a lover or to keep a lover; all that sort of thing. Then through Palo,[4] the sort of subversion, that's just downright nasty stuff; that's where they get into the bits of human beings and the graveyards and so on, and cursing. But then we thought about that negative, even cruel aspect within the diaspora, spreading out from Africa. And, of course, if you violently uproot these indigenous people with complex social systems, spiritual practices going back thousands of years, their own civilisation and dynamism, from Central and West Africa, and you stick them in a huge wooden boat chained to the floor; the women facing up so they can be raped as often as the animalistic sailors choose. Sailors who believe they are naturally superior and entitled despite their base behaviours and entrenched, racist ignorance powered by endorsed religious bigotry. All blessed by priests; servants of the rich as they are sold as slaves; less than human, cheaper than sheep and goats once they were dumped in Western European countries and colonies in the Caribbean and Northern Americas. What will become inevitable?

They're slaves, and they've been abused sadistically, constantly, for decades and generations. No matter how civilised and morally refined they began this journey, in the end there is going to be a resentful, ever more angry aspect seeping into it. Into Vodun. Naturally you're going to start including, "how can we somehow placate that rage with some other form of power?" In Santeria and its similar versions of it in the Caribbean and South America, they've integrated the anger and rage into the religion. So something that was much more obvious over there in Benin was how kind it was, and how it's really been given a disservice by the ignorant Western response to the anger within Santeria. That was really reassuring, because the only bit of Santeria that sometimes bothers me was that undercurrent of channelled anger and revenge, with a sort of nasty tinge to it sometimes. In Benin it was surprising how quickly we were accepted. You know, people in the street would see me and we had the Jumeau around my neck. They would see that and immediately know we wouldn't have that unless a Dah had had it made for me; and that would mean we must have been through those rituals that they went through; therefore there's a connection and a sense of mutual respect.

---

4 Palo is also a synchretic practice/religion, but which stems from the Congo rather than from a Yoruba source.

CA: In this autobiographical process that you're in – which is of course a massive undertaking, because there are so many stories and phases in your life – I'm curious about the overall emotional aspect. When you work on this and you're forced to think back on things and people that you may have forgotten, is it overall a happy or a sad story?

GBPO: Oh, it's happy. Overall it's happy. When we were 18, we'd left school and there was two months or so, maybe three months, actually, before we went to university. We got a job for two weeks cleaning toilets at the Royal Agricultural Show, and had the great honour of cleaning the Queen's toilet. They had different pavilions: the Royal pavilion, the aristocrats' pavilions and then down to the plebs, and guess which were the filthiest toilets? The aristocrats. They would do things like climb up, as high as they could, and shit down onto the wall while they were somehow precariously balanced at the top of the cubicle, and then they would lock the door on the inside and climb out so that it got really stinky. They did that all the time: shit everywhere. There were some little old ladies working there, and some of them also worked at these rich people's houses. We asked them, "what is it with these rich aristocrats and lords and ladies, that they shit everywhere?" The ladies replied, "oh, they do that at home, too. They'll go into their bathroom and then shit on the floor so you have to clean it up. It's a power thing and they all do it." What a nasty, twisted fucking thing. Isn't that horrible? The idea of this arrogant power they feel they've got, and they want to demonstrate that they can make people clean up their shit. Gross.

Anyway, my friend Pingle Wad[5] invited me for dinner to his family home, because he was a year below me, so he and Spydeee Gasmantell[6] and Little Baz[7] were all going to be a year longer at school than me. His mother was an ardent Catholic and had eleven children. Eleven! And there was a big family dinner in this big house. We're all sat there, and she's at the head of the table, and everything's going on, and then she turned to me and said, "so, what are you going to do now with the rest of your life?" And, instantly, we just blurted out, "oh, I'm going to take my daydreams really seriously." She threw me out of the house. She threw me out of the house, and told Pingle Wad he shouldn't bother to be around me anymore; that I was a bad influence. We've been called a bad influence since we were about this big.

We've always taken daydreams and flights of fancy that seemed attractive really seriously, and we have this basic inner drive that if we think it's a good idea, we feel duty-bound to try and do it, whether it be a new position in sex or change

5 Peter Winstanley
6 Ian Evetts
7 Barry Hermon

the laws of the country. It doesn't matter what the scale is, but if it's something that occurs to me that seems like it might improve things in some way, or it might open up some new idea or wisdom, then we feel like we just have to do it and see. We can't just think about it, and write it down, or "that would be fun if we had this or if we had that." It's always, "hmm, how can we do that? What's the nearest we can get to that with what we can achieve and access?" That's kind of the baseline, and as we've stuck to that in different ways and ever since, we've always turned away from temptation to make choices because of money or prestige.

When Virgin Records wanted to sign TG, we sent them a demo tape on a cassette but hit it with a hammer first so it wouldn't play. Those sorts of replies to the corporate attempts to commodify us and absorb us. I've always turned away when it's definitely *not* in my best interest. Jaye said, "sometimes Gen really annoys me because of the level of integrity; the things that Gen'll turn down and not do; but then I really love Gen for that very same reason. Gen's not motivated in the usual ways."

CA: That's a strong quality though, to stick with that attitude, because most people give up before they're even 30 years old.

GBPO: Absolutely. They drop away. A lot of people write poetry when they fall in love and they're in their late teens, and some people still write poetry when they're in their mid-twenties, but when you get to your thirties and you look around there's hardly anyone there anymore; and the same for just creative living. There's lots at the university age group, and so on, and then it fades, and you look around, and there's just a few people still standing on a rock, you know, above the level of the water waving a little flag saying, "I'm still trying," and the rest are gone. It's understandable on a very superficial level, but in terms of satisfying the hunger of a soul, it's not. My soul is too hungry for any kind of knowledge that it can get, and for justice; all those things that are considered so sentimental. Justice and the survival of our species in the most creative, constructive way it can; there's always been that slightly messianic element to it. You should always be trying to save the species! Not the world, the world will always survive until it blows up one day in millions and billions of years from now. I hate it when people say, "the end of the world" when they actually mean "the end of us." I mean, the United States is an empire in decline; get used to it. Copy the English version where they kept hold of so much. All the other ones, Spain and France and Italy, they've all lost theirs completely. And the Egyptians and so on, the Mayans, they all just lost the lot, but the British fucking held on tenaciously. That tiny little speck of dirt? It's ridiculous... How the fuck did they do that?

CA: By ingraining things with customs and rituals and traditions. And not necessarily by military force, because that always provokes a reaction.

GBPO: And then absorbing the local culture.

CA: Or having the locals absorb *their* culture. So suddenly half the world has to have tea at a certain time; that's what changes things.

GBPO: It does, doesn't it? And also you let them have their armies but you dress them like our army, and they all have bagpipes, things like that.

CA: In India, even!

GBPO: Commonalities, and the language of course. Yeah, India is still part of the British empire in its own peculiar way. It's fascinating.

CA: What about creativity and context? Do you feel every morning that you *have* to create something, or do you need a context? Like that you know that an artwork is going somewhere, or that there's going to be a show, or a published text?

GBPO: Oh no, we just do. We like deadlines. Deadlines are really helpful for me, but we've never been able to stop making and doing things. It's a biological activity for me. In fact, we have a huge backlog of things we haven't gotten done yet, and they're not things that we *need* to do for a specific location or event; they're just things that we've imagined and thought that they should exist. There's just not enough of me. That's why we've always collaborated, too. It helps get stuff done. A lot of people are doing things to groom their own self-image and their ego, but whilst we have an ego, it's subsumed by getting stuff done. That's the most important part: can it get done, is there any way to do it? If that means getting a team of other people involved as well, that's just great. We don't feel that the ego appetite has been diminished at all.

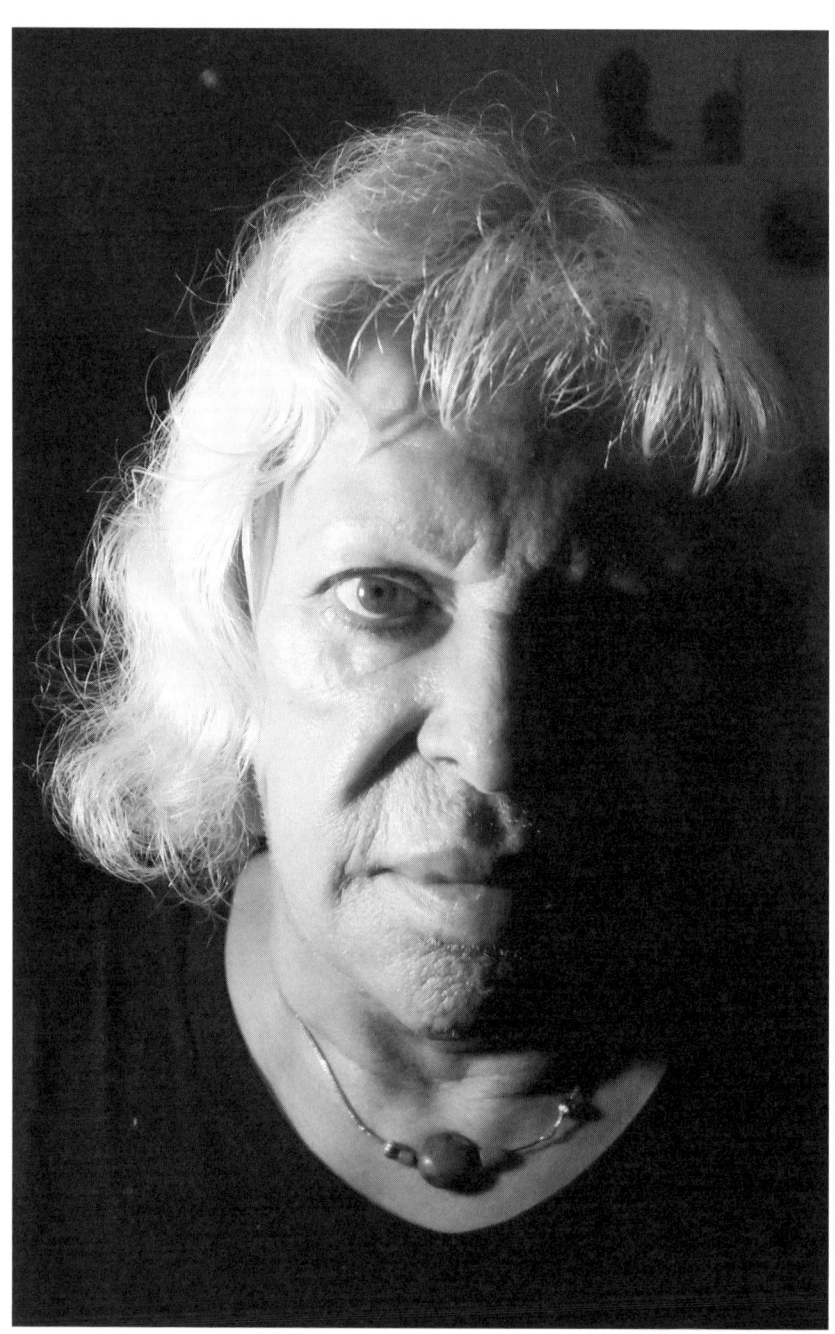

New York, 2018

New York, November 3rd, 2018

*Towards the end of 2018, two relevant projects were being wrapped up, and I wanted to do an interview specifically about them. The first was a lavish art book by Swedish photographer Lars Sundestrand (*To Become Who You Are – FUNTIME Interviews, Documents, Photos and More With Throbbing Gristle, Monte Cazazza, Psychic TV, *on Trapart Books). The other project was our ambient/spoken word album "Loyalty Does Not End With Death," released as an LP on Swedish label Ideal Recordings.*

CA: You were extremely accommodating to people like Lars Sundestrand and myself, who came from the world of small fanzines. The interesting thing about Lars is that you helped boost him into wanting to be a professional photographer, which is what he eventually became.

GBPO: Really?

CA: For me, it was meaningful to see that someone was doing their will for real, not just talking about it like so many of the *poseurs.*

GBPO: Yeah, and doing blow in the dressing room and getting drunk and trying to find girls for a one-night stand.

CA: It seems in the correspondence that Lars actually sent you a lot of the great photographs that he'd taken of TG and PTV.

GBPO: Yeah, he did at the time, definitely. Scotland Yard took every photograph we had so we don't have those anymore; that's one of the reasons it was nice to see the book, because we remembered a lot of the photographs in it but we don't have them. But what you were saying about writing back to people... From 1970 to around 1975 I was doing mail art almost all the time, you know, I would get up about nine o'clock in the morning, walk the dog through London Fields Park to 10 Martello Street, and then go down in the basement and start collaging and typing and rubber stamping and preparing packages to people who'd written. That mail art sensibility definitely spilled over into TG, you know, with the sticker campaigns that we did, and the rubber stamps, and doing everything ourselves, and making newsletters, and doing flyers that were collages and so on.

Nearly all the flyers were done by me, and when people wrote in it was usually pretty easy to tell if they had more than just a passing interest. It was just set in nature to write back. One of the ideas of C.O.U.M. was that everybody has a "genius factor" and everybody has a unique potential hiding inside them, that they just need to be told is okay to let out. That's always been part of what I try and do: to say, "yes, you can do it." It's been really productive. Ryan Martin, when he found the tapes of Early Worm[1] in the archive, he said, "what's this?" I told him that these were just some old tapes that were of no interest from 1967, and he said, "but people will be interested because it shows what you were doing that eventually became Throbbing Gristle." I replied, "well, if you think it's so interesting and it should be a record, why don't you do it?" And he did, and that triggered Dais Records, which has now been going for more than ten years and they have released records by dozens of other people, and re-released rarities by people that otherwise wouldn't be available. There are maybe a hundred records in existence that otherwise wouldn't be, because I said, "why don't you do it?"

Always keep in mind though that an intuitive feeling that the person you proposed was actually going to do that is essential to this process. Ryan was clearly very special and capable of productive focus already. Just a psychic nudge is all it needs.

Same with *Thee Psychick Bible* in Russia. When we were being interviewed some journalist said to me, "how come it's not in Russian?" I went, "well, because I don't speak Russian." He said, "well, it should be in Russian." We said the same thing: "If you think so why don't you do it?" Two years later he wrote and said, "we've finished translating it into Russian, and it will be available at your first concert in Moscow." That simple reinforcement, and that offer, has generated publishing, several record labels, people's careers in different forms. It's not that difficult if you believe in people and you seriously think that there's something special about everyone – which we do. It's important to keep sharing that. People are being tempted with simplicity – with laptops and with smart-phones – and they think that they're being creative by using somebody else's app that has limitations and programming that they didn't choose. So immediately they're in somebody else's territory with that person's imagination's limitations. It might feel as if you're being creative, but really you're just playing with somebody else's toy. If you want to do something creative and new, you have to step away from what's expected and destroy the expected; find what is around you that could

---

1 "Early Worm" was P-Orridge's first recorded album, originally pressed in only one copy. Later on re-issued by Dais Records in 2008.

make a sound, look at what people expect, and do the opposite. If they think it should be on a laptop never use a laptop. Like with TG: if people are used to guitarists that play, have somebody that doesn't play. If drums limit the way that the music sounds, don't have drums. It's really simple. It's a very simple formula, and it's just "use what's available," because it will find a way to be formulated, and be assembled so that you can make something unique together with the people that are available and the materials that are available. No matter how small or unlikely it might seem, you can get those and assemble them in a particular way that's unique and new, and is truly creative.

Lars obviously was listening, and then I guess he trusted me enough to believe what I said, and for that, thank you Lars! I'm glad that you trusted me enough to become you, you know; that's the game. We're all trying to become the true self that's inside; not the one that we're supposed to inherit; not the one that's supposed to placate society. We're supposed to become the one we secretly dream; the one that excited us when we were just reaching adolescence; the thing that we wanted to be when we read the first book that we found exciting, or heard the first record we found exciting, or watched the first movie, you know.

With TG I was trying to be the Velvet Underground, but had none of the skills or the equipment, so it turned into something unique and didn't sound much like the Velvet Underground, which is good. But the impetus was that they'd done something that sounded very different; therefore sounding very different was a good idea, and that would be a good place to begin, and not take note of what's popular or commercial or leads to a career. Do what seems exciting. Can't go wrong!

CA: What's usually your initial response to books like Lars's, or the one by First Third Books?[2] Does it feel awkward or are you proud?

GBPO: The white book, the First Third book, I just think it's nice to give to close friends, and share some of the archive and life story with them; that's basically what we see. We give them away. We're supposed to be selling them but we give them away because we just think it's a great way to share some of life and some of the things happened. We don't look through it and get nostalgic at all, and reminisce; we don't do that. When we finally saw the finished book we checked that it looked okay, that there weren't any glaring mistakes, and then we put it away. It's about getting it done, and then moving on.

Lars's book was more nostalgic, because it was from further back and it contained a lot of things that we'd forgotten. We hadn't realized just how much we'd done with Lars, and we liked that he included letters and things like that, too. It

---

2 *S/HE IS HER/E*, see earlier note.

was very flattering to see that and think that he would go to that much trouble to memorialise events in his life, which is what it is. The pleasure in that came from realizing how much it meant to him, and that it had had a genuinely positive effect on his life.

But we're not a nostalgic person. We're always thinking about what can we do next. It's the same with records: once we get one, we'll play it once to check it's okay. Then we put them on the shelf, and we give them away until we've got none left and then, meanwhile, we're working on something else. It's a constant process; nothing's ever finished; it's just documentation of the process. The process of seeking that unique moment in every day that happens to all of us, and looking for ways to describe it or memorialise it and freeze it. Even in a photograph or a drawing or a poem or simply in a joke; just looking for the special moment of each day.

CA: When we recorded the "Loyalty" album, there were some poems I recognised from before, as well as some new ones. What was it that made you make that particular selection?

GBPO: I do not remember. That's how I do it even live. I'll go through dozens of poems. Some of them are still handwritten; sometimes they're just typed up streams of consciousness. Some of them have been reworked and have been through the mental machine several times. We'll try and leave the body and go to the place where we're performing, and try and feel what it might be like; what the atmosphere might feel like, in an hour or two. Is there something we want to say tonight? Or maybe we can just scry by shuffling them, and then we just look and we throw some to one side and some to the other side, and the ones on this side are the ones that we'll take. There's usually ten times more than we're going to need. And then we take those with us, and we sit around and we pick up more of the atmosphere, and we sense a mixture of people's expectations, and maybe whoever's organizing it – what they feel is happening. It's really a very abstract, internalized thing. And then still, when we go on, we improvise and we'll just change them or go off on a complete tangent. Nothing is ever completely finished in that sense. Certain ones just seem to need to come alive several times, and some don't need to be alive more than once. They're like living things. Just as individual words are living things, so poems are living things, and statements within poems are living things.

CA: One of the things that's so beautiful with your poems is that they can be used for so many different styles. They could be rock lyrics or they could just be pure spoken word, or, as in our case, as a kind of an ambient thing with electronic sounds. I hope that you're happy with the result. I certainly am.

GBPO: Yeah, definitely. Well, I've always trusted your aesthetic anyway. You know that. We've done several of these now, and they always work beautifully. I'm always disappointed that we haven't got a Grammy yet for spoken word, because we certainly deserve one when you listen to the things that win. But it's just that they're not aware that they exist, and we're not on a major label and all the other blah-dee-blah. In certain ways it's the purest form of expression. Or it used to be; I guess it's not always now. We were just listening to "Trip/Reset,"[3] and all the lyrics in that could also just be poems. They're all about certain positive situations that happened because of meeting Lady Jaye. There's a track called "Black Cat," and of course she's the black cat. It says somewhere, "I think I'll sparkle by." Lady Jaye always called DMT the "sparkle," so there's lots of little clues, too. A lot of the poems that we write, and the lyrics and the words in general, they'll have... That's what I'm talking about when I say they're alive; by adding that word "sparkle," it's like a hologram. If you know it's about DMT and Lady Jaye, then everything that's ever to do with Lady Jaye is also in that word, and everything about DMT and Terence McKenna and so on, is also in that word, and yet it just says "'sparkle," which is about light hitting something. One word can contain encyclopaedias of information, and I think that's an art that sometimes gets forgotten. We always use words that way – that they're loaded – and my favourite thing is to use the simplest phrase but know that if only we explained why it's there, it's like the Encyclopaedia Britannica, you know. It's telling you something else, and that journey happens very fast in the brain, and there's this download of information that comes with each word, and each combination of words, and also through the spacing.

I really love doing it. It's amazing to just walk onto a stage and there can be a thousand people, and you could hear a pin drop, and people who speak different languages listen intently to every single thing that we say, and the gaps are just as important for them. It's almost like a liquid that's sort of floating around them; they're in this liquid made out of words. Although they don't know the meanings based on the languages they speak, the voice still projects information; they respond correctly; if it's sad or if it's haunting or if it's a joke, people tend to respond correctly, and that's something that just totally fascinates me. How can we read a complicated, abstract piece of information in ten different countries and get an incredibly positive result each time?

CA: Why do you think that people should buy and listen to this album?

GBPO: Because we are losing the ability to read and write and think faster than ever, thanks to these (shows cell phone), and texting and Instagram. All these

---

3 A Psychic TV album from 1996, re-released by Angry Love Records in 2019.

little games that come from these objects are training people to misunderstand what language is. They're training people to live in the most trivial part of language, which is just emojis. I mean, really... emojis? If you want to remember what language really does, and listen to somebody who's trying to tell you stories that are actually about the depth of human experiences, and the pains and pleasures of life and existence, then you've come to the right place with this record. But if you want to distract yourself and be disconnected from the so-called reality that this particular illusion is, then stick with your telephone. But you'll be missing too much. You really will. You should spend a night with me.

Stockholm-New York, November 2nd, 2019

Although frequently in touch via e-mail and different kinds of text messages, I wanted to talk to Gen "live & direct" again. But as I wasn't planning any New York trips at this time, we decided that a Skype session would be the next best thing. We had by now decided to wrap up the book project, so that it could be published on Gen's 70th birthday: February 22nd, 2020.

CA: You mention pandrogeny already in our interview in 1988. There's a strong sense of consistency.

GBPO: Oh yeah, and it's also mentioned in one of those two red notebooks that Timeless published.[1] There are three pages from 1986 where I say that pandrogeny is inevitable. Jarrett,[2] who did the Polaroid show, found something in an interview where in 1978 or 1979 I mention something called "panthropology." I don't have any new ideas; they all started in 1979.

CA: Yes, but you have very good old ideas.

GBPO: And it takes 40 years for people to understand.

CA: I think also our book will be quite an eye-opener, specifically for people in the art world. There's so much consistency and we have done a good job of, sort of, making little pit-stops in art history and talking about things that have to do specifically with that; and then drifting on into magical stuff, and then back again. By the way, how are things moving along with the autobiography?

GBPO: I'm writing some every day. There's a lot to write! What I've focused on for the last three or four weeks is from being born to going to Solihull School, because that's the least documented part of my life. I just finished the part of

---

1 Genesis Breyer P-Orridge, *Nekrophile*, Timeless Edition, 2018.
2 Jarrett Earnest. The Polaroid show mentioned was "Closer As Love (Polaroids 1993-2007)" at Nina Johnson, Miami. The book/catalog is Breyer P-Orridge, *Closer As Love (Polaroids 1993-2007)*, Matte Editions, 2019.

when I went to Jersey in 1964 and met "Scotch John."[3] You know the story where he asked me to stay and look after the prostitutes?

CA: No, I would love to hear that!

GBPO: I'll send it to you. It's really crazy. So, I'm writing and I'm thinking, "you were 14 years old and you nearly stayed in Jersey to run prostitutes." Bearing in mind that there were no porno mags in Britain at all then; no sex education, nothing. No one had told me what sex was and then this guy shows me all these pictures of his prostitutes doing everything, and I'm thinking now, "is that why I do all these Polaroids?"

CA: Probably.

GBPO: That was my first ever connection with sex; with pictures of sex.

CA: How are you working on the book? Do you work sort of backwards or just drop in at different times in your life that you feel compelled to write about?

G: Yeah, the second. It's just interesting, thinking about threads that appear at times when I didn't think they did. I notice that there's a continuity to certain aspects. Like, one of my earliest memories is being blamed for something I didn't do, which has continued throughout my life. You sort of think, "wow, karma, what is this program that we're all in?" What I'm really finding is just... Is there any kind of free will at all? Are we just living out previous karma? My father wanted to be a professional musician, he performed as an actor, he raced motorbikes, and all this stuff. I then end up hanging out with motorbike gangs, playing the drums, becoming a musician and being a performer.

CA: I know.

GBPO: Am I living out his karma? Is that what I do, and is that what all children do?

CA: Quite possibly. Which leaves no pressure at all on Caresse and Genesse...

---

3 "Scotch John" was the main pimp of of shady tax haven island Jersey in the 1960s. P-Orridge met him during an trip with a Christian youth organisation. When the young P-Orridge had declined the offer of becomning Scotch John's assistant, the pimp went on to show P-Orridge contact sheets of pornographic photos taken in various Jersey brothels.

GBPO: I hadn't thought of that one... Oh, god! What have I done? (laughs)

CA: One of your strong points is not the enormous body of work in itself; it's your sense of integrity. The work can radiate that inspiration just from the fact that it's pure.

GBPO: Perhaps. There is purity of intent, a unity of purpose, and that's why I've always said you have to look at it from the deathbed backwards. Can I be proud of what I do today, should I suddenly die? You know, you can't try and self-analyse on the actual journey or it's too confusing. You remember that we always said that we never wanted to rely on the creative projects we are involved with most deeply for basic living income, for fear of distortion of the central integrity; it inevitably compromises decisions. That's why with TG, for instance, we kept it separate.

Peter "Sleazy" Christopherson paid his bills working as a partner in "Hip-gnosis;"[4] Chris Carter worked for his father's various businesses; Christine Carol Newby worked as a stripper under the name "Scarlet;" and we were on the dole until, after a few years, our Industrial Records label was able to pay me minimum wage for working full-time for I.R./TG, and letting the entire downstairs of my squat be taken over for warehouse and office functions for I.R./TG too. We never joined a label. Not until it was already defunct, and then we just did re-releases. Before that, around 1976, C.O.U.M. hit this point where we were getting incredibly small grants off the Arts Council: like 300 pounds for a year, for an entire performance group... They started writing to me and saying, "now you have to send in scripts for all the performance pieces you're going to do next year so that we can evaluate whether we should give you any more money." We wrote back and said, "look, that's not how art works. You imagine it does, and people may produce things to fit in with your system to get income, but in fact if I want to sit and watch "Coronation Street,"[5] yeah, that's just as valid as me making art objects, because my brain is what makes the art. And my brain is entitled to go wherever it wants; not where you want it to go or fit in with your form."

They just didn't understand what I was trying to say, but that's why we said okay, let's stop C.O.U.M. And then TG started to make enough so that we weren't beholden to anyone. We could still choose whatever records we wanted to do, how we wanted to do them, everything... We had 100% control, and we never did a deal because we knew they would immediately make us compromise. Remember the story with Virgin? When they saw the rave five-star reviews for "The Second Annual Report" they rang up and wanted us to sign to Virgin, and they

---

4 A British design firm, specialising in record covers.
5 A British TV series.

said they wanted a demo tape and they also wanted the cover to feature Cosey showing her tits. And so we sent them a cassette tape; we broke it with a hammer so it didn't work, and said, "no photos, here's your demo."

CA: Demo as in demolition.

GBPO: I want to breathe again, Calle. I'm so tired of this.

CA: I can certainly understand that.

GBPO: It reminds me of Brion Gysin in Paris. That last week, when he was just, "I'm so tired of this." But he didn't have enough to look forward to to keep struggling anymore.

CA: No, and I think you do.

GBPO: Yeah, there's too many books to do!

CA: Exactly!

GBPO: Just when they're starting to think of me as an artist, now we're a writer.

C: Yeah, but that's art too. When you started out, it was with a kind of a violent attitude towards the body as such. I mean, I'm also thinking of Stelarc, of C.O.U.M., Chris Burden, the Viennese Aktionisten, all of that stuff. Why do you think that the transgression was so violent at that specific time?

G: I think it was because we were close enough to the Second World War, and we had seen images of Hiroshima and Nagasaki, and we had lived through the Cuba crisis. All those things made it seem desperate to wake everyone up before we did that to everyone. There was a rage at the stupidity; that people hadn't stopped thinking in terms of war as a solution, because then they had the Korean war, and they had the Vietnam war; it's like it just never fucking stopped. America's been at war ever since the Second World War, somewhere, so I think that was a large part of it. With the Viennese it was an expiation of the guilt to coming to terms with the atrocities that occurred on their side; of course there were atrocities on both sides. Dresden was an atrocity, for example, by the allies. I think they were also trying to expiate and exorcise the demons of their genetic political structures. For people like me it was the sheer rage at the complacency of the

312

middle class. In the 1960s, I think it was Harold Macmillan's[6] slogan to try and get elected that, "you've never had it so good." That was the big slogan. He was a Tory of course, and they were saying, you know, "don't rock the boat, everything's perfect, you've got better wages than you had before the war, you've got houses being built." You know, to replace the ones destroyed in the war. Rationing only stopped in 1953, or 1954. I actually experienced rationing for four years. I was too young to understand it, but I did. It was monstrous, and it was close enough to be both terrifying, and an abomination.

It was like, "for fuck's sake, wake up'!" How do you do that without being violent? You do it by hurting the self, you know; by wounding the self as a symbol of the wounding that's happening from the ignorance of the political structure. Certainly with me there was a lot of that. The hypocrisy and the double standards and the bigotry and the suppression of nature; of the natural order of the human body, our right to control our own skin. All of those things... To me they were just anathema. How could I explain it but say, "it's my skin and I'm going to do what the hell I want to it, and if I have to hurt it and damage it in order to get your attention then I shall, because I need your attention, because this is very, very important."

We have to try and find out if there is any way at all for humane beings to change their behaviour, because for 30,000 years we've been repeating the same violent mistakes with war and invasion and rape and pillage. You would think that any intelligent creature would realize that that was counterproductive.

So it was all those things. You know, when the Cuba crisis was happening and they told Khrushchev[7] that the boats had to turn around that day. My mother waved me off and said goodbye when I was going to school. She gave me a kiss and hugged me, and said, "I hope I see you tonight, but remember I love you if you die."

CA: Wow!

GBPO: That's how people really felt. I've talked to a lot of people from that era, and they all agree that it was really heavy. We thought we were all going to be exterminated by nuclear war. And when we weren't, we thought we'd have a breathing space to try and generate common sense, and that's when you get CND – the Committee for Nuclear Disarmament – which became the nursery of bohemians and beatniks, and eventually hippies. They did all their marches every year to protest the bomb, and that's how the whole London underground grew, from that initiative. All of it grows from that. So that really is the key: the terror of obliteration.

---

6 Harold Macmillan (1894-1986), Conservative British Prime Minister between 1957 and 1963.
7 Nikita Khrushchev (1894-1971), Soviet leader between 1953 and 1964.

CA: In that regard, and taking their experiences into consideration too, did you ever feel an aesthetic kinship with butoh?

GBPO: Yes, but later. I don't know if it was actually a butoh performer, but when we started to be in touch with Fluxus, somebody had a book, or I read a book, and it was exercises by different Fluxus artists. One of the Japanese ones had written, "take 24 hours to get undressed." That was like a Eureka moment. Because suddenly we could be violent in such slow motion that it wasn't violent. Then it was literally how slow can we do it. And that's when it started to really work, because I saw it as very painterly thing. You could take a snapshot of any moment and it would look like a really interesting photograph, but almost like an interesting painting. Or a still from a film. It just looked really intriguing, and we became a great believer in curiosity as being the key to communicating in that really artificial environment of the art world. To still generate enough curiosity, and be non-traditional enough that they had to stop and think and hesitate. They had to take a breath. Otherwise they wouldn't make any connection.

When we did the Paris Biennale in 1975 people were watching us in our box all day long. We have all those photos. And the one in Milan, where there was a scaffolding outside, and my job was to climb the scaffolding up onto the top, and that, again, was meant to last one hour. On the way there I had to hang in all these weird positions. That's a different kind of stress because it looked like ballet, but it hurt more than the other stuff. You know, hanging by one hand trying to find how to get to another piece of scaffolding, but to make it slow.

CA: In moments like that, did you ever think, "what the hell am I doing?"

GBPO: Yes! But I didn't question the transmission. That one in particular, that happened in a dream vision, and somewhere in a notebook there is the original sketch of it. We've always had great faith in those visions. When they come like that we never, never doubt them.

CA: That said, are you still experiencing them in your present condition?

GBPO: Yeah. Not that kind exactly, but we've been having moments where we can see this and another world at the same time. It's quite fascinating. And we have to really concentrate to decide which is the one that I'm still in!

CA: Do you see any kind of hindering or hampering of your creativity in general because of the physical stuff going on?

GBPO: No, not at all.

CA: Good. The new Polaroid book is amazing.

GBPO: It's like when we use rubber stamps and postcards and all kinds of small things. Polaroids are like the everyday stuff that people use. A lot of artists love Polaroids. When it was created it was not seen that way at all. They're crude and romantic at once.

CA: In a way it's like with the film format of Super 8. The Super 8 aesthetic evokes something completely different from other kinds of cinematic stock. There's something having to do with home, and nostalgia and sentimentality. With Polaroids it's this prurient thing, where you're seeing something that you're probably not supposed to be seeing. It always feels like a very private moment. If you see it, it's like a "Peeping Tom" experience.

GBPO: Also it's alchemical, because it's just liquids, basically. The light strikes them and solidifies the image. Visual poetry and making magic. It's not pixels, and it's not the basic effect of light on film; it's a really specific, unique process.

CA: I think it's extra emotional because of the fact that the image also fades. If you leave it in the ligh – the very same light that once gave it life – it will fade away.

GBPO: Me and Jaye fell in love with them. If we saw something we particularly liked, we'd take ten Polaroids of the same thing, and we'd put them in collages and such. I really miss that.

CA: In this phase, do you have good dream recall? Do you dream differently?

GBPO: I dream every night very vividly, but most of the dreams are just... busy. Busy stuff, arguing with people, trying to get things done, that kind of thing. We've only had a few real lucid dreams where we remember everything when we wake up. Those ones we write down because they usually seem significant, and you can always tell the difference in the quality. So there's not a lot of change; maybe slightly fewer lucid dreams, and why that might be, who knows? My sleeping is really off. The other thing that's bothering me is the breathing. But I'm alive and I can function and I can type, so...

CA: Given that you have always looked at things through a kind of matrix of cut-ups, can you see that your situation right now is a cut-up too; in-between sickness and health, and in-between life and death. You're in-between these extreme polarities.

GBPO: It's funny you should say that because the editor, Tim,[8] said to me last week, "have you thought about writing about mortality? Because you're in this unique position." I know what triggered it; it was because the *New York Times* rang him up again about their obituary of me. When I was in the hospital the last time, when I was in the ICU, they actually rang him up and said, "this is the *New York Times* and we'd like a quote about Genesis for our obituary." So they just can't wait to get rid of me!

CA: It's weird. I mean, they're great journalists and all, but I mean, that's just cynical.

GBPO: What is it going to feel like, you think?

CA: What?

GBPO: A world... A world without Gen in it.

CA: I'm trying not to think about it too much. But if I do, I'm just thinking of how blessed I've been. You know, we've worked together since 1986; we've never really had a disruption except for normal disruptions of time. It's just been extremely valuable. We've made these three beautiful albums, and this book, and many other things, and it's just a blessing. I don't think I will have emotional problems with it. It's just a matter of carrying on the work, like you did; you carried on the work. I will carry on the work, and then other people will carry on the work. It feels like a blessing to me.

GBPO: Good. Very good!

CA: Stay strong, and just keep on fighting, and keep working. That's the key to it.

GBPO: It is. It's all I got.

---

8 Tim Mohr: editor of P-Orridge's autobiography (forthcoming).

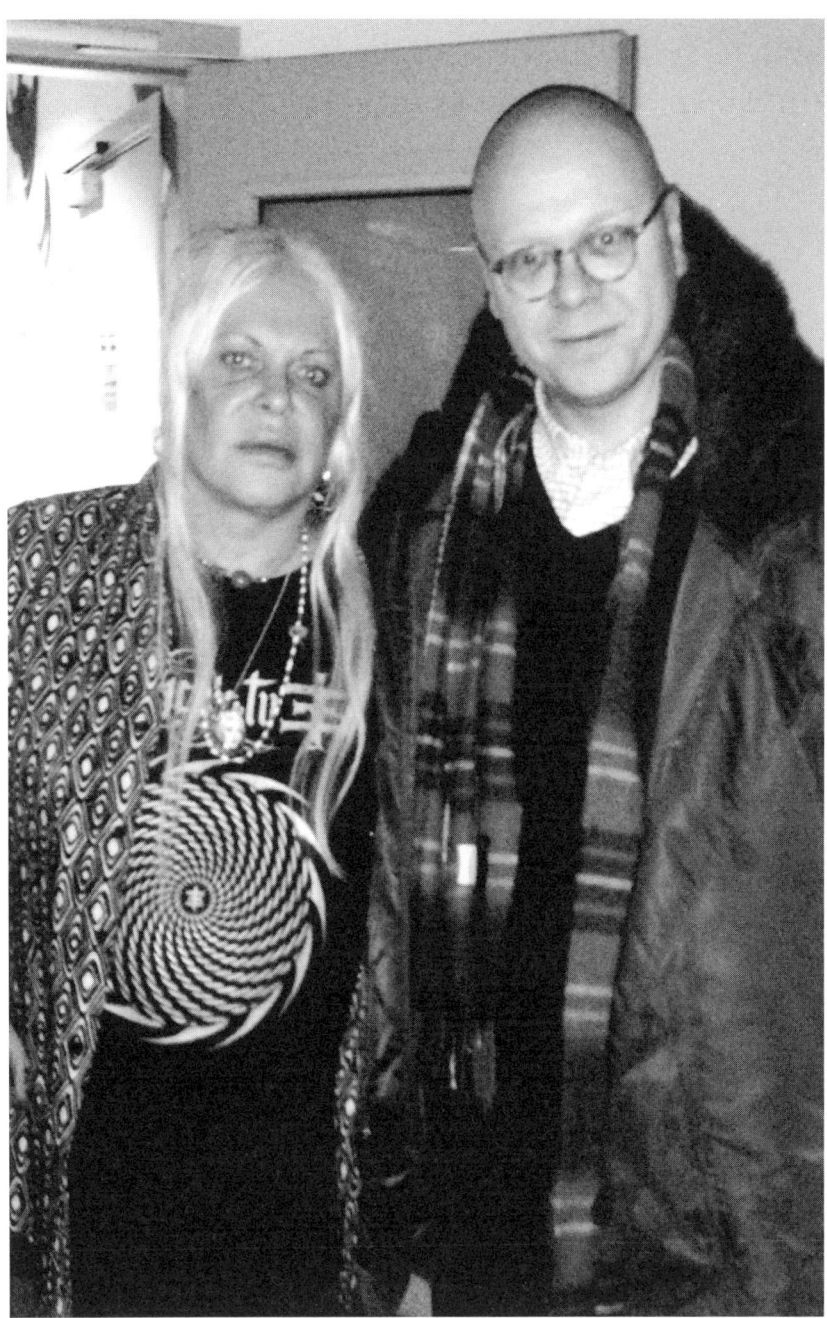

Genesis Breyer P-Orridge & Carl Abrahamsson, Oslo, 2014

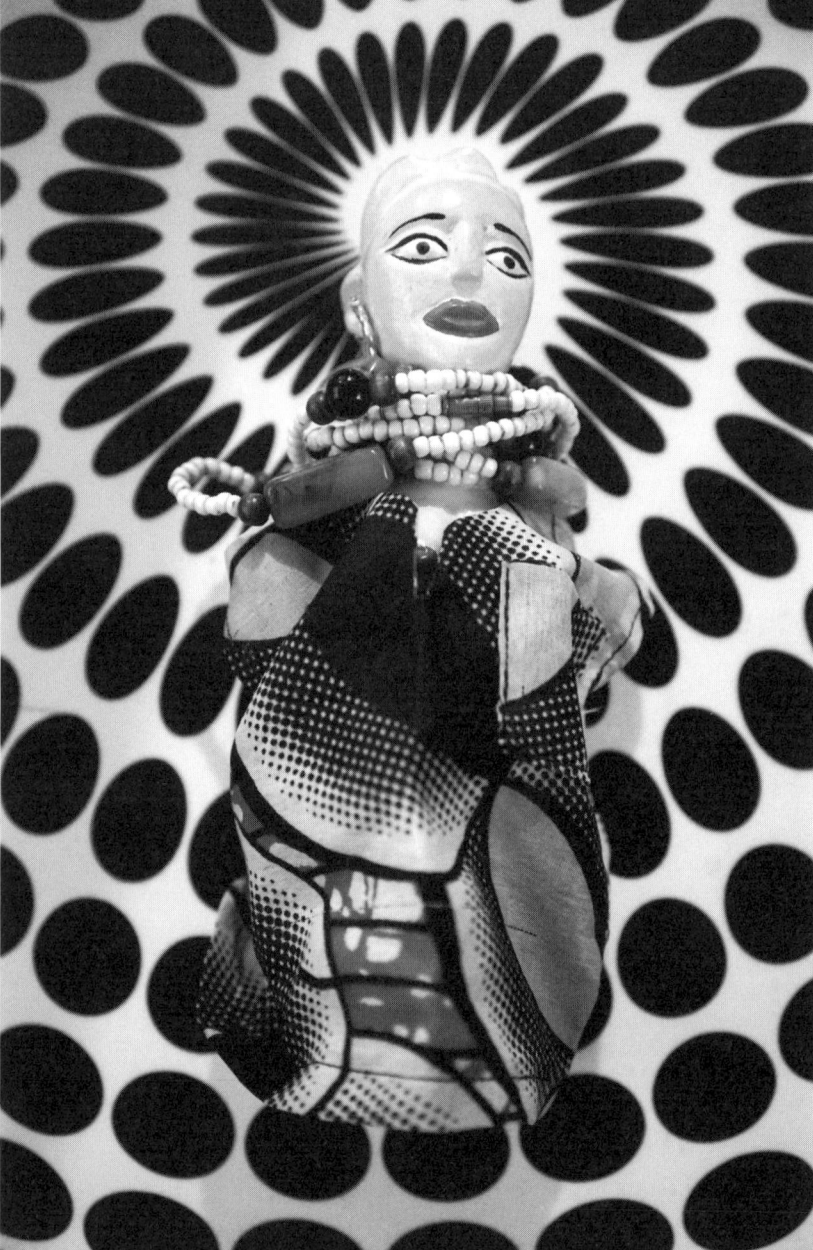

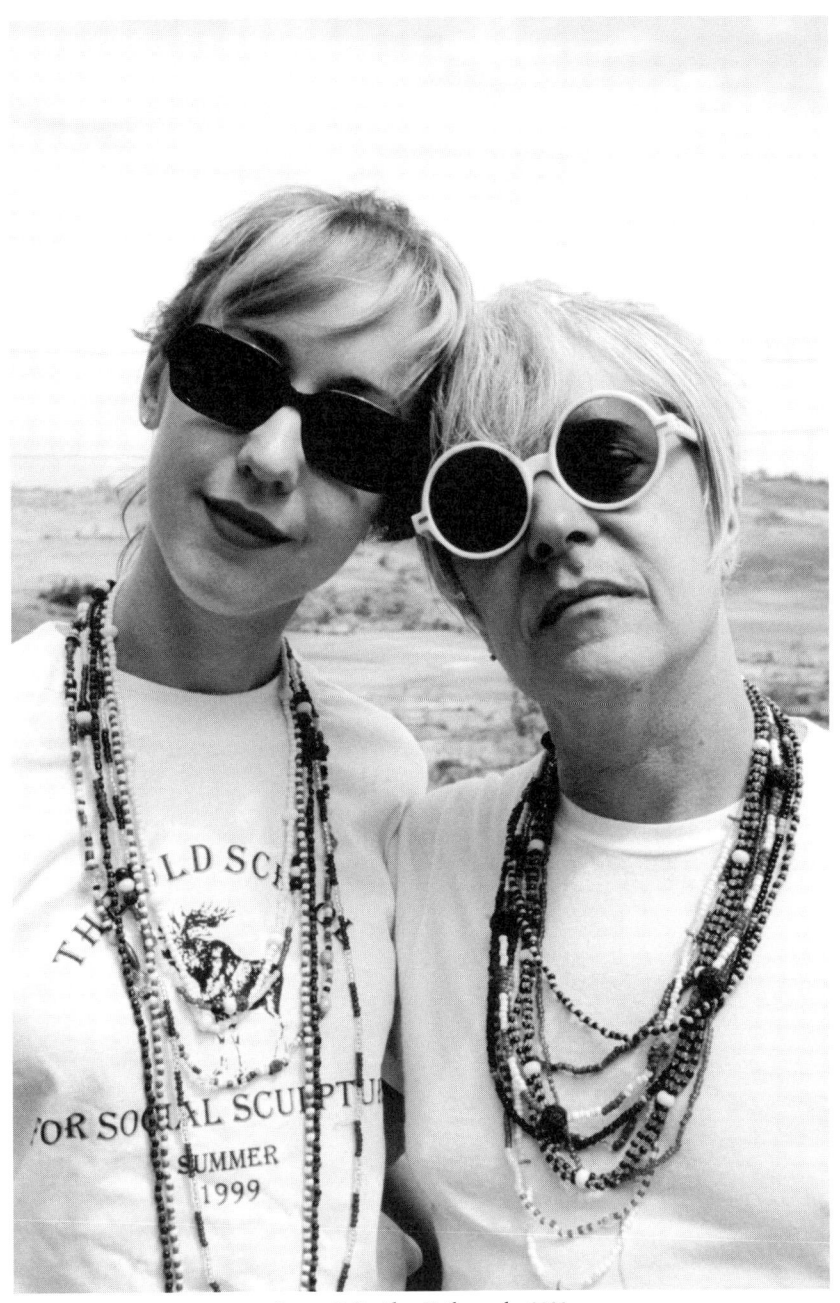

Breyer P-Orridge, Kathmandu, 2000

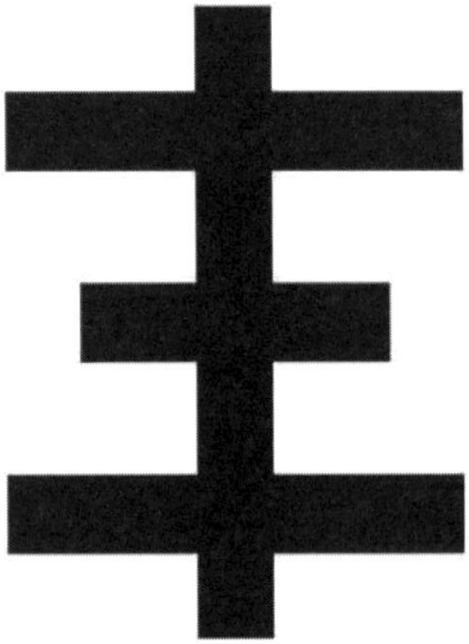